On Hallowed Ground

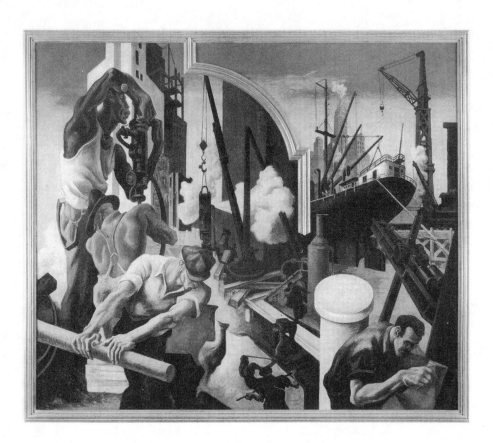

ON HALLOWED GROUND

Abraham Lincoln
and the
Foundations of
American History

JOHN PATRICK DIGGINS

Yale University Press
New Haven & London

Frontispiece: Thomas Hart Benton, *City Building*, from *America Today* (1930). Distemper and egg tempera on gessoed linen with oil glaze, 92 x 117 in. Collection of AXA Financial, Inc., through its subsidiary The Equitable Life Assurance Society of the United States. Copyright © AXA Financial, Inc.

Designed by James J. Johnson and set in E+F Scala types by Keystone Typesetting, Inc.
Printed in the United States of America by R.R. Donnelley & Sons, Harrisonburg, Virginia.

Library of Congress Cataloging-in-Publication Data
Diggins, John P.
On hallowed ground : Abraham Lincoln and the foundations of American history /
John Patrick Diggins.
    p. cm.
Includes bibliographical references (p.   ) and index.
ISBN 0-300-08237-1 (cloth : alk. paper).

1. United States—History—Philosophy.   2. United States—Intellectual life.   3. United States—Politics and government—Philosophy.   4. Lincoln, Abraham, 1809–1865—Influence.   5. Political culture—United States.   6. Liberalism—United States.
7. Enlightenment—United States.   I. Title.
E175.9.D54 2000
973.7—dc21

                                                                  00-035915

A catalogue record for this book is available from the British Library.

The paper in this book meets the guidelines for permanence and durability of the committee on Production Guidelines for Book Longevity of the Council on Library Resources.

10 9 8 7 6 5 4 3 2 1

To the memory of
LOUIS HARTZ *and* CHRISTOPHER LASCH

We can not dedicate—
We can not consecrate—
We can not hallow—
This ground.
    —ABRAHAM LINCOLN, 1863

Locke sank into a swoon;
The Garden died;
God took the spinning-jenny
Out of his side.
        —W. B. YEATS, 1928

In every Tower of Babel the foundation
is more honest than the pinnacle.
    —REINHOLD NIEBUHR, 1952

Contents

PART III: Class, Gender, Race: The Hidden Consensus

Preface

In the 1950s, sometime between sophomore and junior years of college, I lost my faith and found my mind. The forsaking of a set of religious doctrines coincided with a series of personal rejections. During those years I failed to make the traveling squad of the varsity basketball team (height); I failed to pass the physical exam of the Air Force ROTC (sight); and I failed to sustain my belief in the existence of God (Hume). All of this perdition of body and mind took place in the proud decade of the 1950s, when American society began to enjoy the culture of consumption. Young Americans then thought primarily of how best to live well in an environment of increasing material abundance, though unnerved by McCarthyism and the cold war.

An undergraduate course in American intellectual history at the University of California, Berkeley, taught by the learned and searching Professor Henry F. May, introduced me to past thinkers (among them Herman Melville and Henry Adams) who looked to the life of the mind as an endless hunt for lost treasures. The spectacle of the intellect examining every possible external point of view only to arrive at no inner core of reality reminded me of what was once said by Marian Hooper Adams, wife of Henry Adams, of the novelist Henry James: he chewed more than he bit off. Perhaps some of us who entered the field of intellectual history, and who settled for small bites of big thoughts, find we are devoted to other minds even as we strain to hear our own mind thinking.

Today it is considered naive to look to education as the search for truth and wisdom. Instead we are told that the history of ideas demonstrates that "truth" is simply a convention at the mercy of contingency. Knowledge is no longer the discovery of an object; rather, it is a process of "construction" that invents what passes for the true and real. According to this view, nothing can be known except through the unreliable medium of interpretation.

As an ex-Catholic, I have no quarrel with being told that the religious beliefs I once held were simply a matter of the circumstances of my birth. But I do have a problem with schools of thought that claim we can get along without the authority of truth. According to those schools, the truth or falsehood of ideas has no bearing on their historical importance or, more tellingly, political relevance. Curiously, those who see ideas as functioning without foundations in truth seem eager to espouse their own ideas for reasons of expediency and utility; students and scholars are asked to go along with a doctrine that presents itself as subversive of all doctrines.

A few years ago one of my manuscripts was sent to a historian for an endorsement. Because he and I had been antagonists, I hardly expected a word of encouragement. But the historian labeled me with a term that may yet reveal my peculiar situation in the field of American intellectual history. Citing the emergence of a variety of new schools of thought, he claimed that I had "thrown cold water" on them all, chilling their promise of deliverance from our troublesome predicaments. I plead guilty to being a cold water historian, and my confession of imperfect sympathies includes three isms that I thought, and still think, deserved dousing.

The first such ism is Marxism, which had an enormous influence in academic circles in the 1960s. During this decade, many New Left activists went to graduate school and received doctorates in history, sociology, literature, and other fields. Marxists saw society in a state of deep conflict, with ideas functioning as a "false consciousness" that rendered people incapable of understanding the depth of their oppression. Many academics who wrote the "new social history" became labor historians, and they looked to the history of the working class to find "moments" when "false consciousness" was peeled away to reveal genuine "class consciousness," and workers expressed their hatred for capitalism and love for socialism. To me, such scholarship required a willing suspension of disbelief. Having been born during the Depression years and having grown up in a working-class family, I could remember only that members of the working class wanted to find a way out of their class situation, especially for their children. In the 1970s I wrote several articles and two books criticizing the new social history and its Marxist categories. Suddenly I knew what it was like to go against the ideologial convictions of the day. Showing up at a convention in Cambridge, Massachusetts, organized to launch the journal *Marxist Perspectives,* a historian welcomed me with the words: "You're a troublemaker."

As Marxism began to fade in the 1980s, a second ism rose to take its place—republicanism, variously called "classical republicanism" or "civic humanism." Republicanism had a strong appeal for radical scholars because it supposedly juxtaposed "virtue" to "interest" and thus had resisted the advent of commerce and the priority of economics over politics. Historically republicanism actually represented a conservative stance, but it became popular for promising to open our minds to a hitherto unknown ideology in American history. The republican view was first put forth by J. G. A. Pocock in his widely influential book *The Machiavellian Moment,* which claimed that a body of thought that originated in Aristotle, fructified in Machiavelli, and culminated in James Harrington in the seventeenth century actually carried itself across the Atlantic and sank roots in America's political culture. Once again feeling challenged by a misinterpretation, I wrote *The Lost Soul of American Politics,* pointing out that few leading American intellectuals in the past were aware of the presence of such a doctrine in America's political environment and that even the founders deliberately rejected many principles of classical thought when framing the Constitution.

About a decade ago I attended a Liberty Fund Seminar on political thought held at Colonial Williamsburg, Virginia. I accepted the invitation with some apprehension, knowing that Professor Pocock would be present. Pocock turned out to be a friendly critic of my position, yet I'll never forget the two things that he said to me at the reception the night before the seminar. "You liberals," he said, turning to look me in the face, "don't have an answer to the Marxists." Apparently Pocock was writing the history of classical republicanism in an effort to show radical scholars that there had been in the past an alternative to the advent of liberal capitalism, and he believed that I remained blind to such an alternative and continued to write about liberalism as the overriding presence in American history. But the second thing that Professor Pocock said caused me to begin to question my identity. He told me that my work reminded him of "Butterfield." He was referring to the Cambridge University historian Herbert Butterfield, a devout believer and author of *Christianity and History* and the influential *Whig Interpretation of History*. Pocock, who had studied with Butterfield, knew that he was a great historian. But I failed to see the connection with my work and asked Pocock what he was getting at. "Butterfield thought," he replied, "that every step ahead in history was a step away from Jesus." Subsequently in an article Pocock described my stance as that of "some kind of a Calvinist."[1]

It may be true that my scholarship broods with the weight of sin, power, and corruption, but reference to the gentle Jesus would surprise those who know me as more of a Nietzschean, and readers of this book will discover that I advocate assertion rather than submission. On the other hand, I would like to think of a possible Christian residue somewhere in my thoughts. Ever since the sixth grade the riddle of God remains a curiosity in search of a conviction:

> And must put up with having learned
> All proofs or disproofs that we tender
> Of His existence are returned
> Unopened to the sender.
> —W. H. Auden[2]

I wasn't looking for trouble when I ended up confronting the third ism: the older school of American pragmatism and our contemporary varieties of neo-pragmatism. The subject of pragmatism, and of philosophy itself, was far from my mind in the 1970s, and I had no idea it would enjoy an exciting revival in the 1990s.

Having been told as a youth that I had no "respect" for authority, I originally started to write a book about it. I could not help but wonder what genuine, legitimate authority would look like when and if I were to come upon it in either an idea or an institution. But for years I kept getting sidetracked onto other topics, and by the time I returned to the subject of authority, all I could find was power. Was authority then only a fine name that covers the aspects of coercion and domination in modern life, an adornment that hides what it adorns? Because the philosophy of pragmatism rose in the late nineteenth century in response to the collapse of traditional forms of authority, and because its philosophers chose not to see the world, as did the Europeans Friedrich Nietzsche and Max Weber, as a theatre of power in which protagonists vie for control, I wondered whether pragmatism might itself offer an adequate response to the eclipse of authority.

In *The Promise of Pragmatism*, I concluded that America's one original contribution to the world of philosophy, pragmatism, taught us how to think and act, not what to think and believe; it rejected authority for methodology, logicality for experimentation, truth for technique. Pragmatism rested all knowledge on experience, on the premise that nothing could be known unless we engage the world and learn how to cope with it. The philosopher John Dewey believed that students and scholars should turn to current events rather than study supposedly obsolete theoretical ideas, for events transform potentialities into actualities. "When a change occurs," wrote Dewey, "*after* it has occurred it belongs to the observable world and is connected with other changes. The nomination of Lincoln for the presidency, his election, his Emancipation Proclamation, his assassination, after they took place can be shown to be related to other events; they can also be shown to have certain connections with Lincoln's own past."[3]

The philosopher tells us that nothing can be known until it has happened; the historian spends his intellectual life trying to figure out why what happened happened. No wonder Henry Adams, America's greatest historian, concluded: "Experience ceases to educate."[4]

If knowledge cannot easily be derived from experience, why has pragmatism been so influential in our time? Aside from politicians hiding behind the word as a way of avoiding taking unambiguous stands on controversial issues, pragmatism as a philosophical proposition promised a solution to a problem that has bedeviled thinkers throughout centuries of history. For pragmatism taught us that there is no real conflict between "interests" and "virtue," as was assumed in the eighteenth century. John Dewey put the matter incisively when he asked, questioning Immanuel Kant, why it is right to act in the interest of others and wrong to act in our own self-interest. Dewey argued that to realize our interests and desires is to live according to the principles of biological evolution and that "growth" is the life force of history.

The three isms all represented efforts to move liberalism beyond its own limitations. Karl Marx believed that the "Furies of interests" would be overcome once private property had been abolished.[5] Classical republicanism promised to subordinate the sphere of private interest to the spirit of civic virtue and public duty. And pragmatism taught us that interest loses its negative features as society moves beyond its allegedly obsolete competitive character and enters the modern age of cooperation and community governed by the rule of "intelligence." All three isms have posed a challenge to liberalism; none have made a dent on the omnipresence of liberalism in American history and American life.

What, then, do we mean by liberalism? My use of the term in the present text does not necessarily imply a method of government or a mode of thought. No doubt liberalism does mean a constitutional, representative government based on the will of the majority and a temperament that espouses tolerance, openness to experience, and a lofty optimism about human nature. Today the "L word" often suggests sympathy for the poor and those suffering from class or ethnic deprivation, although politicians on all sides of the spectrum betray such concerns when running for office and calling for tax cuts. Modern liberals, as opposed to the classical liberals of the nineteenth century, have also stood for an interventionist state to bring the market economy under control. Yet today one hears everywhere the cry, "No more big government!"

My use of the term "liberal" refers to none of the above. By the phrase "Lockean liberalism," I mean a body of ideas that regards matter and property, comprehended by mind and conscience, as elementary and irreducible realities and views liberty and natural rights as the means by which happiness is pursued and freedom protected. So used, the phrase contains both liberal and conservative connotations. Historically liberalism has been associated with the rise of the middle class and the opening of opportunity to more and more people to gain wealth and status; once these goals are obtained, the liberal finds he has a conservative impulse to protect his position and possessions.

Much of this attitude can be traced to the seventeenth-century political philosopher John Locke, who was the first to include in the meaning of property the value of the labor that went into tilling the soil and transforming the materials of earth. With Locke the relation of labor to land stood as a moral proposition, since the mixture of both led to agricultural improvement and human progress. Lockean liberalism also signified "negative liberty," as Isaiah Berlin has called it— freedom from political and ecclesiastical authority and from the hegemonic rule of higher social classes.

But two centuries later, when the Transcendentalists Ralph Waldo Emerson and Henry David Thoreau, writing in the 1830s, called religion a "corpse-cold" institution and the state an "imbecile," Lockeanism was about to experience an ironic fate in America. The American poets saw, as did the Frenchman Alexis de Tocqueville, that government in America was too impotent to command authority and religion practiced too casually to command devotion. What would influence people and govern their lives was not government itself but society, precisely where Locke had located sovereignty in the democratic will of the majority. People looked not above to God but to each other as they sought the recognition and approbation of their fellows while responding to the vicissitudes of public opinion. With America moving away from its Lockean roots, property and money became separated from labor and work, and with the worship of wealth itself we enter the modern age of Thorstein Veblen, the first social scientist to analyze the status of leisure and the stigma of labor. Today our contemporary consumer culture, wherein more and more people spend and borrow on credit in a fever of frivolous luxury, would bring tears to the eyes of the moralist John Locke. Yet it is the premises of his philosophy that constitute many of the foundations of our culture.

Nowhere were the gross consequences of Lockean liberalism more profoundly perceived than in writings of the German sociologist Max Weber. After visiting the United States in 1904, Weber became convinced that America represented the future that other industrial nations would follow: and it was not a pretty picture. Weber recognized, as did Locke, that early capitalism (then called "commerce") sprang from a religious need to prove oneself in the eyes of God, to win one's salvation through hard work, frugality, and even self-denial. The Enlightenment had replaced this religious orientation toward life with the authority of reason, but reason soon became an instrument of organization and rationalization that undermined the spirit of devotion to labor. Thus we must face the "disenchantment of the world"—a world sustained by mechanical foundations rather than ultimate meanings. Although originally inspired by the spirit of religious asceticism, modern "victorious capitalism," Weber observed, "needs its support no longer. The rosy blush of its laughing heir, the Enlightenment, seem also to be irretrievably fading, and the idea of duty in one's calling prowls about in our lives like the ghost of dead religious beliefs."[6]

The religious asceticism that had, ironically, planted the seeds of capitalism among the Puritans of New England remained alive in the more secular precepts and practice of Ben Franklin, and reached its sublime in Abraham Lincoln's veneration of work and industry. Can this idealistic strand of liberalism be found today, or is it merely a ghost of the past?

"Where are you coming from?" That question is often asked of me and it requires not a geographical but a political answer. Given my criticisms of Marxism, republicanism, and pragmatism, I am suspected of being a conservative or a closet Catholic. Actually I am an intellectual historian impatient with those conservatives who complain of the chaos of our times and the absence of authority, forgetting that America itself had its Lockean birth in resistance to authority. Indeed, authority was overthrown not only in the American Revolution of 1776; sovereignty itself was so dispersed in the Constitution of 1787 that the branches of government spent more time contending with each other than giving leadership and direction to the country. The liberal pluralism of the Constitution offered a pose (or counterpoise) rather than a philosophy, a structure that would balance power relations instead of a moral philosophy that would guide virtuous conduct. Perhaps Walter Lippmann gave the best definition of liberalism when he described it as the overthrow of authority and the endless search for its surrogate.

Many contemporary conservatives complain of the absence of moral and philosophical content in our present society and politics. This position presupposes a golden age of American history in which people tried to live up to the demands of solid virtues, whereas in fact, the divorce of philosophy and morality from politics, the separation of the search for the true and the good from the race for power and position, began at the founding moments of the American Republic. Ironically, the founders drew upon the American mind to create an apparatus in which mind would be replaced by the "machinery of government." The proponents of the new Constitution, debated in Philadelphia in 1787–88, saw themselves as forging a new kind of government in which there would be no need for intellectuals as a separate class of legislators and lawgivers. When the anti-Federalists, the opponents of the Constitution, asked why all the controlling mechanisms were necessary, and why the country could not simply leave controversies to be resolved by forthcoming leaders, the Federalists replied: "Enlightened statesmen will not always be at the helm." Even the rule of law could scarcely be counted upon without checks on the abuse of power. The problem is that human reason may be "timid and cautious" when people conduct themselves as individuals, but when acting collectively people become assertive and irrational. "In a nation of philosophers, this consideration ought to be disregarded. A reverence for the laws would be sufficiently inculcated by the voice of enlightened reason. But a nation of philosophers is as little to be expected as the philosophical race of kings wished for by Plato."[7]

Two centuries before the schools of poststructuralism and deconstruction of our time, and before the "diseases" of the mind that according to conservatives have closed the American mind, the framers declared the end of philosophy by devising a government that had no need to rely on the illusion of reason and virtue.[8] In the Constitution knowledge is understood not as truth but as the phenomenon of power and its effects. Its authors were less concerned about telling people what they ought to do than about predicting what they would do: they would "vex and oppress" each other unless subjected to controls. And the framers were right!

Not, however, according to the isms that seek to save us from liberalism. Marxists see the Constitution as a form of class domination; academic republicans lament its displacement of active civic participation by representation; and pragmatists criticize it for aiming more to control the "passions and interests" than to allow for the expression and nurturing of the "beloved community." Recently two new isms have risen to challenge liberalism as the mainstream of America's political currents: multiculturalism and poststructuralism. In taking on these isms, I may be accused once again of dashing cold water on attractive new doctrines. But these two isms exist in a curious tandem: if they tried in earnest to cling to each other, they would both surely drown.

Poststructuralism holds that we know people and their societies only through the means by which they come to be represented. In our thoughts there is no immediate existence of such subjects, no presence of anything until it is mediated by language, discourse, rhetoric, and other signficant representations. What we know is a function of where and who we are rather than of how other things are. "Am I that name?" asked Desdemona of Iago, bewildered at the thought that her very being was nothing more than how she was called and described by others. Multiculturalism, in contrast, rests on the assumption that ethnic groups have an intrinsic identity apart from how they are regarded; people are who they were born as, rather than becoming whatever descriptions and categories have been imposed on them. Poststructuralists insist that everything is a "social construction" with no reality existing beyond the contrived constructions through which we think, while multiculturalists believe, or profess to believe, in essential characteristics that are natural rather than nurtured.

But whether they call themselves "constructionists" or "essentialists," advocates of both isms are quick to demand their natural, inalienable rights, even when "nature" is regarded as simply a word on a page or an utterance signifying nothing but a sign or a sound. The natural rights of Lockean liberalism were once thought to derive from the "self-evident" truths of "nature and nature's God," from what is there to be apprehended, not constructed. While our fellow ismites reject this principle, they continue to cling to liberalism as a rhetorical strategy, an argument for opportunity and access. Few live for liberalism, but many live off of it.

It may be the embarrassing reality of material acquisitiveness that leads many of us to want to deny the liberal environment in which we live. Yet the philosopher George Santayana once described the American as an idealist who works upon matter, a person who must confront the material necessities of life in order to rise above the mundane and lead a life of principle. Such was the position that Abraham Lincoln advocated for all Americans. With Lincoln, the human desire to fulfill the possibilities of life becomes all the more possible in America, a special country where individual rights had replaced aristocratic privileges and the rule of law assures justice and equality. The Frenchman Tocqueville also saw the energy of ambition being released from all constraint, an "enlightened materialism" sweeping over America in the early nineteenth century. Previously in European history, before the rise of the eighteenth-century Scottish Enlightenment of Adam Smith and David Hume, the ideas of public virtue and private self-interest were regarded as incompatible. But Tocqueville saw something new under the sun in America: a "virtuous materialism" based on the ideals of work and vocation. Lincoln taught and lived such a life, and he asked Americans to live up to the "better angels of our nature." In Abraham Lincoln liberal democracy found its educator, and that is the role I have cast for him in many of the following pages.

As America enters into a new century, a country once born of the old world presently finds itself in a position to lead it. The spotlight may last no longer than the gaslights of the nineteenth century, but while it lasts a question must be addressed: how can America relate to the rest of the world unless we understand ourselves, unless we can define the significance and purpose of our chosen country? We can start by turning to Lincoln, who tried to teach us that to know America is to know the meaning of the American Revolution and its timeless document, the Declaration of Independence.

On the subject of the American Revolution, Lincoln is more of a theologian, perhaps even a mystic, than a historian. Although he did not pretend to understand the event, to know for sure what exactly caused it, Lincoln passionately believed that we could learn from the Revolution the political lessons vital to the country's education. In Lincoln's mind, the struggle for liberty in 1776 started the liberal tradition in America. Yet today some historians tell us that to know America we must understand "the radicalism of the American Revolution," as though the events of 1775–83 had turned colonial society upside down and created democracy in a single blow. High school students subjected to the new national history standards are asked to explain how the American Revolution "influenced" later revolutions in Russia, China, and Cuba. From these versions of American history, one might think that twentieth-century communism evolved naturally from eighteenth-century liberalism when, in reality, Western democratic liberalism has turned out to be communism's graveyard. Ex-communists like the Polish intellectual Adam Michnik and the French historian François Furet study the American Revolution in order to appreciate how the establishment of a liberal political culture made it unnecessary for the United States to fall for the disastrous illusions of utopian radicalism. But what can Americans learn about our Revolution when it is described as both "radical" and "utopian"?[9]

In 1790, the English philosopher Edmund Burke wrote *Reflections on the Revolution in France,* convinced that what had broken out in the streets of Paris was truly revolutionary and deeply radical. Years earlier Burke had stood before the British parliament to defend the the American colonies' quest for freedom as consistent with the sober prudence of English political institutions and values. But he staunchly opposed the French Revolution. He could support one revolution and oppose another because he knew the difference between liberalism and radicalism. Observing the confiscations of property in the French countryside, the violent assaults on authority, and the political will to purify that would culminate in terror, Burke exploded: "Your new constitution is the reverse of ours in its principles; and I am astonished how any persons could dream of holding out anything done in it as an example for Great Britain."[10]

Today we seem to have lost our capacity to be astonished when we are told that America is too radically diverse and multicultural to have its own defining principles. Lincoln had no trouble identifying such principles, and when he instructed immigrants as well as native citizens to look to the American Revolution, he was less interested in comprehending it than in commemorating it as an event whose "proposition" and "axioms" were more important than its causes.

This book is dedicated to the memory of Louis Hartz and Christopher Lasch. In the latter part of his academic career, the historian Lasch courageously confronted the implications of a Lockean America that the political theorist Hartz had articulated in the 1950s. Although Lasch's despair over America's "culture of narcissism" seemed to be an indictment of modernity, the phenomenon could be traced to the country's foundations in a Lockeanism that made "Man, being the master of himself . . . [the] proprietor of his own person,"[11] the ego sovereign unto itself. Both Hartz and Lasch agonized over the problem of liberalism without presuming to have an answer to it. As the poet Joseph Brodsky advises us: "it is better to agonize than to organize."[12] In refusing to run after those seductive organizing isms that promise to give America easy political solutions, both scholars paid honor to the rich complexity of American intellectual history. Anguished about the limitations of a liberalism that cannot imagine a possibility beyond itself, a liberalism that has no second act in history because it cannot liberate itself from itself, Louis Hartz and Christopher Lasch enabled us to see America as it really is.

For helpful criticisms of parts of the manuscript, I wish to thank Paul Berman, David Bromwich, Nick Salvatore, and Ronald Steel; for careful manuscript editing, Julie Carlson; for steady encouragement, Jonathan Brent; for thoughtful guidance, Lara Heimert; for intellectual hospitality, the Social Philosophy and Policy Center at Bowling Green State University.

Introduction

The scariest crisis in the history of the American Republic erupted with the outbreak of the Civil War. The South having seceded from the Union, the nation dissolved into warring sections and the Constitution seemed on the verge of perishing in a long-fated death agony. The American political mind itself, once thought to have derived from the liberating power of the ideas of the eighteenth-century Enlightenment, also fell on the battlefield's bloodied "hallowed ground."

America would, of course, survive the Civil War due to the superior economic resources of the North and the military achievements of the Union army. But the political leader presiding over the ordeal, Abraham Lincoln, accepted victory less in joy than in sorrow. He recognized that winning the war could possibly mean losing the philosophy in which America had been conceived. He once had believed that America could be held together by the unifying ideas of the Lockean-inspired Declaration of Independence; he had been convinced that people are capable, in the words of Alexander Hamilton, of "establishing good government from reflection and choice," so that a political regime can avoid having its origins based upon "accident and force."[1] The Civil War, however, although it succeeded in eliminating slavery, represented a defeat for those Lincolnian ideals. To the extent that victory required resorting to violence to reestablish what the Constitution's framers had intended—the location of sovereign authority in the national government—the American mind had failed to exercise reflection and rational choice.

At the time of the Constitution's drafting in 1787, James Madison feared that without it, the states would "continually fly out of their proper orbits and destroy the order and harmony of the political System." In his special message to Congress in 1861, Lincoln, without naming Madison, quoted him on the possibility of an "inherent and fatal weakness" in all republics. "Must a government, of necessity, be too *strong* for the liberties of its own people, or too *weak* to maintain its own existence?" The secession crisis dramatized the failure of the Enlightenment to come forth with knowledge as an answer to power, to use the institutional inventions of mind to check the drive either to dominate or disintegrate. History had become the battlefield of two opposing forces struggling to prevail, and "So viewing the issue," Lincoln lamented, "no choice was left but to call out the war power of the Government; so to resist force, employed for its destruction, by force, for its preservation."[2]

Herewith, then, a depressing question. When the political reconstitution of America would no longer be an affair of mind alone, when truth inheres in rifles, cannon, and firepower itself, must history prove nothing more edifying than the impotence of ideas in history?

For some astute Americans, Lincoln himself provided an answer to this question. "How to illustrate the distinctive benefit of ideas, the service rendered by those who introduce moral truths to the general mind?" wondered Ralph Waldo Emerson in *Representative Men*. In that book, a series of essays on Plato, Shakespeare, Napoleon, and other titans published in 1850, Emerson was not altogether sure that outstanding leaders could give meaning and direction to the rest of the human race. Emerson lived during a time when democracy and universal manhood suffrage came to be associated with everything vulgar: pork-barrel politics, General Andrew Jackson, the "spoils system," and spittoons. Amidst this crassness, what could the American mind do? Emerson worried that democratic society could well remain indifferent to excellence and genius. But with the death of Lincoln in 1865, Emerson's urgent hope that the democratic masses could recognize great leaders seemed confirmed. Americans came to know and esteem Lincoln because they saw themselves at one with his mind, character, and ambitions; what the fallen president stood for they aspired to. Lincoln could be regarded as great not because he surpassed democracy but rather because he deeply and fully represented it.[3]

Walt Whitman was moved to write an elegiac poem on the death of Lincoln, a poem to which, in the words of Cuban political leader José Martí y Pérez, "all the cultured people of New York listened in religious silence"[4]:

> When lilacs last in the dooryard bloom'd,
> And the great star early droop'd in the western sky in the night,
> I mourn'd, and yet shall mourn with ever returning spring.
>
> Ever-returning spring, trinity sure to me you bring,
> Lilac blooming perennial and drooping star in the west,
> And thought of him I love.[5]

Martí could never forget hearing Whitman delivering his "mystic elegy." Himself a poet, Martí poignantly recalled the event: "Whitman came from the country to recite to a group of his close friends his long poem on that other natural man, that great and gentle soul, 'that powerful western fallen star,' Abraham Lincoln."[6]

It was not only the assassination that led Americans to recognize the good and the great. For years afterward Lincoln touched the minds and hearts of Americans everywhere outside of the South. Even today Lincoln retains a marvelous authority in a land of democracy. Consider the contrast between him and recent occupants of the White House: on the one side homeliness, humility, self-doubt, magnanimity, and the need to know the right; on the other, slickness, hubris, self-righteousness, and the need to know the ratings.

"We love to think of the Great as flawless," wrote W. E. B. Du Bois of Lincoln. "We yearn in our imperfection toward Perfection—sinful, we envisage Righteousness." But that is no way to think of Lincoln, Du Bois advised readers of the African-American journal *Crisis*. "I love him not because he was perfect but because he was not and yet triumphed." Of possible illegitimate birth, Lincoln grew up poor and little educated, Du Bois reminded his readers. "He was one of you and yet he became Abraham Lincoln." We need not dwell on Lincoln's reservations about immediate emancipation and his expedient politics. "At the crisis he was big enough to be inconsistent, merciful;

peace-loving, a fighter; despising Negroes and letting them fight and vote; protecting slavery and freeing slaves. He was a man—a big, inconsistent, brave man."[7]

What should render Lincoln relevant to different people everywhere is his conviction that America's political ideals transcend differences of race, class, gender, religion, and ancestry. He believed that all of humanity possesses certain qualities and endowments. In a speech in 1858, he made it clear that the Declaration of Independence, though it had been derived from white Anglo-Saxon traditions of an earlier age, belonged just as much to subsequent generations of immigrants:

> We have besides these men—descendants by blood from our own ancestors—among us perhaps half our people who are not Descendants of these men, they are men who have come from Europe—German, Irish, French, Scandinavian—men that have come from Europe themselves, or whose ancestors have come hither and settled here, finding themselves our equals in all things. If they look back through history to trace their connection with those days [of the American Revolution] by blood, they find they have none, they cannot carry themselves back into that glorious epoch and make themselves feel that they are part of us, but when they look through that old Declaration of Independence they find those old men say that "We hold these truths to be self-evident, that all men are created equal," and they feel that that moral sentiment taught in that day evidences their relation to those men, that it is the father of all moral principles in them, and that they have a right to claim it as though they were blood of the blood, flesh of the flesh of the men who wrote that Declaration [loud and long continued applause], and so they are.[8]

Lincoln's conviction that a moral sentiment taught long ago in the past "evidences" its relevance to people of today, and indeed to people of all sorts, opens the American nation to an increasing multinational constituency. Lincoln died too soon to witness the massive arrival of Asians and other people coming to America from what today are called "third world" countries. But he seemed to presage that the country would evolve from a series of settlements; first Anglo-America, then Euro-America, and finally today's multicultural America. Lincoln fervently believed that all people could benefit from the Declaration, which he called "the apple of gold," and also from the Constitution, the "picture of silver" that framed it, protected it, and thereby guaranteed its egalitarian principles.

As Lincoln anticipated, people from the rest of the world who have come to America have benefited from the Declaration and the Constitution, from the principle of equality and from the rule of law, from the ideal of open opportunity for all and from a concept of justice that requires people to be treated alike. But even as many constituencies have benefited from equal opportunity mandates, certain educators claim that a multicultural environment necessitates the cultivation of diversity and, hence, the teaching of non-western histories. The assumption is that we need to study the cultures from which immigrants originated, even though in arriving here they may have left such cultures behind. This argument brings back a debate that took place after the period of World War I over the viability of the "melting pot" thesis, dividing those who saw assimilation as necessary to America's political unity and those who saw the sustaining of ethnic differences as necessary to the richness of America's culture. Even though today many racial and ethnic barriers have come down, educators remind us of the early part of the century when America was rife with discrimination against newcomers. American history is presented as having no common culture of inclusion, no consensus of values, and no possibility that the country can be interpreted by means of a unifying synthesis.

The rising conviction today is that the older liberal consensus narratives excluded women, the working poor, blacks, Hispanics, and other members of ethnic minorities, and now that the story of the long-neglected is told, America must be seen as an environment of deep conflict in which each forgotten group shows American history to have been a series of failures rather than successes. This widespread conviction is in part true; those in the past whose histories went untold were often denied access to opportunity and the power and prosperity that often accompany it. But the historical condition of denial and the recent demand to be recognized and included is continuous with the story of liberalism and its claims to rights, opportunities, permissions, and entitlements. Multiculturalists, feminists, Marxists, and other radical activists may see themselves in conflict with the values of liberalism, but are they not actually steeped in it in their common ambition for power and position in the name of "rights"? To be at the disposure of your own will is to be free, wrote John Locke in *The*

Second Treatise of Government.[9] Historically, acquiring freedom and extending it to others depended upon the reaffirmation of liberalism.

The obverse is also true: acquiring freedom and denying it to others also depended upon misuing liberty at the expense of fellow human beings. Liberalism as the central theme of American history offers no unmixed blessing. Liberalism also helps us to understand what Americans have done to others and against others. In Georgia, for example, white men mouthed the acquisitive shibboleths of Jacksonian democracy to rationalize dispossessing the Cherokees of their lands, in defiance of the authority of the Supreme Court. It was antistatist liberalism, derived from Locke, Jefferson, and Thomas Paine, that also retarded the advent of the positive nation-state that would have provided welfare and health measures, industrial accident insurance, and laws regulating the abuses of big business. As Herbert Croly observed in *The Promise of American Life* (1909), liberalism privileged sectionalism over nationalism, individual over community, and opportunity over duty, leaving an America with the heritage of Jeffersonianism at the expense of Hamiltonianism, an impression that the people could do no wrong and government could do no right. A liberalism based on individual natural rights and the cult of self-reliance set the individual apart from society and state.

Liberalism also set people apart from one another. Because liberalism has always been averse to authority, it should come as no surprise that identity politics and multiculturalism flourish in a liberal society that can do no less than allow people to pursue the desires they happen to have and to define themselves in whatever way they wish. More and more Americans, even those in positions of leadership, assume that they are incapable of identifying with anything other than themselves and their ancestral roots. It is as if America is going backward, all the way back to the Old World from which it departed centuries ago. Within a modern democracy have sprouted categories of lineage and even the hereditary claims once associated only with aristocracy. Defining who one is is no longer a matter of will and self-determination but instead a matter of where one comes from. "My grandparents came from Lebanon," declared Donna E. Shalala, secretary of Health and Human Services and former professor and university president; "I don't identify with the pilgrims at the personal level."[10]

Traditionally American youth of all colors, religions, and ethnicities were taught that they could, and should, identify with the pilgrims and take pride in doing so:

> My country 'tis of thee
> Sweet land of liberty;
> Of thee I sing.
> Land where my fathers died
> Land of the pilgrims' pride
> From every mountainside
> Let freedom ring.

The song, composed in 1831, continued to reverberate like a chorus of conviction. Three decades later, when Lincoln issued his Emancipation Proclamation, "colored people joined in" in singing the verses. "I never saw anything so electric," wrote Thomas Wentworth Higginson, the New England abolitionist and Transcendentalist; "it made all other words cheap; it seemed the choked voice of a race at last unloosed. Nothing could be more wonderfully unconsious; art could not have dreamed of a tribute to the day of jubilee that should be so affecting; history will not believe it; and when I came to speak of it, after it was ended, tears were everywhere."[11]

W. E. B. Du Bois also sang those lines as a young student, and he had no trouble identifying with the highest reaches of New England's Brahmin culture. Martin Luther King Jr. invoked the song in his stirring "I Have a Dream" speech; a century earlier the feminist Margaret Fuller had proclaimed that American culture was as "rooted in strength as the rocks on which the Puritan fathers landed."[12] Closer to our time, the great black contralto Marian Anderson felt similarly about the spiritual strengths of her country. When the Daughters of the American Revolution prevented her from singing in Washington's Constitution Hall in 1939, Eleanor Roosevelt made it possible for her to perform a few months later at the Lincoln Memorial. Before 75,000 spectators she sang "My Country 'Tis of Thee," and, according to the press, tears flowed down the cheeks of many blacks as well as whites.

Moving Anderson's performance from Constitution Hall to the Lincoln Memorial symbolized more than a change in venue, for Lincoln had espoused and taught unifying principles that extend beyond the mandates of the Constitution. Lincoln believed that the American

Republic had its origins not in 1787, with the drafting of the Constitution, but in 1776, with the writing of the Declaration of Independence. The Constitution established institutions enabling Americans to preserve their liberties; the Declaration gave them the right to revolt in order to free themselves from domination and thereby gain their liberties. What had been won militarily had to be protected politically. During the Civil War Lincoln tried to read the emancipatory, egalitarian principles of the Declaration into the conservative Constitution, thereby making the national government work for ends that Thomas Jefferson, the Declaration's author, never intended.

Some historians regard Lincoln's effort at using words and speeches to "remake" the Republic as nothing less than the great train robbery in the history of American political thought. In this reading, Lincoln stole the meaning of America from those who founded it by placing equality at the forefront of American ideals and making the national government responsible for realizing what, under the principle of federalism, had originally been left up to the states. Jefferson believed that government should govern least and the people govern most at the local level; Lincoln saw local governments as sanctioning slavery and viewed the national government as the last hope of liberty. "Everyone in that vast throng of thousands," wrote Garry Wills of those who listened to Lincoln at Gettysburg, "was having his or her intellectual pocket picked."[13] According to this view, Americans did not know that right before their eyes a decentralized federalist system was being transformed into a sovereign nation-state.

Why did Lincoln privilege the Declaration over the Constitution? The obvious answer is that the issue of slavery made the Declaration a beacon for black Americans and for the conscience of Lincoln and the abolitionists. Lincoln had not always felt this way. In his early years he had hoped that the Constitution and obedience to its laws would be the Republic's "political religion." As a lawyer, he had believed that the elucidation of legal principles and definitions could help assure social order. But he came to see that the tensions and unresolved contradictions in the Constitution itself had created the very conditions that brought on the Civil War, even though the Constitution's framers assumed, ironically, that such conditions would serve to preserve the Republic. The *Federalist* authors assumed that the presence of widespread diversity, as well as the "auxiliary precautions" of the Constitution's system of checks and balances, would preserve liberty. Factional rivalry would prevent "overbearing" popular majorities from imposing their collective will. Whereas today diversity is supposedly an expression of democracy, the framers saw it as an answer to democracy, the means by which different interest groups could never build a unified coalition. The authors assumed, in short, that conflict could be controlled and the tendency to factions, the "poison" and "pestilence" of republics, safely domesticated.

According to the framers of the Constitution, factional and sectional diversity would preserve the Republic by countervailing power against power and thereby prevent majorities from dominating minorities; for the South, now a minority, this premise became a means of defending slavery and the right of secession. John C. Calhoun simply reminded Americans that the *Federalist* authors had failed to prevent the domination of a majority faction forged "between those whose interests are most alike." Noting vast demographic changes, Calhoun protested that the "equilibrium between the two sections of the government, as it stood when the Constitution was ratified, has been destroyed."[14]

The prospect of a numerical majority "united by a common interests" had already seemed improbable to James Madison, who assumed interests would always be in flux and the American people too factional to be able to hold the same opinions, and even to Thomas Jefferson, who, while believing in the validity of democratic majorities, assumed that individuals are too idiosyncratic to submit to common views. Madison had also assumed that by extending the Republic's sphere to allow for growth and expansion, majority domination could be curbed because of the greater number of different interests and factions, and the consequent addition of new and different factions would curb majority domination. But in fact the growth and development of the "extended republic" led to a dominant alliance of the North and West, with each region sharing a similar political culture based on free labor. Hence the South's case for secession rested not only on the principle of limited government and states' rights but also on a reaffirmation of diversity as essential to liberty. Calhoun's proposal for a concurrent majority, with differing interest groups given a veto power, seemed the only alternative to a majoritarianism that left liberalism the dominant political force in American life.

In rededicating the nation to the Declaration as the document that endowed people with natural rights, Lincoln recognized that the Constitution, poised to handle conflict, had failed to do so. With the Civil War looming as the tragedy of American political thought, Lincoln returned to the Declaration as the redeeming ethical idea. Lincoln was not lifting the wallets of his audience at Gettysburg; he was educating their minds. The object of that education was to make the American people aware of the meaning of their political and moral foundations.

Herewith one confronts curiosities that may seem inconsistencies.

While Madison and the *Federalist* authors told us that "if men were angels, no government would be necessary," Lincoln saw the necessity of government and still believed Americans could aspire to "the better angels of our nature." While the Constitution's amending procedures were designed to adjust to change, Lincoln saw the Declaration as an "immortal emblem" that could possibly endure unchanged through time. And, above all, while the framers had seriously doubted that America could be "a nation of philosophers," Lincoln believed that America was founded on "a philosophical cause"—human equality and the "principle of liberty to all," which he saw as having been articulated in the deeds of those who fought and died in the Revolution of 1776.[15] Lincoln refused to believe that America's foundings were purely historical or, as the *Federalist* authors assumed, empirical—the outgrowth of the new "science of politics." By proposing that America had its defining conception in a philosophical cause, Lincoln wished to rescue an idea of moral life from the merely contingent, and thereby to show that history need not be left to chance and that an idea born of the mind, "liberty to all," could be brought into existence and made into an effect. In doing so, Lincoln sought to give America a ground or reason for its existence.

But the Civil War Lincoln saw as historical rather than philosophical. Humanly unwilled, unintended by North and South, it was a catastrophe without a clear cause. "And the war came" was all Lincoln could say about its meaning. The war was possibly a product of causes of a purely contingent nature or, even more indeterminate, it may have been, Lincoln speculated, divinely ordained, part of God's inscrutable purposes. By contrast, America's foundations in the Revolution were "brought forth" by human will and purpose and "conceived" with specific political ideals in mind. In 1776, Americans self-consciously set out to make history as instruments of their own cause. Lincoln, it must be pointed out, willfully chose to ignore the opening line of the Declaration—"When, in the course of human events, it becomes necessary . . . "—in which Jefferson had implied that America had no choice other than being directed by events instead of determining them, obeying necessity rather than volition, and thus the rebellion could be seen as forced upon the colonies, a last desperate effort when all negotiations had failed. Lincoln chose to see the Spirit of '76 as the triumph of will over circumstance, with freedom an act of creation rather than a simple inheritance. Whereas the Civil War was tragic, a condition without an explanation, the Revolution was heroic, an act created by human agency. The difference between the two events was the difference between fate and freedom, and Lincoln identified America not with its midlife tragedy but with its intellectual and moral birth. In the midst of the Civil War, when history more than ever seemed a meaningless, bloody chaos, Lincoln grounded America's foundations in a renewable idea rather than in a fractured institution.

Did the later Constitution entail the earlier Declaration as a necessary upholding of the principles Lincoln saw as sacred? The framers hardly thought so, and later Southerners were to deny it emphatically. Lincoln would have liked to have considered the two as consisting of a harmonious whole. But even before the Civil War he sensed the differences between the Constitution and the Declaration; between a political apparatus and a philosophical ideal; between a process of institutionalization that systematizes the operations of government, and a moral imperative of actualization that renders equality a challenge to be forever approximated. If the Constitution makes restraint necessary, the Declaration makes redemption possible.

As the framers saw it, with the presence of philosophy missing in the American people, with the absence of reason and its capacity for reflection, and of virtue and its capacity for civic duty, people could only react to promptings and urges they could hardly be counted upon to restrain. The *Federalist* depicts citizens as incapable of responding to anything but economic "interest," political "passion," factional "rivalry," religious "zeal," and other frailties of human nature. But the Declaration, at least as Lincoln read it, endowed people with the capacity for conceptualization as well as action, implying that the Revolution consciously intended what the words in the document meant.[16] Of the Constitution and its political institutions, Lincoln instructed Americans: "We, when mounting the stage of existence, found ourselves the legal inheritors of these fundamental blessings. We toiled not in the acquirement or establishment of them; they are a legacy bequeathed to us."[17] Americans of Lincoln's generation had inherited a Constitution that was designed to check people's abuses of freedom and to limit the state's use of power. What had been won in the Revolution, freedom and power, had to be controlled in the Constitution. It was the Declaration that remained for Lincoln the emancipatory document of political idealism, one that gave human beings of all backgrounds the same rights and freedoms that would make the political and economic conditions of life as voluntary as possible, with each and every American entitled to exercise the faculty of self-determination. "Let us re-adopt the Declaration of Independence," Lincoln urged Americans when debating Stephen Douglas over the expansion of slavery. To ignore the Declaration in favor of the Constitution would be to desecrate both documents. Convinced of the living presence of the Declaration, Lincoln went beyond the founders to find America's foundations in an idea that must not perish from the face of the earth.

In this book I refer to Lincoln's sense of foundations as a liberalism based on Lockean and Calvinist sentiments. Does Lincoln share this stance with others? We have been taught to believe that Thomas Jefferson, the author of Lincoln's cherished Declaration, was America's outstanding Lockean thinker, the "sage of Monticello" who steeped himself in English political philosophy. Yet in the Declaration Jefferson, a slave owner, substituted "happiness" for "property." In this formulation well-being is a civic affair, an elusive social possibility rather than a natural right to self-ownership that would secure the survival of all races. Locke, to be sure, saw human desire moved by the thought of pleasure, joy, and happiness, but he also saw that people seldom act in ways that fulfill their wants and wishes; hence the constant "uneasiness of desire." Whereas in the *Federalist* happiness is equated with "safety" and "security" as well as property, all of which require government's protection, in the Declaration the role of government is simply to stand aside as people seek the good life, a state of existence that cannot be inalienable since it is a matter of "pursuit" rather than a consequence of possession based on productive human endeavor. But is government not to guarantee the very activity that sustains life itself? No mention is made in the Declaration of the dignity of work and the right of labor, which Locke regarded as the basic human need indispensable to the right of self-preservation, a theory of property acquisition that gave one the right to own what one has made and cannot be taken away without the maker's consent.[18]

Lincoln is much closer to Locke than is Jefferson, especially when he taught Americans that the liberty of possession follows from the act of labor. Lincoln also understood that labor not only produces property but creates value as well, for with wealth as a mode of exchange one can purchase the means of nourishment and leisure and hire others to do the work that once was a matter of necessity. The Declaration was, originally, a self-legitimizing text, little concerned with the welfare of other people and their rescue from misery, and in excluding the black race it chose to ignore John Dickinson's dictum that "we cannot be Happy without being Free."[19] In reading into the Declaration the primacy of labor and elevating it to the status of a foundational covenant, Lincoln gave the document a conscience, a moral quality lacking in Jefferson's notion of happiness.[20] The idea of happiness itself, as Nietzsche reminds us, belongs to the "aristocratic mode of evaluation" of life, to the "well born" who *felt* themselves to be the happy" class "and did not have to establish their happiness artificially by examining their enemies."[21] At its worst, the idea could, Reinhold Niebuhr warned, tempt Americans with the sin of pride; at its best it could, in the apt words of Howard Mumford Jones, entitle people to "the ghastly privilege of pursuing a phantom and embracing a delusion."[22]

Jefferson was far from being the only Southerner who could not bring himself to acknowledge any binding relationship of owning to working. But Lincoln, who never equated the love of liberty with the pursuit of happiness, synthesizes a Calvinist conscience regarding the duty of work and the sinful temptations of idleness and a Lockean commitment to labor, industry, and to the primacy of natural, inalienable rights as universal endowments. Lincoln fervently believed that at the historical foundation of America's political culture lay a consensus regarding equality, opportunity, labor, property and ownership, and the will to work and the desire to succeed, to move one's original condition beyond the burdens of birth.

Such ideals were denigrated in the nineteenth-century plantation South, and today in certain parts of our culture they are derided as "bourgeois." But why taunt those who believe in themselves and diligently engage the world in order to seek greater opportunities? Lincoln's law partner William Herndon described young Abe's ambition as "a little engine that knew no rest." It resonated with the aspirations of America itself. To be truly free, Lincoln insisted, is to rise above the contingencies of society and history, to fulfill the possibilities made possible by our founders and thereby to be worthy of our ancestors. It is the will and the imagination that liberates; as William James advised, "a man's vision is the greatest fact about him."[23] Lincoln's vision for America offers the ethic of work and honor as the only answer to the corruptions of wealth and power. A redeeming vision for our tawdry times.

PART I

America's Extrapolitical Foundations

CHAPTER 1

Abraham Lincoln: Toward a Synthesis with Foundations

The Specter of Synthesis

"WHAT THIS COUNTRY NEEDS," WROTE NOVELIST SAUL Bellow in *Herzog*, "is a good five-cent synthesis." Today the very idea of "synthesis," mocked as a product of the supposedly complacent and conservative decade of the 1950s, is all but forbidden in American historiography. At least in academic circles, the idea of consensus is demonized—taken to mean the suppression of differences below and the imposition of authority from above. America is so culturally multifarious and, we are frequently told, so irredeemably divided along lines of race, class, and gender that the search for synthesis may seem futile.

Yet when one considers the ideas and institutions through which hitherto excluded groups have made gains in America, one can hardly ignore that we are living in a rights-based political culture in which claims to opportunity based on the historical tradition of inalienable natural rights are derived from Lockean liberalism, a tradition conspicuously absent in the two perspectives that have prevailed in recent historiography: classical republicanism and Marxist radicalism.[1] Is it not possible that there is more that unites the American people than divides them? The case for consensus can still be made today the way Lincoln made it in the middle of the nineteenth century. More than any other figure in American history, Lincoln both embodied and espoused the principles of right to labor, property, and opportunity, and I treat his political and moral philosophy as a *foundation* that might guide us through our troubled times.

Today, however, one hears only of "anti-foundationalism." In much of contemporary historiography, and especially in philosophy and political theory, we find a widespread conviction that life and mind have no grounding foundations, that what we believe and do are simply what we happen to think and act in a given circumstance and context. According to this view, knowledge itself, rather than being anchored in natural law or religious principles, functions only in the service of power, and people often submit to the exercise of power over themselves without necessarily having consciously consented to it.

Years ago the American government endorsed legislation dealing with "truth in advertising." Such laws would be regarded as oxymoronic to the anti-foundationalist thinker (and perhaps also to the Madison Avenue marketing strategist). According to the logic of anti-foundationalism, there is no knowable reality behind representations that the mind itself constructs; therefore, what need is there to insist on an objective truth beyond the beguiling messages of advertising? From this perspective, consumers remain under the thrall of power, mediated through a language of signs and images. Outside of this system, there is no genuine truth.

This depressing cultural abyss is the result of the confluence of two philosophical systems: European poststructuralism and American neo-pragmatism. The two have joined together to reinforce two claims: first, that we delude ourselves insofar as we believe that truth exists external to ourselves, to be claimed through an act of uncovering or recovery; and second, that this delusion masks the reality that truth-claims are, in fact, only the imposition of our own subjective interpretations. There can be no true knowledge, no access to anything universal, transcendent, and morally binding, and the effort to be "philosophical" about ultimate ideas, to try to ground a principle in some antecedent concept, is dismissed as naive. Many philosophers, particularly poststructuralists and neo-pragmatists, have thrown in the towel and have given up trying to get in the ring with truth as a conceptual antagonist and have happily announced the beginning of a "post-philosophical" era. In the eighties Richard Rorty announced the "end of philosophy" and turned the discipline over to language and

rhetoric, just as John Dewey had earlier seen the limitations of philosophy as he turned it over to science and experimentation. We must, it
seems, get over our yearnings for objective truth.

What is to be done when philosophy is thought to be nothing more
than a nostalgic pining after the there that is no longer there? The
answer, say the poststructuralists and neo-pragmatists, lies within society and its conventions. Instead of reaching for the universal, we
should look to the local and regard as legitimate whatever enjoys agreement and shared sentiment.

More than a century ago, Lincoln had to wage intellectual war
against just this kind of reasoning, for the denial of truth and the claim
that all beliefs are a matter of circumstance was precisely the position
that Southern politicians took to defend slavery. The defense of slavery
was articulated in George Fitzhugh's book *Sociology for the South, or the
Failure of Free Society* and in Henry Hughes's *A Treatise on Sociology,
Theoretical and Practical.* In both books, the realities of the plantation
replaced the ideals of philosophy. In the debates leading to the Civil
War, the South had customs and convention on its side; it was defending local consensus. Lincoln rejected such claims, arguing for larger,
national consensus—the "philosophical cause" of liberty, accessible to
each and every human being. "Whenever the question [of slavery]
shall be settled," Lincoln asserted, "it must be settled on some philosophical basis. No policy that does not rest on some philosophical
public opinion can be permanently maintained." Whereas today many
scholars hail the "end of philosophy," Lincoln hoped that politics could
be elevated to the status of philosophy in order to address the most
crucial moral issues facing the nation. Without a philosophical sensibility, all politics would be power and America would be unable to
recognize the goals that it is failing to achieve.

To some historians today, the outbreak of the Civil War proves once
and for all that American history can be neither consensual nor exceptional. A people who war among themselves can hardly be said to subscribe to a synthesis. In a text that greatly influenced the New Left, William Appleman Williams's *The Contours of American History* (1961),
the author speculates why the American public has been so preoccupied with the Civil War. "Underlying that persistent involvement is
the realization that the war undercuts the popular mythology that

America is unique. Only a nation that avoided such a conflict could make a serious claim to being fundamentally different."[2]

It does seem that the Civil War crisis compromises the idea of American consensus, and certainly it dramatized the breakdown of the constitutional system, which was, after all, specifically designed to control conflict. Yet as the historian Louis Hartz pointed out, that crisis was the one instance in American history when a region of the country no longer identified with its national history and instead asked to be considered separate and different. But this attitude only led to a schizoid political temperament, as Hartz also discerned. For while the South romanticized its own "feudal ethos" in order to rationalize the existence of slavery, and while it chose to ignore the Jeffersonian egalitarianism in the Declaration of Independence, it had, in the writings of John C. Calhoun and others, to return to the Jeffersonian Enlightenment and the doctrine of natural rights to justify its own right to nullification and secession, and to claim as its own the liberal idea of self-determination.

Thus even during the Civil War—so often viewed as a challenge to the idea of national consensus—the North and South argued over the correct interpretation of Lockean principles, rather than over the principles themselves. The North saw property as a reward for labor, and the South regarded property as the right to possess another's labor and perceived state sovereignty as the right to withdraw from a Union that had been based upon the consent of the governed. During 1861–65 the United States was engaged in a war over slavery and, as well, a war over the right to secession, the right to define the nature of the Union, and the right to claim the ultimate seat of sovereign authority. It was a civil war, not a social revolution, and hence consensus survived. It reasserted itself in late-nineteenth-century debates over currency, tariffs, railroads, lobbies, and other issues that agitated what Mark Twain aptly called the "Gilded Age."

Before the Civil War there were, of course, some isolated exceptions: One thinker who posed the most outright—even desperate— challenge to liberal consensus was George Fitzhugh, the southern apologist for slavery and defender of Cavalier chivalry. Fitzhugh, who had been generally neglected in American political thought, intrigued Hartz as one who departed from the liberal tradition to offer a critique

of it from the viewpoint of hierarchy and paternalism, which supposedly created a more humane environment for slaves than the brute
"wage slavery" of the North. Fitzhugh, Hartz observes, tried to steer
the minds of Southerners away from American liberalism. Many felt
that his arguments scarcely deserved an audience. The abolitionist William Lloyd Garrison, for example, refused to answer Fitzhugh's attack
on northern liberalism, declaring: "Argument is demanded—to prove
what?" Fitzhugh himself had a nervous breakdown trying to prove that
his views would unlock America from the prisonhouse of liberalism.

From Politics to the "New Birth of Freedom"

Although Lincoln was lauded by contemporary luminaries,
including Americans such as Emerson and Whitman and the Europeans Tennyson and Tolstoy, he has been treated less kindly by recent
historians. The Harvard historian David Herbert Donald's *Lincoln* is a
case in point. Donald describes Lincoln as a crafty politician always
strategically planning for the next election; a prudent man tempered
by a "pragmatic approach to problems" that rendered him content to
respond to critical situations rather than anticipating them; an upstart
of "unquenchable ambition" who ran for the presidency without having any sense of the depth of secessionist sentiment in the South and
without any clear plan for preventing the outbreak of civil war. Moreover, Lincoln's much quoted remark—"I claim not to have controlled
events, but confess plainly that events have controlled me"—is cited by
Donald as evidence of "the essential passivity of his nature."[3]

When Lincoln uttered those thoughts, in April 1864, he was responding to a complaint that he had violated his pledge in his First
Inaugural Address not to interfere with slavery. He now had to explain
why he had issued the Emancipation Proclamation of the previous
year. Having taken an oath to uphold and defend the Constitution,
Lincoln wrote in a private letter, he came to see the necessity of using
power not to preserve slavery but to rid the country of it so that the
institution could no longer "permit the wreck of government, country,
and Constitution all together." Rather than expressing "passivity," Lincoln was expressing passion tempered by logic. "Was it possible to lose
the nation, and yet preserve the constitution? By general law life *and*

limb must be protected; yet often a limb must be amputated to save a life, but life is never wisely given to save a limb."[4]

Lincoln's rumination on the inscrutability of events, far from demonstrating passivity in the sphere of politics, may well suggest a higher philosophical wisdom in the face of history. The enigma of fate and will has perplexed thinkers for centuries; Lincoln was only expressing the possible illusion of free will in determining the outcome of events, a riddle that he saw dramatizing itself on the bloody battlefields of the Civil War, just as Stendhal and Tolstoy had seen it unfolding in all its gory mystery in the Napoleonic War of 1812.[5] Standing above Lincoln the politician is Lincoln the philosopher, who sees in history the tragedy of human life. "Lincoln's own career," wrote the Dutch historian Pieter Geyl, "furnishes striking proof that the fate of mankind is not from the first to the last governed by reason."[6] The same vision of history resonates in the thoughts of many of the nineteenth century's greatest historians, including Alexis de Tocqueville, Henry Adams, Thomas Macaulay, and Jacob Burkhardt. All saw that in the new democratic age it would be difficult to attribute any influence over the destiny of humankind to the will and conscious decisions of individuals, and it would be even more difficult to discern a rational pattern in the chaos of events. Likewise the protagonist in Stendhal's *The Charterhouse of Parma* wanders about the battlefield at Waterloo "understanding nothing," unable "to make head or tail of what was happening."[7] In his fragment "Meditation on the Divine Will," found after his death, Lincoln wondered about the purpose and will of God and understood nothing.

In contrast to Donald, Garry Wills takes seriously Lincoln's meditations on history and politics, and in *Lincoln at Gettysburg* he offers an eloquent analysis of the symbolic significance of the military battle in America's act of remembrance. As a learned scholar trained in the classics, Wills would have us believe that the American president rose to Ciceronian heights in his speeches and addresses. He contends that Lincoln, in delivering his address at Gettysburg, intended to redefine the meaning of America so that the Civil War would be won not only militarily but also ideologically.

Wills insists that Lincoln "cleansed" the Constitution as a document that had once countenanced slavery and that hence had been "tainted with official sins and inherited guilt." He quietly "altered the document from within," bringing the "legal compromise" that allowed for the continuation of slavery "to its own indictment." By doing so, "he performed one of the most daring acts of open-air sleight-of-hand ever witnessed by the unsuspecting." According to Wills, the crowd departed from the blood-drenched fields of Gettysburg not knowing that they had been delivered a new conception of government, with broadened powers and responsibilities. With Lincoln's emphasis on the proposition of equality, Americans were given "a new past to live with that would change their future indefinitely."[8]

The Gettysburg Address does indeed represent the most powerful of American statements about the nation's own self-definition. But the speech never mentions the Constitution and it has little to do with its legal compromises about slavery. Rather than giving the American people "a new past," Lincoln gave them an old past, the eighteenth-century America that offered "a new nation, conceived in Liberty, and dedicated to the proposition that all men are created equal." Such an orientation, claimed Lincoln, would return the Republic to its definite origins in the Declaration of Independence. The Gettysburg Address was not so much a transforming document as a call to sustain a consensus that Lincoln was sanctifying in the name of the battlefield's fallen dead.

It can hardly be said that the Gettysburg Address "remade" America. More than a decade before the address, Calhoun had noted how the "character of the government had been changed" from the "federal republic" envisioned by the framers "into a great national consolidated democracy."[9] The superior economic strength of the North and the military conquests of the Union Army did the remaking; in the Gettysburg Address Lincoln hopes for "a new birth of freedom" so that the "honored dead" would not have fallen in vain. Ironically, that new birth would have its instrumental enactment in the Constitution when the Thirteenth, Fourteenth, and Fifteenth Amendments were added toward the conclusion and in the aftermath of the Civil War. These civil rights amendments incorporated the egalitarian principles of the Declaration into the Constitution; henceforth America's liberal consensus, which promised rights to life, liberty, and property, would depend upon the authority of the courts and the government for enforcement.

The ideals of democracy, rather than resting upon the consent and sovereignty of the people, would turn on the power of the state in an environment where equality and democracy vie with one another when the wishes of the few struggle against the will of the many.

Where the Constitution's framers saw their task as curbing popular control of government, Lincoln's achievement was to make government serve the needs of unpopular causes. Thus liberalism, which historically rose in opposition to government, was to look to government and the courts to control whatever stood in the way of its ideals. With the civil rights amendments the national government is invested with the authority to act in the name of the whole people in preserving liberty and property and guaranteeing the equal protection of the law. In the post–Civil War era, however, the politics of Reconstruction compromised the authority of the national government, and thus the ideals of racial equality were to lay dormant until the twentieth century. When they finally reemerged in the civil rights movement of the 1960s, the Lockean ideals of liberty and equality had undergone an ironic twist. Once espoused in the act of resistance to government, with sovereignty residing in the will of the majority, they now came to depend upon government for their realization. The liberalism of property and opportunity, once rooted in local sentiment, became nationalized and formally legalized in the U.S. Constitution.

Consensus Historians and Lincoln

Although Lincoln's political values represented the full force of the liberal consensus, consensus historians themselves have treated Lincoln in ways that have obscured his towering place in American history. The first historian to articulate a consensus perspective, Richard Hofstadter, saw the Civil War as sustaining the continuity of America's political culture and considered Lincoln himself to be so much a part of the country's "bourgeois" mentality that his politics became almost synonymous with the sphere of business. Hofstadter's *The American Political Tradition* (1948) offered the provocative chapter "Abraham Lincoln and the Self-Made Myth." In the introduction (which an editor asked Hofstadter to write after he had completed the text), Americans are told what they have been all about since the very beginning of their history: "The sanctity of private property, the right of the individual to dispose of and invest it, the value of opportunity, and the natural evolution of self-interest and self-assertion, within broad legal limits, into a beneficent social order have been staple tenets of the central faith in American political ideology." We should not be misled by the conflicts and antagonisms in American history, for the contestants are motivated by the same ends of self-interest even if expressed in different objects of desire; hence the spectacle of "conflicts between special interests—between landed capital and financial or industrial capital, between old and new enterprises, large and small property." The occasional ferocity of ideological struggles only conceals the common drives of the antagonists. "Even when some property right has been challenged—as it was by followers of Jefferson and Jackson—in the name of the rights of man or the rights of the community, the challenge, when translated into practical policy, has actually been urged on behalf of some other kind of property."[10]

So absorbed was Hofstadter in his own vision of consensus that he treated Lincoln less as a moralist than as an opportunist—one who dared not challenge public opinion, a "professional politician looking for votes," a historical figure who must be judged "among the world's great political propagandists." Hofstadter acknowledged that slavery violated Lincoln's egalitarian sentiments and that if the institution were to be justified as property, Lincoln, in his own words, would place "the man before the dollar." But in opposing the expansion of slavery instead of condemning it outright, which according to Hofstadter Lincoln did only to appease the abolitionists, Lincoln in his view avoided taking a moral stance; instead he appealed to the self-interest of northern laborers whose economic position would be threatened if slavery moved out of the South. Hence the struggle between slavery and antislavery merely represented two forms of property.[11]

Hofstadter's hero in *The American Political Tradition* was the abolitionist Wendell Phillips, the one figure who remained so far outside that tradition that he reversed Lincoln's priorities and preferred to see the South successfully secede so that slaves who had escaped to the North would be freed even if the Union were lost. In contrast to other figures in the book, Phillips alone articulated a socialist critique of the wage system, the maldistribution of property, and the authority of wealth, only to find that his anti-capitalist sentiments left him in "iso-lation." As a vigorous agitator, Phillips, though "a thorn in the side of complacency," nonetheless remained impotent to challenge the liberal consensus.[12]

Whereas Hofstadter desired, as did Hartz, to see if consensus had any loose links in its iron chain, Daniel J. Boorstin sought not to challenge the chain but to celebrate it. Beginning with *The Genius of American Politics* (1953) and continuing in several subsequent books, Boorstin hammered out a reassuring thesis. Ever since Tocqueville, E. L. Godkin, and Lord Bryce, it had been assumed that democracy was at odds with the demands of philosophy, with a high degree of civiliza-tion, and with a classical dedication to a noble conception of public life. Boorstin insisted, in emphatic contrast, that it was America's "genius" to have freed itself from the speculative temptations of mind and to have learned to enjoy what is common, average, and ordinary. Boorstin assured Americans that their country has succeeded historically pre-cisely because politics and society got along marvelously well without the need of intellectuals and their misleading theories. Further, he was happy to report that Lincoln, unlike the more charismatic and vision-driven political leaders of Europe, was a prudent, level-headed back-woods lawyer, and hence among the "respectable spokesmen for the respectable community."[13] Nearly a half-century before our contempo-rary postmodern thinkers, Boorstin depicted America as having no philosophical foundations! Whereas Tocqueville and Weber thought they saw American history as animated by ideas, particularly Anglo-American Puritanism and liberalism, Boorstin wrote an essay titled "The Place of Thought in American Life" to prove that it had no place.[14]

Thus to Boorstin the Civil War represented no disruption to con-sensus because the event lacked "ideology," and by that much dis-puted term he meant an idea or theory resting on philosophical foun-dations, on some solid bedrock that is self-evident and indubitable. We Americans, Boorstin insisted, never needed a philosophy of truth or an ideology that would fixate on the conceptual at the expense of the actual, the purposeful to the neglect of the procedural. Whereas Hartz saw the domination of a single ideology of liberalism, Boorstin praised America for being anti-ideological and hence committed to nothing visionary, theoretical, or moral. Ironically, even as a conservative historian Boorstin anticipated neo-pragmatism and poststructuralism in advising that modern life can do without philosophy because we live by experience alone.

Inspired by his vision of the "givenness" of American history, of the pragmatic temperament of the American people and the robustness of their environment, Boorstin depicts the country's greatest political tragedy as, to use a chapter title, "The Civil War and the Spirit of Compromise." Boorstin's argument is both ingenious and disarmingly simple. He wants us to believe that because the Civil War was fought along sectional lines, because each side professed to be defending its basic institutions and cultures rather than envisioning a new society in the making, any "elaborate philosophizing" about the issues would have been "superfluous." Instead, according to Boorstin, the war provides "an admirable illustration of our tendency to make sociology do for political theory, to merge the descriptive and the normative, to draw the 'ought' out of the 'is.'" Boorstin emphasizes the "hardheadness" and "obvious factual basis" of the pro-slavery argument positing the South's superior wealth, and George Fitzhugh's *Sociology of the South* demonstrates the Americans' peculiar scientific habit of mind. Even the Northern abolitionist Phillips struck this note when he tried to show the opposite, that the South's economic deterioration was due to slavery. In Boorstin's view, Lincoln, too, avoided moral heroics and instead appealed to the material interest of the white workingman. And John C. Calhoun appealed to the past in his effort not to change the Constitution but to defend it. His aim, Boorstin reminds us, was "not revolution but *restoration*."

Thus both sides in the Civil War, in Boorstin's opinion, avoided the pitfalls of ideology and brought the sectional debate down to the hard ground of social facts and the dictates of experience. "Every statistical detail became a clue to a way of life. 'Givenness' was here expressed in the assumption that life as it was in America—whether in the North or the South—gave the outlines of life as it ought to be, that values were implicit in experience."[15] If such were the case, if moral values simply derived from daily experience, if the ethical sprang from the actual, clearly America had no need for foundations. Or did it?

Curiously, Boorstin's thesis about the antifoundational "genius" of

America cannot begin to explain why the Civil War happened. If life as it actually was came to be accepted as life as it ought to be in America, why did the North and South have to go to war? The answer is, contrary to Boorstin's thesis, that reality violated ideology, that the "is," instead of merging with the "ought," blatantly contradicted it. The historical existence of slavery represented a threat to liberty and a shared sentiment involving free labor and humankind's right to land and earned property. The liberal consensus survived precisely because Lincoln took seriously political principles and upheld a covenant with the past—a covenant that became nothing less than an ideology that morally elevated the meaning of America. Lincoln believed in political ideas as "propositions," and nothing was more foundational to him than the Declaration of Independence, the "sheet anchor" of the Republic.

Lincoln, Jefferson, and the Declaration of Independence

What, then, would hold America together? In the context of our contemporary "culture wars," the academic world commonly assumes that America cannot possibly be explained by a fundamental unifying principle. Multiculturalists, Marxists, and feminists, though they may emphatically disagree with one another, are united in their belief that an overarching "synthesis" of American history is repressive and that submitting to a theory of "consensus" is regressive—that it returns us to an older body of scholarship from which women, African Americans, and ethnic minorities had been excluded. The academy assumes that unity masks domination and that only diversity can sustain freedom.

Herewith one of the many ironies of American history. In the nineteenth century, the most strenuous denunciations of the idea of American consensus came not from those who opposed slavery but from those who supported it or remained indifferent to it as a moral issue that deserved to be brought up in politics. Senator John C. Calhoun, for example, demanded that the South be recognized for its differences, especially its "inequality of condition" that made it an oppressed minority region as compared to the politically predominant northern and western states. He also took delight in "deconstructing" the Declaration, thereby demonstrating to his satisfaction that the principle of equality is "contrary to human observation" and that the state of nature on which the idea of equality rests is a fanciful literary fiction. Citing Locke's statement that "all men are born free and equal," Calhoun told the Senate in 1848:

> Taking the proposition literally there is not a word of truth in it. It begins with "all men are born" which is utterly untrue. Men are not born. Infants are born. They grow to be men. And concludes with asserting that they are born "free and equal," which is not less false. They are not born free. While infants they are incapable of freedom, being destitute alike of the capacity of thinking and acting, without which there can be no freedom.[16]

Calhoun attributed such presumably faulty thinking to a "philosophical turn of mind," which is "disposed to look to more remote recondite causes." But Calhoun chose to ignore what Locke had in mind when he insisted that people come into the world from the state of nature equal and free since it is in society, and not nature, that the domination of some human beings over others originated. Calhoun also insisted, as do some postmodernists today, that there is no higher truth in politics than the presence of power and the conflict of opposing interests.[17]

In his debates with Lincoln, Stephen Douglas also denied that America could flourish only with a common moral foundation. Douglas told Americans that Lincoln was completely irresponsible in insisting that a house divided cannot stand and that the country cannot endure half-slave and half-free. Such a position presupposed that there "must be uniformity in the local laws and domestic institutions of each and all the states." On the contrary, Douglas argued, when the country's political foundation was laid, the architects of the Constitution "knew that the laws and regulations which would suit the granite hills of New Hampshire would be unsuited to the rice plantations of South Carolina." Rather than having any synthesizing principles, "our government was formed on the principle of diversity . . . and not that of uniformity." We cannot hold different people to a single standard of truth or morality. "We must take them as we find them, leaving the people free to do as they please, to have slavery or not, as they choose." Sounding like a modern-day poststructuralist, Douglas denied the existence of any moral foundation that would allow us to discriminate between competing beliefs and practices. Denying that the Declaration was a covenant containing binding truths and inalienable universal rights, Douglas held instead that the meaning of liberty simply varied with the meanings and usages it had in different parts of the country. Accordingly, he campaigned on a platform to give people in the territories the sovereign right to vote slavery "up or down."[18]

When Lincoln replied that even in a democracy people do "not have a right to do wrong," he appealed to foundational truths in religious scripture and the Declaration.[19] Lincoln's reasoning proved liberating precisely because he upheld what in our time postmodernists have put down as "essentialism"—the view that truth, reality, and human nature itself can be defined by their intrinsic properties. This view enables moral and political thought to aspire to that which is universal rather than particular; that which is necessary instead of contingent; eternal truths and timeless ideals rather than transitory facts and shifting historical contexts. "The world," Lincoln wrote in 1864,

> has never had a good definition of the word liberty, and the American people, just now, are such in the want of one. We all declare for liberty, but in using the same word we do not all mean the same thing. With some the word liberty may mean for each man to do as he pleases, with himself, and with the product of his labor; while with others the same word may mean for some to do as they please with other men, and the product of other men's labor. Here are two, not only different, but incompatible things, called by the same name, liberty. And it follows that each of the things is, by the respective parties, called by two different and incompatible names—liberty and tyranny.
>
> The shepherd drives the wolf from the sheep's throat, for which the sheep thanks the shepherd as his liberator, while the wolf denounces him for the same act, as the destroyer of liberty, especially as the sheep was a black one. Plainly the sheep and the wolf are not agreed upon a definition of the word liberty; and precisely the same difference prevails today among us human creatures, even in the North, and all professing to love liberty.[20]

Where the postmodernist calls for seeing life as contrived and contingent, and where the pragmatist calls for "turning away" from origins, metaphysical foundations, and first principles, Lincoln sought to recall America to its founding ideals. He looked to the Declaration not only as America's moral and political foundation but also as the "immortal emblem for humanity" everywhere in the world. To Lincoln,

the Declaration endowed America with meaning and value and provided principles that he hoped would unify the country. Ironically, the
Declaration's author, Thomas Jefferson, saw his own creation quite
differently. A localist rather than a nationalist, Jefferson never intended that the Declaration should stipulate principles that would
unify the country, that it should be binding on the individual, or, what
is more crucial, that it was consciously intended to apply to all people.
He had written of equality and natural rights only with white male
citizens in mind. Later, when Lincoln proclaimed in the Gettysburg
Address that "our fathers brought forth on this continent, a new nation, dedicated to the proposition that all men are created equal," he
had a better grasp than Jefferson of the original idea of equality as
formulated by Locke. In criticizing monarchical and patriarchal rule,
Locke wrote that men and women are not born into subjection, and
that in the state of nature no one has the authority to "take away or
impair the life, or what tends to be the preservation of life, the liberty,
health, limb, or goods of another."[21]

The historians Pauline Maier and Garry Wills argue that Lincoln
ignored Jefferson's original intent when he read into the Declaration a
universalist interpretation that extended equality and natural rights
beyond white males.[22] True, but Lincoln's reasoning was closer to
Locke's than Jefferson's was. Referring to a black female slave, Lincoln wrote: "In her natural right to eat the bread she earns with
her own hands without asking leave of anyone else, she is my equal
and the equal of all others."[23] Slavery stood condemned for violating
three liberal principles that Jefferson himself once described as "self-
evident": slavery denied blacks the right to liberty, free labor, and property as a means to the undeniable need of every human being for self-
preservation; it prevented them from exercising the right to consent to
the form of rule over them; and it withheld from them the right to
resist unjust power.

A Lockean liberal with a Calvinist conscience, Lincoln believed that
the Republic could be both explained and guided by a unifying principle. Where Jefferson's Declaration was a manifesto of separation and
dissolution, Lincoln reconceived it as a symbol of national unity. Although Jefferson praised agricultural labor, he often identified with
aristocratic leisure and longed for a "natural aristocracy"; Lincoln, by

contrast, valued work, ambition, and those who struggled hard and took advantage of any opportunity to rise from the lower to the higher ranks of society. Although politics ran in Lincoln's blood, it was the life of labor and industry that he extolled in his sense that the principles of the Declaration made possible the "race of life" in a truly "free society." Speaking in New Haven, close to the scene of a shoemakers' strike, Lincoln stated: "I want everyman to have a chance—and I believe the black man is entitled to it—when he may look forward and hope to be a hired laborer this year and the next, work for himself afterwards, and finally to hire men to work for him. That is the true system."[24]

Lincoln's "true system" has been dismissed by our eminent radical historian Eric Foner. A president of the American Historical Association, Foner regarded the ideology of free labor as important historically but unreliable politically. "In the post-war years," he wrote, "the same cult of the self-made man and economic success would come to be a justification of every action and privilege of the business class."[25] Would it not also become a justification of every advancement and privilege of the academic class? The beginning academic starts out as a "hired laborer" and works hard to become a full professor so that instruction and grading of exams can be turned over to teaching assitants. As Thorstein Veblen pointed out long ago, there is little difference between the business world and the academic world, between profit-minded entrepreneurs and career-minded "captains of erudition."[26] Ambition, the desire to succeed and excel, characterizes the athletic and entertainment world as well as that of business and the academy. To trace an idea to its uses and abuses in one class is a revealing attempt to discredit it by establishing guilt by association. But are we to believe that the "self-made man" can only be greedy and grasping while the collectively made working class is innocent and idealistic and the professorial class is noble and virtuous?

The dismissal of Lincoln's "true system" only indicates that much of what he stood for seemed too caught up in the capitalist culture of ambition, competition, and profits that the 1960s generation rejected, even while its members' own energies would later move in that direction as rock stars went for the big money, black athletes negotiated Nike contracts, and professors demanded higher salaries. Another

subject close to Lincoln, American nationalism, also had little meaning to a generation that saw America as a "one-dimensional" nightmare. The idea of patriotism lost its innocence in the Vietnam War, a
blundering, tragic conflict for which there could be no Gettysburg
Address. Young Americans did die in vain, and the health and continuity of American historiography became discredited. With the ravages of the war, Lincolnian ideals seemed more irrelevant than ever
as historians divided along generational lines. Older scholarship had
once concerned itself with the conditions that made freedom possible;
younger scholars sought—and still seek—to expose the conditions that
made domination inevitable. So caught up were radical scholars in the
paradigm of power, control, and domination, so fixated on structures,
the reification of systems, and the disappearance of the human subject, that they, like many conservatives and even the CIA, failed to
foresee the collapse of communism and the outburst of freedom in
1989.

Appropriately, it was a Hungarian refugee, Professor Gabor Boritt
of Gettysburg College, who had to explain to us in his 1978 book
Lincoln and the Economics of the American Dream the meaning of Lincoln to America and to the world itself. In a 1994 edition, Boritt noted
that he wrote the book

> during the Vietnam war and the post-Vietnam era when American self-
> respect was at a low ebb. I will never forget wandering from one book-
> store to the next in the Harvard Square area of Cambridge, finding vol-
> umes and volumes of Lenin's work but nothing on the shelves by Lincoln.
> Since I felt deeply for America and the troubles of its sorrowful Civil War
> president—their many faults notwithstanding—I realized that to stay true
> to myself I would have to go against the current of mainstream intellec-
> tual life. I also realized that attempting to defend the notion that a histor-
> ical figure may deserve not merely critical analysis but also celebration
> would seem sophomoric to many professional historians. Upon their
> good opinion, in turn, my own life as a historian would depend. I went
> ahead all the same, and things worked out. I am grateful.[27]

When Lincoln declared "I want everyman to have a chance," he
was referring to what Boritt has rightly called "the economics of the
American dream." In an 1861 speech to German immigrants in Cin-
cinnati, Ohio, Lincoln went to the heart of that dream. "I hold the
value of life is to improve one's condition. Whatever is calculated to

advance the condition of the honest, struggling laboring man, so far as my judgment will enable me to judge of a correct thing, I am for that thing."[28]

In its truest and most enduring sense, Lincoln's "everyman" transcends differences of gender, race, and ethnicity and stands indiscriminately for all humanity. A labor theory of value based on equal opportunity for all could well be America's redeeming synthesis; and Lincoln's fervent belief in American nationalism and the Republic as "the last best hope" for liberty in the world could provide the bonds of nationhood.

"It Hath No Relish of Salvation in It"

Much of the historiography in the second half of the twentieth century has downplayed Lincoln's accomplishment as a political and moral philosopher. Although it is true that Lincoln went only as far as the fourth grade in school, he became the most profound president in American history, a thinker who, while recognizing that the profit system was the driving force of society, drew back from deifying the almighty dollar; a philosopher-president who felt deeply that modern humankind is tragically condemned to live in a universe of power and sin. The depth and quality of his thought is evident both in the conclusions he reached and in his mode of reaching them.

Lincoln sought to clarify issues by treating them as "propositions" and "axioms," issues that should be accepted based not on the tyranny of custom but on their intrinsic merits. In the Gettysburg Address, he spoke of equality as a "proposition" that the country was dedicated to, which implied that it was an ideal to strive for, to be upheld even when impossible to realize as an ultimate reality. Where Hartz and Hofstadter saw liberal consensus as expressing little more than different forms of property, Lincoln saw it expressing nothing less than equality as a moral as well as an economic commitment; and where Boorstin believed that Americans wisely refused to dedicate themselves to ideology or any abstract principle, Lincoln explained why principle must determine practice. Thus as a "proposition," equality needed to be proven in thought as well as approximated in action. The South ridiculed the idea of equality as preposterous given the uneven distribution of talents and abilities. But Lincoln drew upon reason and logic to demonstrate that to deny equality to one person or a group is to endanger the rights of all people. In a "Fragment on Slavery" composed privately in 1854, Lincoln reasoned in terms of premises and definitions to illustrate what implications follow from certain assumptions. To Lincoln, knowledge was a matter of method of reasoning. Listen to his mind at work:

> If A. can prove, however conclusively, that he may, of right, enslave B.— why not B. snatch the same argument, and prove equally, that he may enslave A.?—
>
> You say A. is white, and B. is black. It is *color*, then; the lighter having the right to enslave the darker? Take care. By this rule, you are to be the slave of the first man you meet, with a fairer skin than your own.
>
> You do not mean *color* exactly?—You mean the whites are *intellectually* the superiors of the blacks, and therefore have the right to enslave them? Take care again. By this rule, you are to be slave to the first man you meet, with an intellect superior to your own.
>
> But, say you, it is a question of *interest;* and, if you can make it your *interest,* you have the right to enslave another. Very well. And if he can make it in his interest, he has a right to enslave you.[29]

As a politician Lincoln was also an educator, and he sought to have Americans become self-conscious about their own relativistic predicament and recognize that geography divides the American mind. After telling listeners how much he "hates" the institution of slavery, he condemns the sin and not necessarily the sinner. "Let me say I think I have no prejudice against the Southern people," he stated in Peoria in 1854. "They are just what we would be in their situation. If slavery did not now exist amongst them, they would not introduce it. If it did now exist amongst us, we should not instantly give it up. . . . When it is said that the institution exists; and that it is very difficult to get rid of, in any satisfactory way, I can understand and appreciate the saying. I surely will not blame them for not doing what I should not know how to do myself."[30] But while Lincoln possessed a sense of the relativity of knowledge, an attribute that prevented him from rushing to judgment, the texture of his thought was ultimately essentialist and universalist; he believed that humanity had certain qualities and endowments that applied to all people everywhere. In a speech delivered in Chicago in 1858, he made it clear that the Declaration was not restricted to white Anglo-Saxons, as though it belonged only to the descendants of Locke and Jefferson. The Fourth of July, Lincoln declared, belongs to anyone who comes to America in search of freedom. "That is the electric cord in that Declaration that links the hearts of patriotic and liberty-loving men together, that will link those patriotic hearts as long as the love of freedom exists in the minds of men throughout the world [applause]."[31]

Although Lincoln tried to reason logically and ethically, the illogical realities of politics and the amoral nature of power often led him into what appeared to be inconsistencies and hesitations. While he called upon Americans to obey the Constitution and its laws in 1838, he himself thundered against the Supreme Court at the time of the *Dred Scott* decision in 1857 (which denied free blacks citizenship) and suspended habeus corpus during the Civil War. Although in debates with Douglas in 1858 he declared that a "house divided" cannot stand, he was willing to allow it to stand when, in the midst of the Civil War, he acknowledged that if possible, he would accept the reentry of the South into the Union with slavery intact. Although he decried the Russian suppression of Hungary during the European revolutionary uprisings of 1848, by arguing that people have a right to rise up and "shake off" an existing regime and to form a new one, he also insisted, in 1860–61, that the South had no such right to withdraw from the existing Union.[32] As for slavery itself, Lincoln, though repelled by the institution, conceded that white society looked upon racial amalgamation with a "natural disgust," and time and again he warned that the sentiments of society, however repugnant, cannot be disregarded.

Because Lincoln failed to challenge openly a bigoted public opinion, he has been charged with succumbing to it and being more concerned with preserving the Union than freeing the slaves. The charges are accurate but ill-conceived. How could Lincoln win office in a democracy without heeding popular sentiment? Politics to Lincoln was a means to an end, and everything depended on preserving the Union. For if the Union dissolved, how could slavery be abolished? That Lincoln succeeded in both saving the Union and freeing the slaves is testimony to how a genius can confront contradictory principles in action: in this instance the South's right to self-determination and the Union's right to self-preservation.

"Rarely was man so fitted to the event," observed Emerson of Lincoln and the Civil War.[33] Lincoln represented a marvelous fusion of two stances that some postmodernist thinkers regard as completely incompatible. Today it is fashionable to deride the idea of truth as little more than the will to interpret, to regard reality as a representation without a reference to the actually real, and to insist that we must see everything as a product of time and contingency. Many assume that one must be either a sophisticated pragmatist (or poststructuralist) and look upon truth as something made rather than found, or remain a naive absolutist and see truth and value in past first principles. Fortunately for America, Lincoln saw things differently. He succeeded in being as flexible as he was foundational, in practicing an expedient politics of circumstance and an essentialist politics of conviction.

As a politician, Lincoln was a pragmatist willing to adjust to events and to adapt different policies to different circumstances, ever ready to revise positions based on new developments, and determined not to see America bound by the dead hand of history. As a philosopher, however, Lincoln was a moralist and even an absolutist, unswerving in his belief that natural rights are inalienable and hence inviolable, that the Republic's founding principles have the capacity, if properly understood, to remain immune to change, and that the meaning of right and wrong is not relative and dependent upon time and place.

Although historians like to describe Lincoln as operating completely within the "American Pragmatic Tradition," he would probably have had a hard time adhering to the actual philosophy of pragmatism as it arose in the late nineteenth century.[34] Pragmatism insisted then, and persists in claiming now, that there is no knowledge outside of experience. But to Lincoln values are born of remembrance, not forthcoming experience. The pragmatists minimized the importance of the historical past because only the present and future—the true "experience" in their view—could be acted upon and changed. Hovering over the pragmatist's mentality is what Santayana called "the dominance of the foreground." Lincoln, in contrast, sought to have Americans reenact the past in imagination so that the Spirit of '76 would not fade from memory.

The burdens of history weighed heavily in Lincoln's political thought. As early as 1838, in his Young Men's Lyceum Address, deliv-

ered in Springfield, Illinois, Lincoln lectured Americans on the meaning of the rule of law in a democratic society. At the time of the address
America had been reeling from mob violence against abolitionists and
blacks. Lincoln used vivid descriptions to depict lawlessness spreading
as though nature had gone mad—images of "dead men seen literally
dangling from the boughs of trees upon every road side; and in numbers almost sufficient, to rival the native Spanish moss of the country,
as a drapery of the forest."

But why should Americans be law-abiding if obedience is based on
nothing more than fear of punishment? Why respect the rights of
others? Lincoln is not preaching mere legal allegiance to abstract institutions. Instead he wants Americans to understand that the freedoms they enjoy had their origins in the Revolution of '76, an episode
of courage, heroism, and sacrifice, a political struggle born of pure
spirit, a nation so conceived in the blood of liberty that freedom entails
responsibility even more than opportunity:

> Let every American, every lover of liberty, every well wisher to his pos-
> terity, swear by the blood of the Revolution, never to violate in the least
> particular, the laws of the country; and never to tolerate their violation by
> others. As the patriots of seventy-six did to the support of the Declaration
> of Independence, so to the support of the Constitution and Laws, let every
> American pledge his life, his property, and his sacred honor;—let every
> man remember that to violate the law, is to trample on the blood of his
> father, and to tear the character of his own, and his children's liberty. Let
> reverence for the laws, be breathed by every American mother, to the
> lisping babe, that prattles on her lap—let it be taught in schools, in semi-
> naries, and in colleges;—let it be written in Primers, spelling books, and
> in Almanacs;—let it be preached from the pulpit, proclaimed in legisla-
> tive halls, and enforced in courts of justice. And, in short, let it become
> the political religion of the nation; and let the old and the young, the rich
> and the poor, the grave and the gay, of all sexes and tongues, and colors
> and conditions, sacrifice unceasingly upon its altars.[35]

In classical terms, one might say that Lincoln had an intuition for
the bond that exists between *pathos* and *mathos*, between suffering and
its significance. Lincoln could link "sacrifice" to the "sacred" since he
knew full well that politically the Republic was born in violence, and
during the Civil War America would once again see blood flowing on
the nation's "hallowed ground." Almost as though acting out a classi-

cal tragedy, the Civil War dramatized the interrelated themes of guilt, vengeance, and justice. America, the whole nation and not just the South, was morally responsible for tolerating slavery; the South must be retaliated against for jeopardizing the Union with the act of secession; and retribution and redemption could come only by returning to the Declaration and reaffirming equality as a universal principle.

Yet even before the Civil War the note of tragedy resonated in the Lyceum Address. Ironically, although Lincoln called upon Americans to make the Constitution and obedience to its laws "the political religion of the nation," he knew as well as his southern opponents that the Constitution served to protect slavery and hence violated the Declaration. An institution that can do good can also do evil. Abolitionists like William Lloyd Garrison burned a copy of the Constitution, and slave owners understood perfectly well that the Constitution recognized slaves as a species of property. In trying to incorporate the emancipatory spirit of the Declaration into the conservative character of the Constitution and claim that both symbolized America's "political religion," Lincoln was wrestling with a conceptual contradiction. Long before guns opened fire on Fort Sumter, the stage was set for tragedy.

If a label must be applied, Lincoln might best be described as a "Christian pragmatist," to use Reinhold Niebuhr's expression: a thinker who sees history as contingent, politics as morally ambiguous, and God as an inscrutable silent presence; a thinker who, nevertheless, accepts the responsibility for making choices between conflicting alternatives and greater and lesser evils.[36]

But however one describes Lincoln, consider what he achieved in the realm of political thought. He succeeded in balancing an ethic of responsibility that held himself as well as the American people accountable for the consequences of their actions; an ethic of duty that asked Americans to live up to the country's original principles embedded in the Declaration; and an ethic of forgiveness that might have saved America, had he lived, from a politics of hate, malice, and revenge. Above all, even though he was no true believer, he brought religion to bear upon politics and had no hesitation citing the Bible as a source of moral authority. It should be recalled that in both classical republicanism and radical socialism there is no important place for religion; on this Machiavelli and Marx could agree. But Lincoln brings religion into the liberal consensus, and the Gettysburg Address and his Second Inaugural Address asked Americans to ponder "the judgments of the Lord." Earlier, when debating Douglas over the Kansas-Nebraska Act, which proposed to open these territories to slavery, Lincoln thundered: "It hath no relish of salvation in it." The line came from from Shakespeare's *Hamlet*.[37]

Lincoln was also a master of rhetoric, and even though he knew language could be duplicitous, he did not hesitate to use language to define something, to determine its essential qualities and thereby establish its meaning. Lincoln was a master at what philosophers call the "analytic statement," one that turns on its stipulative defining properties and whose truth or falsehood can be established by analyzing the statement itself. "As I would not be a slave, so I would not be a master. This expresses my idea of democracy. Whatever differs from this, to the extent of the differences, is no democracy."[38]

"What pregnant definitions," Emerson exclaimed of Lincoln's way of reasoning; "what unerring common sense; what foresight; and, on great occasions, what lofty, and more than national, what humane tone! His brief speech at Gettysburg will not easily be surpassed by words in any recorded occasion."[39] For Emerson, Lincoln served as an example of an exceptionally American version of nobility: "A great style of hero draws equally on all classes, all the extremes of society, till we say the very dogs believe in him." "Abraham Lincoln," at home with the humblest and admired by the wisest, is "perhaps the most remarkable example of this class that we have seen."[40] Emerson could reconcile genius and democracy, the one and the many, and thereby see a vital unity residing within the diversities of American life. Is it not time to have students and readers understand history the way Emerson saw it and Lincoln lived it? One of the needs of the soul, wrote Emerson poetically, is to have a vision of America as a whole. Abraham Lincoln provided such a vision. In his patriotic nationalism, in his liberal dedication to work and opportunity for all, and in his religious devotion to justice, charity, and magnanimity, American history reached its most sublime synthesis.

CHAPTER 2

America's Lockean Moment: The Revolution and the Spirit of '76

"The Blood of the Revolution"

ABRAHAM LINCOLN TEACHES US HOW TO READ THE Declaration of Independence. What about the Revolution that forged the document itself? For centuries many historians have tried to unravel the "causes" or the "ideological origins" of the Revolution, convinced that if that goal could be achieved we Americans would know who we are and where we are heading. We would establish, at last, our national identity. Lincoln had a different take entirely. He shied away from giving an account of historical events. Convinced that the Revolution could be commemorated without necessarily being explained, he confined its meaning and significance to collective memory rather than causal understanding.

Lincoln paid little attention to the many grievances that the colonists had enumerated in the Declaration to create the impression that King George III was conspiring to subvert their liberties. The causes of the Revolution proved less interesting to Lincoln than the consequences, or what he regarded as the patriotic emotions it engendered as a legacy to future generations. For the Revolution lived in America as a memory passed on as oral history within the family. The glorious "scenes" of the Revolution are to be remembered, and not necessarily its causes. "The consequence was, that of those scenes, in the form of a husband, a father, a son or a brother, a *living history* was to be found in every family—a history bearing the indubitable testimonies of its own authenticity, in the limbs mingled, in the scars of wounds received, in the midst of the very scenes related—a history, too, that could be read and understood alike by all, the wise and the ignorant, the learned and the unlearned."[1]

Exhorting Americans never to forget "the blood of the revolution," Lincoln implied that the event required a narrative telling as opposed to strict causal analysis, for what would sustain moral ideals born of struggle was as much a matter of aesthetics as politics. Thus Lincoln worried that history as visual memorial carried on by story telling had disappeared from view. "Those histories are gone. They can be read no more forever. They were a fortress of strength; but, what invading foement could *never do*, the silent artillery of time *has done;* the levelling of its wall. They are gone. They *were* a fortress of giant oaks; but the all-resistless hurricane has swept over them, and left only, here and there, a lonely trunk, despoiled of its verdure, shorn of its foliages, unshading and unshaded, to murmurs in a few more gentle breezes, and to combat with its mutilated limbs, a few more ruder storms, then to sink, and be no more." Lincoln thus sought not so much to explain the Revolution politically as to express it emotionally. With memory of the Revolution threatened by the passage of time, Lincoln treated it symbolically, as an event whose emotional depth generated passion and whose significance could be maintained only through a return to its original principles. The Revolution is to be preserved in imagination and recollection.[2]

But why did Lincoln avoid dealing with the causes of the Revolution, indeed with the very reasons articulated in the Declaration that justified it? One possible answer is that it may have been the case that the Revolution defies reason and explanation because it involved the riddle of power and sprang from the depths of human passion. This predicament led to a paradox. The colonists were in an abnormal situation in which they may have misunderstood exactly what they were doing, unaware of the meaning of their acts. No one wants to admit, as Tolstoy reminds us, that they cannot know the cause of historical events until they unravel the mysterious ways of power. And no one wants to admit that American freedom grew not only from love of liberty but from hatred of the enemy. "I mean," Lincoln told the Lyceum audience in 1838, the powerful influence which the interesting scenes of the revolution had upon the *passions* of the people as distinguished from their judgment. By this influence, the jealously, envy, and avarice, incident to our nature, and so common to a state of peace, prosperity, and conscious strength, were, for the time, in great measure smothered and rendered inactive; while the deep rooted principles of *hate,* and the powerful motive of *revenge,* instead of being turned against each other, were directly exclusively against the British nation. And thus, from the force of circumstance, the basest principles of our nature, were either made to lie dormant, or to become the active agents in the advancement of the noblest causes, that of establishing and maintaining civil and religious liberty.[3]

A revolution that mobilized the "passions" of the people could only distort their "judgment," thereby rendering the event beyond rational comprehension.

It is curious that Lincoln regarded "hatred," "revenge," and "jealously, envy, and avarice" as "principles," even if the "basest principles of our nature" that transformed ignoble instincts into the "noblest causes." Did Lincoln doubt that the reasons spelled out in the Declaration truly accounted for the colonists' motives in rising up against the British? Are reasons causes? Whatever the answer, when the Civil War broke out in 1861, it should be remembered that Lincoln was to wonder in a similar way whether stated reasons truly ignited and fueled that conflict. In his tragic elegy the Second Inaugural Address, Lincoln stated that "all knew that this interest [slavery] was, somehow, the cause of the war." But slavery itself could be a cause only if Lincoln could confidently specify what course of action might have been taken to control the cause and then, in turn, specify who is to blame for the cause getting out of control. This Lincoln refused to do. The South desired to perpetuate and expand slavery, the North to restrict and confine it. "Neither party expected for the war, the magnitude, or the duration, which it has already maintained," he wrote two years after the war erupted. "Neither anticipated that the *cause* of the conflict might cease with, or even before, the conflict itself should cease." Both sides pray to the same God and their prayers go unanswered. "Let us judge not that we be not judged," the president counseled, citing the Bible. But the war itself was inevitable because neither side was willing to eliminate the conditions that led to it. "Both parties deprecated war; but one of them would *make* war rather than let the nation survive, and the other would *accept* war rather than let it perish. And the war came."[4]

Unsure of what ultimately caused the war or who is to blame for it, Lincoln could only remain convinced of one thing: that he did not control events, a view of history he acknowledged at the time of the Emancipation Proclamation. Yet if Lincoln was a fatalist, how could he be a moralist?

"The Dead Have No Rights"

When studying Abraham Lincoln and thinking about the American Revolution and the Declaration of Independence, we confront a contradiction. The Revolution as an event and the Declaration as a document were meant to overthrow authority, or at least all illegitimate authority that does not emanate from the people themselves; and, perhaps more important, to reorient America so that the people would look to a promising future unburdened by the weight of the past. America broke away from England because it saw itself as a separate entity, and not for nothing did Jefferson advise that "we may consider each generation as a distinct nation, with a right, by the will of its majority, to bind themselves, but none to bind the succeeding generation, more than the inhabitants of another country." It stood as a scientific axiom that generations exist independently of one another. "These are axioms so self-evident that no explanation can make them plainer: for he is not to be reasoned with who says that non-existence can control existence, or that nothing can move something." If the Creator endowed people with natural rights, those rights cease with a given people's death, for the "Creator made the earth for the use of the living and not of the dead. . . . Those who exist not can have no use nor right in it, not authority or power over it." Drawing a sharp distinction between present and future generations, Jefferson denied the value of continuity as well as community. "The dead have no rights," he insisted. "They are nothing, and nothing cannot own something."[5]

Lincoln's relation to Jefferson is more problematic than we have been aware. The common impression was that Lincoln revered Jefferson, since in his speeches on the Fourth of July he paid homage to him. Recently, however, the historian Allen Guelzo has come across evidence that Lincoln's esteem for Jefferson was more a public gesture that concealed his private reservations.[6] Clearly on theoretical matters Lincoln had to distance himself from Jefferson. For Lincoln believed that the dead did indeed have rights; specifically, they had political demands that could be imposed on present generations, and thus the deceased founders possessed a moral authority that extended far beyond their graves. While Jefferson denied the dead a vote, Lincoln sought to give the founders an enduring voice so that America could enjoy an identity that holds across space and time. Here Lincoln comes close to articulating the classical principle that those who made history are more important than those who simply inherit it.[7]

How did Lincoln demonstrate such a daring claim? By taking the Declaration, which Jefferson regarded as a scientific document, and interpreting it as a sacred text, and in the process of doing so he sacralized the whole meaning of the Spirit of '76. What rendered the American Revolution sacred and resistant to the ravages of time was the bravery and sacrifice it entailed for its success. That the patriots were willing to give up their lives for the cause of freedom meant nothing less than a hallowed epiphany at the moment of the Republic's political founding. Fearing that the passage of time undermines patriotic memory, Lincoln called for a "return to the fountain whose waters spring close by the blood of the Revolution." Lincoln hailed the Declaration as the "*political religion* of the nation." In his debates with Douglas, he went so far as to sacralize the document by equating it with the meaning of death itself:

> Take nothing from me—take no thought for the political fate of any man whomsoever—but come back to the truths that are in the Declaration of Independence. You may do anything with me you choose, if you will but heed these sacred principles. You may not only defeat me in the Senate, but you may take me and put me to death. While pretending no indifference to earthly honors, I do so claim to be activated in this contest by something higher than anxiety for office. I charge you to drop every paltry and insignificant thought for any man's success. It is nothing; I am nothing; Judge Douglas is nothing. *But do not destroy that immortal emblem of Humanity—the Declaration of Independence.*[8]

Although Lincoln believed passionately in democracy, he also understood how democracy can be its own worst enemy. His urgent effort to immortalize the Declaration stemmed from his fear that Americans would forget its meaning and significance. Democracy, wrote Tocqueville, "engenders a sort of instinctive distaste for what is old," and the conduct of the American people, pushing always ahead, will "erase the tracks of time." That democracy may obliterate history worried Lincoln as well as Tocqueville. "Since the past has ceased to throw light upon the future, the mind of man wanders in obscurity," wrote Tocqueville. Lincoln agreed, stating in his Second Inaugural Address that the "dogmas of the quiet past are inadequate to the story present." Nevertheless, even though Lincoln declared that Americans "must disenthrall ourselves, and then we shall save our country," he also declared, in the very next sentence: "Fellow citizens, *we* cannot escape history." In the Gettysburg Address, Lincoln sought to endow the valiant deeds on the battlefield with a sacred permanence that could possibly prevent their significance from perishing. But Lincoln wondered whether his sentiments and words could match the deeds and events whose valor surpassed anything that could be uttered in language; yet what took place on the battlefield could be known only by language and the tears of memory. We are gathered to dedicate the earth to the fallen, Lincoln preached:

> But, in a larger sense, we can not dedicate—we can not consecrate—we can not hallow—this ground. The brave men, living and dead, who struggled here, have consecrated it, far above our poor power to add or detract. The world will little note, nor long remember what we say here, but it can never forget what they did here. It is for us the living, rather, to be dedicated here to the unfinished work which they who fought here have thus far nobly advanced. It is rather for us to be here dedicated to the great task remaining before us—that from these honored dead we take increased devotion to that cause for which they gave the last full measure of devotion—that we here highly resolve that these dead shall not have died in vain—that this nation, under God, shall have a new birth of freedom—and that government of the people, by the people, for the people, shall not perish from the earth.[9]

In America's mainstream political culture, ranging from early liberalism to modern pragmatism, from Thomas Jefferson to John Dewey, the historic past had little relevance to the present and its problems. Rather than pondering the past, America must face the future. But with Abraham Lincoln the heroic deeds of history could be made to last out of the act of remembrance. Both the Revolution and the Civil War must be rescued from the futility that accompanies oblivion. The dead have rights due to the sacrifices they made and the living have responsibilities to rededicate themselves to the cause of freedom.

Lincoln departs from Jefferson in another important respect. While Jefferson extolled agriculture as a superior way of life that guaranteed liberty and independence, Lincoln could not wait to flee the farm. Although Lincoln had to pay homage to Jefferson, he was actually closer to Hamilton in seeing farm life as nurturing the same restrictive environment that had bred slavery as much as liberty. Lincoln also tasted the sweet smell of success and, as with Hamilton, he felt deeply the pull of honor and ambition. Lincoln, in addition, saw the need to create the conditions for rapid economic development, and as a Whig he had no hesitation about looking to government to provide capital as well as leadership. He may have had less faith than Hamilton in the "rich, well-born, and able," but like Hamilton he looked to industry and technology as the driving force of America's future. Above all, Lincoln identified opportunity as the engine of human motivation. It was a natural, inalienable right to rise to achievement, and such a rise was rendered possible by the right to labor. Importantly, Lincoln saw support for the right to labor and its relationship to individual progress in the Declaration of Independence—even though its author, the slave-holder Jefferson, says nothing in the document to suggest that the right to work freely conveys the power to act independently in the economic sphere of life.

It was Lincoln's deepest conviction that the ideological significance of the American Revolution expressed itself in the Declaration and that the Spirit of '76 endowed America with its meaning and purpose in human history. Yet a recent study of the Revolution, a widely influential book much read by scholars, students, and the general public alike, a book that represents the reigning interpretation of the event, and a book that will be scrutinized in this chapter, treats the Revolution without even mentioning the Declaration. Why the willful neglect of Lincoln's "immortal emblem"? One possible answer is that to connect the Revolution to the Declaration is to concede that the older liberal consensus school remains valid and that John Locke's political philosophy

still defines America's dominant ideology. Few historians wish to acknowledge that their predecessors had gotten it right. Historians seldom return to older historians; instead they attempt to replace them.

Lockean Liberalism and Property Rights

How can one explain today's rights-based political culture
without considering the legacy of Locke? In the seventeenth century,
Lockeanism represented a radical challenge to political authority and
its pretensions to religious foundations—that is, it ridiculed the mon-
arch's claim to a "divine right" to rule absolutely. But in American
history Lockeanism has come to be seen as conservative because of its
emphasis on property and what recent critics call "possessive individualism."[10] The Declaration itself is Lockean through and through, and
Jefferson sought to prettify its meaning by substituting the "pursuit of
happiness" for what would have been a crass reference to property (or,
actually, "estates"). Perhaps Jefferson recognized that the ownership
of property had little to do with the legitimacy of how this land was
originally acquired through labor and instead saw land being taken in
acts of aggression and violence, as in slavery and the settlers' mistreatment of the Native Americans' habitat. Although the term "happiness" had been regarded as one of the ends of government, Locke's
specific reference to "life, liberty, and estates" makes it clear that those
who find, make, or usefully employ a previously unowned good have a
right to keep it. Curiously, when James Madison proposed a bill of
rights to the Constitution, the First Amendment held that true government consists in the "enjoyment of life and liberty, with the right of
acquiring and using property, and generally of pursuing happiness
and safety."[11] As will be discussed in the last chapter, it was black slaves
who, together with Lincoln, advocated every man and woman's right
to property as the fruit of their labor. Lockeanism has been in the past
and can be in the future a liberalism that truly liberates.

The reluctance to acknowledge the centrality of property to America's political culture is puzzling. One would think that Locke's political philosophy, which challenged patriarchal authority and endowed
women with rights to property and divorce and workers with a labor
theory of value, would be more appreciated.[12] Toleration, education,

life conceived as born free of subjection, government derived from the consent of the people, and the legitimacy of pursuing self-interest all provided some of the liberating ingredients of a philosophy that served seventeenth-century England and America well. Locke, who was in some respects the first male feminist, argued that women, as rational beings subject to natural law, were entitled to the same inalienable right to seek happiness.[13] Locke represents a turning point in history from which there was no turning back; he recast existence as a matter of economics and opportunity instead of duty and politics, especially old classical politics that relegated women and workers to servitude. "Thus in the beginning," wrote Locke of a country without a history where human labor had yet to exercise its productive effects, "all the world was America."[14]

The Mystique of "Republicanism"

In the beginning, according to contemporary scholarship, all America was republican. The idea of republicanism may be more in historians' minds than in history itself. It is certainly a long way from Lincoln's thinking about America. Lincoln's outlook was as much theological as political, resting, as it does, on a Calvinist sense of sin and redemption and a Lockean sense of labor, property, and natural rights. Lincoln's legacy can be both conservative and liberal, with history shouldering the burden of evil and at the same time holding out the possibility of freedom, opportunity, and justice for all. But republicanism is, the historian tells us, not so much conservative or liberal as something far more profoundly different, so different that American history must be reinterpreted to accommodate what has continually failed in American politics—"radicalism."

The idea of republicanism has saturated American historiography. Nowhere is it more insistent than in Gordon Wood's *The Radicalism of the American Revolution* (1992), a highly praised book that was awarded the Pulitzer Prize in history. Wood has convinced himself that long ago in American history there existed a widespread sentiment he calls "radical republicanism," or more exactly, "the radicalism of the republican revolution."[15] A puzzling expression. Historically radicalism identified all hope with the future, while republicanism identified all truth with the past. To link radicalism with republicanism amounts to what Kenneth Burke called "casuistic stretching," a "planned incongruity" that "leads us to be shocked at the idea of putting opposites together."[16] But Wood's book shocked neither history nor Hollywood. It has become so much a cultural artifact that it received prominent treatment in the Academy Award–winning screenplay of the Hollywood film *Good Will Hunting*. The scene that refers to Wood's book was chosen as the film's best picture clip for advertising purposes, and thus it has been estimated that 87 million people saw it on American television alone. The scene takes place in a bar in Cambridge, Massachusetts. The hero, Will, played by actor Matt Damon, a mathematical genius well-read in other fields but resentful of the pretensions of the academic world, challenges a Harvard graduate student named Clark, who, in the presence of attractive coeds, is attempting to prove his intellectual superiority by humiliating Will's working-class friend:

> CLARK: I was just hoping you could give me some insight into the evolution of the market economy in the colonies. My contention is that prior to the Revolutionary War, the economic modalities, especially in the southern colonies, could most aptly be characterized as agrarian precapitalist and . . .
>
> [Will, seeing his friend cornered by the scholarly show-off, walks up to the bar and intervenes in the conversation.]
>
> WILL: Of course that's your contention. You're a first-year graduate student. You just finished reading some Marxist historian, Pete Garrison, prob'ly, and so naturally that's what you believe until next month when you get to James Lemon and get convinced that Virginia and Pennsylvania were strongly entrepreneurial and capitalist back in 1740. That'll last until some time in your second year, then you'll be regurgitating Gordon Wood about the pre-revolutionary utopia and the capital-forming effects of military mobilization.
>
> CLARK [stunned by Will's erudition]: Well, as a matter of fact, I won't, because Wood drastically underestimates the impact of . . .
>
> WILL: Wood drastically underestimates the impact of social distinctions predicated upon wealth, especially inherited wealth. . . . You got that from Vicker's *Work in Essex County,* was it pages 98 to 102, what? Do you have any thoughts of your own on the subject or were you just gonna plagiarize the whole book for me?

As the dialogue suggests, Wood's *The Radicalism of the American Revolution* is the most talked-about book on early American history.

The book argues that the Revolution eliminated hierarchies and traditional social distinctions and deferences that were once associated
with the Old World. The possibility that the advent of new wealth may
have reinstituted old distinctions, that what was created in the Revolution resulted in perpetuating in different forms the old ways of life that
had supposedly been destroyed in 1775–83, that, in short, the rule
of money replaced the role of monarchy, are problems that can be
scarcely considered if the Revolution is to be regarded as radical. Had
the Revolution been authentically radical, as the historian claims, Lincoln need not have explained to Douglas and to the American people
why the Spirit of '76 must be carried forward in the name of true
equality.

Wood's previous major work, *The Creation of the American Republic, 1776–1787* (1969), is one of the great seminal texts in early
American history. The book on the American Revolution, however,
says the right things with the wrong words, to the point that its author
assumes he is writing about republicanism when he is actually narrating a story of liberalism that contains conservative ramifications. But it
has been fashionable lately in historiography to use the term "republicanism" with all of its implications for "public virtue" and "civic humanism." Such expressions caught on in scholarship as an effort to
prove that the liberalism articulated by the older school can now be
challenged and that consensus scholars missed seeing that American
history has had a non-capitalist alternative somewhere in the past.

By no means did Wood intend to refute liberalism. He scarcely
writes from the point of view of the Left, and he has always been
critical of the scholarship of those scholars of the 1960s who would see
in the American Revolution the rumblings of class conflict. Instead
Wood sought to say something new about the origins of America's
political culture. To use the terminology of liberalism would seem
stale and unoriginal; hence he tries on the vocabulary of republicanism. But all this effort of saying the same thing in the guise of a new
lexicon can be confusing.

A few years ago, the Speaker of the House, Newt Gingrich, himself
once a history professor, instructed his followers to read three texts
that he regarded as edifying and essential to the moral health of America's political culture: the *Federalist*, Alexis de Tocqueville's *Democracy*

in America, and Gordon Wood's *The Radicalism of the American Revolution.* The problem with this troika of a canon is that each text, rather than reinforcing the analysis, ideas, and conclusions of the other two, contradicts them to the point that if one is true the others must be false in explaining America. And if two of them are valid, then the Republican Party should rethink its populist premises. Gingrich instructs us to grasp the meaning of America through a canon of immiscibility. The newly won status of the Republican Party, which now enjoys the position of being the popular majority party in Congress, makes it all the more puzzling why its former leader would recommend Tocqueville and the *Federalist* authors, who warned Americans that the problem they would have to face was the majority itself. Neither Tocqueville nor the *Federalist* authors saw the Revolution as radical, and neither could see how republicanism might explain America.

"Gordon Wood's two great works," writes Gingrich in *To Renew America,* "further strengthened my understanding of the enormous gap between America as it was founded and America as it is being mistaught in the academy. The Founding Fathers clearly understood that America was a new idea. They created a vision of self-government in which virtue and patriotism were primary safeguards of freedom's survival."[17] Unfortunately, the idea of virtue gets lost between the two books cited, Wood's first and second book, since the founders themselves concluded that they could not count upon it. As for patriotism, another subject broached by Gingrich, it too proved an unreliable idea. Gingrich is on stronger grounds when he cites such leaders as Lincoln, Theodore Roosevelt, and Franklin D. Roosevelt for inspiration. "I came out of my two years of reviewing American history convinced that our first need is to rediscover the values we have lost."[18] Lincoln did indeed see values emanating from the Revolution, but the values were far from republican—they were liberal.

It is an important and serious matter to try to get straight the terminology of our political culture, for how we call ourselves influences how we think about and define ourselves. Are we Americans radical, in that we are determined to perpetuate the revolutionary spirit? Are we republican, in that we are determined to live the life of civic virtue? Or are we what Tocqueville saw as a new hybrid: liberals who assert their rights, conservatives who protect their property?

The "Radicalism" of the American Revolution?

Republicanism is an old idea, one first articulated in classical antiquity; liberalism, much newer, was first conceived in sixteenth- and seventeenth-century England. After Aristotle, the central figure in republican thought was Niccolò Machiavelli, who taught princes how to use political power; after Thomas Hobbes, the central figure in liberal thought was John Locke, who taught the people how to control it.

It is difficult to see how the American Revolution can be both republican and radical at the same time. Acknowledging that some English republicans sought only to reform the monarchy, the historian hastens to add: "But republicanism was no less revolutionary for all that. In fact, it was in every way a radical ideology—as radical for the eighteenth-century as Marxism was to be for the nineteenth-century. It challenged the primary assumptions and practices of monarchy—its hierarchy, its inequality, its devotion to kinship, its patriarchy, its patronage, and its dependency."[19] From such a reading one would think that it was not liberalism but republicanism that offered a comprehensive critique of patriarchal authority, supplied Americans with a nature-based philosophy with which they would come to enjoy a rights-based political culture, and articulated a radically new theory of happiness as the human desire to avoid misery and choose opportunity. But in fact, far from being about rights or happiness, republicanism is about civic duty and public virtue. Above all, republicanism demands of citizens that they accept the Roman concept of authority, in which action becomes legitimate to the extent that it augments the founding and perpetuates ancestral memory all the way back to a country's remotest beginnings.[20]

How then can the American Revolution be both republican and radical? Thomas Jefferson, Thomas Paine, John Adams, and the *Federalist* authors all rejected the authority of the past. In the *Federalist*, readers are asked why they are objecting to the proposed Constitution simply because it is "new," a "novelty" and "innovation," an "experiment" in the "science of politics."[21] From the beginning the leaders of America's political culture challenged Americans to turn away from the past and toward what Jefferson regarded as the "sovereignty of the present generation" and the principle that "the earth belongs to the living."[22] Republicanism is retrospective; the new American Republic would be prospective and be guided by whatever the future had to offer. The foundations of the American Revolution are inextricably tied to a liberalism that would never allow itself to be bound by the past.

At the time of the Revolution, however, the idea of republican "virtue" could be invoked as an indictment of the extension of the corruptions of Old World parliamentary politics into the New World. Within this rhetoric of accusation, colonists were encouraged to believe that England was conspiring to subvert liberty in America, and thus the colonists were to make a revolution almost for the sake of restoration. This mentality, as we saw Lincoln observing, projected onto the Old World the less than selfless impulses of the New, thereby enabling the colonists to see themselves acting for the "noblest causes." Historians who take seriously the rhetoric used in times of revolutionary upheaval ought to heed the wisdom not only of Lincoln but of Karl Marx himself. It should come as no surprise that colonial pamphlets depicted the rebels desiring to restore lost liberties in the tradition of Whig and republican thought, and hence to see themselves as virtuous and their enemies as vicious. Marx showed how the French revolutionaries gravitated toward similar paradigms, seeing themselves as "resurrected Romans" and "Hebrew prophets" as they dressed themselves in older cultural clothing that was meant to be restored. As Lincoln and Marx observed, revolutionaries cannot legitimate their actions by claiming to bring into existence something daringly new; hence they cling to an obsolete vocabulary while forging a new reality that misleads them into thinking that revolution really means "to revolve." After the initial turmoil had subsided in the French Revolution, in 1799, Marx saw taking place what Lincoln had observed, a decade and a half earlier on the other side of the Atlantic: the "bourgeois transformation" of society in which "Locke supplanted *Habakkuk*."[23]

It is curious that historians have joined together republicanism and Marxism in order to offer a challenge to consensual liberalism and capitalism (the subject of Chapter 8). Marx himself saw republicanism as dubious. Yet its very language has continued to mislead historians who confuse the language of politics with the politics of language, particularly those historians who believe that political ideas and their rhetoric not only represent reality but "create" it.[24]

One revolutionary leader who happened to be a master of political language was Thomas Paine, and he appreciated 1776 as signifying a profound break with the past. Inevitably Paine, along with others, has been described as a republican who supposedly partakes of the recently discovered (or invented) paradigm of civic virtue. In truth, Paine stood adamantly for republicanism to the extent that he had no use for monarchy and championed representative government; nevertheless, he saw ancient republicanism as retrograde and parasitically aristocratic. He also tried to explain to Americans why republicanism has had its day in history. A government based upon republican principles and a nation aspiring to a liberal future must, Paine exhorted, "come close to a final separation," for each is moving in the opposite direction; the former adheres to "precedent" while the latter lives by "improvement."[25]

What, then, did the colonists live by and for? "The republican revolution," according to Wood, "was the greatest utopian movement in American history. The revolutionaries aimed at nothing less than the reconstitution of society." Americans have been misled into assuming that their revolution was less than radical, Wood might say, because the French Revolution is usually held up as the norm. Thus we should question, as he put it, "the myth that has continued into our time—the myth that the American Revolution was sober and conservative while the French Revolution was chaotic and radical. But only if we measure radicalism by violence and bloodshed can the myth be sustained."[26] Are there not other ways to measure the meaning of a revolution?

The Revolution That Wasn't

Neither "radical" nor "conservative" is an appropriate term with which to describe the Revolution. Had there been a revolutionary threat to the existing order and a counter-revolutionary resistance to that threat—that is, a real effort at "the reconstruction of society"— American history would have climaxed in class warfare. The American Revolution was spared not only the blood and terror of the French

Revolution. Consider what else did not take place on this side of the Atlantic. In America there was

1. No discussion, not even a whisper, of questioning the sanctity of property,
2. No confiscation of church holdings,
3. No attack on religion and its relation to the ethical rationality of the coming commercial society,
4. No old-regime aristocracy to overthrow,
5. No landless peasantry and emergent proletariat to fulfill the requirements of class division,
6. No unification of political authority in a single assembly that claimed to represent the "general will,"
7. No "positive" notion of liberty, which instead of freeing humankind from constriction and restraint, leads citizens to believe that individual fulfillment can be actualized only collectively,
8. No moralizing role of politics wherein civic participation promises to regenerate society so that the distinction between state and society can be abolished,
9. No reign of virtue and terror in which a revolution devours its own children before a Thermidorean reaction takes place (as in France when the forces of the Right moved against the Left),
10. No political philosophy that ignores religion in order to put all trust in reason,
11. No theory of history that purports to reconcile rationality, contingency, and freedom,
12. No public philosophy that commands the scrimmage of private interests so that free will aspires to something other than itself,
13. No "ideology" that, in its eighteenth-century context, offers a scientific study of society that unveils illusions and thereby allows reason to be seen as immanent in a history whose processes can now be brought under human control,[27] and, following from the last limitation,
14. No theory of power that permits the political architect to eliminate its causes in order to free humankind from its effects. The American Revolution was unique in leading to a constitutional system that recognized the struggle for power as a fact of human nature whose elimination cannot be attained by cries of corruption or by incantations of virtue.

Far from preserving the power of a particular class, the Constitution was a radical admission of human limitations. All revolutions claim to have an answer to the problem of power, and a revolution that is "radical" should, as the meaning of the term implies, go to the "root" of that problem. The *Federalist* authors, however, were the political philosophers who acknowledged that a government can at best manage power. In the events leading to the Revolution, the colonists were almost paranoid about power and the way it moved silently and conspiratorially to subdue unalert citizens, and hence the generation of '76 saw power and liberty as mutually antagonistic.[28] Even so, in the *Federalist* Hamilton takes pains to point out that power implies not only the meaning of "over," as in domination and coercion, but also "to," as in the ability to make things happen and resist domination. Thus he tries to reassure readers why power should not be feared since its dispersion in a system of checks and balances render its consequences controllable. Power becomes not so much the antithesis of freedom as its expression. Where there is uncontrolled freedom people will, whether they are the few or the many, "vex and oppress" one another. In the new Constitution the principle of resistance to government lies in the very structure of government, indicating that differences and opposition would characterize American politics, and hence the Revolution, although made in the name of "one people," failed to produce it.

In what sense was the American Revolution a "revolution"? The depictions of the many ways the colonists struggled to free themselves from all dependency relations, structures of authority, positions of subordination, and other modes of submission can hardly be described as revolutionary. To resist, oppose, and aspire to be free is more indicative of the waning sentiments of obedience and obligation than of the desire to restructure an entrenched old order. Perhaps a distinction between rebellion and revolution may help us understand that America, in the period 1775–89, took shape as a deliberately self-limiting political experience, a model of moderation that never lost sight of its original aims of declaring independence, restoring liberty, and limiting the power of government.

The American "revolution" was more of a rebellion—that is, it was more of a political event than a social phenomenon. A revolution seeks to transform the entire framework of social relations in order to eliminate power, exploitation, and oppression; a rebellion seeks to rectify grievances in order to reclaim liberties that have been violated. A revolution sets out to topple power in order to create a new regime that offers itself, or imposes itself, as the omniscient instrument of popular consent; a rebellion sets out to bring down an old system of authority whose ending is an end in itself. A revolution seeks to wrest unity out of diversity; a rebellion recognizes that, as Jefferson put it, uniformity is the perfection of monotony.

A truly republican revolution would most likely have taken the course of the French Revolution under Maximilien Robespierre in 1793, when anyone not regarded as helping to bring about civic virtue fell prey to the Terror. But the American colonists, rather than forging political innovation and transformation, actually resisted it. It was the British Parliament that had sought to change the operations of the colonial system in order to make it more efficient and just, at least from the viewpoint of an Englishman burdened with taxes. What, after all, was the American Revolution if not a revolution against taxes and commercial regulations; against government as an external imposition; against civic duty as loyalty to the mother country; and against, from the British perspective, reform itself? Had the Revolution been inspired by the principles of republicanism, one would expect the Declaration of Independence to have demanded the right to participate in politics in the name of public virtue—a subject upon which the document remained silent. Lincoln correctly interpreted the Declaration as granting Americans the right to pursue a life of labor and industry. What about leisure?

Consumerism and Patronage

Could America have experienced a genuine "radicalism" in making the transition from monarchical rule, where social bonds were more organic and structured, to a new regime where all such ties dissolved as society became more democratic and egalitarian? The case made for the radical birth of freedom rests on the assumption that America made a decisive break from past restrictions. But consider the two phenomena that are offered as evidence of the radical character of the Revolution: the rise of consumerism and the decline of patronage.

The extravagant purchase and display of clothes and other possessions were characteristic of the gentry classes of the eighteenth century. Rather than challenging those classes, "emulative consumption" in colonial America helped the emergent middle class to break away from both an older Calvinism that frowned on the pursuit of wealth and "severe republican moralists" who feared the corruptions of luxury. But spending in order to keep up with (or surpass) the possessions of one's neighbors can never be truly liberating. Emulation compels people to take on the mannerisms of the classes above them, and "conspicuous consumption" (Wood's phrase) can serve only to make the bonds of society top heavy. The ability to purchase may signify new opportunities for upward mobility, but as acquisitive, outward-looking consumers the American people allowed society to shape their identity.[29]

Indeed, years after the Revolution it was not government but society that became the force of inhibition. No wonder Emerson concluded that Americans lacked a capacity for solitude and self-reliance and Thoreau saw his neighbors possessed by their own possessions. Tocqueville observed a people who had overthrown monarchy only to give themselves over to the pursuit of money, which, while releasing genuine "energy," allowed that energy to be absorbed in an unremitting search for approbation in a society now regarded as sovereign and determined by the vicissitudes of a public opinion more punitive than the gallows of the Old World. Tocqueville could agree with the Transcendentalists that mass democracy mired in endless acquisition leads to lives of either desperation or docility.

Yes, indeed, we have become consumer crazy. But how "radical" is that squalid spectacle that made possible our present-day shopping malls? It would be more accurate to describe such tendencies as part of the liberal consensus that permitted a *conservative* respect for property to evolve into an acquisitive quest for things that one cannot afford but buys anyway, the very indebtedness that the colonists were trying to escape.

Did America also escape dependency by leaving behind patronage, that political practice that supposedly festered only in the corridors of court and Parliament in the Old World? The allocation of jobs and sinecures by office holders to office seekers is described as peculiar to the corruptions of England. "Patronage was the lifeblood of monarchy," and in colonial America, even the influence of the king could not convince residents to tolerate flagrant appointments and the exploitation of political position.[30] One would think, then, that a "radical" revolution would have extirpated such a monarchist practice. But the rise of Jacksonian democracy and the "spoils-system" is seen by its critics as a "throwback to the old monarchical techniques of the eighteenth century." The historian who defends the supposedly new system of "rotation-in-office," on the other hand, sees it as democratic because it was based on "not worth, not ability, not character, and not reputation, but connection to party"—as though ties with a new party are freer than ties with an old parliamentary faction.[31] In short, the Revolution liberated Americans from subordination and dependency only to have them turn for services and favors to the party machine, an institution that lives by connections rather than for convictions.

For a revolution to deserve the description "radical" it certainly would have had to purge radically Old World institutions like patronage. But the historian Edward Channing saw the phenomenon of "office seeking" as even more prevalent after the Revolution, with the Loyalists driven from their political appointments. By the end of the Civil War, the "spoils-system" had so brought back the same corruptions infecting the monarchical politics of eighteenth-century England that Henry Adams felt it necessary to return to the writings of Robert Walpole, the English statesman and prime minister, to figure out what was going on. What Adams saw was that the widespread existence of patronage, whether in eighteenth-century England or nineteenth-century America, meant that politics remained prey to economics. Political office, once regarded as a "sacred trust," had become a "species of property" to be bought and sold, and politics, once regarded as a civic duty in which citizens rise to virtue, had become simply a form of business transaction. After visiting the United States, Max Weber wrote of American parties as "office patronage organizations" consisting of bosses, administrators, publicity consultants, and other officials who behave like "mercantilists" and "capitalists." Adams and Weber saw that democracy begets bureaucracy. It is difficult to see how the American Revolution freed Americans from dependency when patronage became even greater after monarchical rule.[32]

Another way to evaluate the alleged radicalness of a revolution is to measure its lasting effects. After World War II, the federal government became the official patron of higher education in an American society that is truly interdependent. Today more money flows to politics than during the reign of George III, and with the same intent to buy power and influence as that demonstrated by consumers, who spend wishing to buy status and distinction. If America had a radical revolution, where are its traces?

The Futile Attempt to Liberate Us from Liberalism

One need not cite the realities of the present to refute claims being made about the past. How we got from there to here follows logically from liberalism, not from republicanism. The advent of commerce and consumption is the beginning of the end of classical values to the extent that modern history, unlike the ancient world, has the technological means of enchanting society with promises of the new at the expense of the old. Consumption marks the end of the primacy of politics and the beginning of the domination of economics, the end of values as something that can be stabilized and preserved and the beginning of change as the only thing that matters, the end of looking back to the founding of the Republic to gain inspiration from its original principles and the beginning of looking forward to a life where circumstances prevail over any sense of principle based on historical ideals. As Hannah Arendt pointed out, the meaning of commercial society, where things are produced for no other purpose than to be consumed, completely shatters the metaphysical foundations of republicanism, where the sphere of politics once promised to render the public realm immune to the ravages of time as well as the corruptions of money.[33]

We are a liberal, acquisitive people, and our belief in both things, liberty and property, sufficed to make a successful revolution. But the Revolution was neither republican nor radical. Edmund Burke once remarked that Machiavellian republicanism is "intelligence without property," a marvelous phrase that drives home the point that classical politics bestowed no value on economic liberty and remained separate from modern liberalism.[34] What the founders wrought was something new. Consumption reflects the will to property, the essence of Lockeanism; equality rests on the norm of nature, the premise of Jefferson's natural-rights philosophy; both eventually lead to modern market capitalism. Further, an emergent capitalism that disintegrates the old order has been the historical role of liberalism, not republicanism, and certainly not radicalism, which generally is a response to liberalism and its alleged insufficiencies.

Why does the expression "republicanism" persist as a pervasive paradigm in historiography? The very term "republic" joins together the Latin expression *res publica,* meaning the public good, or what people have in common—the commonwealth and the good of the whole. Thomas Paine explained to Americans that a government that invoked "common interests," as opposed to "common rights," was a government of "conquerors," a regime not to be trusted.[35] Civic virtue as the citizen's obligation to uphold the public over the private has a strong and relentless hold over the minds of many recent scholars. But once the distinction between public and private disappears, we are in the world of liberalism, not republicanism. In liberalism the older priority of politics and duty over interest and opportunity succumbs to the escape from political authority and a new life that has as its end the pursuit of happiness. With liberalism the world opens itself up to commerce, trade, contracts, commodities, labor, wages, property, and possessiveness in general. Ironically, some colonists convinced themselves that the Revolution was being fought to prevent the coming of the self-indulgence of liberalism and to uphold an older republican virtue. In 1778 the *Virginia Gazette* put it this way:

> GENEALOGY OF THE AMERICAN WAR
> Luxury begot Arbitrary Power.
> Arbitrary Power begot Oppression.
> Oppression begot Resentment.
> Resentment begot Revenge.

Although the colonists saw themselves as struggling against the power and corruption that they identified with monarchy and Old World parliamentary cliques, it could very well be, as Lincoln suggested in his Lyceum Address of 1838, that they were struggling with their own temptations of the flesh. Contemporaries also saw this fall from innocence. "Are we not precipitating ourselves into the imitation of every species of Luxury and refinement?" the young artist John Trumbull asked his father after the Revolution. "And does not all this tend to the inevitable destruction of republican virtue and national character?—I fear so."[36]

Considering the aftermath of the American Revolution, one cannot help but think of America immediately following World War II. In the midst of both wars a strong sense of patriotic unity and idealism developed, with people accepting restrictions and the rationing of consumer goods and with youths courageously going off to fight for their country. Then, in the aftermath of the later war, the American people went on a binge of spending and buying, gorging themselves on everything that had been rationed and availing themselves of everything coming off the assembly lines. But no one would describe the squalid spectacle as "radical" or in any way bold or daring. The mass consumption after World War II repeated what Trumbell had called in post-Revolutionary America "an endless itch for imitation." The literary scholar Kenneth Silverman catches the irony in the situation when he observes that the lust for luxuries in the 1780s meant that America won the war with England and lost the war for its own soul. "At the very time that America became politically free, her moral weakness was forging a new social dependence."37

The Impossibility of a Radical Democratic Revolution

The new liberal, consumerist reality emerging in post-revolutionary society that we now discern, two centuries later, failed to be clearly grasped when the Constitution was drafted. The framers were unable to see that the American people would conform to the customs of an emergent American society. More precisely, they failed to understand that a new social order would be sufficiently conservative to guarantee that any future internal revolution would be improbable. Unlike Tom Paine, the framers distrusted a society without the surveillance and control of government, and thus they assumed that the political sphere must dominate the social domain. Hence they drew up a Constitution designed to preserve liberty as well as protect property and the faculties for acquiring it on the assumption that property and democracy were incompatible. One would think, then, that the American Revolution did indeed forge a genuine "radicalism," and the framers had good reason to use the Constitution to control its effects. But the opposite scenario needs to be considered. If the American Revolution was soberly conservative in that it sought to preserve established liberties while leaving property untouched, why did the framers fear the rise of democracy?

It is a common impression that the framers feared modern democracy because they were aspiring to emulate ancient classical republics.[38] In reality, the framers rejected such republics as hopelessly obsolete models of pride and self-delusion. Hamilton dismissed them as so perpetually bellicose and militaristic that economic growth stagnated; Adams believed that the idea of "civic virtue" kept the masses of people in a state of servitude and misery; and Madison sought to demonstrate to readers of the *Federalist* why classical thinkers were wrong to assume that a polity must remain small and restricted geographically, because this was the very kind of environment that generates instability and unreason. The ancient polis, scoffed Adams, might be studied as a "boudoir," a chamber of mirrors in which people could see the reflections of their own vanities and defects. Adams and Jefferson, so apart on other issues, both agreed that classical authors were better at writing about liberty than preserving it. Ultimately, the framers turned away from ancient republics as models simply because all such republics had eventually failed. Those who drafted the Constitution rejected the old republics and their "gloomy sophisms" for a "new science of politics."[39]

But even with a new approach to politics and political institutions, the framers still had deep apprehensions about democracy. The new Constitution, Madison emphasized, must "break and control the violence of factions" so that the body politic would not be endangered by a "rage for paper money, for an abolition of debts, for an equal division of property, or for any improper or wicked project."[40] Herewith a riddle.

The framers did indeed fear democracy as wickedly radical and, seeing property threatened by nothing less than class conflict, they established mechanisms to control such conflict. Yet it turned out that when those controls were circumvented in the Jacksonian era, when popular democracy in the form of universal white manhood suffrage prevailed over republican checks, all the wicked projects that Madison feared vanished like a bad dream. The American Revolution had no substantial radical content because democracy itself was not radical. Popular factions, it turned out, posed no threat to property, the distribution of wealth, and the role of political leadership in the Senate.

As Tocqueville would point out, the people shared the same values as the owning classes and believed in ambition, opportunity, and the freedom to acquire and dispose of property. It was not the framework of political institutions but the social values and mores that held America together, the liberal consensus that had gone unseen in post-colonial America. Had America a real radical revolution consisting in all the tensions that tore apart French society, class conflict would have doomed the American Republic from the start.

Not only did the American founders fail to foresee what Tocqueville described as the "common opinions" that breed "*consensus universalis*," they also failed to appreciate the enduring value of America's Protestant heritage.[41] Perhaps because they saw themselves as philosophers of the Enlightenment, the framers looked upon religion as divisive and thereby missed seeing what Tocqueville and Max Weber later saw: an earlier Puritanism that endowed America with a viable Protestant work ethic that respected property rights. The dictum of Francis Lieber became an axiom in American political thought: Man's "goodness, his greatness, his activity, his energy and industry—everything good and characteristic of him as a man—is connected with the idea of individual property."[42]

The idea that the American Revolution was radical gains some credence when compared to prior revolutions that rarely threatened hierarchy and class domination. But a fixed class structure based on the residues of an ancien régime was precisely what was absent in America. The idea that the Revolution "created" a democratic culture implies that it brought into existence what once had no presence. But such conditions did have a presence. As Weber demonstrated, the value and dignity of labor was recognized by the Puritans in the seventeenth century; an emerging national character that refused deference and "servile dependence" to the upper stratum had characterized American manners before the Revolution, according to Hector St. John Crèvecoeur's *Letters from an American Farmer;* and recently Pauline Maier has demonstrated that the spirit of egalitarianism pervaded American society well before its articulation in the Declaration of Independence.[43]

Here we arrive at a crucial question. Can the people themselves make a radical revolution? To be more precise, can a people who already enjoy liberty consciously will themselves to move to a state beyond liberalism in order to arrive at radicalism? It should be recalled that all historical revolutions that aimed at a radical transformation of the social order took place in non-liberal environments in which people were hardly consulted as to their wishes. Revolutions that are genuinely radical in overthrowing religion, property, and traditional social relations are undemocratic and led by a vanguard of intellectuals and revolutionary leaders that only purport to be acting in the name of "the people." Such revolutions have more to do with conceit than consent.

Since liberal political freedom depends upon the consent of the governed, it is difficult to understand how people would consent to have a revolution change them into something other than what they are. The American Revolution amounted to, among other things, a power struggle between two unyielding forces: a mother country determined to rule, and colonies determined to be free of domination. The struggle itself was part of the modernization of the western world and had little to do with attempts to realize radicalism's unborn ideals. In America the deliberate, conscious equation of liberty and property enjoyed the same status after the Revolution as before. That equation remained at the heart of the American identity, and as long as Americans consented to it, it is difficult to see the possibility of their supporting a radical revolution that would have caused them to give it up.

A people could rise up against a class alien to itself without risking its identity, however. Historically that class had been the aristocracy in one form or another, and in most cases worldwide an emergent bourgeoisie had forged its consciousness in challenging the aristocracy. But in America aristocracy had, outside the deep South, no real form or substance. And without an aristocracy and ancien régime, how can Americans understand different cultures elsewhere in the world that must struggle against those conditions?

America and the World

> The American Revolution created this democracy, and we are living with its consequence still.[44]

Can a revolution create a democracy? No other modern revolution, with the possible exception of the Dutch in the sixteenth century, set in motion changes that would eventually become a democracy resting upon liberal institutions. Yet Holland's struggle against Spain was more of a war for independence than a revolution, as was America's struggle against England two centuries later, and in each instance the presence of an external foe served to unify the provinces in Holland and the colonies in America. As to the classic French Revolution, it created democracy only to see it destroyed. In France a revolution based upon truly radical ideals turned out to be unrealizable. As François Furet put it: "The French Revolution produced a multiplicity of constitutions and regimes and gave the world its first look at egalitarian despotism. It gave lasting life to the concept of revolution defined not as a passage from one regime to another—an interlude between two worlds—but as a political culture inseparable from democracy and, like democracy, inexhaustible, with no legal or constitutional limit because it is fueled by the passion for equality which, by definition, has no threshold of satisfaction."[45]

The American historian Wood, in contrast to the French historian Furet, mistakenly assumes that radicalism can arise out of an established environment of liberalism and that equality has its threshold of satisfaction in consumption. Thus he sought to credit a political event with social significance in order to claim that American democracy was the natural result of its Revolution. But revolutions that are truly social fall disastrously short of achieving political democracy. "Revolution and democracy are contradictory notions," observed Raymond Aron.[46]

Yet the misimpression that a revolution could somehow be democratic and emulate America became a desperate delusion during the Vietnam War. Keeping in mind the earlier questionable thesis that the American Revolution "created" our democracy, consider the following exchange:

> SENATOR MUNDT: Dr. Hartz, I am sorry I came in late, giving me a limited opportunity to scan your statement rather hurriedly. I presume the purpose of these hearings is to try to determine, as a nation which was born in the crucible of revolution, what should be our attitude toward other revolutions in other areas of the world. I take it that you have stated your general concepts in this paper.
>
> Do you feel that this country should seek to mold the rest of the world in its own image?

MR. HARTZ: Let me say, first, Senator, that the burden of my remarks has been to attempt to establish that America did not arise out of a revolutionary experience but rather out of a migration experience. Under these circumstances, I do not think the issue we confront is an issue of exporting our revolution elsewhere. It is true that we have had a revolution for national independence and to some extent that would be involved in the problems of other nations. But if we are concerned with matters of social revolution and social change, the American experience does not give us, if we look inside that experience, anything that we could export elsewhere. I think, therefore, the issue is the rather more complicated issue of whether we should seek to spread automatically to societies experiencing social revolution the results of an historic experience which has arisen out of the entirely different experience of migration. And my answer to that question almost inevitably is that we must not fall into the fallacy of attempting to do that.

This exchange took place before the Senate Foreign Relations Committee hearings on the topic "The Meaning of Revolution" in 1968, at the height of the Vietnam War. Louis Hartz, the historian of liberal consensus who had suffered a mental breakdown in his last years before leaving Harvard (I discuss Hartz further in Chapter 7), appeared lucid as he spelled out before the Senate his thesis about the significance of an American history in which people enjoyed freedom without having to struggle for it:

MR. HARTZ: The legend of the *Mayflower* is the great legend of our history, and yet few Americans realize how thoroughly it excludes from that history the possibility of a social revolution. For if, as we are told, the glory of the Pilgrims was that they fled the social oppressions of Europe, how could they have a revolution against those oppressions after they arrived in America? . . . The fact is they did leave behind the central structure of aristocratic Europe, and in doing so they escaped not only that structure but the need to destroy it on its own ground. Indeed, the very psychology of escape, of getting away, is America's substitute for the European psychology of social revolution. . . . It is not hard to show that it was the flight from Europe which made possible the completeness and the ease with which American liberalism triumphed. . . . The pattern of liberal history on the continent [consists in] a succession of violent moments, compromise victories. America escapes this pattern precisely because it leaves behind the medieval ghosts who will not die in Europe. . . . But curiously this wisdom must be qualified in the historical sphere, for experience

shows that precisely those institutions which a revolutionary cannot destroy he can effectively desert. Indeed I would argue on the basis of the American experience, if it would not confuse my categories too much, that the only really successful revolution is in fact a migration.
SENATOR GORE: You mean anywhere?
MR. HARTZ: If you can find a place.[47]

Other thinkers like Lincoln, Horace Bushnell, Tocqueville, and some of the Transcendentalists are closer to Hartz in believing that the Revolution, with its glorious military battles against the hated British, distracted the American mind from its search to understand what America was all about. America's social freedoms and many of its political liberties had been won long before a bullet was fired because the roots of oppression, like the roots of tradition, had been left behind in the Old World:

> The society transplanted, in a case of emigration, cannot carry its roots with it; for society is a vital creature, having roots of antiquity, which inhere in the very soil—in the spots consecrated by valor, by genius and by religion. Transplanted to a new field, the emigrant race loses, of necessity, a considerable portion of that vital force which is the organific and conserving power of society. All the old roots of local love and historic feeling—the joints and bonds that minister nourishment—are left behind; and nothing remains to organize a living growth, but the two unimportant incidents, proximity and a common interest.[48]

The origins of America's political culture had more to do with the impulse to escape than with any effort to bring to the New World political traditions from the Old. From the *Mayflower* to the Vietnamese boat people there continues a spirit that makes all immigrants, no matter how diverse culturally and ethnically, "a family of man" (Lincoln's phrase) born in flight from deprivation and oppression. Old World republicanism was too elitist and aristocratic to take root in American soil. Classical ideals aiming at civic virtue require a leisure class whose freedom to participate in politics depends upon the labor of others, whether servants or slaves. To paraphrase Werner Sombart's famous question as to why America lacked a strong socialist tradition: Why is there no republicanism in the United States of America? Because aristocrats don't migrate.

Nor do proletarians. Their political consciousness is determined by a fixed class position in a seemingly immobile social order—the true grounds for a radicalism that seeks to overthrow that order precisely because the lower classes are denied any means of entering into that social order. An American political culture without an aristocratic leisure class and without a revolutionary working class should be described for what it is. Were not the framers wrong to fear the democratic masses? Were not Americans wrong to fear the subsequent arrival of immigrants as a radical threat to the dominant culture? Was not the American man wrong to fear giving women the right to vote? Did the Jacksonian worker really pose a threat to capitalism? Did not African Americans define freedom from bondage as possession of their own land and labor and the right to earn and vote? Did not Americans take the Indians' land with the Lockean rationale of use and productivity, write treaties that were later broken—only to come later to the side of Native Americans in the name of occupation and contract rights? Evidence of Lockean liberalism seems to be everywhere in American history and nowhere in American historiography.

CHAPTER 3

American Identity in an Age of Political Correctness

To make us love our country, our country ought to be lovely.
EDMUND BURKE

The *National History Standards*

"LOVE IT OR LEAVE IT!" SUCH WAS THE CHOICE CON-fronting the Vietnam War generation, some of whose members did indeed leave the United States to escape the military draft. Many of those who opposed the war liked to remind Americans that the Communist leader Ho Chi Minh admired George Washington and the achievements of the American Revolution. With this compliment, the struggle in Southeast Asia took on the image of an anti-colonial liberation movement rather than a pivotal point in cold war geopolitics.[1]

At the time that the U.S. Senate held hearings on the meaning of revolution, and as the war dragged out on its bloody course, the American Revolution seemed more remote than ever from class-ridden social revolutions of the twentieth century. Eventually America withdrew from Vietnam still unsure of what it had gotten itself into. Had America been a conservative nation bent on upholding an old order, the government might have stayed the course; a radical America may have even supported the communist assault on property and privilege; but a liberal America came to doubt its ability to bring democracy to the Mekong Delta. To continue the fight, *Look* magazine advised, risks destroying "something precious in the word 'America.' "[2]

Something precious was lost in *The National History Standards*, a document published in 1994 to a firestorm of controversy. The standards, designed to be used as guidelines for state education departments and not as mandates for the nation, were produced by the National Center for History at the University of California, Los Angeles. The center had been founded by the National Endowment for the Humanities (NEH) during the conservative presidency of Ronald Reagan, after reports had circulated of low test scores that revealed students' woefully inadequate knowledge of American history. Apparently the NEH had no idea what the center was up to when Gary Nash, history professor at UCLA, replaced as head of the project Charlotte Crabtree of the university's Education Department. When the center released the standards report, politicians and much of the public were outraged by a document that devoted so much space to multiculturalism and other politically correct subjects and so little to the study of important events and significant political leaders and scientists. A few history professors also protested, but the two leading academic organizations, the American Historical Association and the Organization of American Historians, strongly endorsed the standards. The U.S. Senate voted overwhelmingly to condemn them.

Abraham Lincoln's conviction that America had its foundations in the Declaration of Independence and in the ideals of the eighteenth-century European Enlightenment turned out to be that precious something lost in the *National History Standards*: "Standards for United States history should reflect both the nation's diversity exemplified by race, ethnicity, social and economic status, gender, region, politics, politics, and religion, and the nation's commonalities."[3] The authors of the standards had sought to expand the perimeters of American history so that its subjects would include and fully represent the ethnic rainbow that contemporary America has become. As an exercise in cultural and political inclusion, the *National History Standards* has much to commend it; as a pedagogical effort at historical understanding, the document lies somewhere between comedy and farce. The very meaning of history implies inquiry, and the past remains something we hope to know based on documented facts, eyewitness accounts, and historians' efforts to explain why events happened. The goal of history is causal understanding, to establish connections by means of uncovering sequences and coherent patterns. At one time, for example, it was accepted that the American Revolution was an extension of earlier revolutions in England and Holland, all phenomena of Protestantism as well as liberalism. And it was no coincidence that in such northern areas of the world revolution resulted in liberal, constitutional, representative governments that turned out to be stable and prosperous. It would seem, then, that like causes have like results. To study history is to study events in order to understand how similar conditions lead to similar effects. A momentous event such as a revolution can be explained if it can be shown to follow from antecedent events that compose its determining conditions. But in the *National History Standards* we are given events without explanations. Why?

The answer is that the authors of the standards sought to turn the American Revolution into a social phenomenon involving class conflict, as opposed to a political struggle over power and the goal of reestablishing liberty and limited government. Had the American Revolution been truly a "civil war" consisting of "multiple movements" pitting class against class, as the authors put it, then it may be seen as having influenced other revolutions in that similar causes may have produced similar results, and thus America may be considered as having been part of world history rather than having broken away from it. Accordingly, the document asks students to answer the following question: "How have the the ideas that inspired the American and French Revolutions influenced the 20th-century revolutions in Mexico, Russian, China, Cuba, and Vietnam? How have Americans viewed these modern revolutions?"[4]

The choice of these countries is puzzling yet revealing. As Franco Venturi has shown, in the eighteenth century the American Revolution had repercussions in Holland, Sweden, France, Spain, Turkey, Prussia, and Russia.[5] In the twentieth century, with the exception of Mexico, revolutions were inspired by a Marxist-Leninism that had no use for the liberal doctrines of the American or the French revolutions. Marx once praised the United States as "the highest form of popular government, till now realized," only to change his mind and declare the American Republic "the model country of the democratic imposture." Marx's colleague Friedrich Engels saw what our writers of history standards refuse to see. "We must consider the special conditions of America," Engels wrote in 1851. "The ease with which the overflow of population settles on the land, the necessarily increasing tempo of the country's prosperity, which make people consider bourgeois conditions as a *beau ideal*." Leon Trotsky formulated the "law of combined development" to convince comrades that Russia could skip the liberal stage of history that America enjoyed in the eighteenth and nineteenth centuries. What Fidel Castro thinks of the American Revolution should perhaps not be repeated to schoolchildren.[6]

The authors of the history standards represent a generation of scholars who seem to want to deny that America has a distinct historical identity and enjoys a consensus of political values. That America's Revolution may have limited significance for the world also gets lost sight of when we are asked to trace its "influence" to all parts of the world. "The sad truth of the matter," wrote Hannah Arendt in observing how confusing it is to blur the distinction among revolutions, "is that the French Revolution, which ended in disaster, has made world history, while the American Revolution, so triumphantly successful, has remained an event of little more than local importance." Learned thinkers like Arendt are ignored when we are told today that our understanding of American history, stands or falls with our interpretation of the whole course of human history.[7] Yet in light of the contemporary globalization of the economy, this cosmopolitan approach has some merit in comprehending today's world, if not yesterday's. The question remains whether one can be at the same time a cosmopolite and a patriot.

Let Every Faction Bloom

In the mid-1970s, when the American New Left was beginning to sense its impotence after playing an important role in bringing to an end the tragically long Vietnam War, I was asked to give a talk at the University of Florence on the subject of American radicalism. Italian students and professors, many of them Marxists and feminists, seemed to appreciate my account of a student phenomenon that could never successfully reach beyond the campus. Then came a question from the audience. What did I think was the biggest mistake the American New Left made? I replied that if young radicals desired to reach the "masses," they should have refrained from abusing the symbols of American patriotism. The New Left was almost unique in turning against America's own patriotic heroes and traditions. In Italy,

Antonio Gramsci, who loved his country as much as his cause, was both a radical socialist and an ardent nationalist, a Marxist and a Mazzinian. My remarks were received more with respect than with rancor.

Yet shortly afterward, in Philadelphia at a historian's conference, I made the same reply in response to a similar question regarding the failure of the New Left. This time my remarks about patriotism were greeted with hisses, and I was told that no one could love a country that tried to carry out genocide in Asia.

Among intellectuals, patriotism, like truth, is often a war's first casualty. Before World War I, the Greenwich Village rebels Randolph Bourne, Max Eastman, and John Reed regarded themselves as nationalistic liberators willing to draw upon America's intellectual traditions. Eastman defined himself as an "American lyrical Socialist—a child of Walt Whitman reared by Karl Marx."[8] But when President Woodrow Wilson brought America into the war, the same thinkers saw the outbreak of "blind tribal instincts" among both the masses and other intellectual leaders. Eastman's essay "The Religion of Patriotism" and Bourne's "The State" both depicted the war as having laid bare the "herd impulse" of "military patriotism." More than culture or class conflict, war reached the people and compelled them to acts of self-sacrifice based upon a patriotic identification with country and government. Disillusioned that the masses did not rise up in resistance, Bourne declared, "War is the health of the State."[9]

H. L. Mencken insisted that patriotism derives from fear and insecurity. To a "civilized man," wrote Mencken, patriotism is conceivable only when his country is endangered. "His country then appeals to him as any victim of misfortune appeals to him—say, a street-walker pursued by the police." Mencken, a popular writer in the 1920s, equated patriotism with a mindless, 100 percent Americanism and democracy with a modern mediocrity that could scarcely recognize the greatness of George Washington. His essay "On Being an American" is full of loathing on the part of an American who expects more of America. In one of his writings, he had someone ask him why he stayed in America if he disliked the country so much. For the same reason, he replied, that people go to the zoo.

But the critique of patriotism was no laughing matter in the 1920s. The French writer Julien Benda took it up in his influential *The Betrayal of the Intellectuals*. The "Treason of the Clerks," to use the original title, resulted from eminent cultural figures renouncing universal, cosmopolitan ideals and instead seeking to have countrymen identify with their own race and nation. Benda's argument took some questionable twists and turns, but once again it was World War I, the "Great War," that prompted a writer to accuse colleagues of putting their nation above their love for truth, thereby exalting the provincial at the expense of the universal. Indeed, for much of the twentieth century it seemed that patriotism followed war just as night followed day. To the philosopher Bertrand Russell, such political sentiment, whether stemming from pugnacity or duty, had no rational basis whatsoever. Hence patriotism was the willingness to kill or be killed for the most trivial reasons.

During the Vietnam War of the 1960s, the exact opposite situation prevailed: the young could not be compelled to desire to kill or be killed for whatever the reasons. To the anger of World War II veterans, many activist students stormed draft centers and burned the American flag. Among some, hatred for America grew far more intense and bitter than in Mencken's witty sarcasm. Today in the academy the cult of multiculturalism and the postcolonial studies that often rhapsodize about the third world derive from the anti-patriotic legacy of the 1960s. True, the ethnic composition of America has been changing profoundly with waves of immigrants from South America and South Asia. But multiculturalism has its advocates primarily in the academy, noticeably less so among the immigrants themselves.

Why is patriotism so controversial a subject? If those who praise it think mainly of liberation, those who oppose it think only of subordination. Once again positions taken on the issue seem more generational than geographical, for everything turns on the historical situation confronting the young and the old. When Giuseppe Mazzini made the case for patriotic nationalism in Italy in the mid-nineteenth century, he believed that to unite a divided people was also to free a subject people. This mission he bestowed upon a younger, rising generation, assuming it would be both idealistic and discontented, whereas he believed senior citizens would always be prudent, contented, and conservative. The Mazzinian scenario turns upside down in today's America. While older citizens are calling for patriotic unity, younger ones, especially academics, are making a fetish out of difference and diversity. The classical imperial dictum of divide and rule has given way to a new dictum of divide and prevail by virtue of the demands of differential recognition. Identity politics lets every faction bloom while patriotism, now seen as the snare of subordination, perishes.

For much of the American public, July Fourth is a day for chilling out with beer, hotdogs, and baseball. For the intellectual it is often a day of mourning. The "noble sentiment" that America expressed in its "early youth," wrote Margaret Fuller on July 4, 1845, "is tarnished; she has shown that righteousness is not her chief desire, and her name is no longer a watchword for the highest hopes for the rest of the world." Lincoln called upon Americans to return to the Declaration, but Fuller asked: "What is independence if it does not lead to freedom?"[10] The Transcendentalist warned Americans that to be a patriot is to be prepared to be disappointed.

The Battle over Patriotism

To some writers being a patriot is like being a political virgin, one who has yet to be exposed to historical experience and its disillusionments. To believe in patriotism is to believe in certain words and ideas that still ring true and remain inviolate. Love of country is based on a trust in government and its leaders, which often requires a Billy Budd–like innocence about the ways of authority. The novelist Ernest Hemingway captured this virtuous disposition in *A Farewell to Arms,* where a young Italian patriot spoke to a more cynical narrator:

> "We won't talk about losing. There is enough talk about losing. What has been done this summer cannot have been done in vain."
> I did not say anything. I was always embarrassed by the words sacred, glorious, and sacrifice and the expression in vain. . . . Abstract words such as glory, honor, courage, or hallow were obscene beside the concrete names of villages, the numbers of roads, the names of rivers, the numbers of regiments and the dates. Gino was a patriot, so he said things that separated us sometimes, but he was also a fine boy and I understood his being a patriot.[11]

During the 1960s, when the Vietnam War was raging, many young Americans made sure that they stayed in school in order to enjoy the draft deferment that kept them out of the war. During the early 1940s, by contrast, it had not been uncommon for American youths to drop out of school, some even lying about their age, to join one of the armed services in their eagerness to "see action." Today the generations of the 1940s and 1960s exist in different worlds. When the Smithsonian Institution tried to arrange an exhibit on the use of atomic bombs against Japan in 1945, the 1940s generation believed that the resort to an atomic attack was vital to ending World War II, while much of the 1960s generation remained convinced that it started the cold war.

It is no coincidence that academic intellectuals have had several other recent battles over patriotism. One such flared when the distinguished young philosopher Martha Nussbaum responded to a *New York Times* op-ed piece by Richard Rorty, a relatively senior philosopher who identifies with the Old Left of the 1940s. Rorty had urged young Americans, especially leftists, to cease denigrating the value of patriotism and to take seriously the "emotion of national pride" as essential to a "shared sense of national identity."[12] Nussbaum refrained from denying that nationhood matters, but she refused to accept that it should have any priority over one's loyalties. She called, instead, for a universal citizenship based upon a new civic education that inculcates the values of cosmopolitanism. Regarding national identity as "a morally irrelevant characteristic," Nussbaum held that students should be taught that their primary allegiance is to the "community of human beings in the entire world." Once we regard ourselves as "citizens of the world," she explained, we are better able not only to know ourselves but also to work out differences with others beyond our borders and to share moral responsibility for the rest of humanity.

Nussbaum's response to Rorty resulted in a symposium in which writers of varying generations raised numerous questions. How can a universal consensus be derived from differing countries with varying cultures? Should political refugees be treated the same as native citizens? Can one be a citizen of the world without the existence of a world government?

The more cogent of these intellectual warriors made some basic points. To identify with the entire world is to deny our own heritage based on family, race, religion, history, and culture, and, as well, to deny that democracy depends upon a strong identity on the part of its citizens. Moreover, nationality may be a necessary condition for the rule of law, for we must be responsible for our country's actions. Civilized life without law is inconceivable; so we must have a country, and to take it seriously we must have a patriotic identification with, and responsibility for, our country. "If we boast of our best," wrote G. K. Chesterton years ago, "we must repent our worst." Chesterton was asking the English to own up to their past mistreatment of the Irish. His essay was titled "Paying for Patriotism."[13]

Years ago in the essay "The Case for Patriotism," the political theorist John H. Schaar, noting how that sentiment had fallen into abuse due to the Vietnam War, went on to distinguish patriotism from nationalism, "its bloody brother." To be a patriot is to be part of a legacy with a sense of place and tradition; the nationalist, on the other hand, looks to a militant nation-state that effaces local connections and identifies with the progressive march of history.[14] Another scholar, Maurizo Viroli, sees patriotism and nationalism as deriving from different passions with different purposes. The patriot supports the republic and devotes efforts to the common good, while seeing tyranny and corruption as potential evils within the immediate environment. The nationalist advocates ethnic, cultural, and religious unity, while opposing all that is alien, contaminating, impure, diverse, and plural.[15] The difference between patriotism and nationalism, wrote Benedetto Croce, is "like that between the kindliness of human love and beastly lust or morbid lechery or selfish promiscuity."[16]

Such distinctions between patriotism and nationalism resonate in America, especially in the thoughts and actions of Abraham Lincoln. Lincoln opposed America's war with Mexico, and unlike the more nationalistic Walt Whitman, he had reservations about expansion and the doctrine of manifest destiny. Lincoln looked backward as much as forward, and his sense of patriotism expressed itself in his worship of America's founding principles. Lincoln believed that America could be large enough to reach out and embrace "the family of man."

The recent intellectuals' debates over patriotism offered reasons for and against it. Historians who have written on the subject are less interested in reasons than in conditions. They deal with patriotism as a product of such institutions as education, religion, and the military, or as a phenomenon of war or of postwar reconstruction. They tend to assume that patriotism is a dubious emotion that needs to be taught, instilled, indoctrinated, or whatever means it takes to shape the minds of Americans. As a result, in their eyes patriotism, even if it originally symbolized the virtue and valor of George Washington and the scenes of sacrifice associated with the Spirit of '76, degenerated into appeals to masculinity, chauvinism, racism, religion, xenophobia, monument-worship, or, more positively, a group moral covenant and narratives of collective memory based on the need for self-esteem. And, sin of sins, patriotism is seen as part of the nation's consensus.[17]

Now is the time to rescue patriotism for our past as well as our present and future. But this may be a difficult task when it comes to teaching history. The philosopher John Dewey, the most influential figure in modern American education, worried that good history may prove incapable of producing good citizens. Is it not the case that teaching patriotism requires "avoidance of the spirit of criticism in dealing with history, politics, and economics?" Dewey asked. "The more indiscriminately the history and institutions of one's own nation are idealized, the greater is the likelihood, so it is assumed, that the school product will be a loyal patriot, a well-equipped good citizen."[18] And if the teacher offers instead a discriminating, critical history, what will be the school product?

That question was addressed by an executive committee of the American Historical Association in the summer of 1941. This was a period prior to the attack on Pearl Harbor and America's entry into World War II, when American historians were undergoing much soul-searching. Historians today often scold older generations of historians for having failed to write about race, poverty, women, and other ne-glected subjects, and they point in particular to the reluctance of the country to pass an anti-lynching law and the historians' veneration of American institutions. But Charles A. Beard and Carl Becker had written critically about the Constitution and the Declaration of Inde-pendence, the institution and the document upon which, according to Lincoln, America's future depended. Beard had interpreted the Con-stitution as basically an economic rationale devised to protect the prop-erty classes; Becker had "deconstructed" the Declaration by dem-onstrating that its felicitous language concealed the absence of the philosophical foundations needed to make equality credible. In the year 1941, however, both historians were reconsidering their earlier critiques and each would reaffirm their patriotic faith in America's political institutions. Why this change? Was it simply a response to a country in need of support? The answer comes as part of the historians' response to America's confrontation with European totalitarianism, which raised the concern that by acknowledging the country's shortcomings, historians might play into the hands of fascists and communists, who had depicted American liberalism as decadent and dying. The American Historical Association candidly addressed this multifaceted issue in a "press statement" written by Arthur Schlesinger:

> Genuine patriotism, no less than honesty and sound scholarship, requires that textbook authors and teachers should endeavor to present a truthful picture of the past. Those who oppose this view would seem to believe that the history of the United States contains things so disgraceful that it is unsafe for the young to hear of them. This we emphatically deny. If the men who built the nation had their share of human frailties, the story as a whole is one of continuing inspiration to . . . this and other lands.
>
> To omit controversial questions from the historical account, as is sometimes urged, would be to garble and distort the record. The history of the American people has been hammered out on the anvil of experience. It is a story of achievement, often against heavy odds. Some of the most glorious passages have consisted in the struggle to overcome social and economic injustices. Failures as well as successes carry lessons of which posterity can ill afford to be ignorant. In discussing controversial issues the textbook writer has an obligation to give both sides. By so doing he not only upholds the ideal of presenting a truthful picture, but also of encouraging in young people that spirit of inquiry, open-mindedness and fair play which lies at the root of our democratic institutions.[19]

Many contemporary scholars would dismiss such a statement as naive. Poststructuralists and neo-pragmatists, doubting that a "truthful picture" of the past is possible, would remind us that all historical knowledge depends upon subjective interpretation conditioned by our linguistic conventions, by rhetorical strategies designed to persuade the reader to adhere to the author's ideology. And the new social historians avoid studying the life of the mind and the thoughts of intellectual authorities, military leaders, and elected officials.

Actually, this turn to studying the history of the masses, "history from below," is scarcely a new development. In the nineteenth century, the British historian J. R. Green advocated such a turn while sneering at "mere drum and trumpet history." But how can the post-modernist scholar and the new social historian make critical claims about patriotism without studying those thinkers in the past who thought deeply about the subject? The same question might be asked of today's flag-waving patriots who assume that they are at one with America's founders. While the radical denies that the past can be truthfully known, the conservative assumes to truly know it. "The historian who gets nearest to the truth," wrote R. G. Collingwood, "is the historian who spends most pain in examining his conscience."[20]

One intellectual who examined his conscience as though he held a puzzle in his hand was the novelist Nathaniel Hawthorne. His reflections on the meaning of patriotism came to him while traveling in Italy. A writer drawn to the enigmatic, Hawthorne found patriotism to be as unintelligible as Providence. As an idea, it had no intended meaning; as an emotion, no analyzable content. "It would only be a kind of despair" to forsake one's country to settle in another, he wrote in 1858. "I wonder that we Americans love our country at all, it having no limits and no oneness; and when you try to make it a matter of the heart, everything falls away except one's State; neither can you seize hold of that unless you tear it out of the Union, bleeding and quivering. Yet, unquestionably, we do stand by our national flag as stoutly as any people in the world, and I myself have felt the heart throb at the sight of it as sensibly as other men."[21]

Patriotism and the Founding

Does the future of America depend upon a sustaining sentiment of patriotism? Those conservatives who would like to think so and cite the American founders as exemplars, and those radicals who would have us believe that patriotism has been imposed upon generations of young Americans as an invisible form of domination, should both be embarrassed. For neither the *Federalist* authors nor Thomas Jefferson looked to patriotism as reliable. The *Federalist* authors saw divisiveness as inevitable and hence patriotic consensus impossible; Jefferson saw "uniformity" as carrying the seeds of "tyranny." Even George Washington, in the midst of the Revolution, warned that patriotism was too weak a sentiment to motivate Americans to fight for their country. Speaking of the "rule of action," Washington wrote the Continental Congress: "I do not mean to exclude altogether the Idea of Patriotism. I know it exists, and I know it has done much in the present Contest. But I will venture to assert, that a great and lasting War can never be supported on this principle alone. It must be aided by the prospect of Interest or some reward."[22]

Ironically, patriotism became stronger in modern America than during the Republic's founding, probably due to the later influx of up-rooted immigrants eager to establish a new national identity. In political theory the founding is supposed to be the "moment" when a republic lays down its first principles to which it later makes periodic returns. Why was it so difficult to make patriotism one of those principles?

A clue to the answer may be found in the opening *Federalist* paper by Alexander Hamilton. Here Americans were told, in effect, that if we blunder and give the country an inadequate Constitution, we "deserve the general misfortune of mankind." This prospect should, Hamilton advised, "add the inducements of philanthropy to those of patriotism, to heighten the solicitude which all good men must feel for the event." But Hamilton knew he was facing a difficult problem. To Hamilton patriotism meant a dedication to developing a strong nation-state, whereas most Americans identified liberty with resistance to government. He warned readers that both the statist and the anti-statist are suspects in American political culture, one the accused despot, the other the dreaded demagogue. "An enlightened zeal for the energy and efficiency of government will be stigmatized as the off-spring of a temper fond of despotic power and hostile to the principles of liberty. An over-scrupulous jealousy of danger to the rights of the people . . . will be represented as mere pretense and artifice, the stale bait of popularity at the expense of public good." Americans are reluctant to see that government is necessary to protect liberty and to appreciate, as well, "that a dangerous ambition more often lurks behind the specious mask of zeal for the rights of the people than under the forbidding appearance of zeal for the firmness and efficiency of government."

Between those who identify with people and those who identify with government, who is the best protector of liberty? As Hamilton warned in 1787, "History will teach that the former has been found a much more certain road to the introduction of despotism than the latter, and that those men who have overturned the liberties of republics, the greatest number have begun their career by paying an obsequious court to the people, commencing demagogues and ending tyrants."[23] Two years later the French Revolution broke out, and it would soon follow exactly Hamilton's scenario. In the name of liberty and virtue the bloody Terror began; guillotines were built, severed heads were hoisted on pikes. Hamilton knew what the ancients knew: that democracy as a form of government is conducive to tyranny and that when love of one's country becomes confused with "an obsequious court of the people," pseudopatriotism could be the first step toward dictatorship.[24] Maximilien Robespierre claimed to rule in the name of "the people." Hamilton and Washington saw through the brutal masquerade; Jefferson fell for it completely.[25] With the Jacobins, the French faction that espoused egalitarian democracy during the 1789 revolution, patriotism became the pretext for political violence.

Contrary to what both the Right and Left assume today, the founders did not think that patriotism could or even should be instilled or imposed. Jefferson's loyalties extended no farther than Virginia, while Hamilton, the one true patriotic nationalist who had no local allegiances, realized that the principle of propinquity, the human tendency to identify with what is nearest and most familiar, rendered an overarching national solidarity unrealistic. A half century after the framers made that point, Alexis de Tocqueville reiterated it in *Democracy in America* when he observed that human affections restrict themselves to the customary and habitual: "The Union is a vast body and somewhat vague as the object of patriotism." The state and community, in contrast, are "identified with the soil, with the right of property, the family, memories of the past, activities of the present, and dreams of the future. Patriotism, which is most often nothing but an extension of individual egoism, therefore remains attached to the state and has not yet, so to say, been passed on to the Union."[26]

Historically patriotism, like nationalism, has been associated with a country's struggle for freedom. But such a struggle is the missing episode in the history of colonial America and the early federal republic. As indicated earlier, the American Revolution was more a political rebellion than a full-scale social revolution—it was a war for independence and not a class war fought to end all class systems. During the early stages of the French Revolution the spirit of patriotism joined forces with the aspirations of liberalism, and it was French thinkers like Baron Anne-Robert Turgot who were the first to see that the American Revolution had been different. In the New World, America did not have to contend with a reactionary ancien régime that resisted change and modernization. Enjoying liberty as almost a gift from nature, Americans regarded patriotism as important but far from essential. The French Revolution, however, had drawn its philosophical inspiration from Jean-Jacques Rousseau, who sought, in his *Social Contract* and *Emile,* to reconcile the rights of man with the duties of the citizen. He did so through the concept of the commanding "general will," which he portrayed as a manifestation of the collective will of all individuals *(volonte de tous)*. In France "civil religion" was to guarantee the union of patriotism and humanitarianism, classical virtue and Christian goodness. America needed no such guarantees.

"Where liberty is, there is my country," instructed Ben Franklin, who identified with America. Tom Paine, in contrast, saw America as a universal beacon, and as a "citizen of the world," he left America to head for a revolutionary Paris seething with patriotic fervor. "Where liberty is not, there is mine," Paine replied to Franklin.[27] Inspired by new ideas in philosophy and science as well as developments in politics, trade, and commerce, Paine saw America as leading the way in uniting all countries under the cosmopolitan banner of the Enlightenment and its universal values.

Today multiculturalists and poststructuralists champion difference, variety, and diversity—the very values that the eighteenth-century Enlightenment philosophers set out to scrutinize when they made "reason" a primary value. Many Enlightenment thinkers assumed that there could be no science of the particular or the idiosyncratic, no possibility of understanding things without laws that are general and universal.[28] In certain parts of the contemporary academic world, to oppose multiculturalism in support of national unity is tantamount to advocating oppression and domination. Any proposal for consensus and synthesis, it is argued, amounts to coercing conformity and suppressing differences. Thus the *Journal of American History* ran a symposium on "The Problem of Synthesis," with the conclusion that it remained a problem without a solution. To propose that America could be subjected to a unifying interpretation suffered from, it was held, four alleged deficiencies: such an interpretation would be difficult, if not impossible, to put into a conventional narrative form of writing; it betrays elitism and racism; it smacks of western conceit in failing to see all cultures as equally valid in their differences; and it takes the writing of history backward when it should go forward. The title of Princeton historian Nell Irvin Painter's contribution, "Bias and Synthesis," said it all. Referring to the newer historians of her generation, she insisted "that their kind of work and the sorts of people in the past recently given visibility will be left out in any new synthetic view."[29]

Thomas Bender, an intellectual historian at New York University, made a learned case for the need for a synthesis, calling upon historians to conceive of narratives that would emphasize public culture as the site that brings together people from all walks of life. But Bender's article was immediately rebutted by Eric H. Monkkonen in the *American Historical Review*. In "The Dangers of Synthesis," Monkkonen argued that any synthesis written in the spirit of older Progressive historians "opens the way to erroneous and vacuous statements about American character and culture." Monkkonen found safety in specialization. "Only in 'fragmented' subfields will we see professional-research oriented syntheses that will act as creative opening for more ideas. But these syntheses will not create a sense of the whole past. This condition reveals the achievements of historical scholarship, not its failure." Historians must accept their fate: "We have fallen from the state of grace."[30] The message is clear. Subfields succeed, syntheses fail. So much for "professional research" and its rewards.

The conviction that synthesis presupposes exclusion and that consensus implies oppression is widespread among many scholars sympathetic to multiculturalism. Yet American multiculturalism, in spite of all its hostility toward the Enlightenment and the West, would be unthinkable in any other environment. Tom Paine would remind us that the very rights-based political culture in which multiculturalism now thrives may be seen as a long-delayed product of the eighteenth-century Enlightenment. The singularly "dead, white, European males" against whom teachers of the new social history inveigh were precisely the thinkers who gave modern philosophy its foundations. Multiculturalists see themselves as conditioned by society while craving diversity, and they cannot think of the idea of patriotism without thinking of the threat of authority. Thus they go abroad or venture into the distant past in search of non-western cultures, seemingly unaware of the western origins of exactly what it is they do possess: a precious, unconditional right to be different.

E Pluribus Unum or the Disease of Hegemony?

Who are we, anyhow? The question is on the lips of many Americans today. Not long ago we could assume that understanding history helps us to understand ourselves better. But recently, within a generation, historical consciousness has lost its unity, for historians no longer speak with a single voice. Never before in American history has there been such confusion about the meaning of America and the identity of the American people. Never before have Americans been so deprived of the backward glance of historical understanding unsullied by the idiocy of political correctness.

Whether Americans today identify themselves with others, or identify others with themselves, they have difficulty looking to history as a basis of self-identification, as a way of obtaining a feeling of familiarity and continuity with neighbors and ancestors. The older history focused on likeness and concord; the new fixates on differences and dissonance, assuming that those who had been left out of previous narratives speak in various voices. It is no longer "We the People," protests the conservative National Review; it is now "U.S. History: Nobody Here But Us Peoples."[31] Older claims of consensus and tradition have given way to shouts of conflict and turmoil by formerly silent voices demanding to be heard. Today the Greek concept of history, "to inquire in order to tell how it was," has become fragmented: it depends on which history Americans listen to as well as who is doing the telling, and often the story heard has more to do with ideology than inquiry.

The challenge that Abraham Lincoln had to face was not "us peoples," as it is today; rather it was "we sections," as different parts of the country demanded to be treated as separate but equal entities. Lincoln knew that European immigrants desired to be part of America even while clinging to their Old World cultures and traditions, and he extended to them without hesitation both the Homestead Law, which made available plots of land in the territories, and the Declaration, which secured natural, inalienable rights. During Lincoln's era claims of diversity and the politics of difference derived from sectional and racial conflicts; today's multicultural scuffles derive from the conviction that the poor and powerless enjoy a more privileged understanding of the "real" America than do those who rule over them. Since the Civil War, those who have seen themselves as victims, such as southerners in the nineteenth century and some women and minorities in our times, claim to have a distinct and superior moral authority and, therefore, rightful demands to the power that has been denied them. Lincoln would hardly be surprised by such squabbles. "Let us discard all this quibbling about this man and the other man—this race and that race and the other race as being inferior, and therefore they must be placed in an inferior position—discarding our standard that we have left us. Let us discard all these things, and unite as one people throughout this land, until we shall once more stand up declaring that all men are created equal."[32]

Although radicals have done the most to make history politically correct, if only because they outnumber others on the American campus, conservatives are not exactly free of the taint of ideology. Both radicals and conservatives see themselves as having a stake in the past as well as the present. Conservative political commentators, on the one side, and radical and liberal academics, on the other, have their own take on American history, and each side has no doubt that its adversary has been abusing the past. Conservatives complain about what academics have done to the study of history, and academics complain about what history has done to people themselves. In this growing culture war, all history is contemporary politics. But the culture battles belie the illusion that all factions seem to share—that far back in American history can be found a pre-modern sense of community and identity, an idea founded on virtue, class solidarity forged against class oppression, or those throbbing "habits of the heart."

Using history for the purpose of identity is, as Friedrich Nietzsche warned, fraught with unsuspected paradoxes. If the Right turns to the past to enjoy the pleasures of pride and virtue, the Left does so to remind us of the presence of pain and oppression. The Right prefers what Nietzsche called "monumental" and "antiquarian" history, the study of great leaders and moral exemplars, and the belief in a "oneness and continuity" from the past as a "protest against the change and decay of generations." But sometimes the need to believe in history is so great, Nietzsche noted, that "there is no possible distinction between a monumental past and a mythical romance," and those cultures attracted to mighty myths only betray their own incapacity to undertake bold actions and to respond to the call of greatness. Embracing the past in order to preserve or reproduce it, the antiquarian clings to history like a tree to its roots.

The Left betrays a similar timidity in its search for identity. The Left prefers to see itself partaking of Nietzsche's "critical" history, which attempts to establish genealogically how things have come to be legitimated in the past and thereby to locate the unjust origins of present practices. But a "culture of complaint" may whine too much to withstand the weight of history; those who see themselves and their ancestors as victims will obsessively lick their wounds and never be creative and free. Memories of the hurts of history cripple the will as well as the heart. "The deeper the roots of man's inner nature," advised Nietzsche, "the better will he take the past into himself." This powerful nature "would assimilate and digest the past, however foreign, and turn it to sap. Such a nature can forget what it cannot subdue." The weak, Nietzsche admonished, wallow in history without recognizing that the will cannot will backwards; only the strong know when to remember and when to forget the past.[33]

Today the conservative, radical, and liberal alike seek to increase history's significance; perhaps each feels that memory of the historical past has something to do with power; that it is, as Ralph Waldo Emerson put it, "a presumption of a possession of the future."[34]

If conservatives are convinced of two things, it is that at one time America had a sense of unity, stability, and coherence, and that this reassuring vision has recently been undermined by radical academic scholars in their advocacy of differences and diversity and their denial of philosophical foundations.[35] In response to such divisive claims, conservative scholars cite the "Great Seal" of *e pluribus unum*, adopted by the Continental Congress in 1782, five years before the Constitution was drafted. The phrase roughly means "from many, one," and it referred to the thirteen colonies and the need for all Americans to pull together, both to defeat the British in the nearly finished Revolution, and to create national unity in general.[36]

To the contemporary conservative, America's historical unity lies in its unique heritage. Aware that much of the population in colonial Pennsylvania spoke German, and cognizant that none of the framers of the Constitution suggested that a common religion should unite Americans, conservatives nonetheless emphasize the British origins of American political ideas and institutions, particularly the ideas of natural right and limited government. The specific source often cited as evidence of America's sense of unity is *Federalist* No. 2. "Providence has been pleased," John Jay wrote, "to give this one connected country to one united people—a people descended from the same ancestors, speaking the same language, professing the same religion, attached to the same principles of government, very similar in their manners and customs, and who, by their joint counsels, arms, and efforts, fighting side by side through a long and bloody war have nobly established their general liberty and independence."[37]

The problem with this view of American unity is that John Jay, taken ill, soon disappeared from the *Federalist,* and the authors who wrote the remaining papers, Alexander Hamilton and James Madison, could scarcely endorse such an optimistic outlook toward consensual unity and identity. An even further irony is that contemporary radical historians also accept the idea of national unity, but with a consoling twist.

To the radical scholar, whatever is politically unacceptable must in some sense be "unreal," no matter how long it has endured in historical reality. Thus the idea of unity may have characterized American history but that idea, instead of evolving naturally from America's conditions and circumstances, was imposed from above. One of the favorite authors of the Left is Randolph Bourne, the brilliant World War I Greenwich Village rebel who vehemently opposed the idea that the "melting pot" could have ever sprung from a single source: "English snobberies, English religion, English literary styles, English literary reverences and canons, English ethics, English superiorities." An Anglo-Saxon elite, Bourne complained, including himself in his own accusation, must be seen as "guilty of just what every dominant race is guilty of in every European country: the imposition of its own culture upon minority peoples."[38]

While Bourne traced America's will to impose cultural hegemony to the country's Puritan origins, our contemporary radicals trace it to the very eighteenth-century Enlightenment that offered itself, ironically, as an answer to Puritanism. It is no surprise to be told that Puritanism was repressive; the real shock is to be told that the Enlightenment that was supposed to be liberating actually stifled opposition. In recent academic chatter the Enlightenment is dismissed as a false "project" that sought to have everyone live by the same standards, and it is understood to be no coincidence that the standards were those dictated by white males. Thus the eminent political theorist Iris Marion Young claims that the "republican fathers . . . explicitly justified the restriction of citizenship to white men only on the grounds that the unity of the nation depended on homogeneity and dispassionate reason."[39]

"Homogeneity"? "Dispassionate reason"? Are we in the eighteenth-century world of political reality or the twentieth-century world of academic fantasy?

The "republican fathers," instead of relying upon such expectations of consensual unity, set out to build a political regime that presupposed their absence. "As long as the reason of man continues fallible," wrote Madison, "and he is at liberty to exercise it, different opinions will be formed." The restriction of citizenship to "white men only" can hardly be traced to the Enlightenment alone; in non-western cultures such restrictions have been and continue to be far more pronounced. Indeed, rather than suppressing differences, the American framers sought to protect them. "As long as the connection subsists between his reason and his self-love," Madison continued in the *Federalist,* "his opinions and his passions will have a reciprocal influence on each other; and the former will be the objects to which the latter will attach themselves. The diversity in the faculties of men, from which the rights of property originate, is not less an insuperable obstacle to a uniformity of interests. The protection of these faculties is the first object of government."[40]

Where in the world did the impression arise that the thinkers of the American Enlightenment sought to sustain positions of power by imposing homogeneity? From our contemporary European philosophers, who apparently never read the *Federalist* or the writings of John Adams and others. In recent years the radical critique of a supposedly elitist-generated culture of unity has been reinforced by way of Paris. The writings of poststructuralists such as Jacques Derrida and Michel Foucault and the Italian Marxist Antonio Gramsci have been tenured in the academy. American scholars who subscribe to these European ideas can now see the impressions of a country's oneness and unity as little more than "ideology," a false "social construction" based on language usage and other modes of representation that make the contingent and artificial seem natural and inevitable. Thus radicals acknowledge that in America a dominant culture prevails, but its very presence reflects the phenomenon of "hegemony" rather than natural right, a deliberate attempt by ruling power elites to instill habits of unity at the expense of diversity. According to this view, those in charge seek to have Americans unconsciously see themselves as similar, when Americans should instead experience their vital differences and, so armed, express their potential opposition to the status quo. Under the hegemonic order of syntheses, it is argued, things happen to people who neither intended them nor are conscious of them.

But a more accurate reading of the Enlightenment, such as that found in Arthur O. Lovejoy's *The Great Chain of Being*, opens our eyes to a different universe. The aim of consciousness was to sense the inadequacy of mind when faced with the mutability of all things, and the principle of plenitude in the eighteenth-century Enlightenment, Lovejoy observed, led the intellect to admire the abundance and variety of life. We were taught to convince ourselves, as Locke put it, that we "are not big enough to grasp everything"; thinkers should instead be content "to employ their minds with variety, delight, and satisfaction."[41]

Why the Founders Questioned the Call for Unity

Why would the Constitution's framers have wanted to impose unity on the American people when they viewed such unity as a potential threat to the new Republic? In the *Federalist* papers following No. 5, after the stricken John Jay has dropped out, the text grows gloomy about the prospect of fulfilling the hopeful expectations announced in the first papers. Part of that gloom may have been due to the challenge facing Hamilton and Madison, who had to reason against an entire tradition of western political thought—one that originated with Aristotle, blossomed like a flower of evil in Machiavelli, and fructified in James Harrington and Jean-Jacques Rousseau. According to that tradition, liberty depends on citizens having a strong and common commitment to the public good. Such proposals to wrest sovereign unity from the mundane scrimmage of politics struck Hamilton and Madison as mischievous as well as hazardous, and the French Revolution and almost all subsequent revolutions of the modern age (the Dutch excepted) that disastrously strove to create such unanimity proved their views prescient. Curiously, in both classical and modern socialist thought, in both conservatism and radicalism, what is particular and different is bad, while what is common and general is good. The *Federalist* authors challenged such reasoning. The plea for a common unity is precisely what they rejected.

Many of the anti-Federalists, those who opposed the Constitution, made such a plea. They could not help but wonder why the framers were almost obsessed with checks and balances and other mechanisms designed to control "factions." If the American people are alike in their sentiments and values, asked the anti-Federalists, why should we fear the country falling into factions that supposedly reflect differences and conflicting interests? The *Federalist* authors replied that the causes of factions cannot be eliminated for they are "sown" into human nature: a fallible, unstable aspect of being human whose tendencies express different kinds and degrees of interest in property and the faculty for obtaining it, in admiration for charismatic leaders, in zeal for religious beliefs, and in other passions that divide people. Faction expresses freedom and must be accepted and even nourished, for "liberty is to faction what air is to fire."[42]

But while divisibility cannot be eradicated, homogeneity cannot be tolerated. For what is to be feared is the coming together of various groups with common interests and passions, a possible "overbearing" faction that, left unchecked, threatens property and wealth along with liberty. The *Federalist* authors write frequently of the danger that the "many" pose to the "few," and they expressed no doubt that democracy and liberty were incompatible, that democracy had to be controlled so that liberty could be preserved. How could such control be achieved? The *Federalist* authors offered two ways, one implicit and one explicit.

The first, implicit, method was embedded in the very nature of political phenomena. The *Federalist* authors were encouraged to see political phenomena as dualistic, as always tending to fragment due to human nature and the nature of power. "Free government," wrote Jefferson when later drafting the Virginia and Kentucky resolutions of 1798, "is founded in jealousy, not in confidence." Earlier Madison had assured Jefferson that unanimity could never be achieved, for there would always be minorities breaking away in pursuit of their own interests, minorities who had to be protected from the majority. When speculating what might check mass democracy from using the election process unfairly in order to promote some to the exclusion of others, Hamilton expressed his belief that the composition of the people was too mixed to permit such malevolence. "The dissimilarity in the ingredients which will compose the national government . . . must form a powerful obstacle to a concert of views in any partial scheme of elections." The expressions "concert," "common," and "collective capacity" haunt the pages of the *Federalist,* and at times one wonders why the authors are so fearful of democracy when the people seem always ready to divide into factions on their own. If the phrase "power being always the rival of power" is true, why can't power check itself?[43]

The answer to that question takes us to the explicit technique of the Constitution: the threat of power and usurpation could be checked only if the Republic was to "extend the sphere" of government, to have a political regime that would encompass a large geographic area in order to include a greater variety of people with differing interests and passions. In classical thought republics were to remain small and simple, but the *Federalist* authors saw small communities as the seedbed of despotism that would go unresisted. "The great extent of the country is a further security" against the threat of power to liberty, for opposition to tyranny can better organize in large areas where people are too various to succumb to a single leader or faction. Anticipating Alexis de Tocqueville, the *Federalist* feared the tyranny of the majority, especially collective action in local communities, and sought to check the popular will by constructing a government on the basis of multiple factions incapable of forming mass, democratic coalitions. But their stance hardly presaged Tocqueville. Whereas the French thinker saw democracy as eliminating differences and creating conformity, in Hamilton's and Madison's analysis the diminution of differences in a small-scale republic presents a danger to liberty—thus the task was to ensure that any differences would neutralize one another. Most likely the authors learned from the Scottish philosopher David Hume an important historical lesson: small republics of similar sentiments offer no guarantee that liberty or justice can survive. Diversity, not unity, would preserve American liberty.[44]

If the framers of the Constitution had little faith in unity, they placed even less confidence in community. They had witnessed people abusing power during the Articles of Confederation (1783–87), when debtors had taken control of state legislatures, issued currency, and threatened to abrogate contracts. The framers sought to avoid this inequality by deliberately relocating such powers in the new central government. Nor did the framers have much faith in the people's capacity to act virtuously. Today the topic of virtue has considerable appeal. But many framers saw the idea of virtue as futile and would not allow the Constitution to be guided by it. Classical republics based on civic virtue, the framers reasoned, had no record of success, made no effort to lift the life of common people out of misery and deprivation, and had no understanding of the psychology of human motivation. "What is virtue?" asked John Adams. "If the absence of avarice is necessary to republican virtue, can you find any age or country in which republican virtue existed?"[45]

Religion is another idea and institution that commentators today hope will unify America, but it too was considered by the founders and rejected. Skeptical of the possibility of knowing spiritual truth, and aware of the history of religious persecution, the founders drew parallels between religious sects and political factions, between the "monkery of priests and the knavery of politicians," and they concluded that religion would be more divisive than cohesive. In personal life they did see a role for religious morality, and some referred to the "Supreme Being" as the world's "Great Legislature," while Jefferson attributed the source of inalienable rights to the "Creator." But government itself could hardly count upon religion as a source of obedience. "Neither

Philosophy, nor Religion, nor Morality, nor Wisdom," wrote Adams, "will ever govern nations or Parties, against their Vanity, their Pride, their Resentment or Revenge, or their Avarice or Ambition."[46]

Nor could reverence for law and respect for authority be counted on to preserve the Republic. Although the truths of equality might be declared "self-evident," Adams, Hamilton, Madison, and others doubted that legal authority could compel obedience from the mind, at least not from the collective mind of an entire republic of people. For even if individuals are capable of rational conduct and responsibility, when they act in concert, in groups and factions, they often remain indifferent to reason and morality. "In a nation of philosophers," the *Federalist* instructed, "this consideration ought to be disregarded." But America cannot expect such a nation, and thus virtue and enlightened reason cannot be expected to guide the people.

Pluribus or *Unum?*

Every American should know something about the founders and why they created the system they did. The motto *e pluribus unum* acknowledges that we are supposed to be a nation of diverse people and groups, even if we can also have a sense of oneness. And with the shadow of suspicion that so runs through the *Federalist*, it is clear that no single group is to be trusted to control the government. Yet the U.S. Constitution itself was meant to integrate the young Republic. Its mechanistic devices were so delicately structured as to reflect the will of the people and at the same time to restrain it. Just as the seventeenth-century Calvinists believed that God had created people different and unequal, and yet that order and community could be derived from such materials, so did the *Federalist* authors hope that a good mechanical whole could be derived from its competing and badly constructed human parts. Taking differences into account together with sin and evil, the framers started the Republic by institutionalizing conflict—by tying the country together through means of factional rivalry and interest politics.

It was not the unity but the wonderful variety of people that impressed Jefferson, who celebrated the individual as the fount of freedom precisely because human nature is idiosyncratic. "Differences of opinion, like differences of face, are a law of nature and should be viewed with the same tolerance." Why, Jefferson asked, subject opinion to uniformity at the expense of conflict and dissent? "Is uniformity desirable? No more than of face and statue."[47] The world is better the more variety it contains. In the eighteenth century it was not American thinkers who called for unity but French radicals, philosophers who were demanding that the new Republic across the Atlantic adhere to ancient, classical ideals. John Adams answered the French critics of the U.S. Constitution. Scoffing at Rousseau's dream that the individual could be absorbed into a common unity, Adams rejected the classical idea that government depended upon a human sociability that enriches the noble life of politics. But how would society be held together if not by the binding sentiments of community and solidarity? "Power," advised Adams, "must be opposed to power, force to force, strength to strength, interest to interest, as well as reason to reason, eloquence to eloquence, and passion to passion."[48] The U.S. Constitution was designed not to realize good but to prevent evil, not to unify beliefs and values but to control force and power.

The excesses of diversity, however, were also a threat to the young nation, and the founders realized that the prospect of prosperity was the one idea that could counteract this centrifugal force. The various occupations in manufacturing, and not agriculture, insisted Hamilton, are better able to give "scope to the diversity of talents and dispositions which discriminate men from each other." Yet the variety of different environments in America will by no means render the country disunited, Hamilton noted, particularly when one sees what can bind America together. A half-century before Tocqueville, Hamilton discerned how conflict yields to consensus:

> Ideas of a contrariety of interests between the northern and southern regions of the Union are in the main as unfounded as they are mischievous. The diversity of circumstances in which such contrariety is usually predicted, authorises a directly contrary conclusion. Mutual wants constitute one of the strongest links of political connection, and the extent of the[se] bears a national proportion to the diversity in the means of mutual supply. . . .
>
> In proportion as the mind is accustomed to trace the intimate connexion of interest, which subsists between all parts of a society united by the *same* government—the infinite variety of channels which serve to

circulate the prosper[ity] of each to and through the rest—in that proportion will it be little apt to be disturbed by the Solicitude and Apprehensions which originate in local discriminations.[49]

While many of the theoreticians of the Constitution believed that
America's future depended on the precise construction of its political
institutions, and that such institutions would be required to control
conflict, Hamilton believed that the country's future would depend on
its economic performance, and that however politics may deal with
conflict, the need to satisfy the mutual wants of differing sections of
the country produces consensus. The idea that interests can bind even
a competitive society together became fully appreciated by Tocqueville.
In an egalitarian society people feel all the more the need to prove
themselves, and in an environment without rigid class distinctions
people have little social identity other than what they do, earn, and
pursue. "What serves as a tie to these diverse elements?" Tocqueville
wrote to a friend of America's apparently contrasting social order.
"What makes of them a people? *Interest*. That's the secret. Individual
interest which sticks through at each instant, *interest* which, moreover,
comes out in the open and calls itself a social theory. We are a long way
from ancient republics, it must be admitted, and yet this people is
republican and I don't doubt it will long remain so."[50]

Ancient republics assumed that if interests were pursued openly
and competitively society would tear itself apart and the people would
lose all capacity for republican citizenship. The Roman historian Livy
taught that avarice and luxury bred wantonness and corruption. Modern thinkers like Hamilton and Tocqueville, however, were closer to
Adam Smith in discerning that the pursuit of interests implies wants
that need to be satisfied, and wants imply desires that, however different their objects, motivate people to act in socially responsible ways.
What is essential in these thinkers, and what reaches eloquent expression in the thought of Abraham Lincoln, is the conviction that human
beings possess the common desire to better their condition and that
the wealth of nations is increased when labor as well as capital achieves
its rightful reward. Of the Constitution's framers, Hamilton presages
Lincoln in sufficiently appreciating how a core of consensus could lie
embedded within an environment of competitive conflict.

Hamilton and Lincoln rejected both the classical belief that desire could be disciplined and repressed and the radical belief that it could be eliminated altogether as a filthy lust after possessions. They would channel human wants and wishes into economic activity. Where Karl Marx defined money as the "alienating medium of mankind," Hamilton and Lincoln recognized that money is radically subversive in that it respects neither class, race, gender, nor ancestry.[51] In his essay "Wealth," Emerson tried to teach Americans that money is "power" and commerce is "romance," and he wanted to see both extended to the ranks of all people who would practice not self-denial but self-reliance. A shared understanding of "self-interest rightly understood," Tocqueville observed, is at the heart of the American consensus.

Yet on the question of unity versus diversity the American mind could not make up its mind. As Henry Adams observed:

> Until 1815 nothing in the future of the American Union was regarded as settled. As late as January, 1815, division into several nationalities was still thought to be possible. Such a destiny, repeating the usual experience of history, was not necessarily more unfortunate than the career of a single nationality wholly American; for if the effects of a divided nationality were certain to be unhappy, those of a single society with equal certainty defied experience and sound speculation. One uniform and harmonious system appealed to the imagination as a triumph of human progress, offering prospects of peace and ease, contentment and philanthropy, such as the world had not seen; but it invited dangers, formidable because unusual or altogether unknown. The corruption of such a system might prove to be proportionate with its dimensions, and uniformity might lead to evils as serious as were commonly ascribed to diversity.[52]

Americans seem to be a people who accepted the unity of their nation while looking to their differences as the way to prevent corruption from the center, particularly if the country were to become "one uniform and harmonious system." Thus we are still left with the question of American identity. Are we to emphasize the *pluribus* or the *unum,* the many or the one? Hamilton, the patriotic nationalist, was almost alone among the founders in seeing that consensus could go hand in hand with conflict, and he looked to the unity and oneness of America. But most other founders saw little basis for consensus, and the specter of "factions" that haunted the constitutional debates in Philadelphia in 1787 suggests the extent to which the government would be erected on the basis of ineluctably conflicting tensions. American thinkers also worried that the rise of political parties would be divisive, and that various regions of the country would clash over economic policies.

We arrive, then, at a quandary. If the human mind is hopelessly divided and people are antagonistic toward one another—if, as Madison put it, "ambition must be made to counter ambition"—how is it possible to achieve stability and order? The authors of the Constitution leave us with an impression of an America trembling with conflict, rivalry, opposition, division, and faction. To understand how and why "consensus" emerges from such a disparate scenario, we must take up the question of "American exceptionalism."

CHAPTER 4

American Exceptionalism

"You Americans Believe Yourselves to Be Excepted"

SOME YEARS AGO PRESIDENT RONALD REAGAN WENT before the public to deliver his first inaugural address. He spoke of America as "a shining city upon a hill" that had in its power the capacity "to remake the world all over again."[1] The first expression came from the Puritan John Winthrop, the second from the rationalist Tom Paine. Both believed that America had been endowed with a special mission in the world. Yet neither believed in what the other believed. What one sought to uphold—the authority of religion and the spirit of hierarchical community—the other wished to see destroyed. Winthrop and Paine did see America as different and carrying out a unique role in history. But again the orientations diverge. One believed that America must remain separate from Europe; the other contended that America must rejoin it.

From the moment that settlers first set foot on American shores there has been disagreement about what set apart the New World from the Old. America may not have been "The Virgin Land" that was once described in scholarship; today we know too much about the original native populations to regard the North American continent as vacant when European explorers arrived. Still, the settlers, looking back, felt that America was a blessing compared with the lands from which they came. America is young, vigorous, experimental, optimistic, and open to the future; Europe, old, tired, doctrinaire, pessimistic, and wedded to the past. "You Americans believe yourselves to be excepted from the operation of general laws," scoffed Baron Jacobi, Henry Adams's character in the novel *Democracy*. "I have lived seventy-five years, and all that time in the midst of corruption. I am corrupt myself, only I have the courage to admit it, and you others have not. Rome, Paris, Vienna, Petersburg, London, all are corrupt; only Washington is pure!"[2]

The theory of American exceptionalism—the idea that America is and would continue to be distinct from Europe—is as old as American history itself. Or at least as old as American history the way it was understood prior to the contemporary multiculturalists's claim that America had its foundation in a "convergence" with pre-Columbian native populations and with the later arrival of Islamic West African slaves. This new view of America, which is being taught in many high schools, sees America as part of a tripartite ethnic culture, "red, white, black," with little to distinguish the New World from the Old.[3] To many scholars today, American exceptionalism is a conceit, a false notion that the country into which we ourselves were fortunate to have been born is in some sense better—or simply luckier—than other places in the world. While American exceptionalism inculcates pride, what the country needs, according to its critics, is guilt and a well-deserved inferiority complex.

It is time to restore a simple truth: of course America is exceptional. Every student and citizen should be taught as much. Further, "exceptional" does not mean merely different from other countries; indeed, most countries are different from each other and have varying histories and traditions. Instead, "exceptional" signifies special qualities characteristic peculiarly of America. Yet the controversial word has more than one meaning, and from the beginning many writers have had difficulty deciding whether their country's uniqueness is to be celebrated or lamented.

Embedded in the phrase "American exceptionalism" are two contrasting meanings, one upholding differences, rare conditions, and a sense of destiny; the other concentrating on deficiencies and common shortcomings that cast doubt on whether America will succeed. Thus while the European writer Goethe envied America for having no ancien régime, the American novelist Henry James wondered how his own country could produce great literature without aristocracy or inspiring castles.

American exceptionalism can mean either deliverance or deprivation; it can imply the presence of spiritual convictions that promise
salvation—the hope of the religious Right; or the absence of social
conditions that preclude revolution—the frustration of the radical Left.
One segment of the population thinks that America is superior and
delights in looking forward to divine rewards; another believes that
America is inferior and dreads looking to a future without the dream
of socialism. As for myself, I believe that it comes close to the sin of
pride to think one's country is so different that we should either celebrate it or complain about it. One of my heroes, Reinhold Niebuhr,
made us aware how tentative and contingent America was and still
remains because it is always subject to the flow of history: our course
remains too mysterious for us to identify with either Providence or
proletariat.

Yet the idea of American exceptionalism contains a certain irony.
For at the beginning of American intellectual history, with the arrival
of Calvinists to New England in the early seventeenth century, American exceptionalism could mean *both* deliverance and deprivation, so
much so that those who made America a success saw lurking in the
future a rendezvous with failure.

The first American settlers capable of deep intellectual reflection
could be regarded as halfway exceptionalists. The Puritans thought
that they were witnessing Christianity coming to a foreordained consummation in the Jerusalem that was America. They saw that the
Massachusetts Bay Colony would be, in the words of their greatest
historian, Perry Miller, "an exception to all the cities that ever before
had been set upon a hill," a migration into the wilderness to prove that
in the New World there might be a chance to escape the "wrath of
Jehova."[4] But they were also haunted by a sense of universal sin and
depravity and by a sense of history that dramatized the eternal sameness of all things. Nowhere was history more paradoxical: the peculiar
sense of existential dread that compelled Puritans to seek the salvation
of their souls through work and thrift had also undermined piety and
created the conditions of prosperity. But with the coming of Yankee
materialism, Puritans could no longer be assured that what was lacking in Europe could be nurtured in America and that the New World
would remain different from the Old.

A century later Thomas Jefferson and Tom Paine had a more hope-ful attitude toward material happiness that made America seem dif-ferent and once again exemplary as well as exceptional. To Jefferson and Paine it was the Puritans who were unexceptional in adhering to Old World religions and servile social relations. What, then, rendered America exceptional? "Human nature is the same on every side of the Atlantic," wrote Jefferson, "and will be alike influenced by the same causes." It was not the national character of Americans but the unique natural environment that offered special opportunities for human growth, particularly a rural environment with the potential for endless expansion. America's open landscape, which stood unfettered by mon-archy, aristocracy, and peasantry, and its political liberty, which was free of the "*canaille* [riffraff] of the cities of Europe," embraced a greater variety of possibilities for cultivating the mind and working the land. "We can no longer say there is nothing new under the sun," Jefferson wrote to Joseph Priestly. "For this whole chapter in the history of man is new. The great extent of our republic is new. Its sparse habitation is new." In contrast to the sin-struck Calvinists, Jefferson and Paine looked to prosperity itself as evidence of America's special destiny.[5]

In American politics today, for all the insistence on religion and family values, it is the comfort of the people that determines electoral success. "The taste for well being," wrote Tocqueville more than a century ago, "is the prominent and indelible feature of democratic times." The French writer was intrigued with America as exceptional; his paragraphs often begin with the statement that "Nowhere is the tendency toward . . . more widespread than in America," when dis-cussing traits such as the work ethic, the passion for wealth, or the compulsion to conformity. Tocqueville hoped that if a people could practice "self-interest rightly understood" they just might remain un-corrupted by "vicious materialism."[6] But with Jefferson's frankly epi-curean "pursuit of happiness" prevailing over the conscience of the Calvinist, the "city upon a hill" takes up residence in Beverly Hills.

Tom Paine and the "Cause of America"

The subject of America's relationship to the world came up again and again in American history, from the time of the Revolution to the period of the cold war. The term "American exceptionalism" itself actually originated in the 1930s among Marxist intellectuals in New York City. At that time certain factions that had broken with the American Communist Party refused to take orders from the Soviet Union and its international organ, the Comintern. Dissidents began to insist that the historical development of Soviet Russia and that of the West had so diverged that the Comintern had no authority to issue directives to other countries. Revolution, the Americans argued, "proceeds along varying paths with varying rapidities," and thus the Bolshevik seizure of power in Russia in 1917 scarcely constituted a model for America to emulate. Instead, it was explained, each nation must find its own road to the goals of Marxism.[7]

Crucial to understanding the idea of exceptionalism are the stages of historical development. Karl Marx himself believed that the most progressive countries are those that have proceeded through each and every stage of history. He looked to the West, particularly England and Germany, as the most advanced countries, whose working-class socialist parties would show other countries the way. But what about America? Marx and his cohort Friedrich Engels knew that America had spawned socialist parties in the late nineteenth century, yet they saw no hope for revolution on the horizon. Indeed, Marx and Engels saw what Tocqueville saw a half-century earlier, what Louis Hartz so brilliantly analyzed more recently, and what veteran Old Left radicals observed years ago before New Left historians entered the profession and dismissed their works from the canon.

The American people, wrote Engels in 1890, "are born conservatives just because America is so purely bourgeois, so entirely without a feudal past and therefore proud of its purely bourgeois organization." Such "special conditions" meant that the American working class would be far removed from class-conscious politics. "It is quite natural that in such a young country, which has never known feudalism and has grown up on a bourgeois basis from the first, bourgeois prejudices should be so strongly rooted in the working class." The Americans had not had a radical but a conservative revolution, and thereafter it was the "necessarily rapid and rapidly growing prosperity of the country which makes bourgeois conditions look like a *beau ideal* to them."[8]

If the term "American exceptionalism" was first used to deny

Soviet Russia's claim to lead the revolutionary world, a half-century earlier Marx and Engels had cited America's "special conditions" to deny America any prominent role in the world. Here the study of history as the reflection of a present age on its own past seems to come to an end. Does not a country's peculiar past preclude it from relating to the rest of the world? It would seem that the special features of America's historical development left our country in a state of frozen isolation. For if America was exceptional, could it also be exemplary?

"The cause of America," declared Paine in *Common Sense,* "is in great measure the cause of all mankind."[9] Untroubled by exceptionalism, Paine believed that the downfall of royal government in America would be the prelude to its downfall elsewhere and that the triumph of liberty in America would be the beginning of its victory throughout the world. Since Paine's time, America seems to have interested itself in nobility and aristocracy only when romance or tragedy is involved. Indeed, despite the mass love and mourning for Diana, Princess of Wales, Paine has clearly been proven correct: liberal democracy has triumphed in the modern world. Jefferson has also been vindicated. He agreed with Paine that America could be both new and different and still be "a standing monument and example for the aim and imitation of the people of other countries."[10]

On the eve of the French Revolution, *philosophes* looked to America as "the hope of the human race" and as a "model for the future." But within a year the true meaning of America's uniqueness had struck home as France began to veer toward bloody violence. Writing to Jefferson in 1790, Elisabeth d'Houdetot emphasized that "the characteristic difference between your revolution and ours is that having nothing to destroy, you had nothing to injure, and laboring for a people, few in number, uncorrupted, and extended over a large tract of country, you have avoided all the inconveniences of a situation, contrary in every respect. Every step in your revolution was perhaps the effect of virtue, while ours are often faults, and sometimes crimes."[11]

That the American Revolution destroyed little and threatened no one who went along with it clearly rendered the new Republic unique. But by the time the Constitution had been drafted and debated, in 1787–88, many thinkers had lost sight of the country's peculiar conditions and, with Daniel Shays's uprising and other disturbances that

threatened creditors and property owners, the "faults" and "crimes" of Europe seemed to be descending upon America. The *Federalist* authors, as we have seen, were haunted by a dread of class conflict. They were equally apprehensive about the fate of the republics from antiquity to the Renaissance. Such worries perhaps explain why they missed seeing America's exceptional circumstances; hence they came up with a Constitution designed to control differing factions.

Such devices as a bicameral legislature with an upper and lower house, separation of powers among the three branches of government, and division of powers between the federal and the state governments all indicated that unanimity and homogeneity were not to be expected in the new Republic. A few of the more democratic-leaning founders thought such devices unnecessary. A system of two legislative chambers, grumbled old Ben Franklin, was "like putting one horse before a cart and the other behind it and whipping them both." Franklin predicted either stasis or breakdown. "If the horses are of equal strength, the wheels of the cart, like the wheels of government, will stand still; and if the horses are strong enough, the cart will be torn to pieces."[12]

The idea that a divided political regime could be workable had a certain resonance in Newtonian physics, where action generates reaction and the laws of motion itself seem to result in a counterpoise of individual parts. Long before modern science, the idea of "balanced" government had deep origins in classical antiquity, particularly in the writings of Polybius, and it remained current in contemporary French thought, particularly in the writings of Montesquieu. Yet it was the French thinkers themselves who criticized the new American Constitution for what they thought was its excessive checks and balances. To the French, the U.S. Constitution that we revere today as the mainstay of liberty was unnecessary.

The Principle of "Liberty to All"

When news of America's constitutions, those of the states and of the national government, reached Paris, French thinkers could not believe that the framers had completely missed seeing the blessings of exceptionalism. Baron Anne-Robert Turgot complained that America had no need for controls over power and for bicameral legislatures:

the country's social constituencies were homogeneous and lacked the monarchist, aristocratic, and peasant strata that would otherwise have to be controlled by political means. John Adams replied that America would, indeed, reproduce such classes, as had all other countries of the past regardless of their form of government. Thus, as Louis Hartz pointed out in his brilliant *The Liberal Tradition in America,* the framers gave the country a Constitution for a land of conflict that turned out to be successful only because America was from the beginning a land of solidarity.[13]

Today much attention is given to Tocqueville's purported abiding faith in America's capacity for starting up voluntary civil associations. Tocqueville's observations on that subject take up only about six pages in his massive, seven hundred–page *Democracy in America,* and the observations are tempered by his more telling perception that the American people have little will to sustain organizations—they seem to dissolve as quickly as they are formed. Those who cite Tocqueville as advocating communal civil society scarcely confront what undermines it every day. "Why Are Americans so Restless Amidst Their Prosperity?" is the title of one of his chapters. What Jefferson promised, specifically happiness and equality, was precisely what Tocqueville believed drove Americans to move ahead while leaving community behind. It was not democracy, the Polish journalist Adam Gurowski noted, that animated Americans, but "a devouring mobility." Americans were indeed different. "In all recorded history," observed Hilaire Belloc, no people were as restless as early Americans, "not even the nomads of Asia."[14] The civil society that is so often invoked today requires a staying residency that Americans historically have proven incapable of maintaining.

Tocqueville offered what might be called "the sociological turn" in modern thought, for he suggested that the American framers were mistaken to look to political institutions, instead of social conditions, for answers to the problem of class pressures. Whereas the *Federalist* authors saw conflict between the few rich and the many poor, Tocqueville saw consensus arising in a society of mobility that lacked an aristocracy. America's Constitution functioned precisely because the conflict between property and democracy anticipated by the framers never developed. When full suffrage for white men was achieved in

the Jacksonian era (1828–48), most Americans turned out to value property and, instead of using the ballot to appropriate it, worked hard to acquire it in an environment of abundance. In America, Tocqueville observed, there would be no class-conscious "proletariat."[15]

The framers thus failed to see that America would be distinct from Europe in escaping older class antagonisms. They also neglected to notice something else that would have eased their apprehensions about social conflict. When Max Weber visited the United States in 1904, he came to appreciate all the more the country's Puritan heritage, which had produced Ben Franklin, and the Protestant ethic, which had given birth to capitalism. Both Tocqueville and Weber believed that the key to America lay in its Puritan origins. "It was religious passion that pushed the Puritans to America and led them to want to govern themselves there," wrote Tocqueville.[16] But where Tocqueville believed that America would be free of class tensions due to the absence of an ancien régime, Weber, writing years after the Civil War, saw that episode as deriving from a kind of class warfare. In a speech at Saint Louis, Weber reminded the audience of the social character of their country. "Even in America, with its democratic traditions handed down by Puritanism as an everlasting heirloom, the victory over the planters' aristocracy was difficult and was gained with great political and social sacrifices." Would America, then, follow the pattern of the Old World with its class conflicts and other problems?

> The United States does not yet know such problems. This nation will probably never encounter some of them. It has no old aristocracy; hence tensions caused by the contrast between authoritarian tradition and the purely commercial character of modern economic conditions do not exist. Rightly it celebrates the purchase of the immense territory [Louisiana], in whose presence we are here, as the real historical seal imprinted upon its democratic institutions; without this acquisition, with powerful and warlike neighbors at its side, it would be forced to wear the coat of mail like ourselves, who constantly keep in the drawer of our desks the march order in case of war. But on the other hand, the greater part of the problem for whose solution we are now working will approach America within only a few generations. The way in which they will be solved will determine the character of the future culture of this continent. It was perhaps never before in history made so easy for any nation to become a great civilized power as for the American people. Yet, according to human calculation, it is also the last time, as long as the history of mankind shall

last, that such conditions for a free and great development will be given;
the areas of free soil are now vanishing everywhere in the world.[17]

Weber's phrase "last time" echoes Lincoln's warning that America's offers "the last best hope of earth" to a world trying to break free
from the historical conditions of power and domination. As did Weber,
Lincoln recognized that history as the story of freedom has no second
acts and that the combination of circumstances that gave rise to human
liberty may be incapable of repeating itself. Thus the American Revolution must be remembered because it could not be reenacted, and while
the Civil War, Lincoln told Americans, offered the possibility of "a new
birth of freedom," freedom itself depended upon the preservation of
the Union. Lincoln grasped America's uniqueness among other nations of the world. America was not founded upon dynastic succession,
ethnic identity, religious community, or political authority. At the same
time, America did not just happen. "All this," he wrote in his thoughts
on the country's political institutions, "is not the result of accident. It
has a philosophical cause. Without the *Constitution* and the *Union*, we
could not have attained the result; but even these are not the primary
cause of our prosperity. There is something back of these, entwining
itself more closely about the human heart. That something, is the
principle of 'Liberty to all'—the principle that clears the path for all—
gives hope to all—and, by consequence, *enterprise* and *industry* to all."[18]

Like Weber, Lincoln recognized that America's exceptionalism lay
in its culture of entrepreneurial capitalism, which left behind the class
systems of the Old World. Few of the framers saw America the way
Lincoln and Weber later appreciated it. Some, like Adams, assumed
that America would have an aristocracy; others, like Madison, missed
seeing that the availability of free land would mitigate class tensions;
and even Hamilton scarcely recognized that the vast oceans would
render America diplomatically isolated so as not to be in a constant
state of military alert and burdened with defense-related expenditures.
Above all, few of the framers saw the American people the way Weber
did: he discerned an angst-driven people motivated by a work ethic
that made property a sign of both spiritual well-being and social success. With the coming of modernity, Weber realized, this original
"spirit" of capitalism would atrophy and the value once placed on work

would succumb to the sirens of wealth and the seductions of consumption. But significantly, it was precisely what the framers did not count upon that rendered the Republic stable and prosperous. It was not a "mixed," power-controlling government that made America what it became; it was instead a dynamic culture animated by what Tocqueville called "enlightened materialism" and "self-interest rightly understood" (as opposed to the decadent materialism of the Old World with its leisure class waste and aristocratic frivolities). It was, as Lincoln put, the principle of "liberty to all" that gave "hope to all."

Thus there resides a consensus position within the idea of American exceptionalism. Tocqueville insisted that Americans were "born equal" because as a people our predecessors had no need to struggle against established class systems in order to become free. Marx and Engels insisted that Americans were "born conservative" because the absence of feudalism deprived our predecessors of the need to develop class consciousness against an idle aristocracy. Americans were all of the same "estate," and their uniqueness lies in accepting property and wealth as the single yardstick of success. Classes exist in America, wrote Marx, although they "have not yet become fixed, but continually change and interchange their elements in a constant state of flux." America was a "bourgeois republic" with no class stratification, a political culture where wage-laborers, landlords, and capitalists are all driven by the "Fury of private interests."[19] But whereas Marx saw the pursuit of interest as alienating, Lincoln saw it as fulfilling.

Marx, Tocqueville, Weber, and other Europeans saw America as different and as destined to a unique pattern of historical development. Yet the very unanimity that European thinkers recognized in America our own Americans thinkers missed seeing. Hence from the time of the founders to the Civil War, America lived with a paradox: its political institutions had been designed to restrain the actions of a democracy that itself happily accepted the existing social order. "The European," Hartz observed, "wonders at two things in America: our elaborate majoritarian controls, and our marvelous moral agreement."[20]

The framers were not the only ones to misinterpret the social meaning of America. If the Republic was founded upon conflict only to turn out to be about a consensus, where does this irony leave the radical perspective on American history?

From a Whig to a Wail Interpretation of History

America was born in resistance to authority—the authority of Britain, the mother country. This fact creates problems for our present-day conservatives, who would like to see respect for authority restored and a common culture renewed. But our contemporary radical academics are up against an even greater embarrassment. They would like to see class conflict—the same struggles for power that the *Federalist* authors expected to arise in America—released from the controls placed upon them in the very structure of the Constitution. Curiously, the radical shares the assumption of the conservative framers that the forces of democracy, the "many," are a constant threat to the holders of property, the "few." This is not to claim that Madison was a "Marxist" *avant la lettre;* it merely suggests that the *Federalist* authors, unlike the French critics of the Constitution, saw social classes forming in the new Republic, and thus they did not see America as unique and exceptional since the inevitable rise of factions would render the New World conflictual rather than consensual. Yet the precise opposite happened, and what happened is what the radical Left wanted to see happen, the rise of democracy escaping the controls of the Constitution and making conflict possible. Herewith the irony. Instead of class conflict intensifying itself, as in the Marxist scenario, consensus sprang up everywhere in America as democracy shook hands with property and both set out in "pursuit of happiness."[21]

Because according to radical historians what happened should not have happened, those scholars needed to present a counternarrative to the consensus interpretation of America, and the story told by the Academic Left has prevailed in much of American historiography.[22] It is a romantic story recollected through desire rather than from data, a tale that postulates a mythical past lost to the forces of change. Ironically, like contemporary conservatives, who are frustrated about the present for different reasons, academic radicals also assume that the past enjoyed unity and harmony, and that this convergence of two contrary ideologies suggests a new way of looking at history.

Many years ago the British historian Sir Herbert Butterfield wrote *The Whig Interpretation of History* in an attempt to question all assumptions about progress, continuity, and the "rise" of whatever was worthy

of rising. The conceits of the present generation led historians of Butterfield's era to look to the past for "roots" and "anticipations" of
the convictions of their own time, and to praise only those parties that
had successfully fought causes precious to their own political values—
liberty, toleration, humanitarian reform, abolition of slavery, and democracy. In America today we are witnessing the writing of a history
that reverses the old Whig scenario to focus our attention on not what
rises but what is allegedly repressed. Instead of narrating the progress
of liberty and freedom, the radical historian describes what comes
close to a "fall" from an Edenic paradise. In this new scenario, which
could be termed the "wail interpretation of history," American democracy itself, instead of ascending, succumbs to something outside itself,
some alien intrusion that works like a "microbe" on the body politic.
The resulting historiography sounds like a chorus of complaint against
all that had once been celebrated as the story of freedom.[23]

The new labor history coming out of the academy reads like a long
whine about paradise lost. In this poignant scholarship, we are told
that American workers once lived in a harmonious, pre-industrial
society of provision and mutual welfare, a "moral economy" that precluded profit and competitive striving in order to practice "virtue,
equality, citizenship, and commonwealth." But then came the capitalist market revolution of the early nineteenth century; henceforth
America's worldly paradise was lost to an alienating force that, in the
telling words of one historian, "fostered individualism and competitive pursuit of wealth by open-ended production of commodity values
that could be accumulated as money." White workers were not the
only virtuous people to be driven out of the Garden of Eden. "Native
Americans lived in communal, cooperative, and egalitarian bands of
related families" until they "were destroyed by the lack of immunity to
both the microbes and the market brought by whites."[24]

Native American women might have seen things differently, existing, as they did, under conditions of patriarchal domination; and some
tribal chiefs may have been surprised to be told that they had once been
"immune" to a market economy, and hence had no desire to trade
pelts for tools, no history of competitive rivalry and warfare over claims
to turf and herds, no understanding of an economy of exchange and
circulation, and, today, no interest in opening up gambling casinos.

The new labor history feeds upon an anti-capitalist bias that has found a home in parts of the academy. But the scholarship scarcely accounts for the actual behavior of workers in the pre-capitalist colonial era, workers who were forever in court suing for unpaid wages, contesting breaches of contract, and engaged in other bitter litigations that cast doubt on the idea of class solidarity.[25] The idea of "moral economy" derives from the British Marxist historian E. P. Thompson, but its limited significance has been expanded by American historians to reach three un-Marxist conclusions: (1) human nature changes with the stages of history, (2) the rise of capitalism entails the fall of democracy, and, therefore, (3) the promise of America has been squandered. Like the conservative, the radical and often the liberal also believe that the best that America has to offer is behind us. But Tocqueville and Weber, along with the older consensus historians, saw capitalism and democracy rising together—they interpreted President Andrew Jackson's war against the Bank of the United States, for example, as signifying how much Americans wanted to destroy a monopoly the better to get their hands on money. The American worker was no more immune to acquisitiveness than the capitalist, and Tocqueville saw only two possibilities for both, either a materialism "enlightened" or one "pernicious."

As to "the habits of the heart," those community mores that made up for the absence of a government-oriented civic virtue in America, Tocqueville could only wonder whether private moral sentiments could withstand the forces of change. He saw what George Santayana later observed: liberal democracy has no respect for tradition and succumbs to the "dominance of the foreground." The two faiths of American liberalism, Santayana wrote, "are the gospel of work and the belief in progress." As well as being pragmatic and looking forward to life as an experiment to be acted upon, America was also Emersonian. "Freedom," said Santayana of Emerson, "was his profoundest ideal, and if there was anything which he valued more than the power to push on to what might lie ahead, it was the power to escape what lay behind. A sense of potentiality and a sense of riddance are, as he might have said, the two poles of American liberty."[26] The combination of capitalism and democracy specifically produces, wrote Tocqueville, a culture of energy, motion, and transformation that wreaks havoc with habits and "erases the tracks of time," resulting in an environment in which "each man is forever thrown back on himself alone," with the "danger that he may be shut up in the solitude of his own heart."[27]

Lincoln once told Americans that we must "disenthrall" ourselves from the past, "and then we shall be saved."[28] He saw people clinging to older categories no longer relevant to the modern era and to old visions about an orderly past that may have been more imagined than real. Today the conservative and the radical in particular remain so enthralled, and it is curious that both imagine that at one time America enjoyed a wholesome unity that is much sought today. Both look to the past for some kind of redemption.

Refusing to acknowledge that the framers were modernists, the conservative looks to them to give us the abiding truths that will save us from relativism; refusing to acknowledge that the workers were materialists, the radical looks to them to give us the abiding virtues that will save us from capitalism. Positing some golden age in the past, the conservative and radical alike ask us to think backwards, as though history can save us from ourselves.

No such golden age of consensual harmony and altruism existed. The conservative, faced with the farce of multiculturalism, calls for unity, unaware that the framers identified "uniformity" with potential tyranny, and liberty with dissent and inescapable diversity. The radical, faced with the unified consensus of liberal "bourgeois" society, calls for a curriculum of diversity and a politics of ethnic identity, seemingly unaware that in the past the only hope of the Left lay in broad mass movements of "solidarity."[29] America has become a spectacle of fragments living on fictions.

The Paradoxes of American Liberalism

What then is America's identity, its core value? European thinkers saw nineteenth-century America as a "bourgeois republic" driven by materialism, and Santayana added a twist when he remarked that Americans see themselves as idealists working upon matter. Should we weep over our materialism? Hardly. The taint of self-interest afflicts all human action; as William James warned, "the trail of the serpent is thus over everything."[30] Yet human beings have the potential for being ethical creatures; endowed with mind and conscience, they can respond to moral arguments. The audience of the Lincoln-Douglas debates applauded after being told that it was logical as well as moral that they extend to others the same rights that they claim for themselves. America did, after all, emancipate its slaves and give women equal political rights. A liberalism that left classical virtue behind can still be moral and responsible. As Locke noted back in the seventeenth century, the world looks to America because it is the land where self-preservation and spiritual salvation walk toward one another.

Yet the world can scarcely look to America, nor America to the world, if our condition is truly exceptional. As Louis Hartz pointed out at the end of his brilliant and often misunderstood *The Liberal Tradition in America,* we are our own worst guardians. Rather than conveying a cold war message of triumphalism, as his critics charge, Hartz laments America's parochial isolation and the people's lack of insight in understanding who they are. American political thought, cut off from the rest of the world due to the country's unique social environment, has been unable to confront the challenge of clarifying the meaning and direction of world history.

The last pages of Hartz's book are haunting. Hartz hoped to see the country's final "coming of age," an "inward enrichment of culture and perspective," as it made more and more contact with the outside world. "What is at stake is nothing less than a new level of consciousness, a transcending of irrational Lockeanism, in which an understanding of self and an understanding of others go hand in hand." Writing in the midst of the cold war, Hartz accurately prophesized the implications of liberalism for the rest of the world. "For if America is the bizarre fulfillment of liberalism, do not people everywhere rely upon it for the retention of what is best in that tradition?" Soviet Russia had long ago turned against that tradition, wrote Hartz, which leaves America as the last remnant of freedom in a divided world. But how can a people with an exceptional historical experience have anything in common with those still struggling under entirely different conditions? "Can a people 'born equal' ever understand peoples elsewhere that have to become so? Can it ever understand itself?" Hartz makes us aware of the paradox of a liberal America that presumes to lead a world from which it has been so cut off that it cannot even comprehend its situation in that world.

Such probing questions as those raised by Hartz have been neglected in the teaching and writing of American history. Today liberalism, the "L" word, is the kiss of death in politics and a term of abuse in
much of the academic world. Multiculturalists dismiss liberalism as
too western, Marxists identify it with capitalism, and other scholars
reduce it to the ingredient of individualism that can be dismissed as
"myth."[31] Yet Tocqueville himself, often associated with liberal individualism, believed that history could better be grasped by studying collective phenomena. "I do not speak of individuals, who do not effect
the essential phenomena of history," advised Tocqueville; "I speak of
classes, which alone should concern the historian."[32]

One wonders whether Tocqueville would have been surprised by
the recent entry of different people into American politics and such
developments as multiculturalism and affirmative action. Did he not
foresee that democratic society extends the spirit of egalitarianism
and, at the same time, lacks an aristocracy capable of imposing cultural standards from above? Tocqueville paid little attention to institutions in pre-industrial America, but he did anticipate what Max Weber would see developing everywhere in the modernizing world: that
to achieve more equality by eradicating class and racial differences,
groups must look to the state—for the state alone has the power to
enforce democratic ideals, and the very act of enforcement leads to the
administrative state and its bureaucratic agencies.

Bureaucracy is not the only tragedy of our identity. The liberal consensus often threatens to go beyond mere individualism to reach what
Tocqueville feared: an *égoïsme* that is unashamed of itself. Tocqueville
hoped that this would not happen, that the pursuit of interest would be
"enlightened" and "well understood" enough so that it would be re-
flective and restrained, resulting in "a sort of refined and intelligent
selfishness." But whether refined or rapacious, Tocqueville saw nothing else animating America in the period of Jacksonian democracy.
"Picture to yourself if you can, my dear friend," Tocqueville wrote
home from America,

> a society formed of all the nations of the earth: English, French, Ger-
> man . . . all people having different languages, beliefs, and opinions: in a
> word a society without roots, without memories, without prejudices, with-
> out habits, without common ideas, without national character; a hundred

times happier than ours; more virtuous? I doubt it. There's the starting point. What serves as a tie to these diverse elements? What makes of them a people? *L'intérêt*. That's the secret. Individual *intérêt* which sticks through at each instant, *l'intérêt* which, moreover, comes out in the open and calls itself a social theory.[33]

The "equality of conditions" that Tocqueville saw as the most "novel" aspect of the American environment, however, fed the people's demands for fulfillment of their selfish interests. When the lust after material happiness develops more rapidly than the enlightened mind, people lose control of themselves, become envious, and can no longer practice self-restraint. Hence liberty is threatened as people succumb to the temptations of consumption, cease valuing independence and self-reliance, and lose all sense of their own worth.

The *Federalist* authors also saw Americans as actuated by "interests and "passions," so much so that there could be little appeal to reason and virtue. The individual, they noted, might well respond to a sense of honor and reputation and hence be persuaded to do the right thing. But with groups and factions, individual egoism takes on a collective character indifferent to ethical appeals. Much more recently, the theologian Reinhold Niebuhr appreciated this insight, too. In *Moral Man in Immoral Society,* Niebuhr formulated a Christian realism close to that of Tocqueville and the framers. "In every human group," he observed, "there is less reason to guide and check impulses, less capacity for self-transcendence, less ability to comprehend the needs of others, and therefore more unrestrained egoism than the individuals who composed the group reveal in their personal relationship."[34]

Tocqueville, Niebuhr, and the framers of the Constitution would scarcely be surprised at the goings on in today's politics. For early American history begins with the same paradox of liberalism that continues today, a politics that would seem self-contradictory if we were to forget the relentless play of *l'intérêt* in daily life. Just as the colonists remained satisfied to benefit from England's colonial system while protesting paying its costs, so too do we witness today the spectacle of a government being denounced and then having demands placed upon it by its very denouncers. Tocqueville hoped that *égoïsme* could shame itself into self-restraint. Today, however, specific groups continue to insist that their needs and desires be satisfied, and there seems to be no awkwardness in asserting that their own particular interests take priority over all other considerations.

Hence the paradox of an electorate both in revolt against Washington and at the same time expecting more from the officials it elects to office. Voters hate taxes and like receiving checks from the Treasury Department; citizens bemoan the growth of government agencies and demand comprehensive health-care coverage; bankers protest bureaucratic overregulation and then request to be rescued with government bailouts; farmers complain of crop-acreage restrictions only to ask for price supports; owners of beach homes prohibit public access to the waterfront and continue to lobby for publicly financed flood insurance. What Hartz called the "submerged Lockeanism that governed the New Deal" and the welfare state scarcely prepared America to grasp the ways in which government would always remain a resource to draw upon while seldom becoming an institution worthy of respect.[35]

Are there still traces of the "submerged Lockeanism that governed the New Deal" in today's America, where politicians, even Democrats, no longer embrace the New Deal and its welfare state? One place we may look to is the American campus. It could well be one of the ironies of modern American history that the campus radicals, who years ago abused the symbols of patriotism and saw government as a monstrous, oppressive bureaucracy, ultimately turned to government to fulfill what had been frustrated in the normal channels of democratic politics. What Tocqueville called the relentless presence of *l'intérêt* in democratic society plays itself out in various academic programs that strive to sustain the "equality of conditions" that he saw as vital to American history. Even though many campus activists would never deign to see themselves as carrying on the liberal tradition, their own behavior reveals it in their demands to be included in its benefits.

Critics of the recent "culture wars" on the campus, the controversies about affirmative action, multiculturalism, and identity politics, might well argue that such trends depart from the integrity of Lockean liberalism. Locke himself saw no role for government as a provider for the poor and dispossessed; nor did he believe that the doctrine of natural rights extended beyond individuals to specific groups and their demands. The liberal individualism that derives from the Renaissance, and the Lockean individualism that derives from the Enlightenment, would treat each and every person similarly, ignoring differences of sex, race, religion, and ethnicity.

Such a criterion of universalism, however, while upholding political ideals, slights the phenomenon of power. The *Federalist* authors saw that power moves in concert and that the aim of government is to deal not so much with individuals as "factions." But we must go even beyond the framers to get a sense of today's political realities; we must, in short, update Locke and Madison with Max Weber. If in the past it was believed that power follows property at the top of society and moves collectively through groups and factions, today power follows bureaucracy, residing, among other places, in the administrative state and its programs. We should not be surprised, then, that different groups hail their differences to benefit from such programs. "What," asked William James, "is truth's cash-value in experimental terms?"[36] Those students and professors who defend different ethnic programs and identity politics could well reply that the truth of such stances lies in their cash value in negotiating opportunities for employment and career advancement. It pays to be different.

The recent "culture wars" have much to do with American exceptionalism. In no other country have multiculturalism and affirmative action had such an impact on government, education, and the teaching of history. The legal system that such programs depend upon is essentially American, with its equal protection of the laws; due process; the rights, privileges, and immunities of citizenship; and court-ordered decisions on affirmative action. Yet many of the beneficiaries of such liberal institutions are reluctant to acknowledge the depth of consensus in America's political culture, and they have convinced themselves that to study the oppressed and powerless is to uncover challenges to that consensus and to expose exceptionalism as a national conceit.

The Meaning of Exceptional Foundations

The manner in which the idea of exceptionalism is dismissed by many contemporary scholars may be seen in a symposium on the subject in the *American Historical Review.* Professor Mary Nolan, who teaches modern German history at New York University, speaks the conventional wisdom when she cites a book by Sean Wilentz, the historian who assumes that any utterances made by workers against banks and wealth arise from righteousness rather than resentment. Nolan writes: "Arguments about American exceptionalism invariably culminate in the proud conclusion that America had no socialism. Such a sweeping assertion hardly captures the complex nature of class politics and class consciousness in the United States." Referring to the German debate over *sonderweg*, the idea that German history had a "special path" that took the country down the road to fascism, Nolan advises us: "In both Germany and America, exceptionalist arguments produce inadequate history, limited self-understanding, and arrogant politics."[37]

Self-understanding would indeed be limited were we to continue to believe that the American Republic saw itself as special at the moment of its founding. On the contrary, our own founders were not exceptionalists: they saw the American people as no different from the rest of the human race. The foundations I write about—and this needs the utmost emphasis—are not the political foundations founded by our founders. America's foundations lie in the egalitarian ideas that Lincoln expounded to the world, and they took hold precisely because "liberty to all" became possible in an America that was exceptional. The founders, who were concerned as much about the abuses of liberty as about its accessibility, saw America as unexceptional. The architects and theoreticians of the Constitution were concerned about the exact operations of its mechanisms because of their low regard of people—they believed that everyone's actions needed checks and controls. Americans were not expected to behave any differently than the people of class-ridden Europe. The founders looked to well-established institutions, particularly political institutions, to secure the future of liberty and property. "The institutions now made in America," John Adams wrote in 1788, "will not wholly die out for thousands of years. It is of the last importance, then, that they should begin right. If they set out wrong, they will never be able to return, unless it be by accident to the right path."[38]

And if indeed they did begin wrong?

The premises of the framers of the Constitution—that the branches of government are meant to resist one another, that a new liberal regime will work only by the opposition of interests, that property is threatened by democracy and thus the first object of government is to assure its protection, that conflict, in short, must be controlled since it cannot be eliminated—such premises scarcely explain the remarkable durability of American democracy. Most of the framers feared democracy as permissive, as a reign of unfettered desire unleashing the "passions," as a principle of government governed by no principle. They also assumed that each branch of government must reflect the orders of society, and from classical authors they inherited the fear that each branch has its own degenerating tendencies, with a monarchy (or "monarchical element" to use Adams's phrase) in the executive branch succumbing to tyranny, an aristocracy in the upper-house Senate relenting to oligarchy, and a democracy in the lower House of Representatives deteriorating into anarchy. The idea of a "mixed" government was meant to balance class against class and to prevent an unchecked, single-assembly democracy from prevailing.

Yet the Constitution's mechanisms proved inadequate for controlling a democratic will that would level differences and make government subordinate to mass opinion—and, today, to the ubiquity of poll ratings. Society, in short, stumped the state. What truly influences society—social norms, cultural values, religion, even morality itself—is all but missing from the *Federalist*, the theoretical manifesto of the new national government. The framers assumed that the "machinery of government" itself would suffice to hold the country together. Lincoln, however, as we explored earlier, lauded the Declaration as a value-generating document that had the moral weight of a spiritual covenant. When Lincoln invoked the Declaration as the "moral emblem" of the Republic, he saw the document as embodying the country's exceptional social conditions from which it in turned derived its unique cultural preconditions, particularly the idea of equality and the natural right to work freely and rise socially.

When honoring America's founding, Lincoln seldom used the classical language of political virtue. The founders themselves, however, were often ambiguous about this idea, almost to the point of inconsistency. In drafting the Constitution the framers made it clear that the character of the American people suffered from "the defect of better of motives," the absence of civic virtue that made it necessary to have the "auxiliary precautions" of institutional controls.[39] Yet often in private communication the founders waxed nostalgic about a once-honored idea. Consider the following two observations:

> The only foundation of a free constitution is pure virtue.
>
> John Adams, 1807

> The Americans are not a virtuous people, and nevertheless they are free.
>
> Alexis de Tocqueville, 1835[40]

It took two European visitors to America, first Tocqueville early in the nineteenth century, and later Max Weber during the opening of the twentieth century, to see that the stability of America's political culture had little to do with civic virtue or even the country's political institutions. Instead, the key to America lies in its social values, which derived from its unique origins. Both European thinkers considered early Puritanism to be the source of America's liberty and prosperity. What determines a country's development, observed Tocqueville, is its original "point of departure," and thus he thought he saw the "whole destiny of America contained in the first Puritan who landed on these shores." Weber esteemed the liberty that grew out of Puritanism as America's "everlasting heirloom," and he worried what might become of a country that lost its spiritual heritage to the forces of modernity.[41]

That spiritual heritage appears to be in disarray in the teaching of history in many of our high schools and colleges. Today it is fashionable to believe that America has no important heritage and that any call for a unifying synthesis of the American past is simply "ideology," an attempt to impose a false identity so that people can better be dominated. It was not always this way.

The journalist Richard Rodriquez, brought up in a barrio and educated in Catholic schools in Sacramento, California, remembers that he was taught to believe he belonged to America and America belonged to him:

> Our teachers used to be able to pose the possibility of a national culture—a line connecting Thomas Jefferson, the slave owner, to Malcolm X. Our teachers used to be able to tell us why all of us speak Black English. Or how the Mexican farmworkers in Delano were related to the Yiddish-speaking grandmothers who worked the sweatshops of the Lower East Side.[42]

Today we seem to have lost that desire to imagine the possibility of possessing a national culture based upon a common consensus that makes America exceptional. That possibility is the object of my desire in being so bold as to try to reinterpret something as complex and elusive as American history. It should be clear that consensus hardly implies uniformity, nor does exceptionalism imply superiority. Both can breed a politics of arrogance, but that dismaying fact alone cannot fully undermine their value in understanding history. How, then, should history be taught?

PART II

Of Thee I Sing

CHAPTER 5

The Pride and the Pain: History in the Classroom and in Public Controversy

TYRONE. Mary, For God's sake, forget the Past!
MARY (with strange, objective calm). Why? How can I? The past is the present, isn't it? It's the future, too. We all try to lie out of that but life won't let us.
EUGENE O'NEILL, *Long Day's Journey into Night*

Returning to Washington High and Lincoln's Library

SOME YEARS AGO I HAD OCCASION TO VISIT A CLASS OF eleventh-grade students and their teacher of American history. Their school, San Francisco's George Washington High, covers a full two city blocks and is located on top of a hill in a foggy section of the city near the beach. The visit brought back memories from my teenage years of a striking school in my neighborhood. From the football stadium—on whose field ran the great backs Ollie Matson and O. J. Simpson, and on whose track galloped the champion high hurdler Johnny Mathis—one could look out at the Golden Gate Bridge, a towering monument to art deco design with its narrow, vertical fluting and reddish tone.

Washington High had been built in the 1930s as a Works Progress Administration project. Such projects were intended to put back to work the unemployed of the Depression era, including artists as well as laborers. Some of the hallways in the school displayed splendid murals and frescoes composed by associates of Diego Rivera and David Alfaro Siqueiros, leftist Mexican painters who combined brilliant colorist technique and angular lines to produce a bold social

realism of monumental dimensions. The works in the hallways depict brawny proletarians with bulging biceps joining scrawny bespec-
tacled engineers holding plumb lines and slide rules, a mélange of
muscle and measurement working together to build a new society of
solidarity.

A half-century after the building of Washington High, the campus
continued its spirit of progressive politics. In the classroom I visited
more than a dozen years ago, the walls were covered with posters
depicting revolutionary scenes with vague images of Vladimir Lenin
and Mao Tse-tung in the background; pictures of black leaders Frederick Douglass and W. E. B. Du Bois; the anarchist Emma Goldman;
César Chávez, the saintly Hispanic farm-worker leader; "Wobbly"
strikers from the Industrial Workers of the World (IWW); women
suffragettes marching to their cause; Native American tribal chiefs;
Asian workers laying down railroad ties; and the grand old man of
American socialism, Eugene Debs. One had to look hard to find pictures of Thomas Jefferson, Abraham Lincoln, and the school's name-
sake, George Washington.

Things may have changed at Washington High. Today many students in American high schools arrive wearing baggy pants and carrying skateboards, with their heads bopping to rock music beating from
earphones. Girls gush over jocks, guys cruise for a pickup, and occasionally school officers stand at the hallway's entrance to moni-
tor arrivals who might carry knives or other weapons and to dis-
courage them from careening up to the school's steps on rollerblades.
In high school, the subject of history has much to compete with, and
its teachers are heroically trying to make the past relevant in a youth
culture that lives not for the imagined future but for the delights of
the immediate present—this afternoon's soccer match, tonight's date.
While history should not be expected to compete with sports or sex,
one might well ask why young people should be interested in history.
And if they are at all interested, what should they study?

Today many students derive their knowledge of history from the
media, especially popular films and television documentaries. More
recently, with the advent of the internet, students can "surf" hundreds
or even thousands of web sites and discover interesting course outlines on various historical subjects. Knowledge of history is digital, at

the command of the finger punching the keyboard to call up a seemingly infinite array of topics and discussions.

It may disturb some scholars that the learning of history has begun to leave the library. But more than a century ago, in his famous address "The American Scholar," Ralph Waldo Emerson worried that the education that took place inside schools and libraries and depended upon the printed page might become passive and boring. "The theory of books is noble," he wrote, but their authority should not get in the way of youth's potential creativity. "Meek young men grow up in libraries, believing it their duty to accept the views which Cicero, which Locke, which Bacon, have given; forgetful that Cicero, Locke, and Bacon were only young men in libraries when they wrote these books."[1] How, then, should one study history?

Almost as though presaging the new social history of our times, Emerson advises, in his provocative essay "History," that we avoid the "battles and leaders" view of the past, which is so "barren and wearisome [a] chronicle" that the "unity of the story is secured [only] by concentrating attention to the man or woman on the throne." Emerson insists that what is important about the past is what it can do for us living in the present, how it may help us identify with others across space and time. Unless we use our imaginations to try to grasp the experience of others, "we shall see nothing, learn nothing, keep nothing." It is possible, Emerson instructs, to share a kinship with whomever we read about regardless of his or her race, class, or gender. This "stupendous fact of the radical identity" of all men and women, this ability to transcend the historical context in which we find ourselves, means that "we are not children of time." History, when properly taught, is more than dry chronology. "The Indian, the child, an unschooled farmer's boy stand nearer to the light by which nature is to be read" than does the antiquarian. But of history specifically, the student "must learn by laborious reading."[2]

Emerson's address was delivered in 1837, not long after Abraham Lincoln, "an unschooled farmer's boy," had begun his own self-education. As a youth working on neighbors' farms, Lincoln "borrowed and read every book he could hear of for fifty miles around." Born to an illiterate mother and an uneducated father, he was determined not to see his mind go to waste.

Lincoln read voraciously and widely. As a congressman in Washington, D.C., in the late 1840s, he frequented the congressional library, with his eagerness to learn so great that a fellow member of the House called him a "bookworm." Earlier he and and a few of his young friends had read Robert Burns and William Shakespeare. Lincoln had even memorized long passages from Shakespeare and cited him in his political debates and in his advice to politicians and military officers. Lincoln also knew the neo-classical writers Joseph Addison and Alexander Pope, whom he similarly drew upon to proffer advice. To Gen. David Hunter, one of several officers who, in the early years of the Civil War, thought it wiser to delay than to attack, Lincoln advised that it is better to do something rather than nothing. "Act well your part," he wrote, invoking Pope; "there all the honor lies."[3]

In addition to delving into the Bible, especially the Book of Psalms, and *Aesop's Fables,* Lincoln also became absorbed in reading history and legal philosophy. He knew by heart Parson Weems's *The Life of Washington* (1809), the text that first started the myth of young George's refusing to tell a lie about cutting down the cherry tree. No doubt Weems instilled in Lincoln a sentimental and mawkish view of America's first president, but it is a measure of Lincoln's own romantic nature that he remained unsatisfied with more factual biographies of Washington. Lincoln also knew William Grimshaw's *History of the United States* (1845), a more reliable, straightforward narrative. When riding circuit court as a young lawyer, Lincoln picked up a copy of William Blackstone's *Commentaries* and, he later wrote, "went at it in good earnest."[4] Reading legal theory prepared Lincoln for the many grave constitutional problems that arose over slavery and the crisis of the Civil War, when the president felt compelled to wield extra-constitutional powers.

According to his law partner William Herndon, Lincoln also read Edward Gibbon's *The History of the Decline and Fall of the Roman Empire* (1836). In today's terms, Gibbon would be called a true multicultural scholar, one interested in the histories of the Orient and the Arab world. But ancient Rome's decline from greatness haunted Gibbon, as it did Henry Adams and other Americans who wondered about the young Republic's fate. The idea that the American Republic might perish continued to trouble Lincoln as he contemplated an uncertain future.

If knowledge is power, reading is the mind's means of empowering itself. Reading books was Lincoln's way out of the impoverished environment into which he was born. Without the knowledge that he had gained from reading and pondering texts, Lincoln would never have been able to think clearly about complex issues, to establish the meaning of ideas by arguing from definition, to present a thought or enforce a position by apt illustration. Compared to the founders, Lincoln did not read a large body of writing; but what he read he absorbed deeply and could distill in simple, wise statements. Above all, studying history enabled Lincoln to face history, to contend with the movement of human actions and events and to try to understand the ways of power. Lincoln had to undertake this task again and again in order to lead America through its greatest crisis.

History and Citizenship

Today the teaching of history in the schools faces another hurdle. Many educators and public officials assume that a knowledge of history will make American youths into better citizens. The claim was prominently made in the *National History Standards,* and with good reason. The ancient historians Herodotus and Thucydides used history to demonstrate that the health of the Greek city-state depended on citizens' intelligent and active participation in the operations of government. Centuries later, with the rise of the Enlightenment, John Locke taught that the only way political power could be controlled was by giving a country's citizens the right to elect delegates to office and hold them accountable to preserving liberty and security. But by the time Alexis de Tocqueville had written *Democracy in America* in the 1830s, citizenship had less to do with the national government, which then was weak and insignificant, than with "voluntary associations" that sprang up in local communities. What impressed Tocqueville about America was not so much citizenship as workmanship and the dignity of labor in the eyes of the people. From the time of Ben Franklin, hard work and the earning of money were regarded as far more important than politics in leading a life of freedom and independence; and, as Tocqueville saw it, Americans' passion for "self-interest rightly understood" rendered them too individualistic to devote themselves to civic life and the public good on the national level. This description of the American character leaves the teacher of history in a dilemma. Should he or she instill in students the value of voting, or, alternatively, the value of earning?

Both can coexist, as they readily do in contemporary America. But from the point of view of citizenship, voting should be directed toward the public good while earning is an affair of private interests. In theory, the former leads to "civic virtue," the latter to "possessive individualism."

Which activity has done more to empower people? Compare Ralph Waldo Emerson's essays on "Politics" to his "Wealth," and we find that while politics can give us only cunning," wealth offers us "power."[5] One of the great political documents in American history is Henry David Thoreau's essay on "Civil Disobedience" (1849), which declares Thoreau's opposition to America's war with Mexico. But neither Emerson nor Thoreau is of much help to the teacher of citizenship, who is supposed to convey why people should obey authority and why they have obligations to serve and defend their government.

In American history those who were born into slavery often knew well what it meant to struggle for the freedom to be citizens. The former slave Frederick Douglass identified citizenship as the liberty to labor, earn, and own, all enterprises that nurture the spirit of independence. "All that any man has a right to expect, ask, give or receive in this world, is fair play. When society has secured this to its members, and the humblest citizen or the republic is put into the undisturbed possession of the natural fruits of his own exertions, there is really little left for society and government to do."[6]

Technically, citizenship means that people owe allegiance to and are entitled to protection from a sovereign state. In American history, however, the spirit of liberty has often been conceived in resistance to government. The idea of sovereign authority was obliterated at the time of the founding, for example, when political power came to be dispersed among the states and within the branches of the federal government. At one time citizenship was also meant to flourish in small, simple republics where people could gather together and cultivate human excellence by taking part in the operations of government and being responsible for its decisions. Such a definition of citizenship required the leisure with which to study and grasp the political issues of the day. In American history, however, the idea of a small republic was rejected in the *Federalist,* and even the leading political philosopher who likened the minimal to the moral, Thomas Jefferson, left behind his ideals when negotiating the Louisiana Purchase, thereby assuring that America would be an expanding, continental empire. Into that region poured wave upon wave of immigrant workers, who were employed by others and hence lacked the independence and free time essential to citizenship. Toward the end of the nineteenth century, liberal and socialist writers advocated programs to reduce economic inequalities and class divisions so that true citizenship might be possible for all Americans.

But historically citizenship has also been used as a tool of discrimination and exclusion. In the nineteenth century, women, blacks, and Asians were denied the constitutional entitlements that go with citizenship, particularly the right to vote and to serve on juries and, in some instances, to inherit property. The antagonism between native citizens and alien foreigners eased in the twentieth century, when political rights as well as civil rights extended universally to women and minorities as either a matter of birthright or through the naturalization of immigrants.

Throughout much of American history, citizens have been torn between responding to the plight of the disenfranchised lower classes and ethnic minorities and preserving the rights and interests of the privileged majority. Yet despite such struggle and conflict, it is hard to deny that a basic liberal consensus resides within America's political conflicts. Nowhere was this reality more clearly manifested than in the debates over African-American citizenship in the years before the Civil War. First in the Missouri Compromise of 1820, then in the Supreme Court's *Dred Scott* decision of 1857, the country divided along Lockean lines over the status of black Americans born in free states. Slavery apologists argued that the consent of existing citizens was required to admit blacks as new citizens into a given community, and they reminded Americans that the framers of the Constitution had been silent on how African Americans were to be made citizens. Northern critics replied that free blacks had, by reason of birth in free states, a constitutional right to travel in the territories as a privilege of citizenship guaranteed in the Fourth Amendment. This conflict between social consensus and natural right is at the heart of American liberalism.

Ultimately the question of citizenship turns on how America's political culture has defined itself historically. The two major exponents of classical republican citizenship, Niccolò Machiavelli and Jean-Jacques Rousseau, taught that people must practice political virtue, either to enable a republic to rise to greatness by calling on its citizens to renounce private self-interest in the name of patriotism, or by steering a republic away from luxury, complexity, and acquisitive individualism in order to reembrace the ancient ideals of Sparta and Rome. But the *Federalist* authors and other theoreticians of the Constitution rejected both Machiavelli and Rousseau when articulating the principles of America's founding. Drawing instead on the Scottish philosophers David Hume and Adam Smith, as well as the English author John Locke, whose ideas legitimized the right of revolution in the Declaration of Independence, the founders made a decisive break from the past and offered a new approach to politics: a representative form of government that would require neither the demands of virtue nor the duties of citizenship. It was only natural that a country that had recently fought a successful war against its own mother country would inaugurate a new regime that had more to do with economic opportunity than political responsibility. In the *Federalist,* James Madison announced that government must recognize not the people's duties but their rights, particularly their right to what they had created and earned as individuals. "The protection of different and unequal faculties of *acquiring* property is the just object of government."[7] Madison's dictum is pure Lockeanism.

Today's radical school of historiography has its own dictum, which sees "participatory democracy" as prior to property and posits civic involvement as the basis of true citizenship. But participatory democracy and civic involvement rest awkwardly with the framers' shift from politics to economics, from virtue and leisure to work and labor, from the state and the polis to what Jefferson specified as "the plough and the hoe."[8] The framers recognized that the shift from virtue to commerce risked resting the future of the Republic on the basis of hitherto untested theories; historically it had long been assumed that republics must remain small and simple or they would perish from the perils of prosperity. Like older Puritans, the framers worried about the corruptions of wealth as they saw Americans accumulating it, fearful that the last vestiges of citizenship could easily fall prey to luxury and the wasteful pleasures of consumption. But except for John Taylor of Carolina and one or two others, the founders realized that once a country commits itself forward toward a commercial society, there is no turning back to classical virtue.[9]

Ultimately what undermines citizenship is consensus itself. Without conflict and crisis, our political culture lacks the authority to appeal to the people to accept responsibility for the public good over the passions of private interest. Of the crisis that led to the drafting of the new Constitution in 1787, Tocqueville observed of Americans a half-century later: "The consequence of prosperity itself made men forget the cause that had produced it, and, with the danger passed, the Americans could no longer summon the energy or the patriotism which enabled them to get rid of it."[10] During the Civil War, Lincoln could make such appeals, even going so far as asking Americans to undergo sacrifices and engage in days of fasting. But in Jefferson's "pursuit of happiness" there is no place for the authority of the state, which in his estimate governs "best" when it governs "least"; and no clear role for citizenship, which, when he referred to it at all, usually specified the years of residency required to qualify for it. Only a political culture of shared values that takes its ends for granted can regard government so cavalierly or so expediently. Americans need not worry that they might "betray" their ideas about citizenship and government, observed Henry Adams, for they have none whatsoever. Both political parties, he wrote in reference to the Federalists and Republicans in the early nineteenth century, "cared nothing for fine-spun constitutional theories of what government might or might not do, provided government did what they wanted."[11] How can there be genuine citizenship in a democracy that reduces government to the people's will to fulfill their own wants and wishes? In classical thought governance aimed to discipline desire, in liberal thought to realize it; classicism demanded of citizens that they participate in the polity, liberalism that they involve themselves in the economy.

Wars over History

History may be too important to be left to historians alone. Clearly the public thinks so, and for centuries historians have been their own worst enemies by undermining the validity of narratives written by their predecessors. At times it seems that the only relationship historians have to history is to repeat it by revising it.

Perhaps at no time has our own consciousness of the historical past been so acutely felt as it is today. The press screams with reports of hotly debated controversies. One such recent argument divided the country not along lines of class, race, and gender but according to age and chronology. Among other issues, it became a fierce generational battle between those who had proudly fought in World War II and those who refused to fight in the Vietnam War or took to the streets to oppose it.

Officials at the Smithsonian Institution's National Air and Space Museum had no idea that a planned exhibition of the *Enola Gay*, the B-29 that dropped the first atomic bomb on Hiroshima, would set off a firestorm of controversy. On November 27, 1994, in the dark of night, the front half of the plane, under wraps in a long tube, arrived at the Smithsonian. Only a handful of protesters were in sight. One sang verses written by people known as *hibakusha*, those who had survived Hiroshima; others were pacifists waving a banner that said "Disarm." Within weeks, however, the nation would be bitterly divided over the exhibition. The *Enola Gay* controversy reveals much about the state of American historiography.[12]

When the Greek historian Thucydides introduced his book *The Peloponnesian War*, he insisted that first-hand, "eye-witness" accounts of the battles were the most reliable, even if such accounts often contradicted one another.[13] Curiously, critics of the Smithsonian exhibition are closer to the spirit of the historian Thucydides than are the American historians themselves. For the *Enola Gay* dispute represented a division between those who had experienced history, the veterans, and those who later wrote about it, the historians. While those who fought in the Pacific saw the bomb as a savior, as the instrument that had ended the war and allowed soldiers and sailors to return home, the historians who advised the museum's curators saw the bomb as a destroyer, as the instrument that not only took the lives of nearly 100,000 Japanese civilians but also destroyed the possibility of a future world of peace and freedom, a world without superpowers engaging in dangerously tense confrontations. According to revisionist historians, Hiroshima may have ended World War II, but it started the cold war. Moreover, the historians insisted that the number of anticipated casualties in a possible land invasion of Japan had been exaggerated, that the United States should have been more responsive to reported Japanese peace overtures, and that the bomb should not have been used. The Air Force Association, the American Legion, and the Veterans of Foreign Wars, all of which represented those who had actually witnessed the war, accused historians of having "hijacked history." The exhibition as conceived by historians was canceled and shortly afterward the Smithsonian postponed a planned exhibition of the Vietnam War.[14]

The *Enola Gay* controversy was the first in recent times to have put historians themselves on trial. Could they be counted on to tell the truth about the past? Thucydides believed that events could best be explained by those who had taken an active part in them, and history was to be seen through the eyes of one's countrymen and even of their enemies on the field. Does history belong to those who fight or those who write?

Controversies over history can often divide historians and scholars themselves, sometimes to the bemusement of the public. When the Library of Congress planned to hold an exhibition called "Freud: Conflict and Culture," intellectual historians and psychoanalysts jumped all over one another about a thinker who claimed to have been the "conquistador" of the unconscious. The exhibition planned to display the analyst's couch as well as his writings. But scholars could not agree whether he had been a liberator of the emotions or whether he had offered a pseudoscience for the rich, well born, and emotionally disabled.[15]

Immediately after the Library of Congress caved in to pressure and postponed the Freud exhibition, it did the same for a proposed show, "Back of the Big House: The Cultural Landscape of the Plantation." Several members of the library's own staff, especially African Americans, had found it offensive to walk past the temporary exhibition outside their offices and be greeted by photos of slaves. The exhibit was transferred to the Martin Luther King, Jr., Library of the District of Columbia, and the theme was altered to depict the human deficiencies of plantation masters and the human qualities of slaves and their more nurturing "community." The message of the critics had been clear: give us hope, not shame.[16]

Clearly such controversies occurred not because of what was exhibited, but because of how it was represented. The depiction of an event, a figure, or an episode from the past could be so emotional as to divide not only the country but even the members of a specific ethnic group. When in March 1996 the "Gaelic Gotham" exhibition opened at the Museum of the City of New York, it barely survived bitter disagreements among Irish Americans and the institution's staff. Should the show display pretty dresses and bowls decorated with shamrocks, or should it retell the harsh conditions of the life of the laborer on the waterfront and the racism-fed draft riots of the Civil War years? One thing Irish Americans could agree upon is that Ireland's tragic potato famine of the 1840s must be included in New York State's high school textbooks, along with the other better-known horrors of history.[17]

But in the history wars it is mainly American history that has been put on trial. Even before the *Enola Gay* controversy, hints that America was about to be trashed emerged in an exhibition named "The West as America," put on by Washington's National Museum of American Art in 1992. Throughout the galleries, paintings—and particularly the texts that accompanied them—depicted Native Americans overrun by the white man's drive toward frontier expansionism, the environment ravaged by the spread of cowboy capitalism, and the whole triumphalist version of manifest destiny dramatized as the will to conquer and control. But the exhibition drew back from representing Western expansionism as having its impulses in the rise of Jacksonian egalitarianism and the "common man." In the new history, only capitalism, and certainly not democracy, is the destroyer.

In the history wars that follow, or often precede, an announced public display, it is clear that history is not a thing of the past. Rather than dying or fading away, history returns to haunt the present, and often what one group experiences as pride another experiences as pain. It has been said that all politics concerns the present and the future, periods and situations that can be addressed and perhaps changed. But the politics of the history wars are decidedly retrospective, and the past remains an ever-present prologue.

In California in the mid-1990s, a debate raged for a half-dozen years over a statue that had survived the earthquake of 1906. The monument, "The Pioneer," a huge 820-ton granite pedestal, included several life-sized figures: an Indian on the ground, a friar pointing to heaven, and a Spanish vaquero raising a triumphal fist. The statue was meant to celebrate California's history from the Spanish conquest and the founding of Franciscan missions to the Gold Rush. Many California cities have Spanish names, and at the end of the nineteenth century "mission revival" became the style of architecture in everything from school buildings to train depots. During this same period, textbooks hailed the arrival of padres as humanitarians who had rescued the Indians from ignorance and backwardness.

While Californians looked to the statue with civic pride, Native Americans were pained by it and were delighted when scholars began to punch holes in "The Mission Myth." It was revealed, for example, that the leader of the padres, Junípero Serra, was considerably less than the saint that the Roman Catholic Church was about to canonize. The San Francisco Arts Commission was pressured either to remove the statue or to reword its plaque to describe the sufferings and deaths at the hands of the missionaries. The statue, declared Martina O'Dea of the American Indian Movement Confederation, "symbolizes the humiliation, degradation, genocide, and sorrow inflicted upon this country's indigenous people by a foreign invader, through religious persecution and ethnic prejudice." One American Indian recommended naming a street after the warrior Geronimo. Another person suggested that the name San Francisco be changed so that the city would be free, at last, of the Franciscans.[18]

Martina O'Dea's complaint may not sit well with California's suntanned citizens, but it is consistent with the kind of history written long ago. The Roman historian Tacitus believed that the guardian of the past must "restrain vice by the terror of posthumous infamy," and the English historian Edward Gibbon insisted that justice can be done in the writing of history. The purpose of getting the record straight is "to render posterity a just and perfect delineation of all that may be praised, of all that may be excused, of all that may be censured." Such ethical imperatives were perhaps best expressed in the early nineteenth century by a native American himself. When the Hapsburg prince Maximilian arrived with a French army to make himself emperor of Mexico, the Indian Benito Juárez warned: "It is given a man, sir, to attack the rights of others, seize their goods, assault the lives of those who defend their nationality, make of their virtues crimes, and of one's own vices a virtue, but there is one thing beyond the reach of such perversity—the tremendous judgment of history."[19]

What Is History?

The question begs for a simple, clarifying answer, but any answer may vary from country to country and take on different meanings in different epochs. At its most basic formulation, history concerns itself with what happened in the past and why. In certain civilizations the past has represented a lost treasure of wisdom, while in modern societies thinkers cannot decide whether the past is a curse or a blessing. Hence George Eliot: "The happiest women, like the happiest nations, have no history."[20]

In the ancient world history meant "inquiry," to seek information, to look into whatever arouses the mind's curiosity. If philosophy begins in a general wonder about the nature of things, history begins in a specific wonder about how things come to be the way they are, how they grow from the simple to the complex, and how they stop growing, decline, and fall. "It is by looking at how things developed naturally from the beginning that one may best study them," wrote Aristotle. In the Islamic world, history took second place to theology until Ibn Khaldin (1332–1406) proceeded to study the rise and fall of dynasties without resorting to religious explanations. In classical antiquity, history provided the means by which a republic could engage in a *ricorso*, a periodic return to its first, founding principles. Herodotus was fond of contrasting Greek liberty and its norm of simplicity against Oriental despotism and its acceptance of luxury. But in ancient China the study of history also offered the possibility of rediscovering the great virtues that had been lost, the principles of normative order (*dao*) that have fallen away with the passage of time, and thus intellectual history, the investigation of ideas and doctrines, functioned as a hopeful act of recovery. During the European Renaissance, writers also entertained hopeful attitudes toward history as either the witness to experience, the voice of memory, the messenger of truth, or the vision of destiny.[21]

More recent attitudes about the past tend to be less hopeful and more cynical, sometimes nihilistic. Voltaire dismissed history as "a pack of tricks one plays on the dead," while Napoleon looked upon it simply as "a fable agreed upon." When Frederick the Great would call for his secretary to read history to him, he would say, "Bring me my liar." George Orwell suspected that history served as an instrument of power, with scribes rewriting the past in order to control the future. Jacob Burkhardt, offering only a slightly more positive view, believed that history enables us to discern the shams of today by studying the scandals of yesterday. Henry Ford, who perhaps needed no advice, summed up history in one word: "Bunk!"[22]

Often the modern intellectual feels history to be more threatening than edifying. Seeing mythology and history as two futile and nearly indistinguishable efforts to ascertain a chronological order of things and events, the novelist James Joyce felt history to be "a nightmare" of incoherence, discontinuity, and random action. To the poet T. S. Eliot, history loomed as a series of "contrived corridors" with endless passages leading everywhere and nowhere. Fyodor Dostoyevsky found history to be almost horrifying since it refused to reveal its reasons: "One might say anything about the history of the world, anything that might enter into the most disordered imagination. The one thing that one cannot say is that it is rational."[23]

Some thinkers fear history because, of all the disciplines, it lends itself to the most abuse. One reason is that history is not the here and now; it is long gone, far removed from anything present and observable, yet somehow its reality must be "re-presented." Knowledge of the past cannot be derived from observation or verified by scientific experiment. Historical understanding is a matter of reading words contained in texts rather than witnessing the events themselves; thus the temptations for its misuse are great. The historian can either glorify the past and cater to a country's nationalistic conceits, or debunk the past and follow contemporary fashions by portraying the bad and the good according to our own likes and dislikes. But to simply praise or condemn is not the purpose of history. "As praise is the shipwreck of historians," warned Lord Acton, "his preferences betray him more than his aversions."[24]

Two further temptations of history are submission and deception: History can either paralyze the will with the excessive weight of memory, or it can release the will to invent whatever the heart desires. Nietzsche, noting that knowledge of history could be the worst thing for those who were its victims, believed that Europe "suffered a malignant fate of history" caused by "man's prodigious memory, his inability to forget anything"—a pathology so severe that man came to be gripped "by a fear of his own memory." But while Nietzsche feared that people would sink into passivity by submitting to history, the French poet Paul Valéry feared the opposite—that the writer would make history into whatever his readers demanded. "Give me a pen," he stated, "and I will write you a history book or a sacred text. I will invent a king of France, a cosmogony, a moral or a gnosis. What will warn an ignorant person or a child of the fact that I am deceiving them?" In "De l'Histoire," Valéry warns us: "History is the most dangerous product made by the chemistry of intellect. Its properties are well known. It produces dreams, makes people drunk, gives them false memories, exaggerates their reflexes, keeps old wounds open, torments them in their sleep, leads them to delusions of grandeur or persecution, and makes nations bitter, arrogant, insufferable and vain."[25]

History may be abused for fervent nationalistic and ethnic ends. But it can also be used more constructively. The ancients looked to history to remind citizens of the great, heroic deeds of their country's past. Today military historians study ancient history to discover truths about power and victory. At military academies, "officers study previous battles and interventions, and the political circumstances surrounding them, the way law students study torts. The underlying message is that knowledge of the past helps foresight, and those with foresight accrue power."[26]

History can also be used to find out where we are amidst the rushing movement of time. The present may seem less perilous when it is seen in respect to the past. In *The Ground We Stand On*, published in 1940, after World War II had broken out in Europe, John Dos

Passos wrote: "In times of change and danger, when there is a quick-sand of fear under man's reasoning, a sense of continuity with genera-tions gone before can stretch like a lifeline across the scary present." Some writers regard historical continuity with the past as indispens-able to a nation's coherence and a people's identity. In *Reflections on the Revolution in France,* Edmund Burke insisted that history consists of a contract among three categories of people, only one of whom is pres-ent: it is an association among the living, the dead, and those who have yet to be born. History enables a country to be not only continuous but also possibly generous as its people come into contact with others. "It is the mission of history," wrote José Ortega y Gasset, "to make our fellow beings acceptable to us."[27]

Yet in America, history has seldom carried such authority that it can fulfill the purposes of continuity or generosity. Here a continuous commitment to the past becomes highly problematic. America was founded in an act of escape from the Old World, and from the earliest pioneers to Huck Finn to today's Asian boat people, we have been running away from the confinements and miseries of the past. Indeed the very orientation at the Republic's founding was prospective rather than retrospective. The American founders did think of the past as something genuinely worth knowing about, but they conceived it pri-marily as lessons in what to avoid rather than as ideals to be honored and perpetuated. The Constitution's framers recognized that the his-tory of the Old World was the history of failure, and the new Republic would look to history in order not to repeat the mistakes of the past.

The peculiar way that American culture developed also tended to negate history, particularly with the rise of political parties, something that the framers looked upon with apprehension. With party politics, Henry Adams observed of the early Republic, older theories and ide-ologies were abandoned as each faction followed the pull of power in the struggle for domination. Adams, America's greatest historian, failed to unravel the "spool of thread"—he was unable to locate a singular theme with which to tie together the sequence of cause and effect in America's historical development. But how could he? Thomas Jefferson said one thing and did another, adjusting his politics accord-ing to new developments, which themselves seemed to be governed by forces beyond the control of political leaders. Adams taught history at

Harvard for seven years. But what is a history teacher to do when history reveals conviction surrendering to circumstance and order breaking down into a swirl of incoherence? "Not that his ignorance troubled him," wrote the history teacher in *The Education of Henry Adams:*

> He knew enough to be ignorant. His course had led him through oceans of ignorance; he had tumbled from one ocean into another till he had learned to swim; but even to him education was a serious thing. A parent gives life, but as a parent, gives no more. A murderer takes life, but his deed stops there. A teacher affects eternity; he can never tell where his influence stops. A teacher is expected to teach truth, and perhaps may flatter himself that he does so, if he stops with the alphabet or the multiplication table, as a mother teaches a truth by making her child eat with a spoon; but morals are quite another truth and philosophy is more complex still. A teacher must either treat history as a catalogue, a record, a romance, or an evolution; and whether he affirms or denies evolution, he falls into the burning faggots of the pit. He makes of his scholars either priests or atheists, plutocrats or socialists, judges or anarchists, almost in spite of himself. In essence incoherent and immoral, history had either to be taught as such—or falsified.[28]

Adams was not alone in seeing that politics trumps history as the lust for power and that electoral success leaves behind all principles. The New England Transcendentalists also saw politics as a vulgar scrimmage, and Ralph Waldo Emerson, who insisted that "there is no history, only biography," best expressed the impulsive forces of the American self that break out of its very birth mold: "The past has baked your loaf, and in the strength of its bread you would break up the oven."[29] The Transcendentalists Emerson and Henry David Thoreau felt deeply a tension between freedom and history, with the impulses of autonomy and self-determination trying to break away from the dead hand of the past.

Alexis de Tocqueville, the French contemporary of Emerson and Thoreau, discerned the same tension, and observed that a democratic society is far from the best environment in which to nurture a historical sensibility. In America, wrote Tocqueville a century and a half ago, the ever-changing environment obliterates time and memory so that "not only does democracy make every man forget his ancestors"; it also "hides his descendants and separates his contemporaries from him."[30] At the end of the nineteenth century, with the rise of the philosophy of pragmatism, America's culture was further reoriented toward the future at the expense of the past. William James's "the will to believe" could scarcely be applied to the past for, as Nietzsche reminded philosophers, "the will cannot will backwards."[31] John Dewey thought that history should be relegated to secondary importance in the high schools and elementary schools. Why? Because genuine knowledge is experimental and involves acting upon and changing that which is capable of change—not the past but the present and possibly the future if one could get one's hands around history, defined as the movement of events, and thereby control it.[32]

In view of America's peculiar political culture and historical development, its flight from the past and its pragmatic orientation toward the future, how has the teaching of history fared in the United States of our time?

The Teaching of American History

We have all heard the reports. Many students cannot explain why the Fourth of July is celebrated, other than that it gives us a break from work and an excuse for barbecues and beer. Few know what the term "cold war" referred to, and fewer still can identify Daniel Webster, Samuel Gompers, or Frederick Douglass. Questions on chronology and geography fare no better than questions of identity. In one eleventh-grade American history class, two-thirds of the students could not situate the Civil War within the time frame of 1850–1900; a third were unaware that the Declaration of Independence took place between 1750–1800; a similar percentage had no idea that Columbus had set out for the New World before 1750; the same number of students failed to locate Britain, France, and Germany on a map of Europe; nearly a third did not know which nations were America's enemies and foes during World War II; half the class had no clue to what the Supreme Court's *Brown* decision was all about, and questions about who Winston Churchill and Joseph Stalin were left half the students scratching their heads.[33]

It was not always this way. Toward the end of the nineteenth century, history was rigorously taught and learned in American schools. At that time a distinguished panel of historians, including the future president Woodrow Wilson, proposed an eight-year course in history, which would be started in the fifth grade with biography and mythology, and in subsequent years would take up American history and government, ancient Greek and Roman history, French history, and English history. "The historians insisted," writes Diane Ravitch, "that the history program should be offered to all children, not just the small minority who were college-bound."[34]

The serious emphasis on history continued into the early twentieth century and had the attentive guidance of the American Historical Association. But with the advent of progressive education and the child-centered curriculum of the late 1920s, the four-year high school curriculum came to be challenged by the new field of social studies, which sought to teach skills that would help students cope with the problems of the present, rather than dwell on issues of the past. Gradually courses in specific national histories collapsed into courses in "Western Civilization," which in turn took second place to civics and the study of neighborhood and local governments. By the 1960s, many states had lowered requirements for the study of American history to just one course.

Certainly the way history has been taught has much to do with its demise in the classroom. Traditionally it had been an exercise in sheer rote memory, with students trying to keep straight which bill went through which Congress presided over by which president during which years in office. As the documentary filmmaker Ken Burns recalled of his years in high school, without the drama and larger significance of persons and events, "the residual history became a kind of castor oil of dates, facts, and events of little meaning—something we knew was good for us but hardly good-tasting." Burns is in good company, for it seems that the obsession with dates plagued young British students as well as American. George Orwell tells us what it meant when history becomes a meaningless recitation of right answers to wrong questions. "I recall positive orgies of dates, with the keener boys leaping up and down in their places in their eagerness to shout out the right answers, and at the same time not feeling the faintest interest in the meaning of the mysterious events they were naming.

"1587?"
"Massacre of St. Bartholomew!"
"1707?"
"Death of Aurangzeeb!"
"1773?"
"The Boston Tea Party!"
"1520?"
"Please, Mum, please, Mum! Let me tell him, Mum!"
"Well; 1520?"
"Field of the Cloth of Gold!"[35]

The historian Paul Gagnon thinks that the problem with the way American history is taught is that its beginnings are situated in America itself. American history cannot be made intelligible "without a firm grasp of the life and ideas of the ancient world, of Judaism and Christianity, of Islam and Christendom in the Middle Ages, of feudalism, of the Renaissance and the Reformation, of the English Revolution and the Enlightenment. The first settlers did not sail into view out of a void, their minds as blank as the Atlantic Ocean." Gagnon argues that to broaden the horizons of American history is to deepen and enrich it, to appreciate that "those who sailed west to America came in fact not to build a New World but to bring to life in a new setting what they treasure most from the Old World." From this perspective, he continues,

> ours is one of the great multifarious adventures of human history. Boring? Dull? It can fascinate the young, who want to find themselves in the stream of time, to see where their life histories join the history of the race. The blood of American students ran in men and women working the soil of Burgundy and the Ukraine, of China and Africa, before the Normans set out on their conquests. Our ideas of good, evil, honor, and shame weighed upon Jews and Greeks and Christians centuries before Rome fell, and came to us by way of the Middle Ages, the Renaissance, and the Reformation. But we do not like to look so far back. We prefer the myth of the New World, innocent of the sins of the old. It has been our special sin of pride, shutting out the possibility of knowing ourselves or of understanding others. Its educational consequence has been the shrinking of American history to mean only United States. . . . Ignoring Tocqueville's pleas not to forget our heritage, we leave the young to a kind of amnesia.[36]

Gagnon may offer an eloquent plea for a cosmopolitan perspective, but it needs to be qualified. The Calvinists who arrived in New

England from England and Holland in the seventeenth century would have been surprised to hear that they were creating "the myth of the New World," one that would be "innocent of the sins of the old." And the *Federalist* authors could write about power and politics in view of "fallen" human nature precisely because they thought of the Old World and its corruptions and felt the same "interests and passions" within themselves and their countrymen. Nor was the Frenchman Tocqueville imploring Americans to remember "our heritage" in the Old World: in fact, he was asking just the opposite.

Vive la Différence: Enter Alexis de Tocqueville

In Tocqueville's estimate, the uniqueness of America lay in its having escaped almost every aspect of class conflict with which Europe had been burdened: feudalism and aristocracy, the monarchy and the established church, land scarcity and poverty, large populations and standing armies, and other oppressions. Tocqueville saw the nineteenth century as a profound rupture from the long history of the human race, and America, as a democracy without confining traditions, represented an entirely new proposition as a new national character arose from a novel environment that had no precedent in history. "It was there," Tocqueville wrote of America as a whole continent, "that civilized man was destined to build society on new foundations, and for the first time applying theories till then unknown or deemed unworkable, to present the world with a spectacle for which past history had not prepared it."[37]

Tocqueville's sense of the novelty of America renders him an embarrassment to those who look for either a radical alternative or a multicultural potential. In America, he observed, the privileges of the Old World gave way to the competitive hustle of the New World, and with status no longer depending upon inherited class position, the possession and display of money has become the only means of social distinction. Tocqueville also saw American democracy as a melting pot in which differences among people and classes gradually dissolve. In Tocqueville's analysis, a truly multicultural society that values diversity would be characteristic of aristocracy, where the individual has the strength to stand alone and group differences, even eccentricities, are admired. But democracy, rather than satisfying desires, feeds illusions and has everyone trying to be different by pursuing the same thing, a sameness that hides itself until it is too late.

> Among democratic peoples men easily obtain a certain equality, but they will never get the sort of equality they long for. That is a quality which ever retreats before them without getting quite out of sight, and as it retreats it beckons them on to pursue. Every instant they think they will catch it, and each time it slips through their fingers. They see it close enough to know its charms, but they do not get near enough to enjoy it, and before they have fully relished its delights, they die.[38]

Tocqueville, it should be remembered, was defending democracy and equality even while demonstrating their tragic implications. A man of aristocratic sensibilities, Tocqueville concluded *Democracy in America* by praising equality as both a political and economic proposition. Equality promotes "not the particular prosperity of the few, but the greater well-being of all. . . . Equality may be less elevated, but it is more just, and in its justice lies its greatness and beauty."[39]

Where some historians desire to see America as part of world history in order to accommodate the many ethnic groups who come here from all parts of that same world, Tocqueville sought to demonstrate the ways in which America separated itself from the rest of the world. Historians who embrace multiculturalism seem to be more interested in preaching the virtues of appreciation, which is far from teaching the more demanding goals of historical understanding. To appreciate is simply to think well of; to understand is to comprehend the how and why of things, specifically how America broke out of the fixed order of other historic cultures and why democracy represents an irreversible tendency entirely distinct from pre-democratic conditions. This Tocquevillian way of seeing things has little to do with the alleged supremist assumptions of western culture, for the French thinker makes it clear that America's beginnings were fortuitous and its people not so much wise and virtuous as simply the beneficiaries of good luck. "Two thoughts have occupied me to this point," Tocqueville wrote to his father shortly after arriving in the United States. "First, that this is one of the most fortunate nations in the world; and second, that it owes its enormous prosperity far less to its own peculiar virtues or to a form of government superior in itself than to the particular conditions in which it finds itself."[40]

Like Tocqueville, I have no wish to regard America as the center of the universe. But Tocqueville was trying to explain America, and historical explanation involves causes and conditions, the very categories that illuminate different circumstances that account for America's historical development. With Tocqueville it is as though political philosophy ran up against the American environment and, stopping to scratch its head, slumped into a question mark. America confounds the socialist, who looks to the polarization of classes; the republicanist, who looks to the teaching of virtue; and even the capitalist, who looks to the privatization of the economy in a self-regulating market. Tocqueville wanted materialism to be "enlightened" and "well-understood," that is, regulated by rational reflection rather than the workings of the free market that responds to consumer desires.

While the author of *Democracy in America* may have brought with him his concerns for France, it was Americans themselves he listened to, and in many respects they told him what to write and why life in the New World had to be explained on its own terms. Here is a conversation that Tocqueville had with a member of the Livingston family, which had reigned in New York in the pre-Revolutionary era as a kind of gentry aristocracy. Tocqueville asked Livingston why America lacked a class that would concern itself with culture and "intellectual questions."

> HE. Chiefly because of the law of inheritance. When I was young I remembered the country peopled by rich landowners who lived on their estates as the English *gentry* do, and who used their minds, and had a sense of tradition in their thoughts and manners. Then there was distinction in the behaviour and turn of mind of one class in the nation. The law making shares equal has worked continually to break up fortunes and form them anew; our former standards and conceptions have been lost and this process goes on from day to day. Land changes hands incredibly quickly, nobody has time to strike root in one place, and everybody must turn to some practical work to keep up the position his father held. Almost all families disappear after the second or third generation.
>
> I. Is there anything analogous to the influence, the patronage, of large landholders?

HE. No, only individual merit counts here.

I. How do the wealthy classes put up with such a state of affairs?

HE. They put up with it as something inevitable since there is nothing whatsoever to be done about it.

I. But is there nonetheless some resentment between them and the common people?

HE. None. All classes joined together in the Revolution. Afterwards the strength of Democracy was so paramount that no one attempted to struggle against it. Generally speaking the people show no distaste for electing the very rich or well-educated.[41]

Although Tocqueville recognized that the striking phenomenon of all classes joining together in the Revolution could not be expected to take place elsewhere, he did hope that America, then underdeveloped but rapidly modernizing, might provide some clues as to what the western world would be in years to come. Yet in recent scholarship the very idea of "the West" has fallen into disrepute. If Tocqueville saw democracy in America as a relative success, other thinkers closer to our time perceived it as a disastrous failure heading toward suicide.

CHAPTER 6

The "Last Best Hope" or the "Suicide of the West"?

"To Immancipate the Mind"

IDEAS OF THE WEST AND OF WESTERN CIVILIZATION have taken many hard knocks in most areas of academic thought and life. The notion is that teachers of courses in western civilization require students to read primarily the works of dead white European males, works that supposedly represent a canon of conservatism and conformity. Yet criticism of society and revulsion against civilization date well back into western history itself: in the early nineteenth century the New England Transcendentalists Ralph Waldo Emerson and Henry David Thoreau expressed their alienation from the coming of industrial society while turning to the mystical East to help America find the "Oversoul."

Abraham Lincoln, however, an educator as well as a politician, tried to teach Americans about the meaning of the West as a culture of restless wonder, and celebrated America as the best place on earth where the mind could be free to pursue its curiosities. In one of his first campaign statements, delivered in 1832 to the people of Sangamon County, Illinois, Lincoln focused on economic development to make clear the vital connection between opportunity and democracy. He spoke of the coming of railroads and the necessity of banks and commercial intercourse. Equally important was education, a subject that Lincoln felt shy in talking about since he had received so little formal instruction himself:

Upon the subject of education, not pretending to dictate any plan or system respecting it, I can only say that I view it as the most important subject which we as a people can be engaged in. That every man may receive at least, a moderate education, and thereby be enabled to read the histories of his own and other countries, by which he may duly appreciate the value of our free institutions, appears to be an object of vital importance, even on this account alone, to say nothing of the advantages and the satisfaction to be derived from all being able to read the scriptures and other works, both of a religious and moral nature, for themselves.[1]

Lincoln believed fervently that Americans should study the histories of their own country and others so that they "may duly appreciate the value of free institutions." Today such a position would seem unacceptable in certain circles. The idea of the "other" and "otherness" (alterity) is said to be regarded with deep anxiety by those threatened by people of different color and cultures, and thus out of insecurity and a "guilty conscience" dominant white society refuses to recognize legitimate differences. The notion that we can better value our own political institutions by studying the histories of places where these institutions have failed is also dismissed. Such a position is thought to be merely an arrogant parochialism that should yield to a relativistic appreciation of the equal validity of all cultures. To hold that one culture is freer and more advanced than another is, it is charged, a recipe for the politics of exclusion.[2] The idea is that in scholarship and teaching, such exclusion results in a "historical amnesia" that leaves us with a "white-oriented hero worshipping history." What we should be studying instead, some say, is how non-European Americans were so "actively and intimately" involved in determining the course of American history.[3]

Lincoln himself, I hasten to add, hardly advocated teaching history in a way that could exclude others. On the contrary, he argued that it was precisely because America happened to enjoy political freedom that the country should be open to different people everywhere. The Declaration, he emphasized during the Civil War, offered "liberty, not alone to the people of this country, but hope to the world for all future time," the promise that "*all* should have an equal chance." America's development of republican liberty represented the "last best hope of earth" to the whole "family of man," for the idea of self-government, if it can withstand the test of the Civil War, has the potential to "liberate the world."[4]

Lincoln understood, long before today's theoreticians of modernization, that humankind would be liberated not only by politics and education but also by science and technology. The fact that Lincoln cited scripture to support the idea of spiritual morality and the Declaration to buttress political ideals implied that he thought America needed to be led back to truth. Yet Lincoln saw America as moving in two directions at once: while the country's political ideals are to be found in the past, its economic development depends on a turn toward the future, toward technology. And when America looks ahead, it must learn, Lincoln advised just shortly before the coming of the industrial revolution, the meaning of technological transformation.

Lincoln tried to drive home that lesson in a speech he gave in 1859 on "Discoveries and Inventions." It begins with a subtle, witty spoof on "Young America," the group of expansionists who invoked manifest destiny as the country's rationale for moving west and taking possession of everything in sight. A member of this group "owns a large part of the world, by right of possessing it; and all the rest by right of *wanting* it, and *intending* to have it. As Plato had for the immortality of the soul, so Young America has," Lincoln states using an expression from Addison, "a pleasing hope—a fond desire—a longing after territory." Lincoln, ever the Lockean, then mocks the American who would claim to be bringing liberation by acquiring land but forget that land belongs only to those willing to work upon it. "He is a great friend of humanity; and his desire for land is not selfish, but merely to extend the area of freedom. He is very anxious to fight for the liberation of the enslaved nations and colonies, provided, always, they *have* land, and have *not* any liking for his interference. As to those who have no land, and would be glad of help from any quarter, he considers, *they* can afford to wait a hundred years longer."

It is not only the labor theory of value that Young America has forgotten in its march west. There is also the matter of "*Discoveries, Inventions,* and *Improvements,*" which in turn are the result of "*observation, reflection,* and *experiment.*" Lincoln describes how for centuries human beings had watched boiling water raise the lids of containers "with a sort of fluttering motion," but since no one had thought to ask why hot water could lift a pot lid, and no one had bothered to experiment with the phenomenon, the principle of steam power had remained undiscovered. Lincoln then explains the methods of scientific discovery as though he had presaged the writings of the pragmatist Charles Sanders Peirce. Technological advance requires an inquisitive mind and a method of asking questions. It is as though a natural phenomenon cries out "Try me," and the curious investigator does try. The resulting "trial gives to the world control" over elemental forces.

To Lincoln, scientific progress is an aspect of culture, and he has no difficulty stating it as peculiar to the western, secular world. He even goes so far as to suggest that other cultures, like the original Adam, lack curiosity and remain reluctant to penetrate into the reason of things, to make an effort to "Try me" and thereby eat of the forbidden fruit even at the cost of losing the state of grace and innocence. Invention requires the habit of observation:

> But for the difference in *habit* of observation, why did yankees, almost instantly, discover gold in California, which had been trodden upon, and over looked by indians and Mexican greasers, for centuries? Gold-mines are not the only mines overlooked in the same way. There are more mines above the Earth's surface than below it. All nature—the whole world, material and moral, and intellectual—is a mine; and in Adam's day, it was a wholly unexplored mine. Now, it was the destined work of Adam's race to develop, by discovery, inventions, and improvements, the hidden treasures of this mine. But Adam had nothing to turn his attention to the work. If he should do anything in the art of invention, he had first to invent the art of invention—the *instance* at least, if not the habit of observation and reflection. As might be expected he seems not to have been a very observing man at first; for it appears he went about naked a considerable length of time, before he even noticed that obvious fact. But when he did observe it, the observation was not lost upon him; for it immediately led to the first of all inventions, of which we have any direct account—the *fig-leaf apron.*

Lincoln's unfortunate reference to "indians and Mexican greasers" would be sufficient evidence to dismiss everything he stood for as racist. Yet what Lincoln was stating was later reiterated by Max Weber when he visited the United States in 1904. Weber observed that between the two populations inhabiting Utah, the Indians and Mormans, one can choose as superior either those who desired to live in harmony with the environment or those who chose to transform it, and there is no authoritative way to judge whether the romantic or the technological way of life is preferable. Rather than judging people superior or inferior, Lincoln presages today's economic historians by raising a crucial question: why does habit give way to a curiosity that can lead to technological innovation? Lincoln's explanation is biblical. Cultures unwilling to invent are like Adam before the Fall; they are unwilling to disobey God as the first step toward the right to know. The will to inquire and to know occurred in European society before it arrived in America to transform the environment with the turbine engine. First sin, then steam.

Ultimately what makes scientific progress possible, Lincoln went on to tell his audience, is language. Here Lincoln sounds as though he is presaging late-twentieth-century poststructuralism with his sensitivity to linguistic representation. Whether speech is an invention of humankind or a gift from God, the mode of communication depends upon verbal utterances having a reference to actual objects. Of the fast creation of sounds and syllables in speech, Lincoln asks: "What other *signs* to represent *things* could possibly be produced so rapidly?" Yet speech alone is not what makes progress possible. What enables communication "with the dead, the absent, and the unborn" is writing, the means by which knowledge of inventions is preserved and spread. Lincoln then discussed how the coming of printing rescued history from "the dark ages" and how discoveries, inventions, and improvements rapidly followed. Why did it take humanity so long to lift itself out of the caves of ignorance? Once again Lincoln's answer is equality, and he has no difficulty suggesting that that principle is peculiar to the West. In the distant past,

> it is very probable—almost certain—that the great mass of men, at that time, were utterly unconscious, that their *conditions,* or their *minds* were capable of improvement. They not only looked upon the educated few as superior beings; but they supposed themselves to be naturally incapable of rising to equality. To immancipate the mind from this false and underestimate of itself, is the great task which printing came into the world to perform. It is difficult for, *now* and *here,* to conceive how strong this slavery of the mind was; and long it did, of necessity, take, to break it's shackles, and to get a habit of freedom of thought, established. It is, in this connection, a curious fact that a new country is most favorable—almost

necessary—to the immancipation of thought, and the consequent advancement of civilization and the arts. The human family originated as is thought, somewhere in Asia, and have worked their way principally Westward. Just now, in civilization, and the arts, the people of Asia are entirely behind those of Europe; those of the East of Europe behind those of the West of it; while we, here in America, *think* we discover, and invent and improve, faster than any of them.

Does not Lincoln's position come close to the Christian sin of pride in claiming America to be more advanced and hence superior to other nations? Would it not be more honest and humble to see America as continuous with the rest of the world? Lincoln's answer is that the world itself sees America as different, even exceptional. "*They*," he said in reference to those in other countries responding to his claims about America,

> may think this is arrogance; but they can not deny that Russia has called upon us to show her how to build steam-boats and railroads—while in older parts of Asia, they scarcely know that such things as S.B.s & RR.s exist. In anciently inhabited countries, the dust of ages—a real downright old fogyism—seems to settle upon, and smother the intellects and energies of man. It is in this view that I have mentioned the discovery of America as an event greatly favoring and facilitating useful discoveries and inventions.[5]

Today in some academic circles the idea of the West is discredited in favor of non-western cultures, and Lincoln's faith in education and in language in its written form, as well as his belief in science and technology, could well be dismissed as a naive faith in the supposed forces of liberation that actually, when properly analyzed, have more to do with domination. Lincoln valued passionately freedom and equality, and he looked to history to appreciate the conditions of their possibility. Today many poststructuralist academics concern themselves with the opposite—with power, domination, subjection, incorporation, exclusion, manipulation, language as a "prisonhouse" of words without references, and writing as a "discursive formation" that turns human beings into "social constructions"—which leaves us with the sense that we have been made into something not of our own making. Modern social theory is about as far away from Lincoln's outlook and values as one can imagine. How did we get into such a predicament?

To answer that question, something of a confession is in order.

Until this point in the book, I have been pretty hard on the "new social history" for minimizing important events and leaders and their ideas. But the turn toward poststructuralism and other theories of power and domination derives from, I regret to say, my own field, from intellectual history itself. And in this instance it is curious that many intellectuals thought about the world in ways far different than most people did.

Critical Theorists and Cold War Intellectuals

If you were to read the daily news or watch televison and then flip through some of new history textbooks, you would feel as though you had been learning about two different worlds. Evening news reports frequently strike the viewer as a mosaic of misery. Not only do visions of the past pain the mind—Hiroshima, the death camps, the "killing fields"; today graphic sights of the present remind us of the wretched of the earth. Recall the "boat people," those surviving on sampans off the coast of Vietnam; the illegal Chinese immigrants on a decrepit freighter who had to jump overboard as their vessel ran aground in New York's harbor; the fugitives on rafts with tattered sails approaching Florida's beaches in desperate flight from Cuba and Haiti. Everywhere the poor and oppressed are trying to move from South to North, from Latin America to the United States, from North Africa to southern Europe; and also from East to West, from Seoul to Seattle and from Saigon to Paris. How has this movement of humanity registered itself in the curriculum on the college campus?

North America and western Europe, the two regions of the world whose political ideals were founded in the Enlightenment, loom as a haven to those driven out of their own heartless countries. Yet in parts of the academy the whole idea of the West and the "Enlightenment project" have become objects of contempt among multiculturalists and others who challenge the notion of a culture shared by all Americans. Ironically, the more attractive America becomes in the eyes of the world's oppressed people, the more repellent it becomes in the writings and teachings of intellectuals who like to put "free" in quotation marks and refer to their country as fascist "Amerika."[6]

The cult of multiculturalism behind the new history, which diminishes the importance of the West in the expectation of giving us a new history, is itself ahistorical. The genuine multiculturalists were actually western intellectuals of the late nineteenth century, historians like Max Weber and Henry Adams, who studied Samoa, China, India, and the Islamic worlds as well as medieval and ancient Judaism. The ideas of these dead white men are still alive today with insights into the origins of institutions and social customs.

Today, when people from all over the world are flocking to America, students are told that they must study precisely that from which people are fleeing. It is as though America was not blessed in having skipped the feudal stage of history, and students must begin to think backwards and value pre-modern non-western societies. How did contemporary thought come to such a state of mind? The answer to that question involves two ironies.

First, almost all the ancestors of Americans came to this country to escape either religious or political repression or economic oppression. Although some thought nostalgically about the old country, and some encountered prejudice and exploitation in America, most felt exhilarated by the freedom and opportunity offered by their new country. In more recent times, in the 1930s, another generation of immigrants arrived on these shores in escape from repression, in this instance Hitler's Germany. But the German refugee intellectuals felt no such exhilaration, and they were to write books that sagged with the weight of gloom. Ironically, those intellectuals who taught a younger generation to question America as part of western culture and its "Eurocentric" biases had themselves been saved by America. Yet they feared that America, like Germany, would give up democracy in favor of fascism. T. W. Adorno and others, fot example, wrote *The Authoritarian Personality* and applied the "f-scale" test to a sample of American people to uncover their suspected fascist tendencies. Whence would come fascism? "I certainly knew what monopolistic capitalism and the great trusts were," wrote Adorno years later, "yet I had not realized how far 'rationalization' and standardization had permeated the so-called mass media."[7]

Adorno's reference to "rationalization" takes us to the second irony. The critique of the Enlightenment and western liberalism that the German intellectuals brought to America derived to some degree from a scholar who actually admired America: Max Weber. The German

philosopher had worried that reason, the liberating idea of the Enlightenment, could easily transform itself into "instrumental reason," or
rationalization—the tendency to organize, integrate, manipulate, and
dominate. But Weber believed, as did the American Transcendentalists
Emerson and Thoreau, that liberty lies in the human capacity to resist
the institutionalization of life, to oppose bureaucracy with spontaneity.
And when Weber visited the United States in 1904, to speak in Saint
Louis at a conference celebrating the world's arts and sciences (as well
as the centennial of the Louisiana Purchase), he reminded Americans
of the country's "democratic traditions handed down by Puritanism as
an everlasting heirloom."[8]

But many later German scholars, influenced by Marx and Freud,
saw religion as repressive. In particular, the émigrés who came from
Frankfurt to New York and started a school of thought known as Critical
Theory remained convinced that liberty is an illusion. Why? Because
liberty requires power for its realization, and power by definition is an
organ of exclusion and repression. Ironically, the *Federalist* authors,
long before the critical theorists or even the influential Michel Foucault, had realized that empowerment and the tendency to control go
hand in hand; hence to check power and prevent its consolidation it was
made multilateral and dispersed among countervailing institutions.

Many of the German émigrés who taught in America, however,
never deigned to consider America's liberal foundations as liberating.
But right after World War II, German professors sought to have others
feel the alienation they felt. "Because they were displaced themselves,"
recalls Anatole Broyard of émigré scholars teaching at the New School
for Social Research, "or angry with us for failing to understand history,
the professors did their best to make us feel like exiles in our own
country."

> All the courses I took were about *what's wrong*: what's wrong with the
> government, with the family, with interpersonal relations and intraper-
> sonal relations—what's wrong with our dreams, our loves, our jobs, our
> perceptions and conceptions, our esthetics, the human condition itself.[9]

The critical theorists T. W. Adorno and Max Horkheimer wrote
Dialektic der Aufklarung in 1944, and when it appeared in America in
1972 as *Dialectic of Enlightenment,* students and scholars who read it

became convinced that liberal capitalism is little more than a state-regulated social formation in which freedom is the illusion of the bourgeoisie. Earlier, in 1940, Horkheimer wrote "The End of Reason," which insisted that the rational faculty of mind, by questioning all illusions and norms, ended up destroying itself. The English philosopher John Locke, Horkheimer noted, had hoped that reason would support the natural, inalienable right to self-preservation. We must now see this as a contradiction, Horkheimer insisted: in modern society, which is buffeted by monopolization, centralization, collectivization, and bureaucratization, there is no authentic self to preserve, and reason itself functions as an agency of dissolution.[10] It was these German philosophers who sowed the seeds that would lead to the current politics of difference. The argument was that the "logic of identity" creates a false impression that all things relate rationally to one another; thinking about things relationally reduces them to "unity" and as a result differences are repressed.[11]

The Frankfurt school, as the group of German intellectuals was called, inflicted immeasurable damage on western liberalism. When the school referred to liberalism it was always "liberal capitalism," supposedly a noxious mixture that could endure only momentarily before giving way to fascism.[12] Given the cataclysmic climate of the 1930s and early 1940s, such expectations are understandable (later Frankfurt scholars would try to come to terms with the dogged staying power of liberal capitalism). But the German critique of the Enlightenment is incredible. How the notion of a "logic of identity" ever caught on in academic circles is curious when we consider that America's founders saw a unifying identity as threatening and differences as inevitable. Comparing the Frankfurt school to the *Federalist* results in one of the quandaries of modern intellectual history. The German scholars saw power everywhere and reason nowhere; the *Federalist* authors trusted in reason less because they felt power more. They never assumed, in short, that mind would come forth with the knowledge that would master the abuses of power. The "machinery of government" could be so devised that power would control itself. Thus they successfully erected a system that aimed to govern the people and at the same time could control itself through checks on its own potential abuses. Needless to add, the German scholars never read the

Federalist, and as a result they taught a generation of Americans to scorn liberalism while Louis Hartz was trying to teach them that, in America at least, liberalism was the only game in town.

The political implications of the German school are as disturbing as the intellectual ones. In the years 1940–41, when America was about to be drawn into a war against the Third Reich, some German philosophers exiled in the United States could not foresee an Allied victory or even draw a distinction between American liberalism and European fascism. The West was finished to the extent that its philosophical foundations had been exposed as fictions.

It was not only the Marxists manqués from Frankfurt who served as prophets of doom. The critique of western culture came from conservatives as well as radicals. It should be noted, however, that while German thinkers in America had come to gloomy conclusions about western political thought, it was liberals, particularly the historians Charles A. Beard and Carl Becker, who overcame their earlier skeptical relativism and reembraced the truths of the Enlightenment, even those truths that must now be accepted as "myths" and "glittering generalities."[13] "What Is Still Living in the Philosophy of Thomas Jefferson?" asked Becker, as he reconsidered his own earlier deconstruction of the Declaration of Independence that he launched in 1922. While Beard and Becker were reappraising the Enlightenment, Reinhold Niebuhr, the Protestant existential theologian, wrote *The Children of Light and the Children of Darkness* to defend liberal democracy against those who had tossed it into the dustbin of history. "Man's capacity for justice makes democracy possible; but man's inclination to injustice makes democracy necessary." Power cannot be eliminated, Niebuhr noted, as did the *Federalist* authors, but its effects can be controlled, and the Christian's role in politics is to see that evil is resisted.[14]

But in America in the early 1940s many thinkers on the Left and Right believed that liberalism would prove incapable of resisting and controlling power. The year that Horkheimer published "The End of Reason," the ex-Trotskyist James Burnham published *The Managerial Revolution,* which informed Americans that liberal capitalism would be superseded by bureaucratic collectivism. That book was followed by *The Machiavellians* (1943), which held that history is the study of power struggles among ruling elites. Burnham's thinking about new power alignments in the world culminated in *Suicide of the West* (1964). Whereas German critical theorists had convinced themselves that America would become hegemonic in collaboration with other authoritarian regimes, Burnham, now a conservative cold warrior and supporter of presidential candidate Barry Goldwater, insisted upon an entirely opposite conclusion. The West was becoming so weak and irresolute that it would soon have no capacity to control or even influence the world. Instead of striving to dominate the world, the West had lost its "will to survive":

> The great harbor of Trincomalee, commanding the western flank of the Bay of Bengal, southeast Asia and the Strait of Malacca, ceases to be a western strategic base. Gone too are the mighty ports of Dakar and Casablanca, looming over the Atlantic passage. Of the guardian bases of the north African littoral, southern flank of Europe, only Mers-el-Kebir remains, no longer of any importance and scheduled soon to be abandoned. Bombay, overlooking the Arabian Sea; Basra, watching the Persian Gulf and opening toward the northern plateau and the passes from the steppes; the staging areas of the Middle East and those of East Africa guarding the Indian Ocean—all abandoned; Hongkong, left as a pawn in the arms of communist China; Singapore, shedding its strategic utility for the West as it phases into an independent Malaya; the mighty NATO air base at Kamina in Katanga, air power axis of sub Saharan Africa, abandoned; the half-billion dollar system of American-built air bases in Africa's northeast salient into the Atlantic, hub of a great wheel holding within its compass all north and central Africa, the Near East, and Europe right out to the Urals, and linked at its western rim to the Americas: abandoned. Suez, the Canal and the Isthmus: the watery passage from Europe to Asia and East Africa, the land bridge between Asia and Africa, abandoned.[15]

Both the Left and the Right, the German radical theorists and the American conservative cold warriors, concluded that liberalism is the ideology of western suicide. Even though radicals saw the West continuing as a power system, while conservatives saw contraction and defeat everywhere, both criticized the Enlightenment's faith in the redemptiveness of reason. The eighteenth-century assumption that humanity's rational capacity to comprehend the world and thereby change it promised that knowledge would conquer power and issue in a universe of freedom. The author of *The Managerial Revolution* could

agree with the Germans that the new ruling class would be bureaucratic elites and that modern technology would provide the new instruments of domination and control—but he doubted that the West still
had the will to employ such instruments.

With the end of the cold war, the perspectives just described have
undergone ironic reversals. If the West "won" the cold war due
to its will to prevail using superior technology and more efficient
economies—the very resources derided by the Critical Theorists—it
has, on many campuses at least, lost the culture war to the forces of
multiculturalism.

The Mystique of Roots and Race

Throughout history the image of the West stood opposed to
that of the East. From ancient times the West referred to a place of
striving, wandering, exploring, in contrast to the more settled and
venerable East as a place of holiness and wisdom.[16] With the French
Revolution, philosophers pondered further the meaning of such divisions. G. W. F. Hegel declared that the "history of the world travels
from East to West, for Europe is absolutely the end of History, Asia the
beginning." In Asia, Hegel saw an "oriental despotism" where only
the one is free; in Greece and Rome he saw an aristocratic republic
where some are free; and in modern Germany he hailed the unfolding
of a world spirit where a universal freedom rises with the ascension of
the state and everyone is free. In Hegel's view, America remained
outside this cosmic vision because it had no sovereign state, no classes
striving to possess it, and no authority capable of clarifying the course
of world history. With Hegel, the American philosopher George Santayana quipped, "history begins in Eden and ends in Berlin."[17]

There is, as Santayana noted, a certain "egotism" in identifying
one's country with the march of history, and there have been American thinkers, first the Transcendentalists Emerson and Thoreau and
later the Beatnik poets of the 1950s, who turned to the East to practice
a life of meditation. But there is no getting around the reality that the
West has been the center of dynamic change and innovation. Out of
the religious wars in the West grew the idea of toleration, out of the
political conflicts there grew liberty and freedom. In the early years of

the American Republic, a free society was regarded as incompatible with the tyranny of either religion or government. Jeffersonian political philosophy opposed all authority that would impose itself on the individual, whether that authority be the absolutism of church or of state. Today, however, some historians seem to agree with Hegel that history begins outside the West:

> The study of American history properly begins with the first peopling of the Americas some 30,000 years ago. After students learn about the spread of human societies and the rise of diverse cultures in the Americas, they are prepared to delve into a historical convergence of European, African, and Native American peoples, beginning in the 15th century. In studying the beginnings of American history it is best for students to take a hemispheric approach. This broader context of American history avoids provincialism and drives home the point that the English, as latecomers to the Americas, were deeply affected by what had already occurred in the vast regions of the hemisphere.[18]

At first glance, such an approach to history seems harmless and actually edifying in its attempt to reach the needs of America's increasingly diverse ethnic populations, and professors who see themselves as standard setters may be commended as among the few academics in the country genuinely concerned about the education of students. But such ambitions rest awkwardly on a stubborn, persistent, and apparently unrevisable frame of mind that props itself up on three premises: that the truths of political freedom can be taught with the materials of social history, that young students will enjoy a certain self-esteem by virtue of knowledge of ancestry, and that American history "begins" well before people were capable of comprehending their existence and thereby achieving self-consciousness.

Abraham Lincoln, it will be recalled, tried to teach America that its beginnings lie not in a "convergence" with other past cultures but in a decisive break with them. Scientific progress took place not when humankind carried on a culture's conventions but when the mind questioned them. History is controlled by the advance of knowledge, and America was to be the land of the future precisely because it had left the past behind.

Eighteenth-century thinkers did speculate on where human existence had originated in the new world, but they did not believe, in contrast to some contemporary scholars, that such "discoveries" had any bearing on the demands of historical understanding or the political education necessary for citizenship. This is not to maintain that American history begins only with the "discovery" of America at the end of the fifteenth century. On the contrary, the founders were intrigued by the state of nature, the original condition of humankind, and surmised that knowledge of that subject might tell us something about ourselves.

Hence John Adams: "Whether serpents' teeth were sown here and sprung up men; whether men and women dropped from the clouds upon this Atlantic island; whether the Almighty created them here, or whether they emigrated from Europe, are questions of no moment to the present or future happiness of man. Neither agriculture, commerce, manufacturers, fisheries, science, literature, taste, religion, morals, nor any other good will be promoted, or any evil averted, by any discoveries that can be made to answer these questions." Voltaire would have been even more impatient with an obsession with beginnings. "If it should be asked," he said, "from whence came the Americans, it should be asked from whence came the inhabitants of Terra Australis; and it has already been answered, that the same providence which placed man in Norway, planted some also in America and under the antarctic circle, in the same manner as it planted trees and made the grass grow. . . . It is no more surprising to find men in America, than it is to find flies there."[19]

Today it is widely believed that students cannot be motivated to study anything other than their own ancestry, and hence that American history must begin beyond America. Will students be exhilarated to find the remains of their ancestors in archaeological digs as the first step in discovering their roots? There seems to be little evidence for this premise. "Few people can extract solutions to their problems from their roots," observed the Oxford historian Theodore Zeldin. We need to give up the "illusion that humans can be understood simply as example of their civilization, or nation, or family." Historical understanding is not a matter of categorical ethnic identities; nor is an enchantment with one's early family members of much value in making free choices and freely developing one's own self-identification:

To know who one's ancestors were, and what they were proud of, can no longer suffice for people who think of themselves as different from their parents, as being unique with opinions of their own, and who feel uncomfortable with traditions embedded in violence. People who want to be free need to dig over a much wider area, and deeper, to understand their personal emotions and ambitions. Looking at one's most obvious roots does not automatically equip one to choose one's friends, one's partner, one's life work, nor to cope with anger, loneliness and other inadequacies. To discover in what direction one wishes to go, one needs to acquire memories with a new shape, memories which point into the future, and which have direct relevance to one's present preoccupations.[20]

One premise of the new school of history has recently been challenged by educators themselves: the notion that students can learn only if they have sufficient self-esteem—an attribute based upon identity with historical role models of their own particular ethnic background. Such "sentiment," writes the psychologist Roy F. Baumeister in *American Educator,* a journal of the American Federation of Teachers, "reflects the widespread, well-intentioned, earnest, and yet rather pathetic hope that if we can only persuade our kids to love themselves more, they will stop dropping out, getting pregnant, carrying weapons, taking drugs, and getting into trouble, and instead will start achieving great things in school and out. Unfortunately, the large mass of knowledge that research psychologists have built up around self-esteem does not justify that hope." No doubt it is helpful to make students familiar with leaders and achievers in their own ethnic heritages, but it should be remembered that early America's greatest achievers, the very people who transformed the country and successfully resisted political oppression, were New England Calvinists, hardly a people overrun with self-esteem. As Baumeister has pointed out, self-esteem can make students confident and productive, but it can just as readily make them "conceited, arrogant, narcissistic, and egotistical."[21]

Radical history has often been associated with multiculturalism, the cult of diversity, and other schools of thought that emphasize non-western traditions. According to those paradigms, it is perfectly legitimate, perhaps even a moral duty, to study those in other parts of the world who had to deal with conditions different from our own. It is true that one purpose of history can be to rescue the obscure from oblivion. But the theoretical difficulties of writing and teaching such history are daunting. How is it possible to understand what members of a long-gone society were doing if they lacked literacy and practiced unfamiliar customs? It would require an all-comprehending understanding and sympathy to teach and write about those alien to ourselves. But one need not go outside America to understand America.

Lincoln's version of American history is precisely what is under attack in much of the academy. Today, as the Harvard historian David Landes notes, "the very idea of a West-centered (Eurocentric) global history is denounced as arrogant and oppressive. It is intended, we are told," writes Landes, quoting the Mideast scholar Islamoglu-Inan, "to justify Western domination over the East by pointing to European superiority." Landes wryly adds: "What we should have instead is a multicultural, globist, egalitarian history that tells something (preferably something good) about everybody."[22] One need not cite a non-American for evidence of this bias. Gary Nash, professor of history at University of California, Los Angeles, and director of the *National History Standards,* echoes it perfectly. In explaining why, in his view, high school teachers are ill-prepared to teach history as it should be taught, Nash raises the question: "Why was it that the flowering of social history in the universities, which made such important gains in breaking through Eurocentric conceptualizations of American history and world history, made only limited gains in bringing a less nationalistic, white-centered, hero-driven, and male-dominated history to the schools?"[23]

The answer to the question is not a little embarrassing. For while the radical school seeks to teach history "from the bottom up," when it comes to devising a curriculum and a set of standards for the nation, history should be instructed from the top down, from the universities to the high schools.

But why should history not be taught from the bottom? The argument for such an orientation derives from two premises, one supposedly empirically scientific, the other contritely sentimental.

The scientific view upholds the old nineteenth-century Marxist notion that to understand history we must study the ascendancy of the working class. Investigation should direct itself not to the "political actions of princes and States," which "share the illusion" that history takes place outside ordinary life ("something extra-super terrestrial"), but instead to the human productive activity of labor, the real "driving force of history."[24] The second premise is the contemporary conviction that to study history from below is to include all those people who had been left out, especially the poor and the powerless. One perspective asks us to do history as a scientific enterprise, the other as a moral duty. Proponents of each perspective spend little time concerning themselves with the origins of human freedom; perhaps they are convinced, and with good reason, that its subjects have yet to enjoy it. But would not those coping with the brute conditions of life be better prepared to struggle toward freedom by understanding how it came into existence in the modern world?

The Right to Have Rights

Many of those who have jumped on the bandwagon of multiculturalism—feminists, gays and lesbians, ethnic minorities, and Marxists manqués and their mystique of the proletariat—are the very ones whose causes have least advanced in non-western cultures. Although Castro's Cuba has eliminated racism, it remains brutally hostile to homosexuals and hardly allows workers an influential voice in political decisions. The Islamic world should cause feminists to shudder. The journal *Foreign Policy* reports that while many women in western countries are beginning to share in the power of the ruling class, women in developing countries across the world bear the brunt of brutal living conditions, and the plight of their families is even worse in factories where child labor brings back the "dark satanic mills" of the nineteenth-century industrial world. In a symposium entitled "Is Multiculturalism Bad for Women?" twelve leading feminist scholars, including the poet Katha Pollit and the sociologist Saska Sassen, agreed with the political theorist Susan Moller Okin that whenever and wherever in the non-western world minority ethnic cultures command group rights, women lose out.[25]

In America, however, it turns out to be the other way around. Here women have benefited from rights based upon what Iris Marion

Young calls "the politics of difference." The political scientist Young argues that gender differences should be recognized in public policy. Citing what has been going on in such areas as bilingual education and American Indian causes, she argues "that sometimes recognizing particular rights for groups is the only way to promote their full participation."[26]

Here one runs up against a number of paradoxes. Rights deriving from custom in non-western cultures inhibit women; rights deriving from nature in western cultures benefit them. Rights themselves in their original context implied universalism; today the politics of difference requires assenting to what is not general but specific to a group or gender. Such conflicting imperatives could lead to schizophrenia. As Charles Taylor notes, the idea of equality calls upon us to treat people in "a difference-blind fashion," whereas the politics of difference requires that we recognize and foster particularity.[27] Equality negates identity by treating everyone as similar; recognition politics negates equality by treating different groups differently. Whatever stand one takes in contemporary politics, few people doubt that they have a right to rights, whether it be the right to equal treatment and opportunity or the right to separate status and preferences. But where do rights come from historically?

Many of those who compose the new history use the vocabulary of liberalism. Hence their texts, and particularly the *National History Standards,* are replete with such terms as "citizenship," "democratic ideals," "choices and decisions," "alternatives," "consequences," and the like, all of which presuppose the possibility of being free in a society open with options to be considered and visions to be acted upon. But how is one to teach such ideas and values when America is supposed to have "converged" with non-western cultures rather than having decisively departed from them? What do fifteenth-century Africa and pre-Columbian America have to do with modern "democratic ideals"? The two questions that today's students should address, it seems to me, are Where did the right to have rights originate? and What historical conditions are needed to allow freedom to break the bonds of domination? At the risk of oversimplification, consider the following:

West	Non-West
Liberty and democracy	Patriarchy and hierarchy
Rights and representation	Rituals and kin councils
Diversity and factions	Solidarity and tribes
Science and technology	Sorcery and totems
Work and productivity	Hunting and gathering
Pragmatic experiment and future consequences	Sacred traditions and ancient origins
Sin and vanity	Animism and idolatry
Egotism, angst, and the restlessness of desire	Mysticism, acceptance, the absence of longing

How can one arrive at the political values of the West by having students begin with the non-West, where rarely do values come into being as an act of choice rather than as an inheritance? To suggest that the noble idea of human rights is solely of western origin is far from denying non-western cultures the importance of their own values. In China, for example, duty and responsibility are more important than equality and liberty, and the fulfillment of obligations takes place through personal and familial relationships. Some Asian scholars do insist that a theory of human rights can be drawn from Confucius and Mencius, who believed that people have the right to engage in speech and disputation and to choose the good while "tolerating the bad."[28] But in Asia rights have more to do with personal behavior than with political assertions and protections based on theories of nature and social contract, and political philosophy is addressed more to leaders than to subjects, especially those leaders who might abuse power instead of using it to work for the welfare of the powerless.

In the recent book *We Are All Multiculturalists Now,* author Nathan Glazer is as worried as I am about the right location of the origins of rights, even while he defends multiculturalism and affirmative action. Glazer, a Harvard sociologist, quotes me referring to the authors who wrote the history standards for the country. "The most glaring contradiction is that its authors seek to inculcate values characteristic of the Western World that cannot be derived from what they would learn from the non-Western world." "This," Glazer adds, "strikes me, as a reader of the standards, as quite true."[29]

Not since the Nazi propaganda has a document like the *National*

History Standards so minimized the importance of the western Enlightenment and replaced political knowledge about human nature with cultural mystiques about races and racial heritages. To privilege primitive cultures over political ideas is to become fixated on the organic metaphors of community and solidarity, to see as precious those peoples who are at one with nature, who are endowed with nonrational group characteristics that submerge the individual, and who are blessed with a faithfulness to tradition—characteristics often found in fascist literature (particularly when authors depict races preying upon one another and native populations being victimized by alien intruders). The races are reversed, of course, with whites the conniving predators and the natives nothing less than virtuous innocents betrayed by unfulfilled treaties.

The cult of antiquity appeals to those who see a nation as having been wrongly defeated. The task is to prove that such a nation or tribe is older than the victor. "To buttress Nordic supremacy," writes the historian David Lowenthal in *Possessed by the Past*, "Nazi archeologists found sites and artifacts 'proving' a Germanic family tree antedating Romans, Celts, and Slavs. To chauvinists, only their own antiquity counts."[30]

The indictment of whitey needs to be faced, but so, too, does the indecision of the Indian. "History," we are told by the standards authors, "opens to students the great record of human experience, revealing the vast range of accommodations individuals and societies have made to the problems confronting them, and disclosing the consequences that have followed the various choices that have been made."[31] Without for a moment dismissing the rapaciousness of many white colonists, should not students consider the consequences for those Native American tribes who chose not to choose, who preferred to remain Indians, to keep their identity and cling to their customs in the face of inexorable change? Those who seek to teach an indiscriminate openness to all of history risk misleading students into thinking that one can have the best of both worlds: a culture of lineage and a politics of liberty. "The despotism of custom is a standing hindrance to human advancement," wrote John Stuart Mill in *On Liberty*.

The national standards document reads more like a directory of ethnic categories than an analysis of freedom based on natural rights or an interpretation of power as individual growth and self-development. The document also straddles an embarrassing incompatibility in trying to teach the values of freedom while insisting that history is the sole locus of one's identity. "Historical memory is the key to self-identity, to seeing one's place in the stream of time, and one's connectedness with all humankind. We are part of an ancient chain, and the long hand of the past is upon us—for good and for ill—just as our hands will rest on our descendants for years to come."[32] The first sentence is psychologically questionable, the second historically debatable.

With all the emphasis on "one's place" and "one's connectedness," the standards refused to acknowledge that people in the past had no say about the place where they found themselves and the culture into which they were born. Customs and cultures are seldom selected, observed Ernest Gellner; "they are our fate, not our choice." The multicultural bias that runs through the history standards presupposes that the identity of each ethnic group originates in respective past cultures, and hence that the purpose of history is to find identity through memory. Yet Franklin, Jefferson, Emerson, Margaret Fuller, William James, Ralph Ellison, and other American thinkers show us that whatever is worthwhile in life is not inherited but chosen, not derived from fixed antecedents but created from new challenges. "To be free," wrote Ortega y Gasset, "means to be lacking in constitutive identity, not to have to subscribe to a determined being, to be able to be other than what one was."[33] Rather than helping people free themselves from the past, the history standards trap them in their ethnic differences. In so doing they make a virtue out of diversity at the expense of both American history and the possibility of a common curriculum that will enable students to identify with something other than themselves.

Will students know whence the idea of equality sprang when there is so much emphasis on the non-West in the new teaching of history? This emphasis is where the new social history and the old intellectual history meet, with some of the younger scholars who have been influenced by the 1960s culture agreeing, although for different reasons, with older German refugee scholars on the limited importance of the western Enlightenment. And the critique of the Enlightenment involves two accusations, each misleading.

The German scholars, whose ideas were also to influence French poststructuralists, claimed that the Enlightenment offered a false promise about the possibilities of what knowledge could do to liberate humankind. The Enlightenment, the story goes, claimed that the criterion of reason would render new forms of knowledge valid since they would be accepted under non-coercive conditions and, as such, would advance to constitute a challenge to power. But the Age of Reason failed to see, it is charged, that knowledge itself becomes power as it carries out its will through organized institutions, lays down rules, and pursues its goals with claims to expertise and, hence, without interference. This critique of the Enlightenment, one hastens to point out, has very little to do with the American Enlightenment, where the founders scarcely expected knowledge to challenge power; power was to be checked and countervailed by power itself.

Central to the idea of the West is the eighteenth-century Enlightenment. If twentieth-century European intellectuals blamed the Enlightenment for history's misplaced hopes, several American historians fault it for holding inconsistent ideas that amount to hypocrisy. This is the second accusation against the Enlightenment. When one comes across a discussion of the Enlightenment in American history textbooks, one can count on a brief treatment of the subject followed by a discussion of the Declaration of Independence, after which the subject of slavery comes up—and there, inevitably, students are asked to explain the "contradiction" between the statement "all men are created equal" and the fact that the author of that statement happened to own slaves. Now at this point a student of American intellectual history might investigate an even deeper paradox. Why was it that those who professed to believe in equality (Thomas Jefferson and Patrick Henry) justified slavery, while those who emphatically did not believe in equality (John Adams and Alexander Hamilton) condemned the institution? An answer to that question would take students into the higher reaches of intellectual history, where "great men" grapple with great ideas—an area declared out of bounds by the new radical history.

The temptation to expose the founders as hypocrites may be irresistible, but what does this have to do with teaching knowledge of history as "the precondition of political intelligence"?[34] Wouldn't it be more fruitful to investigate how and why the idea of equality emerged in history out of a particular context that had nothing to do with the "convergence" of differing civilizations, particularly those that simply reproduced rites of servitude for centuries? This point was made by the Mexican author Octavio Paz, who wondered whether the pre-Columbian world could even be subjected to historical analysis based upon temporal significance. "Meso-American civilization negated history more completely" than did China in preferring symbolic, atemporal thinking to the disruptive road to change, Paz wrote. "From the Mexican high plateau to the tropical lands of Central America, for more than two thousand years, various cultures and empires succeeded one another and none of them had historical consciousness. Meso-America did not have history but myths and, above all, rites."[35]

The political ideals of the West emanated from a western culture conscious of itself. Yet even though the ideas of equality and natural rights are a product of western culture, that culture often failed to face its own heritage when racial relations came to the fore.

A Lesson in Lincoln's Failure of Nerve

Abraham Lincoln, who felt deeply the meaning of American exceptionalism, had at least one failure of nerve. It occurred in 1852, when in a eulogy on Henry Clay he turned to the subject of colonization. In his remarks, Lincoln explained that the senator had been president of the American Colonization Society, an organization that aimed to return black slaves to Africa, specifically to Liberia. Quoting Clay, Lincoln announced that "there is a moral fitness in the idea of returning to Africa her children, whose ancestors had been torn from her by the ruthless hand of fraud and violence." But black Americans have the opportunity of carrying "back to their native soil the rich fruits of religion, civilization, law and liberty." Lincoln emphatically endorsed Clay's policy as "the ultimate redemption of the African race and African continent," and of the hope that colonization would be carried out successfully, Lincoln exclaimed with biblical imagery:

> May it indeed be realized! Pharaoh's country was cursed with plagues, and his hosts were drowned in the Red Sea for striving to retain a captive people who had already served them more than four hundred years. May like disasters never befall us! If as the friends of colonization hope, the present and coming generations of our countrymen shall by any means,

succeed in freeing our land from the dangerous presence of slavery; and, at the same time, in restoring a captive people to their long-lost fatherland, with bright prospects for the future; and this too, so gradually, that neither races nor individuals shall have suffered from the change, it will indeed be a glorious consummation.[36]

Lincoln returned to the subject of colonization several times, but it was during the Civil War, with the prospect of emancipation looming, that the matter became most urgent. Many northerners, Lincoln realized, would not tolerate seeing slaves freed without their deportation to Africa or Central America. So in 1862, Lincoln invited to the White House a delegation of free black leaders. Soon after they made their introductions, he went to the cold heart of the matter. Even though you may have been free all your lives, Lincoln told them, "your race are suffering, in my judgment, the greatest wrong inflicted on any people." Lincoln called upon free blacks to set an example and consider colonization even if it meant sacrificing some of the comforts enjoyed in America. Then Lincoln informed them that many Americans remained indifferent to the plight of black people, even though slavery had brought on the war. "I repeat, without the institution of Slavery and the colored race as a basis, the war could not have an existence. It is better for us both, therefore, to be separated."[37] The black leaders, the first African Americans ever to be invited to the White House, politely rejected Lincoln's appeals.

One wonders whether Lincoln was trying to convince American blacks or himself about recolonization. Did he really believe that former slaves could return to Africa with, in the words of Clay, "the rich fruits of religion, civilization, law and liberty"? All along Lincoln spoke of America as the "last best hope of earth" for the fulfillment of such ideals. From his White House meeting with freed blacks, however, it became absolutely clear that African Americans had no desire to return to Africa. In this instance they, and not Lincoln, understood the meaning of American exceptionalism.

Yet today in many schools young black students are told that they should study Africa as vital to knowledge of their heritage. Recent identity politics encourages young black children to believe in an idea that blacks of Lincoln's generation had rejected.

Students could well study early African history to learn something about the brilliance of its art and music—especially the magical power of sound, rhythm, and beat that has influenced modern jazz—the diversities of its tribal customs, and perhaps even the intricacies of its languages. But freedom is a distinct phenomenon born not in cultural transmission but in political conflict and struggle, and human rights do not grow on trees, nor do equality, tolerance, and democratic self-government drop from the sky. Look again at the earlier list of categories, particularly the last two, egotism and mysticism.

The State of Nature and the Idea of Equality

The juxtaposition of western angst to non-western acceptance is meant to suggest that early Africa and pre-Columbian America did not experience the existential dread that gave rise to modern politics as we know it. Politics entered history as an expression of human nature and brought up all sorts of questions about intentions and actions. In the Enlightenment the ultimate controversy was whether man was good or evil, benign or aggressive, innocent or dangerous. In the early stages of the Enlightenment, philosophers addressed political questions precisely because the ideas of a self-sufficient community, a coherent and unified solidarity, and fixed customs and unchallenged standards, all of which are supposedly inherent in pre-modern, non-western cultures, were nowhere to be seen in England. It was the moral deficiencies, not the cultural superiorities, of the western world that required thinkers to address an environment threatened with extinction. Western political philosophy subjected itself to self-interrogation. The stakes were high, for the desire for freedom arose out of fear of death.

Thomas Hobbes wrote *The Leviathan* (1651) amidst the bloody civil wars tearing England apart, and the story of the history of American liberty begins not in the supposedly tranquil pre-modern, hierarchical, and authoritarian non-western world but in the turbulent seventeenth century, where authority had broken down. In the state of nature, Hobbes postulated, all men are equal and have the same desires and hence are prone to prey upon one another. With no established culture or government or economy, humankind's natural state is a war of everyman against everyman. It bears noticing that Hobbes sees, as would Lincoln centuries later, the undevelopment of industry and enterprise as leading to the repression of human energies and the perilous insecurity born of frustration:

> In such condition, there is no place for Industry; because the fruit thereof is uncertain; and consequently no Culture of the Earth; no navigation, nor use of commodities that may be imported by Sea; no commodious Building; no instruments of moving, and removing such things as require much force; no knowledge of the face of the Earth; no account of time; no Arts, no Letters; no Society; and which is worst of all, continuall feare, and danger of violent death; And the life of man, solitary, poore, nasty, brutish, and short.[38]

Government has its origins in the people's willing consent to surrender some liberties in exchange for protection in an insecure and hostile environment. Humankind's basic, essential right, derived from nature and hence inalienable, is the right of self-preservation.

When John Locke amplified the social-contract theory of government to include "life, liberty, and estates," he saw humankind endangered not so much by fellow man as by an environment of scarcity in a landscape subjected to the whims of nature. Threatened by the prospect of hunger, the preservation of life turned less on politics than on economics. The right to property derives from the need to appropriate the fruits of the earth, and to the extent that a person "mixes" his labor upon the soil, he is the rightful owner of property. This right, incidentally, is independent of the consent of others; for if members of society had to wait upon such consent to begin growing and gathering, that society would soon disappear from history. The right to life, liberty, and property is a matter of survival, and it belongs to the individual, whether the right be endowed by God or by nature.[39]

When Jefferson announced that "all men are created equal" in the Declaration, and when he then thought the opposite in *Notes on the State of Virginia* because African Americans supposedly did not measure up to his standards of ability and achievement, he was reasoning as someone other than a Lockean. The idea of the equality of humankind as members of the same species has little to do with society's attitudes toward abilities and talents. Originally, in the state of nature, human beings are under no government and hence are not subjected to the rule of authority or the will of others. All men are equal because none is subordinated by nature or God and no one has rightful authority over others.

As indicated earlier, Locke was the first philosopher to challenge the idea of patriarchy; he also defended women's right to divorce, education, and property inheritance. The doctrine of natural rights, which became incorporated into the Constitution and which today endows women and minorities with civil rights and equal protection of the law, was alien to Islamic Africa and to the Aztec cultures of pre-Columbian America and subsequent Catholic Mesoamerica. But here we must look beyond an irony to face a tragedy about which we can at least apologize.

While today constitutional rights have empowered many ethnic groups, and have indeed done more than their respective ancestor cultures to advance their causes and opportunities, in colonial American history Lockeanism was used to make a case against Native Americans and their claims to land ownership. Locke himself protested the trade of American Indians as slaves and, writing a constitution for Carolina in 1672, he sought to offer Native Americans individual plots of land. But the colonists ignored Locke and proceeded to dispossess Native Americans of their land by using Lockean arguments, especially the right to self-preservation in a threatening environment and the right to property by virtue of having labored upon it.[40] Uncultivated land, even though occupied, was seen as vacant, and colonists had no hesitation appropriating it on the grounds that they would improve it and wrest value from it. Long before the Indian wars of the nineteenth century, the intellectual seeds of dispossession had been planted. Locke and liberal individualism explain America, for better and for worse.

Obviously a Lockean sensibility did not work historically for everybody. It was not only Locke's theory of property rights and labor value that accounted for why some cultures advanced and others clung to familiar conventions. According to David Landes, the Harvard economic historian and author of *The Wealth and Poverty of Nations: Why Some Are So Rich and Some So Poor*, economic development depended upon a capacity for scientific curiosity and technological innovation, which began with the fifteenth century's age of exploration.[41] The rise of capitalism in particular may have required religion as well as science, or what Max Weber called, in *The Protestant Ethic and the Spirit of*

Capitalism, an alienated spiritual striving stirred on by an inner anxiety about the state of one's soul. This striving resulted in a devotion to hard work, frugality, and self-denial, which encouraged the production and saving necessary for capital formation.[42] Whatever the origins of economic progress, the validity of Lockeanism appears to have fully withstood the test of history. Locke insisted, it will be recalled, that property and liberty are vital to a country to safeguard its people from hunger and starvation. In Amartya Sen's *Resources, Values, and Development,* the point is made that "no substantial famine has ever occurred in any independent and democratic country with a relatively free press." The Irish potato famine of the 1840s resulted not only from natural blight but also from the brutality of British colonial domination. Elsewhere in the world the sources of starvation were internal—note the examples of the Russian Ukraine in the 1930s, Communist China and the "Great Leap Forward" in the 1950s, or, more recently, Ethiopia, the Sudan, Somalia, and North Korea, where hundreds of children perish from starvation every day.[43]

Is it "Eurocentral triumphalism" to teach students that the freedoms they enjoy, and the comforts they take for granted, come from western political thought and not from non-western cultures? The history of colonialism is instructive. As Fareed Zakaria has noted, colonialism is by no means democratic, but the English presence in the non-western world brought constitutional liberalism: the right to life and property, checks and balances on each branch of government in order to limit power, equality under the law, and freedom of religion and speech. Zakaria also informs us that political scientists detect a striking connection between a constitutional past and a liberal democratic present. As of 1983, "every single country in the Third World that emerged from colonial rule since the Second World War with . . . a continuous democratic experience is a former British colony."[44] America, we need to remind ourselves, was also once a British colony.

Lincoln reminded America of this historic fact when the *Dred Scott* decision was made in 1857. Chief Justice Roger Taney had argued that when the Declaration of Independence was written, the founders "were speaking of British subjects on this continent being equal to British subjects born and residing in Great Britain." Lincoln protested that such an interpretation precluded "not only negroes but white people outside of Great Britain" from benefiting from the document. "The English, Irish and Scotch, along with white Americans, were included to be sure, but the French, German and other white people of the world are all gone to pot along with the Judge's inferior races." Lincoln could have reminded his audience that the Declaration does not specify nationality or ethnicity as a means of including British heirs and excluding all others. But he did remind Americans that unless the Declaration is read as an instrument of inclusion, the meaning of the Revolution becomes meaningless. "I had thought the Declaration promised something better than the condition of British subjects; but no, it only meant that we should be equal to them in their own oppressed and *unequal* condition. According to that, it gave no promise that having kicked off the King and Lords of Great Britain, we should not at once be saddled with a King and Lords of our own."[45]

Always Lincoln returns to the meaning and significance of the Revolution, as he does in the immortal Gettysburg Address. Here he makes clear that "a new nation, conceived in Liberty," was "dedicated to the proposition that all men," and not just British subjects, "are created equal." As in the Revolution, so too in the Civil War Lincoln is less interested in political explanations than in moral convictions about America's historical foundations. He seeks to bring the past into a meditative association with the present. The meaning and purpose of American history for Lincoln is to make its political ideals a vital part of the contemporary national culture—and culture is not only what a country has accomplished but also what it has chosen to remember about itself.

CHAPTER 7

Politics at the Center, Professors at the Peripheries: The Legacy of the 1960s

"What an odd thing—to be in the Italian army."
"It's not really the army. It's only the ambulance."
"It's very odd though. Why did you do it?"
"I don't know. There isn't always an explanation for everything."
"Oh, isn't there? I was brought up to think there was."
ERNEST HEMINGWAY, *A Farewell to Arms*

History in the Streets

THERE MAY NOT BE AN EXPLANATION FOR EVERYTHING, but one hopes there is for some things. Traditionally history as a discipline has addressed the issue of explanation, the attempt to account for why things were the way they were, the motives and causes of human actions. Often this task has called for relating one event to another in a sequence that makes what happened understandable. Today, however, much of historiography is preoccupied, if not obsessed, with representation—the attempt to bring into the story all those people in the past who had been left out, and often this task requires not so much explaining events as convincing readers and students that making present the hitherto absent is itself a sufficient exercise. "*Sie konnen sich nicht vertreten, sie mussen vertreten werden,*" wrote Karl Marx in *The Eighteenth Brumaire of Louis Bonaparte,* declaring that those who cannot represent themselves must be represented. Fair enough, but how?

With the poignancy of a young boy standing outside a lavish party and gazing inside with envy, F. Scott Fitzgerald's novels offer parables about the meaning of success and its costs. Today many writers of the new radical history are so fascinated with the forgotten and obscure, with those at the "margins" of the "system," that it almost seems better to be at the bottom of society than in the vanguard of history. Success itself has come to be suspect.

Much of the new history reflects the political ambitions of the 1960s generation, many of whom currently do a good deal of the teaching and writing of American history. As student activists they had once looked to the powerless and the poor to redeem America. After finding virtue in the down and out, and taking politics to the streets, they naturally wrote a history of street demonstrations, with the American Revolution itself becoming the "urban crucible" in which one watched for the forging of "class consciousness."[1] Never mind that in the course of American history, political action has made history, win or lose, triumph or fail, without necessarily changing the nature of society and its persistent political culture and value system. In the 1770s, for example, America successfully won a revolution without a class consciousness rising to challenge property and alter positions of power and social relations; two centuries later, in the 1970s, America successfully lost a revolution (Vietnam), and its social relations remained similarly intact. For the radical school, the idea that America has enjoyed a consensual social environment was a call for desperate measures as its activists expanded the perimeters of American historiography, expecting to find evidence of something unsettling, perhaps even subversive. If traditional history demonstrated continuity and consensus, the new history would reveal disruption and opposition.

Thus in recent years historians have sought to tell the story of those missing from older narratives, especially racial minorities, Native Americans, women, and workers at the subterranean depths of society. This is a perfectly legitimate exercise, and one that is long overdue. But an awkward fact must be faced. As long as members of the radical school write only about conflict and opposition—as "radicals" generally do—they cannot illuminate significant progress and success. Resistance politics did help bring the Vietnam War to an end and has opened our eyes to problems of race and poverty. But no radical generation has succeeded in reaching beyond the critique to offer a new path for America—one that can transform the nature of American society or redirect the course of American history. (Popular culture can be influenced by a radical agenda, but even here success comes at the price of commercialization; a culture's ambitious youth is soon followed by a capitalist middle age.) At one time it was widely assumed among young activists that the Vietnam War could not end without America's undergoing a radical transformation. When it did end, there was no dancing in the streets. But America survived the 1960s intact, and since then it has become not radical or even liberal but more and more conservative. In fact, America today is so conservative that the two political parties, once so divided in the Franklin D. Roosevelt years, have become almost indistinguishable, with politicians of all persuasions calling themselves "pragmatists" not because they know what the term means but because such a label allows them to run for office by running after public opinion instead of leading it and educating it. Yet if leftist activism failed to change the present, leftist scholarship has been changing our views of the past. While politics moves to the center, historiography searches the peripheries.

Hence we confront a curious disjunction in contemporary American life. Whereas in the realm of politics America has become increasingly conservative—in economic and social policy though not necessarily in culture and lifestyle—in the world of American historiography its radical authors have remained adamantly radical. Such a situation is scarcely surprising when we consider the genius of Louis Hartz's *The Liberal Tradition in America* (1955). Hartz was the first to detect that American liberalism contained a conservative time bomb, and he also knew, as someone who taught in the 1960s, that radicalism had a shelf life only on the American campus, where it was powerful enough to perpetuate its views but impotent to spread its message beyond a captive classroom. As to conservatism as a political philosophy—that is, as a Burkean affection for prudence and moderation and perhaps even a literary sensibility of irony and tragedy—it too rarely sank roots in America. But an earlier liberal consensus had an inevitable rendezvous with conservatism in that the former carried the seeds from which the latter sprouted.

The Pilgrimage of Louis Hartz

Hartz first spelled out this argument in his doctoral thesis, which later was published as *Economic Policy and Democratic Thought: Pennsylvania, 1776–1860* (1948). Although the work is often read, when read at all, as a defense of the New Deal on the grounds that America had not had a laissez-faire economy but instead an interventionist state, the implications of what Hartz had unearthed go much deeper. Hartz explained why America became what Hamilton had feared: a nation without a nation-state.

In the Jacksonian era, the rise of the corporate economy that depended upon state-issued charters that authorized a private company to run a specific enterprise was attacked from all sides: by exponents of entrepreneurial individualism who regarded business as more efficient when free of government, and by labor organizations that saw such charter grants as a form of class legislation that threatened the sovereignty of the people. But instead of invoking the European idea of socialism to challenge these charters, the American worker invoked the Lockean idea of natural law and the Jeffersonian-Jacksonian concept of the moral superiority of the worker over the banker. The anti-charter case was also voiced by real-estate holders and other interest groups, which feared that all proposals for state-government investment in private enterprise would increase taxes. Thus although anti-investment and anti-charter interests represented different class strata, both uttered sentiments that defended liberty in negative terms: as resistance to government and as skepticism toward the idea of the state as the domain of unity, civic spirit, and justice.

What appeared to be liberal and even radical turned out to be a potentially conservative stance that was to characterize the future of American political thought. For after the Civil War, corporations appropriated the anti-charter and anti-investment sentiments and used them against government itself. Hartz's book hinted strongly that in attacking the idea of a mixed economy, Democrats and even many Whigs left America's industrial future to the domain of free enterprise. The Jacksonian notion of "equal rights" originally meant to assure that all people would enjoy the free exercise of their "talents and industry"; it was thought that all pretensions of the public good merely bestowed on select classes privileges not equally enjoyed by others. Then the suspicion was that the wealthy relied upon government while genuine workers pursued their ends apart from the state and its laws. Today, as we witness the twilight of the welfare state, the same Jacksonian sentiment prevails. In politics Democrats as well as Republicans shout: "No more big government!" A century and a half ago one heard the same shibboleth. "Too much legislation is more to be dreaded than the entire want of it," complained a Pennsylvania Senate committee in 1834. "The maxim is true that 'the world is governed too much.'"[2]

With the New Deal of the Depression years liberalism became identified with government, but it was a tenuous identification that had enjoyed only one earlier expression—in the Progressive era of Theodore Roosevelt, during which he preached his belief in government and the importance of the public good over private interests. Hartz himself was a Progressive liberal who credited Franklin Roosevelt's New Deal for addressing social issues long neglected, and he valued diversity and dissent more than consensus and continuity. But Hartz never mistook his own values for the liberal, individualistic capitalism that had pervaded America's political culture. Liberalism, which claimed to be against all dogma, itself became a dogmatic fixation that led people to assume that what they believe is simply what is good and useful to believe. People were sovereign, and no political leader, with the exception of Abraham Lincoln, dared challenge their sense of right and wrong.

Two years after Hartz published his study of Pennsylvania, Lionel Trilling published *The Liberal Imagination* (1950). Like Hartz, Trilling recognized that America had no genuine radical or conservative tradition but instead only a liberalism that refused to face reality. One of Trilling's targets was Vernon L. Parrington, the Progressive historian who had led a generation of readers and students to see American intellectual history as a battleground of moral categories: Jefferson, Franklin, and Emerson stood for democracy, reason, and the promises of the mind; Jonathan Edwards, Hamilton, and Hawthorne for sin, property, and the paradoxes of the heart. The Parringtonian paradigm resonated with conflict: the Enlightenment versus Calvinism, Transcendentalism versus materialism, agrarianism versus capitalism. Trilling hoped that scholars and students would overcome such simple dualisms and think in terms that would make the materials of American intellectual history more complex, tense, ironic, and perhaps even dialectical.

In some respects Hartz sought to do the same in the area of social thought. In one of his lectures at Harvard, Hartz, citing Marx and Rousseau, told students that "the liberal world was held to be untrue, since it contained frightful coercion." The answer to such coercion can be nothing short of the socialization of the economy and the abolition of the class system. "Marx is saying that conflict is so basic that you can never expect capitalists to be reasoned into a solution or even a compromise. Marxism is the final dissolution of the idea of a harmony of interests."[3] While Marx may have been correct in his conviction that the capitalist would be reluctant to compromise with the socialist, would the worker feel the same hesitation in compromising with the capitalist? Are interests always in conflict? We turn to *The Liberal Tradition in America*.

One of the great achievements of Hartz's seminal book is that it succeeded in doing what Marxists have long encouraged scholars to do even though they themselves seldom do it: combine an analysis of a social structure with an exploration of the political ideology that emanates from it. Hartz sought to show that American liberalism became pervasive because it grew silently out of two interrelated but hitherto unnoticed factors: the absence of feudalism and the presence of Lockeanism.[4] The first condition meant that America had no aristocracy that would have, as a class, resisted social change, denigrated the value of labor, and ridiculed the idea of equality (the plantation South was, of course, the exception). The second condition meant that Americans were property conscious, valued individual natural rights even if they were more sensed than understood, and regarded liberty as consisting more of a resistance to political authority than the classical duty of participating actively in the workings of government. Such conditions produced a mentality that precluded the possibility that America would have either a reactionary aristocracy or a revolutionary working class.

"But is not the problem of Fitzhugh at once the problem of De

Leon?" asked Hartz, in part feeling the anguish of both George Fitz-hugh, an antebellum exponent of southern feudal chivalry, and Daniel De Leon, a Marxist exponent of class struggle.[5] The problem was also, one might add, the mutual quandary facing Irving Howe and William F. Buckley Jr., whose respective journals, *Dissent* and *National Review,* came out at about the same time as Hartz's book. If the Left could not forge a radical transformation of American liberalism, could the Right create out of the same materials a conservative tradition?

It should be noted that Hartz's interpretation of American history presaged schools of European thought that became influential in the 1960s and thereafter. He anticipated the French Annales school in suggesting that to focus solely on politics, as in the older history, conceals the long-term hold that a *mentalité* has had over the American mind, *la longue durée* of liberalism. As in the writings of Michel Foucault, Hartz's work also portrays political thought as a discourse that interlocks itself, particularly in America, around the idea of property; hence liberalism is an "absolutism," an "irrational" phenomenon that cannot be rationally transcended through critical self-reflection. The hegemonic hold of liberalism also approaches a totality whose boundaries go unperceived, and the many Americans who fail to feel the presence of liberalism are unconscious of who they are. Finally, Hartz managed to join together the *savant* and the *populaire,* high political philosophy and popular culture in mass society, as he showed how Jeffersonian liberalism culminates in the figure of Horatio Alger. Those millions of late-nineteenth-century Americans who read his tales were expressing their preference for the Algerian world of pluck and luck. Locke knew, as did the ragged newsboy, that what moves human beings is the idea of happiness and happiness alone.

Nowhere was the idea of ambition, hard work, and material happiness better articulated than in the speeches and writings of Abraham Lincoln. Lincoln recognized that human self-preservation depended not so much on politics as on work and access to land. A man of the soil as well as the law, Lincoln saw the origins of private property as the beginning of human history, and he raised the doctrine of "free labor" to a spiritual principle, convinced that self-ownership was the driving impulse of western civilization. Lincoln loved to recall his humble beginnings just as he reminded Americans of the poor and uprooted

people who first landed on these shores. As did later consensus scholars, Lincoln saw that the differing worlds of capital and labor could
well be a matter of disputation but not of irreconcilable conflict because in commercial society the status of the productive worker is as
mobile as the flow of money. He also insisted that it was interest—
not, as some contemporary historians contend who deny consensus,
"virtue"—that motivated human conduct. On this matter America enjoyed a Lockean psyche residing in the majority of the population.
"Farmers being the most numerous class, it follows that their interest is the largest," wrote Lincoln. "It also follows that that interest
is most worthy of all to be cherished and cultivated—that if there
be inevitable conflict between that interest and any other, that other
should yield."[6]

The validity of the liberal school as a synthesis of American history
goes to the heart of our foundations. But the proposal that a unifying
theme may illuminate American history is met with much resistance
by the radical school, which presumes that the entry of new ethnic
constituencies into historiography undermines liberal consensus and
that a multicultural society shatters it beyond repair.

The late Louis Hartz would have been very interested in this new
turn toward non-western cultures. After he left Harvard University in
the early 1970s, he spent his last years traveling throughout the third
world; in January 20, 1986, he collapsed on a street in Istanbul and
died at the age of sixty-six. He once told a former graduate student that
he thought America could understand itself only by opening up its
mind to other cultures and religions, and his last book was on Islam,
Buddhism, Hinduism, Confucianism, and other world outlooks. *A
Synthesis of World History* (1983) is almost mystical in its longing, and
not a little impenetrable in its prose; yet Hartz's interest in comparative world religions was nothing less than part of his search for a
solution to the human condition.

With a mode of reasoning that resembled Augustine's, Pascal's,
and, at times, Tocqueville's, Hartz saw humanity as divided within the
core of its "soul," with men and women active and passive—oscillat-
ing between high ambition and quiescent resignation, "Promethean"
struggle and "Buddhist" surrender. This restlessness, driven by fear
and anxiety, compels people to cling to their identities, which are based

on family, religion, tribe, clan, or country—all of which Hartz regarded as "absolutisms" deriving from an inner psychic terror that brooks no analysis and questioning. Even if such institutions were abolished, the fear that forged their creations may remain as haunting as ever. "Unless there is a change in the nature of man for which history offers no precedent," observed Hartz, "the problem of his liberation from the inner fear generated by action and quiescence will remain. You and I can achieve that liberation. We have already done so, travelling again and again around the earth." Hartz then paraphrases Marx's *The German Ideology*, where a socialist future promises that one need work only in the morning and then can go fishing in the afternoon and read poetry in the evening.

> There is a well known utopia, not disassociated from a belief in the passing of cultural institutions, that urges that man be free to be an engineer one day, an accountant the next, and an artist the next. I suggest an alternative: that man be free to be Chinese one day, Indian the next, and European the next. And I suggest more still, that man be free to add a thousand other choices smothered in history by the absolutism of these. This is to transform all choice and it is to match abundance with a human dignity that terror has denied.[7]

Can we believe our eyes? The very scholar who was dismissed as a "consensus" historian ends his life calling upon people in all parts of the world to understand the conflicting tensions within themselves that prevent them from accepting the infinite possibilities of diversity and even the transvaluation of identity. Rather than conforming to an American consensus, Hartz fled from it. Today more and more Americans cling to their identities and thereby allow free choice to be smothered in the folds of history. How our contemporary "identity politics" emerges naturally from a political culture of liberal consensus is the subject of the concluding chapter. But it should be emphasized that Hartz was acknowledging consensus in order to figure out how it might be overcome; hence his pilgrimage to the non-western world to find elsewhere what liberalism had denied him in America. Having seen America imprisoned within an unseen and unfelt monolithic ideology, he alone assumed the obligation of finding a door of escape. He failed, of course, but even in trying he lifted the story of American history to heroic heights.

A "Botched Civilization"

Louis Hartz remains the bête noire of the radical school, which assumes that the continuity of liberal consensus can be challenged by creating a history from below and at the margins. But what is involved in trying to rescue from oblivion the forgotten, especially those who left no written record? As Michel de Certeau observed, in seeking to find the vanished the historian joins the mystic:

> Something has been lost that will not return. Historiography is a contemporary form of mourning. Its writing is based on an absence and produces nothing but simulacra, however scientific. It offers representations in the place of bereavement. Doubtless it is not certain that we know the present any better than the past. . . . At least in the present we can nourish the illusion of overcoming what the past has rendered insurmountable. Thus it is that the historian or the mystics . . . repeat their experience in studying it [what is missing, lost, forgotten]. . . . A mirrorlike structure: like Narcissus, the historian-actor observes his reflection. . . . He seeks one who has vanished.[8]

In the 1970s Christopher Lasch, one of the most morally sensitive historians of our generation, wrote *The Culture of Narcissicism*. The public and even the publishing world expressed surprise when the book became a best-seller, a rare feat for a work by an intellectual historian. But narcissists like to read about themselves, and similarly, they like to write about themselves. When one examines the work of much of the new history, which deals with many nameless subjects, it is difficult to tell whether the historical subject is speaking or a politically frustrated generation is still chanting its own radical aspirations through the vanished voice of that subject, as though the historian ventriloquist observes his reflection in the mirror of history. Whatever the case, in much of the new radical school, which seeks a kind of redemption by means of representation, the famous must make way for the anonymous because the silent shall be heard, the invisible seen.

The teaching and writing of American history has undergone profound changes. Its color has changed from a monotonous white to a rich rainbow of different hues, each representing a distinct minority group. Its focus has shifted from top to bottom, from studying political leaders and intellectual elites to investigating the lives of ordinary,

common people; and from the center to the periphery, from studying
the masculine world of power and authority to discovering the wom-
en's world of spheres and roles. And American history has, as the public is well aware, turned from celebrating the country's achievements
and successes to confessing its failures and violations of humanity.
Finally, the teaching and writing of American history no longer enjoys
a synthesis, an overarching interpretive framework for understanding
the past based on persistent themes and ideas. How can we account
for these changes?

What happened between the generations of the 1940s and 1950s
and those of the 1960s and 1970s left the country with two opposing
outlooks at the end of the century. Historical events and episodes
immediately come to mind: the Vietnam War, the civil rights movement, women's liberation, the ecological awakening, and the "Great
Society" program and its war on poverty. But there is no reason why
any or all of these events should have divided America along generational lines, at least not in the world of scholarship. Many older historians opposed the war and supported civil rights and other causes.
Why, then, did the academic mind become politicized in the field of
American history? One reason is that the New Left of the 1960s became convinced that America had to face such problems as war and
poverty because previous historians had misinterpreted the nature of
America itself: they had perceived consensus and relative content-
ment where they should have seen conflict and seething resistance,
they wrote about harmony when they should have been documenting
misery. Does the blundering tragedy of Vietnam and a past record of
indifference to race and poverty mean that previous interpretations of
American history must be thrown out? When it comes to interpreting
American history, who is right?

To begin to answer that question, I offer three scenes: one from
testimony by Adolph Strasser, secretary of the Cigarmakers' International Union, given to U.S. Senate hearings on "Relations Between Labor and Capital" in 1885; the second from a film documentary on the
life of Harry Bridges, the communist leader of the San Francisco longshoremen; the third from the movie *Reds*, about the life of John Reed,
the romantic revolutionary who championed Bolshevism and helped
found the American Communist Party. The first scene is Strasser's:

Q. Does the existence of your trade unions, as a rule, make any difference in the prices paid for labor in other industries as well as your
own?

A. The working classes think they do not receive their fair share of the
proceeds of productive industry. As individuals they ask for more.
The demand is refused. They combine; they call it a "trade union." As
a union they ask for more.[9]

The second scene takes place in the 1950s in the office of the
Matson Navigation Line.

MANAGEMENT: "Mr. Bridges, what is it that you and your men want?"
BRIDGES: "Exactly what you want."
MANAGEMENT: "And what's that, Harry?"
BRIDGES: "Profits!"

The third scene takes place in Portland, Oregon, in 1914, after
World War I had broken out and the public wanted to know why.

CAPITALIST: "Jack, tell us what the war is all about."
REED: [Rising from his chair, the handsome Warren Beatty, dressed in
black tie, utters a single word . . . and then sits down] "Profits!"

The New Left of the 1960s cheered the film *Reds,* as it had Beatty's
earlier film *Bonnie and Clyde,* which shows a glamorous gunslinging
couple racing around the country holding up banks in the midst of the
Depression. The first two scenes, though actual history, were anathema to the activists in the academy. Communists, as well as anyone
claiming radical credentials, were not supposed to seek profits or anything "more" that smacked of bourgeois comfort. On this bedrock issue of where working-class leaders stood and what workers themselves
wanted, the unity of American historiography shattered to the point
that eventually the whole of American history, from the colonial period
to the present, came to be reinterpreted, and colonial artisans were
depicted as interested less in material gain than in taking pride in their
skills and craft traditions and retaining control over the workplace.

Such a reorientation had been attempted before, but previous generations, which had assumed that America could be saved from materialism by revealing its hidden enclaves of cultural, moral, and political idealism, came to the conclusion that "Profits!"—or as Van Wyck
Brooks put it, "catchpenny opportunism"—was precisely what America was all about.[10] They then wondered if there was any escape from

this condition, which supposedly had come from three sources: the inhibitions of Puritanism, the acquisitive impulses of capitalism, and the cultural sterility of a once-frontier society. All of these tenets had combined to make America a "business civilization," a "botched civilization," and an "old bitch gone in the teeth" (Ezra Pound) supposedly dead from the neck up that the "Lost Generation" indicted in the 1920s while fleeing to Paris.[11] In America, observed the philosopher George Santayana, the will was always felt to be deeper than the intellect. In addition, the will to wealth and "aggressive enterprise" overtakes modern society, leaving intellectuals and scholars with no way out of a consensualized Jeffersonian culture where nothing counts save the realization of material happiness.[12]

For decades it has been fashionable to romanticize, if not sentimentalize, the working class. Such ideological history only points up the poverty of radical theory when confronting the nature of liberal reality. "To understand oneself is the classical form of consolation," wrote Santayana in "The Genteel Tradition in America"; "to elude oneself is the romantic." Does the new radical history, with its emphasis on representation often at the expense of explanation, enable Americans to understand themselves? Or do we elude facing who we are by allowing ourselves to believe that we had no hand in becoming who we are? Most of us cannot claim to have made history; does it follow that history has made us?

Cunning and Its Discontents

It is a common cliché today that one's identity has been conferred rather than achieved; that to know who we are is to find out how we became products via some mysterious process called "social construction." Many scholars focus on race, class, and gender as social or cultural artifices that have inhibited the full development of human freedom by denying people any conscious choice in the decision to become who they are or who they wish to be. It is tempting to see historical and social phenomena as externally formed and contingent upon circumstances, for any phenomenon so conceived can easily be deconstructed by demonstrating the artificial conditions of its construction. One can readily understand why women and ethnic minorities prefer to see their situation in history as socially constructed rather than biologically mandated or religiously foreordained. Those who have yet to make a front-line appearance on the stage of history are entitled to see their fate as arbitrary. If history teaches anything, it is chance, misfortune, and the accident of birth and the irony of fate. When Henry David Thoreau complained that society "paws" at him, he was warning Americans not to allow themselves to become formed creatures when they should be free creators. To be free is to know thyself in order better to determine it, to resist society's pawing constructions and, as much as possible, history's random contingencies. But it may also be the case that people consciously decided to become one thing and ended up becoming something else.

The section's title, "Cunning and Its Discontents," is meant to suggest a series of ironies involving unintended consequences. The idea of cunning, of the notion that people are barely conscious that they are bringing about a new stage of history that actually defies their purposes, has run through American history long before the New Left succumbed to it. From the very beginning of American history the impulse toward capitalist profits grew stronger where it was unsought—that is, in Puritan New England—than where it was much sought, in what became the plantation South. One part of the country sought to save its soul and instead, through hard work and frugality, produced prosperity and Yankee materialism; the other strove for the profits with which to enjoy the life of the gentry leisure class and instead, shirking labor and imposing it on others, ended up with an economic system that bounded master as well as slave.

The American Revolution itself, a war fought in part to uphold simple republican virtue and independence, brought about an environment of consumer indulgence and social dependence. Feminism, too, has its cunning. The recent movement of women out of the household and into the workforce and professions, originally seen as the first steps in reforming society by means of a more devoted feminine conscience and sensibility, has left society pretty much intact, with women elected to political office and behaving much like men, as insensitive to scandal as a rake is to guilt. The original intentions of agents may have little to do with the deeper meaning of events.

Ironies tend to compound themselves. Thus the very institutions that the New Left derided—Calvinist religion and its sense of guilt and duty, and Lockean liberalism and its sense of natural rights and the value of labor and property—proved more liberating in American history than did the New Left's academic causes. One celebrated cause of the New Left, for example, was the "new labor history" and its idealization of the working class, but the attitudes of the working class toward Native Americans, African Americans, Asian immigrants, and women and their struggles remained unsympathetic if not downright racist and chauvinist. If American history is to be the study of freedom marching onward and upward, who were freedom's friends and who were its enemies? Or is the story simply one of domination and victimization?

The radical school should be severely scrutinized for the same reason that the American founders examined and rejected the classical school. The founders realized that classical history was little more than a record of systematic failure, a legacy all the more questionable when its thinkers such as Machiavelli distorted political reality as they sprinkled their texts with paens to civic patriotism. The founders also saw ancient republics as fragile, so precarious that John Adams described them as having "foamed, raged, and burst, like so many water-sprouts upon the ocean." One cannot look back upon the "petty republics of Greece and Italy," wrote Alexander Hamilton, "without feeling sensations of horror and disgust at the distractions by which they were kept in a state of perpetual vibration between the extremes of tyranny and anarchy. If they exhibited occasional calms, these only serve as short-lived contrasts to the furious storms that are to succeed."[13] The founders saw through the classical rhetoric of public spirit and civic virtue and revealed, instead, a record of petty strife and failed hopes.

The liberalism that was present at the creation of the Republic enjoyed the darker wisdom of skepticism, derived from Calvinism, perhaps, or from David Hume and Scottish philosophy. In the eighteenth century Adams and Hamilton adopted modern, skeptical liberalism as a critique of classical virtue. Today the situation is reversed: the radical school adopts classical republicanism and the idea of civic virtue in an attempt to present a critique of contemporary liberalism. It seems that many of today's labor historians have taken on the old role of classical authors in assuring us that something glorious can be found in the past. They tell us, for example, that the noble cause of workers enjoyed a "moment" of realization, a "zenith," that their activities constitute a "transitory" phenomenon of "solidarity" that could not be sustained and hence passed into oblivion.[14] This is history as storytelling about the possible rather than the factual. "It is the business of fiction," observed the literary critic Harry Levin, "to explore what might have been, what may be, what is not; and, in this respect, our story-tellers are no less prone than those of the Middle Ages to remind us that they are recounting dream-visions."[15]

What's wrong with dreams? The historian and sociologist John H. M. Laslett and Seymour Martin Lipset edited a comprehensive anthology titled *Failure of a Dream? Essays on the History of American Socialism.* What is questionable is the question mark itself, which implies that the story of radical socialism amounts to more than recounting dreams. Perhaps. Yet as the political theorists Karen Orren and Stephen Skowronek have noted, American historians seem always to be discovering some radical "alternatives 'from below' " that disappear from the scene faster than they appeared, making history the study of that which is about to happen but doesn't and the past little more than a poignant expectation that can never be realized.[16] Such historians seem to have a fascination with failure, with that which can rarely make itself felt and win its object. So determined are they to uncover an implacable consciousness among workers that they cannot help becoming true believers; and for those who believe, the substance of things hoped for, to use Santayana's formulation, becomes the evidence for things not seen.

Why are conflict historians of the radical school so obsessed with what ends up aborting? Ralph Waldo Emerson advised us never to equate latency with life itself: "Everything is impossible until we see a success."[17] But the labor historian, instead of allowing us to see a success, remains a materialist who can scarcely make his subject materialize, and he wonders why this critic of labor history remains "pessimistic." Perhaps he or she has forgotten Mark Twain's definition of the pessimist: "The optimist who didn't arrive."[18]

If the radical school had created an imagination more willed than true, it might be forgiven its temptation of solipcism. History, when not a "nightmare from which I am trying to awake," is also "a tale like any other often heard," wrote James Joyce. "He found in the world without as actual what was in his world within as possible," reflects Stephen Daedalus in *Ulysses*. To make the mentally possible into the historically actual renders the historian the creator of history rather than its discoverer, and what never happened could have happened if the living speak for the dead. But as Joyce put it when referring to historical events, "can those have been possible seeing that they never were? Or was that only possible which came to pass? Weave, weaver of the wind."[19]

Historians may "weave" history from the heights of the creative imagination or the depths of political desperation. Should they adhere only to empirical data rather than to longings? Some philosophers believe that it is legitimate to take either position, providing it is done with honest self-awareness:

> You are secretly convinced that to perceive facts is a blessed privilege, and to create imaginary beauties a disgraceful self-delusion. You would, I think, express your moral judgement better if you acknowledged them to be vapours of your private soul, and not implications of your alleged science. It is perfectly indifferent to me whether what gives me pleasure is a solid body or an airy illusion. Whichever object is the more delightful seems to me the better, and I no more care whether it exists within or without my skull, than I ask whether the zephyr that refreshes me blows from the east or the west.[20]

Surely thought cannot be based on only what gives pleasure. The founders remained convinced that ideal republics existed only in the "warm imagination" as "airy phantoms" and "idle theories," retrospective speculations with no basis in real experience, linguistic constructions waiting to be deconstructed.[21] But the new radical school, like the mythmakers of old, asks us to believe in the viability of an autonomous "working class culture" and, against bourgeois capitalism, in "its dialectical counterhegemonic counterpart among workers"; "artisan republicanism," a "women's sphere," "republican motherhood," or a "civic humanism" that they constructed out of "the language of republicanism" itself.[22] Would Thomas Paine, the Revolution's most popular voice, have preferred a classical politics of deference and subordination to a modern economics of energy and freedom? Would Mercy Otis

Warren and Judith Murray Sargent have championed a republicanism that never denied the distinction between the *oikos* and the polis, between the household to which women were confined and the public sphere to which they aspired to be liberated?

Scholars who see history as conflict and struggle can seldom come up with a success story. Yet those who deny consensus are denying their own successful, if ironic, role in history. As Hegel understood, unintended outcomes show how agents in historical movements remain unconscious of what they have wrought and how easily they come to accept what they started out rejecting. Thus the radical activists of the 1960s who set out to bring down the "system," and particularly a higher educational "multiversity" that loomed as the "iron cage" of bureaucracy, now find themselves comfortably ensconced within that very system.[23]

So situated, the radical school has written a body of scholarship that aims to replace a good deal of prior historiography, particularly the school of liberal consensus. And here we confront another of the ironies in the study of American history. For the presence of the liberal consensus has been challenged by two episodes in our past, and both ended in lost causes.

In the nineteenth century, the plantation South tried to refute the country's foundational consensus by insisting that Jefferson had only white men in mind when writing the Declaration and that work can be best left to servants and slaves. In our time, ironically, certain radical historians who have successfully expanded the perimeters of historiography to include blacks, women, workers, and ethnic minorities have also challenged the liberal consensus at the foundation of our political culture. Both the Right and the Left see liberalism as the cause of two wars, the Civil War and the cold war, each of which were brought on, it is alleged, by liberalism's refusal to see that matters of race and issues of class are inherently conflictual and cannot be resolved by returning to America's historical foundations. Both wars were ideological, for just as the Soviet Politburo opposed liberalism and the right to private property, so did the plantation South oppose Lockeanism and the right to free labor. If Vladimir I. Lenin legitimated Bolshevik rule as the "dictatorship of the proletariat," John C. Calhoun legitimated the South's economy as a paternalism offering black people the

safety and security of bondage, a position that earned him the epithet,
"the Marxist of the Master Class."[24] Both the South and the Soviet
Union denied the liberal principle that an individual exists for his or
her own sake and not for the good of "organic" society or social "solidarity." George Fitzhugh as well as Karl Marx blamed Lockean liberalism for the atomization of modern society. "Isolated and individu-
alized," complained Fitzhugh, human beings are "the most helpless
of animals. We think this error of the economists proceeded from
their adopting Locke's theory of the social contract. We believe no
heresy in moral science has been more pregnant of mischief than this
theory of Locke."[25] Both systems of slave labor (which is what Russia
became under Stalin) insisted that capital and labor were in conflict
and that capitalism could never emancipate workers from conditions
of servitude; neither system could countenance liberalism and the
doctrine of natural rights as guaranteed liberties. Yet as I have suggested throughout this book, liberalism as a foundational consensus is
the missing ingredient in contemporary historiography. The following
sections may help explain why.

New History versus Old History

It is often forgotten that the scholars who wrote from the perspective of the 1940s and 1950s "liberal consensus" school—Daniel J.
Boorstin, Richard Hofstadter, and Louis Hartz—had at one time been
leftists who, following the Marxist tradition, saw history in terms of
class struggle with conflict the driving force ("the midwife") of modernization and liberation. That perspective had risen in the radical
1930s when Boorstin, Hofstadter, and Hartz had been graduate students. But having experienced the years of the Great Depression and
the war against Hitler's Third Reich, events that were supposed to
heighten class tensions and bring down capitalism, such scholars began to question not only Marxism but liberalism itself, especially the
early Progressive historians Charles A. Beard, Frederick Jackson Turner, and Vernon L. Parrington, who also had made conflict, whether
class, sectional, or moral, the animating force of American history.[26]

Recent historiography has dismissed the consensus scholars in
favor of a newer conflict school of thought that emphasizes not only

class but also race and gender as divisive issues that went unacknowl-
edged in past narratives. Why did the older school embrace consensus
and neglect to deal with the more volatile issues of American political
life?

The critics of consensus offer two explanations. First, the consensus school of thought happened to have taken hold in the 1950s,
the era of the cold war when McCarthyism had created a climate of fear
and paranoid insecurity. Reacting to the anti-communist hysteria of
the times, those who had once expounded a Marxist conflict interpretation of history ran for cover and, it is held, wrapped themselves in
the mantle of patriotic consensus. Moreover, the consensus scholars
happened to be mainly Jews living in urban America, and the older
conflict scholars were Protestants born and raised in the Midwest.
Confused about their ethnic identity and suffering from status insecurity, the Jews as outsiders felt compelled, it is claimed, to give up the
idea of social conflict and write about America as a country of consensual harmony. Thus for both political and cultural reasons, it was safer
for historians of the 1950s to think one way rather than another and to
write expediently rather than critically.[27]

The problem with the first allegation, that of fear of anti-communist
reprisals, is that consensus historians began to conceive of their work
during World War II in the early 1940s, before the cold war had
hardened its grip on the world and Joseph McCarthy had made his
accusations about the menace of communism not to America, but in
America.[28] The problem with the second allegation, that of insecurity
by the Jewish consensus scholars, is that older Protestant conflict scholars had already been moving toward a consensus interpretation after
the outbreak of World War II. In 1943, *Life* magazine serialized chapters of Charles Beard's *The Republic*, and Americans were told that they
in fact live by a common core of political ideas emanating from the
eighteenth century. The same year Hofstadter began writing *The American Political Tradition*, which appeared in 1948 but was, the author later
wrote, "to a very large extent an intellectual product of the experience of
the 1930's."[29]

The false impression that the anti-communism of the cold war required historians to take up the cause of consensus is easily refuted
when we consider Arthur Schlesinger Jr.'s *The Age of Jackson* (1945) and

The Vital Center (1949). The first work explained why in America's early historical development the conflicting antagonisms of social classes proved more important than sectional rivalry or any sense of national unity. The second work demonstrated that it was Stalinism, not liberalism, that imposed a coercive consensus that would brook no dissent or conflict, while America upheld a centrist pluralism of unending struggle and contestation. As the *Federalist* authors had observed almost two centuries earlier, while the sources of factional conflict cannot be eliminated, their effects can be controlled. The inexorability of conflict lies at the very foundation of the American Republic.   ·

Whence, then, arose the confusing idea of consensus? In truth, consensus scholarship had less to do with the cold war and Jewish sensibilities than with the radical political climate of the 1930s and the need to explain why both communism and fascism will not happen in the United States. To go back and read the radical journals and books of the 1930s—all of whose authors were thrilled by Wall Street's sudden crash at the end of the 1920s, certain that the subsequent rise of Hitler meant the end of the liberal state, and convinced that the apparent heightening "crisis" of capitalism made socialism inevitable—is to read about the coming of another even more cataclysmic crash, and one that never came. But waiting for it to come was absolutely exhilarating, as Lewis Corey exhorted in *The Crisis of the Middle Class* (1935):

> A world is dying. It is dying as the old feudal world died, accompanied by revolutions and wars. Capitalism emerged slowly, agonizingly, almost blindly, for there was no real understanding of the control and drift of social forces. It took 500 years of struggle to create the new world of capitalism. But the struggle for socialism, in the midst of the dying world of capitalism, is more purposive, easier, more capable of speedy realization. For our struggle is animated by the purposive understanding and control of Marxism, which is communism: the perceiver of a new world and its creator. It is the new Enlightenment, and it calls to struggle for a new world already appearing on the horizon. The Marxist Enlightenment, too, urges the challenges of the old: Dare to understand—forward, not backward![30]

The challenge of Boorstin, Hofstadter, and Hartz was to explain why a world that was supposedly dying refused to die, why the collapse of America never happened, and why all Marxian prophecies about conflict and the "contradictions" of capitalism turned out to be only the wish fallacy of the Depression generation. Hence they turned toward the themes of consensus and continuity, and while Boorstin celebrated an America supposedly characterized by an absence of ideology, Hartz and Hofstadter almost lamented in finding a liberal America mired in a consensus based on shared values about property, opportunity, and the pursuit of material happiness. A century earlier Alexis de Tocqueville had called such a consensus, at its best, "enlightened self-interest" and "self-interest rightly understood," or, at its worst, a "pernicious materialism" incapable of disciplining itself.

The liberal school, the last to attempt a "synthesis" interpretation of American history, held that the conflict between labor and capital and the idea of "class conflict" never caught hold in America because it is a land of social cohesion where most Americans share the same interests and values, particularly, as Lincoln reminded citizens, the ambition to work economically as a means of rising socially. To be sure, conflicts had broken out as soon as the first colonists had landed on these shores: disputes between owners and their indentured servants, debtors and creditors, orthodox believers and dissidents; and, later, between land grabbers and Native American tribes, abolitionists and slave holders, farmers and railroads, female aspiration and masculine obstinacy, union and management. But such conflicts scarcely signified the will to change the world by radically transforming the nature of America's political economy, which for Karl Marx was to be the specific role of the working class, the potential revolutionary "proletariat," the one class that, in struggling against an alienated society, is "in a position to realize humanity."[31] It was the integration of America's working class into the culture of capitalism that intrigued, and often despaired, scholars of consensus of the 1950s, who more and more began to agree with Tocqueville that America was different from Europe in lacking rigid class systems—the controversial idea of "American exceptionalism."

In the 1960s a newer body of scholarship emerged to challenge everything that the liberal school stood for. This later radical school depicted American exceptionalism as a myth concocted during the cold war both to reassure America of its presumed superiority and to cite conditions that "have muffled and destroyed dissent, especially working class dissent."[32] Significantly, the new radical school convinced

itself that "class consciousness" could be uncovered in American history by looking at places that had gone uninvestigated. "Men make
their own history," advised Marx, "but they do not make it just as they
please."[33] Marx had oriented inquiry at the point of production; the
radical school seeks to make history just as it pleases by taking inquiry
to places of pleasure, not the life of backbreaking labor but the life of
enjoyable leisure, not the factory but the tavern.

Homogeneity and the Challenge of Diversity

The recent entry of racial and ethnic minorities and women
into the mainstream of American politics is purported to represent a
challenge to consensus, a new perspective that the Yale political theorist Rogers Smith calls "multi-traditions." Supposedly an entirely new
feature of American history, "multi-traditions" is said to be based on
an ascriptive politics of identity that has as much to do with personal
recognition as economic redistribution.[34] Although Tocqueville
showed us why democracy tends to purge society of differences, the
1960s generation saw itself as different and elevated diversity to the
status of an axiom. Ironically, in the nineteenth century, as noted
earlier, it was the reactionaries and racists who claimed that America
was founded on the principle of disunity and diversity, while movements of the Left appealed to unity and solidarity. On the issue of unity
versus diversity, America's political founders took curious positions,
with the proto-feminist Mercy Otis Warren joining the conservative
Alexander Hamilton in believing that the new nation's development
called for a patriotic devotion to a national community, and with
Thomas Jefferson suspecting that all calls for unity were a threat to a
liberty that has its true home only in diversity. Hamilton, who believed
in power and authority, wanted to see slaves freed; Jefferson, who
believed in variety and liberty, wanted them to remain enslaved.

The Discovery of Republicanism

The older consensus school of thought was based on a modern
liberalism derived from the writings of John Locke, the philosopher
who made "life, liberty, and estates" (property) the foundation of mod-

ern freedom and security. The purported discovery of some alleged legacy of ancient classical republicanism, with its juxtaposition of "virtue" with "interest," supposedly undermines the claim that there has been only a single liberal tradition and makes civic duty and participatory politics the basis of the noble life.

Amazingly, when the radicals of the 1960s generation later became academics, they came to have more faith in citizenship and civic life than did even the founders of the American Republic. The few times the founders used the term "republicanism," it signified a form of government that derived its power from the people and prohibited titles of nobility, and the expression "republic" and "republican spirit" merely meant opposition to monarchy in favor of representative government and opposition to aristocracy in favor of simplicity. Indeed in the colonial period the very expression "republicanism," rather than signaling a "radical" opposition to Lockean liberalism, often functioned the way "Americanism" did in the cold-war era of McCarthyism: as an accusation directed toward those suspected of betraying liberty to tyranny. (It was no coincidence that the charge of betrayal was leveled at elites, whether Alexander Hamilton or, closer to our time, Adlai Stevenson.)[35] As to those colonial thinkers who believed that America could rely upon classical civic virtue, they "suffered from," the theoreticians of the Constitution scoffed in the *Federalist*, "a blind veneration of antiquity."[36]

Capitalism and the People

According to the radical historians, if America is to be called a capitalist country, it is up to the historian to show how the "market revolution" and the "corporate system" were imposed upon the people themselves.[37] Property consciousness, ambition, and the lust for profits are the results of the domination of the ruling class and its control over culture and education. Market economics betrays political democracy; to say that it expresses it is to commit the fallacy of consensus and believe that people share a core of common interests and values.

An example of opposition to consensus, we are told, may be seen in the nineteenth-century Populists who, while finding themselves "debt ridden agrarians" demanding "an increase in money supply," cleansed themselves of capitalist temptations as they spoke of "a classical republican emphasis on the need to enhance public virtue."[38] So speaks the historian. But when the Greenwich Village intellectual Randolph Bourne studied the Midwest, he saw its people seeming "to live in apocalyptic sociological—not, socialist, however—dreams." Bourne advised Americans to read Thorstein Veblen's essay "The Country Town," which should remind today's historians never to confuse rhetoric for reality. The "business-like . . . character of real estate speculation" in the Midwest, wrote Veblen, "affords a common bond and a common ground of pecuniary interest, which commonly masquerades under the name of public patriotism, public spirit, civic pride, and the like."[39] To mistake the masquerade for the motive is to judge the people to be as innocent as the historian is naive. With such mistaken assumptions, capitalism remains like a disease: Americans got it without wanting it. Populists who raged against the wealthy classes were considered honest producers, not resentful losers. And history's victims are to be thought of as virtuous losers.

The anti-consensus school that began to dominate the writing and teaching of American history upheld a series of positions, not all of which were consistent. Often a romantic populism merged with a hard-headed Marxism so that those past Americans who resisted change in the name of the people could be interpreted to be as radical as those forging it in the name of the masses. In more recent years some scholars interested in American history, particularly feminism and women's history, have turned to French poststructuralism and deconstruction for theories of power and domination. But all such episodes and theories tend to perpetuate a misunderstanding rather than face it. The idea of consensus versus conflict may be one of the most misleading ideas ever to befoul the landscape of American historiography.

How could there have been conflict unless different people and groups strove after the same things in life? Conflict, rather than excluding consensus, presupposes it. Liberal consensus thrives in a competitive environment of power, struggle, and self-assertion. Indeed only with conflict do freedom and the development of consciousness become possible; confronted with preferences and priorities, the mind engages in moral choices and willed actions, and since different human ends are not necessarily compatible, the possibility of conflict and even tragedy cannot be eliminated from history.

The coming Civil War, as Lincoln well understood, involved nothing less than a conflict over interpreting the meaning of equality and liberty; a struggle over a foundational consensus that was once regarded as "self-evident." It was a cultural battle over the basis of America's political values, a sparring over the right to another's labor as property and the right to work as an essential aspect of self-expression and the need for self-development and human fulfillment. Conflict can be found almost everywhere in American history. Often it has involved competing claims to property and profits, indicating that acquisition, possession, and their justifications are part of America's animating élan and that democracy is the environment where desire seeks its elusive objects—Gatsby's "green light" that beckons us on.

Lincoln saw "a house-divided" at the very basis of America's values, dividing a South that saw slavery as right and sought to extend it from a North that saw it as wrong and sought to confine it. When the North emerged victorious from the Civil War, slavery had been purged once and for all. Yet America's foundations would still need to confront the legacy of racism and other discriminations and exclusions. Expanding the foundations to include the hitherto excluded would present conflicts that would, ironically, only reaffirm the consensus at the heart of the foundations themselves.

But "class conflict"—that's the rub!

PART III

Class, Gender, Race:
The Hidden Consensus

CHAPTER 8

What Do Workers Want?

Is not then the demand to be rich legitimate?
RALPH WALDO EMERSON

The Recovery of Presence

ABRAHAM LINCOLN LOOKED TO THE AMERICAN REVO-
lution as the defining moment in the nation's history. He also knew
that it would be difficult to sustain the ideals of the Revolution in
peaceful, normal times when politics becomes little more than the
strategic adaptation to opportunity, the systematic sacrifice of integrity
to the siren of success. Lincoln proved prophetic.

Recently we have been told that after the American Revolution the
growing presence of wealth and consumption brought about more
equality and freedom and less exclusion and dependence. That the
Revolution led to no egalitarian redistribution of wealth is acknowledged. Yet these possibilities of pursuing wealth freed Americans to
challenge traditional social conventions and hierarchies. Consider the
following perspectives:

> We have one material which actually constitutes an aristocracy that gov-
> erns the nation. That material is wealth. Talents, birth, virtues, services,
> sacrifices, are of little consideration with us.
>
> John Adams[1]

> To clear, cultivate, and transform the huge uninhabited continent which
> is their domain, the Americans need every support of the an energetic
> passion; that passion can only be the love of wealth. No stigma attaches to
> love of money in America, and provided it does not exceed the bounds
> imposed by public order, it is held in honor.
>
> Alexis de Tocqueville[2]

Man was born to be rich, or grows rich by the use of his faculties, by the union of thought with nature. Property is an intellectual production. . . . We rail at trade, but the historian of the future will see that it was the principle of liberty; that it settled America, and destroyed feudalism, and made peace and keeps the peace; that it will abolish slavery. . . . Power is what they [the entrepreneurs] want, not candy. Is not then the demand to be rich legitimate?

Ralph Waldo Emerson[3]

True as this is [no egalitarian redistribution of wealth and power], it misses the point of what happened as a consequence of the Revolution and misunderstands why people in the early Republic could legitimately believe they were living in an egalitarian world. Wealth, compared to birth, breeding, family, heritage, even education, is the least mortifying, the least humiliating means by which one person can claim superiority over another; and it is the one most easily matched or overcome by exertion. From this point of view, the popular myth of equality in the early Republic was based on a substantial reality.

Gordon Wood[4]

The demand to be rich is indeed legitimate, but this economic side of liberalism legitimates capitalism, which some anti-consensus historians regard as the scandal of America's political culture. Thus Gordon Wood has himself been reprimanded by his colleagues for depicting the Revolution as a radicalism that leads not to socialism but to capitalism and a consumer's cornucopia.[5] In a historiography that had been influenced by the 1960s ethos of "participatory democracy," politics is privileged over economics, and Emerson's dictum that wealth is a species of power is seldom acknowledged. In contrast, Virginia Woolf, in *A Room of One's Own*, asked why men are "so prosperous" and women "so poor."[6] She answered that women mistake the vote for power and refuse to see that what really empowers people and renders them free is money. Ben Franklin had also seen that wealth is meant to be used and enjoyed as well as earned. Yet many social historians are less interested in "the way to wealth" than in class, race, and gender as a gateway to historical understanding.

Those who knew something about class and gender, as did, respectively, Franklin and Woolf, knew why those at the bottom and at the margins were powerless. W. E. B. Du Bois, who knew something about "the color line," often referred to the Greek legend of Hippomenes, who won the race for Atalanta's hand in marriage by placing golden apples before her and thus defiling the temple of love. Du Bois worried that African Americans could also be seduced into thinking that riches are the be-all and end-all of life. "Work and wealth are the mighty levers to lift this old new land; thrift and toil and saving are the highways to new hopes and possibilities; and yet the warning is needed lest the wily Hippomenes tempt Atalanta to thinking that golden apples are the goal of racing, and not the mere incidents by the way."[7] Du Bois had no desire to see his people, or America itself, become slaves to riches; doing so would have been a violation of the New England Calvinist culture that had nourished his youth. Yet he also knew that there cannot be power without wealth, and if a subsequent loyalty to socialism precluded him from admitting this openly, in his later years he moved closer to an Emersonian equation of freedom and self-sufficiency.

Wealth, power, self-reliance, and other characteristics of liberal capitalism are far from the categories used in modern scholarship to bring back the past. The three missing persons in American history were workers, women, and blacks. Actually workers were never really missing, and labor history has had a long, honored place in American scholarship. But the "new labor history" claims to tell us something new, and, as in the study of black Americans and women, working-class history also insists on inhabiting a world beyond or before liberalism.

Those who study women's history, black history, and workers' history also share other assumptions. All such scholars aim at "the recovery of presence," at finding the absent persons and placing them in the story. Often this requires looking to ordinary people and the masses rather than to great leaders, and accounting for the ensemble of social relations may be more important than explaining the causes of events. Moreover, many historians believe that recovering the presence of those left out of history will subvert the old liberal consensus perspective—on the assumption that those who had been excluded from the synthesis represented a challenge to it. Many consider democracy to have been the historical force enabling the downtrodden to rise (though some black scholars are more astute and prudent on this point). Finally, almost all in the radical school assume that any explanation of absence or subordination must reveal discriminatory behavior involving either class, gender, or race, all of which are supposedly "social constructions," categories that emerged as part of history's contingencies and hence have no basis in nature. By such reasoning, workers, women, and blacks can be rescued from oblivion, from what E. P. Thompson has called "the enormous condescension of posterity."[8]

"To Recover Past Struggles"

Without denying the extent of class divisions, racism, and chauvinism in American history, we may have a better take on the harsh realities by looking at the "spring of action" that may drive these inequities, the way the *Federalist* authors and John Adams did in the eighteenth century, when they were analyzing human motivation. These writers presaged Max Weber's theory of "social closure," the process by which groups or factions seek to maximize their own interests by restricting access by others to resources and opportunities. In much of American history the justification of exclusion may have been class, race, or gender. But such categories are simply the means by which a competitive society shuts the door to rivals and outsiders. Ironically, historians themselves use class, race, and gender in an attempt to break through such closures and contest the position of privileged insiders. It is tempting to use such classifications, for they provide convenient accusations with which one can charge history and society for its mistreatment of peoples of the past. But the pattern of exclusion at the top and usurpation from the bottom is part of the phenomenon of power, with one side desiring to contain change and the other clamoring for it. It is difficult to blame power for behaving as it does. Yet when historians write about workers, women, and blacks, those without power somehow occupy a morally superior position until they themselves obtain it, and thus what starts out as a narrative of conflict ends up as a narrative of consensus when the outsiders become the insiders and behave accordingly. Behavior and its motives, not language and self-description, is the key. One might say about class, race, and gender what Edmund Burke said about government and its relation to people: "Obedience is what makes government, and not the names by which it is called."[9]

As to those deemed by historians as belonging to a class, race, or gender, what is it that commands their obedience? One of the most exciting developments in American intellectual history and political theory in the past quarter-century was the idea of classical republicanism. Numerous historians jumped on the republican bandwagon and tried to recover the history of missing persons in American history by employing such ideas as citizenship and civic virtue, as though such ideals could command obedience. But of what use could republicanism be in rescuing the obscure? Labor historians thought they saw in republicanism an answer to capitalism that seemed even more useful than Marxism because politics, the passion of the 1960s generation, could now replace economics. Yet in republicanism, unlike Marxism and even Lockean liberalism, not only is there no labor theory of value but work itself was associated with servitude. As to women, in the long tradition of classical republicanism stretching from Aristotle to Harrington and Rousseau, it was assumed almost as a law of nature that wives, daughters, and mistresses must remain outside the public realm of politics and be happy with their domestic duties. Slavery, too, was regarded as a natural condition in classical political literature, and southern apologists for "the peculiar institution" had no hesitation citing ancient sources to justify their way of life. If workers, women, and blacks had obeyed the doctrines of republicanism, they would have participated in their own subordination to class, gender, and racial segregation.

But even in liberal, democratic America, workers, women, and blacks remained outside the perimeters of power and prosperity. To explain this condition of exclusion and subordination, many historians prefer to cite reasons of class, sex, and race, as though they are declaring their solidarity with those whose plight they narrate. Could the explanation possibly lie elsewhere? Gordon Wood emphasizes, and rightly so, the importance of wealth as a means to opportunity, and such figures as John Adams, Tocqueville, Emerson, Du Bois, and Virginia Woolf were quoted earlier to suggest why wealth became a sign of status and a species of power and, more importantly, a means of pursuing ends with no assurance that their realization would be a benefit. Wealth, far more than politics, makes choices plausible and freedom possible.

The relationship of wealth to power and freedom seems so obvious that readers may wonder why I need make the point. The answer is that in the Marxist tradition that has informed the new labor history, to accept wealth as a norm would be to deny conflict in favor of consensus. It would also be to deny that wealth results in the curse of alienated existence. The 1960s generation went bananas over the idea of alienation, and most of its members uncritically accepted Karl Marx's version of the phenomenon.

Here the new radical historians run up against three tensions standing between their school and the views of their mentor. First, whereas Marx saw the American Revolution and American democracy as emergent middle-class phenomena aiming to preserve property relations, the New Left looked to democracy itself as excitingly radical and hence a resource on which to draw. One scholar, speaking of Merle Curti, the beloved intellectual historian at University of Wisconsin in the 1960s, recalls: "His deep-seated commitment to American grass-roots democracy made a deep impression on me."[10] The idea that American democracy could be considered radical and revolutionary was precisely what Tocqueville had considered and rejected more than a century earlier. Moreover, Marx, a guiding mentor to the radical historians, had seen the development of wealth as an inevitable stage, one necessary for any country to realize its full economic potential before making the transition to socialism. Some radical historians, however, seemed to be desperately looking for episodes in the American past when the coming of wealth and bourgeois society was rejected, particularly by workers. Finally, the third tension: while historians looked to the past for guidance, Marx advised that we draw our "poetry" from the future; he proclaimed that the past, the scene of class oppression and unsuccessful struggle, is not all that inspiring. Yet the Marxist seeks to study the past in order to prove the existence of class conflict and thereby refute the liberal thesis of moral consensus. Hence an editor of a Marxist anthology of historical essays declares that the aim of history is "to recover past struggles in order to create a politics for the present," and that politics should be confrontational rather than integrationist, a daily posture of conflict with the system rather than a strategic immersion into it.[11]

The whole Marxist idea of a conflict between labor and capital rests more on philosophical speculation than on empirical fact. This is not to say that wealthy power elites would not, given the opportunity, exploit the working classes. In the *Federalist*, Americans were warned that all classes, the many as well as the few, would "vex and oppress" one another if left unchecked by institutional restraints. But in Marx's philosophy of history, derived from Hegel's dialectic of the struggle of opposites, we are taught that the conflicting struggle of economic classes is the driving force of history. Why?

"The Proletariat and Wealth Are Opposites"

It is more than baffling to read Karl Marx and be told that wealth is alienating rather than fulfilling: indeed, one does not know whether to laugh or cry. It reminds me of my own experience many years ago when the nuns used to tell me that seeking material happiness would endanger the salvation of my soul; hence, get thee to a seminary! Marx told generations of young students the same thing about the bourgeois life of comfort and pleasure. He did not claim that those who engaged in it would lose their soul; rather, he alleged that they would never find it, never be able to recover the "essential unity of man with nature."[12] Marx had no Adam and Eve myth to account for humankind's fall, but he remained absolutely certain that the very act that produced human alienation, coerced labor, would be overcome by the realization of a universe of free labor. The key to everything for Marx, as it is for many contemporary radical scholars who study working-class history, was labor. Today, if the study of the life of labor fails to yield to these scholars the reason why capitalist society continues to prevail, they shift from labor to culture in search of that reason, and, once discovered, reveal yet again to society how alienated it remains—from nature, from spirit, and from fellow human beings.

In Marx alienation arises with private property and the division of labor; estrangement comes between human beings and the products they make; and reification takes place when people begin to desire the products possessed by others, when what has been produced no longer has immediate use value but only impersonal exchange value. What comes to be prized is no longer work and production but money and consumption in a market system that obeys its own laws. Under such conditions the wage earner is not only exploited but more importantly experiences work as coercion rather than creation, in a process that makes humankind unable to relate to itself. Having lost freedom, having become alienated from itself, humanity's only solution is a proletarian socialism that will overcome the "icy water" of capitalist circulation-and-exchange economics that oppresses workers everywhere. Hence "the proletariat and wealth are opposites. . . . It does not suffice to proclaim them two sides of one whole," wrote Marx. Workers are "compelled to abolish" the rule of wealth in order to liberate themselves from their oppressors.[13]

To suggest that consensus rather than conflict explains American history is to hold that labor's only conflict with capital is its denial of a fair share of profits in a system in which the powerful prey upon the vulnerable. With Marx, however, profits themselves become the problem to the extent that the owners reap them and workers lust after them. Many members of the 1960s generation, at least those who emanated from the campus rather than the rock concert, were ecstatic over the discovery of Marx's "Economic and Philosophic Manuscripts of 1844." But the piece contains one of the most bizarre passages in modern social thought. Marx, after discussing Goethe and Shakespeare, explains why money must be repudiated precisely because it is power:

> Money's properties are my properties and essential powers—the properties and powers of its possessor. Thus, what I *am* and *am capable* of is by no means determined by my individuality. I am ugly, but I can buy for myself the most *beautiful* of women. Therefore I am not *ugly*, for the effect of *ugliness*—its deterrent power—is nullified by money. I, in my character as an individual, am *lame*, but money furnishes me with twenty-four feet. Therefore I am not lame. I am bad, dishonest, unscrupulous, stupid; but money is honoured, and therefore so is its possessor. Money, besides, saves me the trouble of being dishonest: I am therefore presumed honest. I am *Stupid*, but money is the *real mind* of all things and how then should its possessor be stupid? Besides, he can buy talented people for himself, and is he who has power over the talented not more talented than the talented? Do not I, who thanks to money am capable of *all* that the human heart longs for, possess all human capacities? Does not my money therefore transform all my incapacities into their contrary?[14]

Most economists see money as a medium of exchange and a preserver of value. Marx, more a moralist than a realist, saw it as alienating because it turned human beings into helpless creatures of desire driven by a Midas complex and a Faustian paradox: he who lusts after everything can enjoy nothing. On this stance Henry David Thoreau and other nineteenth-century romantic writers would agree. The problem is that Marx has no compelling theory of value with which to replace the capitalist system. Without that new theory, the entire Marxist project collapses, leaving historians researching the right people for the wrong reasons. Marx, to be sure, attributes all value to the act of labor. But his effort was less an empirical demonstration than a moral repudiation of an economic system that assumed, as did the people themselves, that in production one experiences only pain and in consumption one finds pleasures. Such a pervasive assumption implied that human beings work hard to obtain wealth in order to enjoy a freer and more fulfilling life apart from the field and factory. Abraham Lincoln believed in that assumption, as did W. E. B. Du Bois, the black radical scholar, and Andrew Carnegie, the white conservative industrialist. Karl Marx would have no part of it. Instead, he attributed all value to labor and viewed the productive processes of work as so fulfilling that alienation could be overcome and humankind could be at one with itself and with all others.

Was Marx, as Max Weber suggested, futilely trying to recover the handicraft economy of the Middle Ages, where labor was honored? Was he, as Thorstein Veblen suggested, confusing labor with spirit, and thereby hopelessly trying to reconcile English natural right with Germanic Hegelian teleology? Whatever the case, Georg Simmel would point out in *The Philosophy of Money,* labor alone cannot create value because "economic objects have no significance except directly or indirectly in our consumption and in the exchange that occurs between them."[15] Marx sought to locate value in production rather than in consumption because in his view, true, uncoerced labor expresses humanity's essence, whereas the capitalist world of exchange relations transforms people as they become mesmerized by the fetishism of commodities. Thus Marx draws upon Shakespeare's *Timon of Athens* to specify two properties of money:

> (1) It is the visible divinity—the transformation of all human and natural properties into their contraries, the universal confounding and overturning of things: it makes brothers of impossibilities.
> (2) It is the common whore, the common pimp of people and nations. The overturning and confounding of all human and natural qualities, the

fraternization of impossibilities—the divine power of money—lies in its
character as men's estranged, alienating and self-disposing *species-nature.*
Money is the alienated *ability of mankind.*[16]

The hostility toward wealth and money that boils over in Marx's
manuscripts has saturated the writing of American labor history, where
more time and space is spent on discussing workers' picnics than
union's profits.[17] Labor history declares its opposition to such economic matters by labeling them "possessive individualism" and "bourgeois self-interest." This history also tries to show how capitalism
brought about the "market disruption of the household economy";
how it transformed leisure "from a largely participatory to a mostly
passive, consumptive activity"; and how it "pierced an older ritual life
and set expectations" and, with women employed outside the home,
"helped to erode an earlier nexus of authority relations that ran from
community patriarchs down through workers' families."[18] The unquestioned premise of labor historians is that there once existed some
moral order and essential human nature that have been lost to change
and transformation.

Hence much of the teaching of history often treats the "pre-
modern" world as morally superior to industrial society. This dichot-
omy is a strangely nostalgic position to assume in an era when poststructuralism informs us that all assumptions about an essential natural state of existence are projections born of need and desire. The
strictures against wealth and money also miss the point that Locke and
Adam Smith had tried to make when they emphasized that such institutions brought humankind closer to one of its entitlements, the right
to happiness and security in possessing property. In liberal thought,
freedom means the development of individuality, the desire to grow
out of a static condition, and money makes possible the opportunity of
exercising free choice.

The possibility of freedom under capitalism has no place in the
Marxist scheme of things, where all work is seen as coercive, all human activity is subjected to the irrational forces of the market, and all
effort to get ahead is defeated by a profit system that denies the real
growers and producers the fruits of their labor. Marx had written his
early works on economics in the 1840s, shortly before Abraham Lincoln had to deal with questions of political economy. In Lincoln's

address to the Wisconsin Agricultural Society, delivered in 1859 (when Marx was expanding his thoughts on why capitalism results in the increasing impoverishment of the worker and why, therefore, private property begets its own negation), he denied both the primacy of capitalism and the suppression of labor. As one whose own father had hired him out to neighbors to work their land, Lincoln knew what it was like to be forced to work with little or no pay, and so, unlike Marx, he didn't imbue the act of labor with the magical ability to reconnect people to their true being. Labor to Lincoln was not an end in itself; rather it was a means to move beyond life's beginning conditions. But it is labor that creates value by adding something to the universe that did not exist before. Thus Lincoln rejected the notion of orthodox political economy that capital precedes labor, that savings must be invested before production can begin, and that "nobody works unless capital excited them to work." On the contrary, declared Lincoln, "capital is the fruit of labor, and could never have existed if labor had not *first* existed." Lincoln also rejected the Marxist notion that classes, once forged, remained barriers to human effort. The Civil War itself he saw as a contest between two cultures—one a closed, stratified environment where the few lived off the labor of the many, the other an open-class society where mobility follows industry. "There is not," Lincoln announced in his first annual message to Congress,

> of necessity, any such thing as the free hired laborer being fixed to that condition for life. Many independent men everywhere in these States, a few years back in their lives, were hired laborers. The prudent, penniless beginner in the world, labors for wages awhile, saves a surplus with which to buy tools or land for himself; then labors on his own account another while, and at length hires another new beginner to help him. This is the just, and generous, and prosperous system, which opens the way to all—gives hope to all, and consequent energy, and progress, and improvement of condition to all. No men living are more worthy to be trusted than those who toil up from poverty.[19]

While Lincoln and Marx may have shared a common sympathy for the plight of workers, the liberal and socialist perspectives diverge considerably on other matters, particularly social mobility and the legitimacy of honestly earned wealth. Once it is assumed that wealth is the enemy of the worker, it is not difficult to understand why Marxist

labor historians would grant the acquisition of wealth so little significance as an aspect of freedom and self-determination. Instead, these
social historians, when writing about workers in the past, focus on
virtue, community, family, and piety.

Workers and the Myth of a "Moral Economy"

The "consensus" historians of the 1950s took a hard look at
American history in the nineteenth century and saw developing "a
democracy of cupidity rather than a democracy of fraternity."[20] Such
judgments by Richard Hofstadter and Louis Hartz could only lead to
the conclusion that the story of American history is the story of emergent bourgeois liberalism. To the generation that followed the consensus school, the New Left of the 1960s, such a description had to be
refuted if anything new could be said about America. Yet in rewriting
the past, New Left social historians returned American historiography
to the condition from which the early Progressive scholars had tried to
free it. During the Jacksonian era, George Bancroft persuaded generations of nineteenth-century Americans that the spirit of freedom ani-
mates American history, that the people are sovereign and can do no
wrong to each other, and that the purpose of writing history is to justify
democracy to a world that had yet to accept it. This assumption that
freedom and justice are achieved by democratic action, and that such
action must struggle against some vague forces alien to the people
themselves, may be called neo-Bancroftian.

A long tradition of writing about the political environment of the
early Republic has continued to insist upon one theme: democracy as
deliverance from a supposedly false consensus about capitalism. Beginning more than a century ago in Bancroft's writings, especially his
address "The Office of the People"; continuing in Arthur Schlesinger
Jr.'s Pulitzer Prize–winning book, *The Age of Jackson;* then amplified
as "history from below" in Sean Wilentz's *Chants Democratic;* and,
more recently, seemingly coming from above in Charles Sellers's *The
Market Revolution*, readers have been told that the American people
wish to remain simple and virtuous, yet find themselves preyed upon
by economic forces that are alien to their very being. Reduced to its
simplest formulation, American history is portrayed as having no con-

sensus. In contrast to what Tocqueville observed when he emphasized the attitudes and preferences that people shared, our history is characterized by conflict and critical antagonisms among different classes, each holding different values. Such a formulation had been put forth in Vernon L. Parrington's *Main Currents in American Thought,* which depicted America divided at its core, with Jeffersonian idealism opposed to Hamiltonian materialism, the moral majority against the rapacious few.

It should be remembered that Alexander Hamilton and other founders did not believe America would be free of conflict, a reality implied in their use of the term "factions." What John Adams and others did deny, however, was that one class could claim to be morally superior to others, to stand for ideals higher than self-interest. It is that claim of basic moral equality that many of the new labor historians affirm with a vengeance. But the claim cannot necessarily be traced to Marx, who saw workers as victimized by the "Furies of interest," and it cannot be traced to liberal historians of the 1950s who, like Arthur Schlesinger Jr., saw all classes as interest-driven. Where, then, did the idea come from that "history from below" would turn up a saving moral sensibility, a critical self-consciousness that could be found nowhere else in modern society?

It arose from, among other places, the 1960s generation of student activists and their discovery of racism, their opposition to the Vietnam War, and the resulting identification with the poor and oppressed. During this decade, activists saw themselves as participating in what one member called a "movement of all the powerless and exploited." Tom Hayden, an organizer of Students for a Democratic Society, extolled the "consciousness of persevering through historical suffering," and he instructed radicals to "identify with all the scorned, illegitimate and the hurt." One civil rights leader even exalted those who showed the virtuous "strength of being poor."[21]

The urge to romanticize the down and out became irresistible to a generation that, in desperate opposition to the Vietnam War, looked to the poor and powerless to save America from its follies supposedly being carried out by "the power elite." That generation also discovered the writings of the British historian E. P. Thompson, who coined the term "moral economy" to insist that in pre-capitalist conditions workers treated one another with caring and respect. American historians now had an idea that they read into the life of workers in the past, an idea that had workers practicing among their ranks community and solidarity instead of competition, and regarding themselves as radical in their opposition to private property and the advent of industrial capitalism. Then, coming from an opposite direction, not from a Marxist but from the intellectual historian J. G. A. Pocock, the world of scholarship discovered classical republicanism, a body of thought that seemingly could be used for radical purposes because, at least in Pocock's formulations, republicanism historically stood opposed to the coming of commercial society.[22] Thus in recent scholarship we are asked to feast upon new ideas like "moral economy," "artisan republicanism," and "millennial democracy," as if those ideas had existed in the past and had actually inspired workers to behave in brotherly solidarity and resist the temptations of capitalism.[23]

In a desperate marriage of Marxism and republicanism, one historian tells us that Jacksonian workers not only partook of "artisan republicanism" but were "radical" in their "class consciousness and "egalitarian" in their "Painite" conviction[24]—quite a stretch since the pro-entrepreneurial Tom Paine himself was anti-republican, not as a form of government but in its much heralded resistance to commerce and its veneration of antiquity.[25] Another historian would have us believe that the "mythology of consensual capitalism renders incomprehensible the massive resistance that rallied around Andrew Jackson," claiming that those people who cheered when Jackson vetoed the re-chartering of the Bank of the United States were resisting the "market revolution" that was being imposed upon them against their democratic will. "Contrary to liberal mythology, democracy was born in tension with capitalism and not as its natural and legitimizing expression."[26] Both historians presupposed that democracy stood radically opposed to capitalism because workers enthusiastically supported the bank's demise. But that was the national bank. What about the local banks, where people had a better chance to get their hands on money?

Rather than juxtaposing democracy to capitalism, Jackson looked to what he called the "bone and sinew" of the country, specifically the laborers, farmers, and mechanics, to take capitalism away from the capitalists by decentralizing it in the states and local communities. In

light of the financial speculation that afterward spread like wildfire
under Jackson's own scheme of "pet" banks, the historian Eric McKitrick was right to observe the parallels between the greed of a Jacksonian psyche that hated banks but loved money and the "S&L" crisis
that followed Ronald Reagan's deregulation of monetary controls.[27]

Historians are fond of quoting Bancroft to dramatize Jacksonian
democracy as "the eternal feud between the house of Have and the
house of Want." But then it must be admitted that in the end the Democratic Party trailed after the Whigs in accepting as inevitable the coming of "a bourgeois Republic." A worker of the time is quoted as saying
that it is clear that the Whigs were out to "make the rich richer and the
poor poorer" and thereby serve their class interests. "But the Demo-
ocratics," the worker lamented, "what shall we say of them?"[28]

Actually, the question was answered almost perfectly by Theodore
Parker, the Boston theologian who asked for proof of democracy as
much as evidence of divinity. Can there be any real differences in a
two-party democratic system when, as John Stuart Mill put it, what one
party has in possession the other wants in expectation? Parker observed precisely this behavior in Jacksonian America. The Whig orga-
nizes around the dollar and "sneers" at lower classes, wrote Parker.
And the Democrat?

> The Democratic party appeals to the brute will of the majority; it knows
> no Higher Law. . . . There is no vital difference between the Whig party
> and the Democratic party; no difference in moral principle. The Whig
> inaugurates the Money got; the Democrat inaugurates the Desire to get
> money. That is all the odds. . . . There is only a hand rail between the two,
> which breaks down if you lean on it, and the parties mix. . . . A Democrat
> is but a Whig on time; a Whig is a Democrat arrived at maturity; his time
> has come. A Democrat is a young Whig who will legislate for money as
> soon as he has got it; the Whig is an old Democrat who once hurrahed for
> the majority—"Down with money! There is a despot! And up with the
> desire for it! Down with the rich, and up with the poor!" The young man,
> poor, obscure, and covetous, in 1812 was a Democrat, went a privateering
> against England; rich, and accordingly, "one of our eminent citizens," in
> 1851 he was a Whig.[29]

How can there be genuine class conflict when different classes
aspire to the same thing and thereby betray consensus in doing so?
Parker advised that the difference between parties and classes is so

thin that it would break if you leaned on it. Our contemporary historians, however, so emphasize the differences between classes that the
truth of social relations in a bourgeois culture cannot break through
the persuasive seductions of narratives. Hailing the late Herbert Gutman, one of the most influential historians in modern American history, a scholar who reoriented the study of labor history, the historian
Michael Kazin writes:

> Gutman's essays typically give the experience of hunger, unemployment,
> and government repression only a passing glance before they undertake
> their quintessentially populist mission—to demonstrate how the com-
> mon people had created, out of their ethnic traditions and dense net-
> works of kin and neighborhood relations, ideologies and institutions that
> the dominant classes could not destroy. For this frankly partisan histo-
> rian, the workers were invariably filled with a spirit of cooperation while
> their class opponents were ruled by ambition, the desire for profit, and an
> unshakeable belief in the rights of property.[30]

How do we know that workers had a culture distinct from that of
their class opponents? In the older labor history, scholars dealt with
shop conditions and wage negotiations, and scholars such as John
Commons concurred with Harry Bridges and Theodore Parker that
what one class has the other wants. But in the new labor history as
represented in such texts Alan Dawley's *Class and Community,* Paul
Johnson's *Shopkeeper's Millennium,* and Leon Fink's *In Search of the
Working Class,* we are told that workers of the past regarded themselves
collectively rather than individually, that they carried forward older
household economies of mutuality, that they looked to the community
as the fulcrum of struggle, and that there is no conceptual problem
with the idea of class if we regard it as a "process" in the act of formation. Nowhere to be found in such scholarship are statements by workers themselves that they have freely chosen the position in which they
find themselves, any indication that they aspire to a better life, or any
suggestion that they would gladly give up the life of labor for something more pleasurable and profitable. Imagine a coal miner coming
out of a shaft in the fields of Pennsylvania in the 1890s:

REPORTER: Do you see yourself as belonging to a class-conscious la-
    bor movement consisting in daily working-class struggle against
    capitalism?
MINER: No, not really. I'm part of a "process."

The entire edifice of labor history's thesis that American workers posed a challenge to consensus stands or falls on whether historians can define class—and further, whether they can articulate the ramifications of this definition for class consciousness and class conflict. But when something is described as a "process," thought ceases to explain, as language functions without an object in order to begin to appropriate and lay claim to knowledge with the deceptive simplicity of a linguistic act. The language of "process," as Nietzsche pointed out, is "directed not at knowledge but at taking possession of things. . . . One takes possession of the process (one invents a process that can be grasped)."[31] What labor historians do is take possession of a field or genre by giving names and concepts ("class," "moral economy," "mutuality," "solidarity," "artisan socialism," and so forth) both to create the impression of a process or movement (the new word is "moment") that most likely has no basis in any past reality and to give the working class an identity and consciousness that it did not bother to articulate for itself.

But when well-spoken working-class leaders do make clear what it is that labor wants, we can hear only the voice of consensus. On this issue Harry Bridges the communist and Samuel Gompers the conservative speak in one voice and no doubt speak for workers far more reliably than does the academic historian. "What does labor want?" asked Gompers. "We want more school houses and less jails; more books and less arsenals; more learning and less vice; more constant work and less crime; more leisure and less greed; more justice and less revenge."[32]

The Neo-Bancroftians

One would never know what labor wants from reading the new labor historians, who strain to read about every patriotic festival and cup their ears to listen for any chant of democracy and virtue. The neo-Bancroftians cannot bring themselves to believe that democracy itself might be the problem because it provides freedom for some at the expense of others, liberty for the majority to the detriment of the minority. If we were to disabuse ourselves of democratic cant we might better see how a Lockean sense of material reality, together with a Calvinist sense of sin, persisted in nineteenth-century society, when property could be both the basis of freedom and the reason for domination. Within the framework of democratic government, liberty and power remained dynamically active and interrelated as both the will to be free and the impulse to impose and exclude continued unrestrained by the language of politics.

Looking behind the democratic rhetoric of the Jacksonian era, one sees freedom expressing itself as the desire to take whatever the will wanted, as though the possession of power and property meant that politics would be the actualization of potential—rather than a dedication to principle, as in classical republicanism or in socialism. One sees this liberal acquisitive impulse in the legal ramifications over family inheritance; in the lands lived on by Indians and coveted by whites; in the forced labor expropriated from black slaves; in the activities of banks circulating money and controlling credit; in riverboat gambling and entertainers offering their talents as commodities to be sold at the best price; in western expansion and the claims made upon natural resources; in the "spoils system" that turned American politics into "the great barbecue" (Parrington's phrase); and in the American male's rule over wives and women, who were denied a Lockean challenge to patriarchal authority and the freedom to dispose freely of their own bodies and minds. A political culture founded on the right to property gave way to a mentality in which man assumed the right to hold property in man and in woman.

Many of these tendencies, especially the white workers' oppression of blacks and their domination over women, are embarrassing missteps in the story of democracy. The neo-Bancroftians of the Left assume with their nineteenth-century ancestors that democracy is the ultimate norm and hence that there can be no objective standard by which it may possibly be critical of itself. As with Bancroft, the radical school assumes that democracy is synonymous with freedom, that it values tolerance and aspires to justice, that it is both republican and radical and thus untainted by interest politics, and that only the villain (the capitalist, never the worker) would think of others as instruments for his own purpose. "Artisans," writes Sean Wilentz, in addition to advocating independence, "also shied away from endorsing the pursuit of self-interest for its own sake: each citizen, spokesmen explained, had to be able to place the community good before his own, exercising what they called, in classical republican style, virtue."[33]

Wilentz may have found in America the heroic image of the worker so romanticized by the poet Walt Whitman. Such an image, however, escaped Tocqueville, Emerson, Thoreau, Parker, Margaret Fuller, and numerous other writers who saw laborers as no different from other members of commercial society in leading lives of grasping desperation. Intellectuals of the era sympathized with the dignity of manual labor as much as they rhapsodized about the wholesomeness of agrarian life. But they saw workers as well as entrepreneurs in the grip of the same fears and hopes, as though they shared the same liberal consensus, the same ambivalence about desiring change and dreading revolution. Listen to Emerson on "The Superstitions of Our Age" (1847):

> The fear of Catholicism;
> The fear of pauperism;
> The fear of immigration;
> The fear of manufacturing interests;
> The fear of radicalism or democracy;
> And faith in the steam engine.[34]

Can we really believe that the Jacksonian worker had no interest in interest? Where the Jacksonian political culture "shied away" from advocating interest politics, so we are told, an earlier culture consisting of Madisonian and Jeffersonian temperaments, and Federalist and anti-Federalist politics, regarded interest as so inevitable that to deny it was to deny people and factions their basis of representation. According to the historian Gordon Wood, the Revolution "unleashed" so many different interest groups that no American felt shy about mouthing the following dictum of colonial society: " 'Self-interest is the grand Principle of all Human Actions' and 'it is unreasonable and vain to expect Service from a Man who must act contrary to his own Interest to Perform it.' "[35]

Labor historians labor under three delusions. First, they assume that if they can show workers deeply involved in family or community, categorize them in terms of ethnic identities, or reveal them practicing religion or civic politics, somehow "interest" disappears, as though it

rears up only in private economic activities and rarely in social engage-
ments. The idea that egotism is an impulse of only the private individual and not the public actor would have surprised Adam Smith, Adam
Ferguson, and other Scottish philosophers who saw capitalism as a social phenomenon involving reputation and the desire for approbation.

Equally dubious is the argument that a culture of capitalism could
not take place in the neighborhood or the farm until the community
broke down or until an external market arose to invite production for
profit and exchange (as opposed to subsistence and use).[36] On the
contrary, anthropologists have demonstrated that pre-modern societies value exchange, and an environment of community, such as labor
historians extol when they depict the bonds of neighborhood, is really
a situation of necessity that tells us nothing about freedom—that is,
what people would do if they wanted to and could do it. It was commercial society, not the labor historian's much vaunted "moral economy,"
that enabled the masses of people to escape the debasing dependency
relations of the past. As Adam Smith pointed out in his debates with
Jean-Jacques Rousseau, modern commercial society may not offer virtue and complete equality, but it is just and allows more people than
ever before to enjoy the freedoms that opportunity affords.[37]

The third delusion might be called the myth of origins. Historians
assume that if they can demonstrate a labor union starting out under a
radical banner of some version of socialism, then they have successfully disputed the thesis that America's political culture remained saturated by consensual liberalism. Yet there is a difference between a trade
union that failed in its organizational efforts and ones that succeeded
and left a record that can be scrutinized. The International Ladies
Garment Workers Union had its origins in European socialist and
anarchist doctrines. Once firmly established, garment and textile workers engaged in the same ethnic discrimination and exploitation that a
half-century earlier the union movement had theoretically opposed—
the only difference was that Jews and Italians were denying equal
opportunity to blacks and Puerto Ricans. That a union had radical
historical beginnings is no evidence that it behaved radically throughout history. The teamsters union was founded by Trotskyists, but ask
César Chávez about its conduct when it tried to seize control of the
Farm Labor Union in California.[38]

but inherent and systemic as labor union after labor union turned its back on black freedmen, native Americans, East Indians, peoples from southeast Asia, and others whose interests were neither recognized nor represented. Racial antipathy characterized not only conservative unions like the American Federation of Labor, which evicted blacks from jobs in mines and mills, but also the progressive Knights of Labor, which excluded Chinese workers in California, and even the revolutionary Industrial Workers of the World, which shut out Mexican workers in the Southwest.[43]

Nowhere was the phenomenon of an ethnic group coming to see itself as exclusively white more manifest than in the case of Irish immigrants in America. The more the Irish saw their situation as similar to that of blacks, having been denied the vote in Ireland and driven out of the country by famine, the more the Irish tried to identify themselves as white and thus different from the blacks and Mexicans who had been denied suffrage in America. Oppression itself creates oppressors: most of the downtrodden Irish refused to support either the abolitionists or open immigration. From the Civil War riots in New York City in the 1860s to the battle against busing and racial integration in Boston a century later, Irish Americans, according to some scholars, took their stand as a white race.[44]

The temptation to regard racism as a "construction" is irresistible to scholars on the Left for if racism is seen as such, then it is not an expression of human meanness, much less of evil and sin—which could be restrained by the religious and moral mandate to treat others as we would treat ourselves. On the contrary, these scholars present racism as a symptom of the condition that produced it, an arbitrary feature of the environment that must be radically transformed. The notion that what had been unconsciously constructed can be consciously deconstructed presumes that the mind can solve problems by knowing their origins. Such a presumption commits what Hayden White calls "the fallacy of historical self-consciousness," that is, the conviction that we can change the world simply by knowing how it has come to be, how it has affected us, and how we have constructed and produced it.[45] But why was racism constructed to begin with?

It is hard to deny that self-interest, (which is hardly a contingent, arbitrary phenomenon), as well as racial prejudice drove the Jackso-

"The Construction of Whiteness"

Years ago a scholar reviewing my book on the Left scolded me for criticizing a labor historiography that refused to deal with such unmentionable sins as racism, bigotry, racketeering, drunkenness, battered wives, abused children, sexually harassed waitresses. Apparently the working class has no bigots and no brutes, no Bull Connors and no Stanley Kowalskis.[39] Indeed, for a long time only the scholar Herbert Hill addressed the issue of racism in labor, to the chagrin of Herbert Gutman's disciples.[40] More recently, Stanford Lyman, David Roediger, and Alexander Saxton have uncovered the extent of exclusion and discrimination in the unions.[41]

But working-class racism has not been simply a matter of members of one ethnic group distinguishing themselves from others, particularly from blacks supposedly "below" them. Recent scholarship, especially that influenced by deconstruction and genealogy, claims that we can trace how social relations have evolved and thereby show how the "construction of whiteness" came to take hold of immigrant workers who feared and resented people of different colors. Once the genealogical basis of a given "social construction" is established, the historian is then prepared to deconstruct race identity as artificial and arbitrary—never as natural and inevitable. The same deconstructionist assault can be directed against any system of authority that results in hierarchies or any cultures where positions of subordination are regarded as part of the chain of being. Show me how hegemonic domination came to be produced as a "social construction," the theory goes, and I'll show you how such a formation is actually a "mutable" phenomenon that will someday disappear in a "withering away of whiteness."[42]

Such an approach to history makes racial hostility simply a matter of different people having different skin color. But as events in Africa and Northern Ireland indicate, people of the same race can behave brutally toward one another. Stalin and Pol Pot had no need to engage in social constructions to kill people of their own color. Nor was the "construction of blackness" needed when one African tribe enslaved another. If racist notions are simply constructions, they would be contingent and short-lived; they would disappear as conditions changed. In America, however, racism was not incidental or episodic nian Democrats' treatment of African Americans. The Democrats refused to allow the subject of slavery to be brought up in Congress, just as historians refused for years to address the issue of working-class racism. Historians who set out to prove the "radicalism" of American democracy are scarcely in a position to see freedom moving through a culture of democracy to gain power over others. That the supposedly virtuous artisan republican turns out to be a racist is less a belated discovery in historiography than a rediscovery of the older truth that he is an egotist who pursues interest and profit at the expense and exclusion of others. One can no more deconstruct whiteness than the *Federalist* authors could eliminate factions, and for the same reason: it points to a fundamental aspect of human nature, in this case the desire to acquire power and exclude others. But even if the passions and bigoted biases of humankind cannot be eradicated, they can be controlled.

The category of race, like that of class and gender, remains at the surface of life and cannot penetrate to the deeper and darker truths of history and human nature. Such categories are derivative rather than determinative; they express forms of behavior but cannot necessarily command motives of conduct or account for objects of desire. Often the categories are cited to explain why some people are excluded and others included. Yet exclusion, rather than being an act of racism, may very well be a basic aspect of the human condition, whether its roots lie in pride or in power: it goes on almost everywhere in life regardless of ethnic or class identity; it is nothing less than power expressing itself as it moves toward its object of control. And the formerly excluded can become exclusionist themselves. A close look at a campus now dominated by veterans of 1960s activism reveals whites excluding other whites in the name of democracy, authority, and political correctness.

What went on in race relations in nineteenth-century America cannot be explained if we continue to ignore America's Lockean political culture. The case of foreigners who sought to come to the United States in search of political freedom, economic opportunity, and social mobility and found themselves barred because of immigration laws serves to remind us that Hartz's idea of the American Revolution as the experience of migration is only half of the story. The treatment of non-white peoples by Americans, themselves of immigrant ancestry, represents part of the other half of the story, and it indicates why labor historians can write about success only with sadness, if not despair.

One key to how liberalism loses its heart to its stomach may be seen in the life of George Wilkes, as told by Saxton as "Mutations of Artisan Radicalism." Saxton correctly notes that the idea of equality did not rest with politics but moved on to economics as the desire for opportunity. "Equality, in its radical republican context," writes Saxton, "had meant that craftsmen and mechanics, even saloon-keepers, ought to have the same right as wealthy merchants and Hudson River landlords. But why should young white America rest content with political rights if access to wealth was equally part of its birth right?" Saxton describes Wilkes and others starting out as working-class radicals sympathetic to the plight of all workers, only to grow more elitist and racist as they came to believe in the cult of individual success. Eventually, Saxton laments, they turned away from Reconstruction, the Paris Commune, and workers of all ethnicities to take a stand for capitalism, the "business of the country."[46]

Such behavior had less to do with "artisan radicalism" than with modern liberalism, which prizes opportunity and achievement above all other political values. Saxton is simply describing America's fate as predicted in older consensus scholarship, but apparently he thought he could help America avoid that liberal fate by devising a new political vocabulary of "artisan radicalism." As the philosopher reminds us, however, and as Wilkes's life itself indicates, reality has the capacity to resist false linguistic representations. However Wilkes was described, or redescribed, he behaved as Locke had theorized and Lincoln had expected: he identified access to wealth with freedom.

Lincoln once observed, when defending banks and the system of loans and credits, that "it is pretty to see what money will do." No one was more passionate in his belief in the rights of workers than Lincoln, and he saw no basic conflict between capital and labor if an environment of open opportunity could be sustained. Lincoln saw, as did Tocqueville, what Marx completely missed seeing: that an environment that esteems labor will lead not to socialism but to capitalism.[47]

If white workers harbored racist sentiments against people of color and native Americans, we should not confuse the effect with the cause. The lust after someone's land and the wish to prohibit the competition of someone's labor spring from the same motive of self-aggrandizement and self-protection, which means only that if Lockean opportunity is present, Hobbesian fear cannot be far behind. The "social constructionist" interpretation of race relations assumes that the racist is a person whose true humanity has been repressed by the conditions of capitalism. But another way of looking at America's dreadful disgrace is that in nineteenth-century liberal democracy there was no authority sufficiently effective to prohibit racist behavior. Hence in 1838 young Abraham Lincoln had to make the trip to Springfield, Illinois, where nearby the abolitionist editor Elijah P. Lovejoy had been lynched, as well as many blacks, and call upon people to "swear by the blood of the Revolution, to never violate in the least particular, the laws of the country; and never to tolerate their violation by others."[48]

The quandary of American history is that democracy itself freed humankind from the bonds of authority that might possibly have mitigated the extent of racism. The same holds true for sexism. Whatever parity has been achieved for women and blacks has been a result not simply of democracy but also of the authority of law and the judicial system. There is no paradox between freedom and slavery when freedom presents the opportunity to enslave others. To conceive American history as the story of freedom alone is to present only half the story. Freedom is inseparable from power—the power to acquire and exclude, but also the power to rise up and participate. In this sense, power has eluded women as much as workers, even women of wealth. Why?

CHAPTER 9

Outside Demanding In: Women between Republicanism and Lockeanism

Human beings have *rights*, because they are *moral* beings; the rights of all men grow out of their moral nature; and as men have the same moral nature, they have essentially the same rights. These rights may be wrested from the slave, but they cannot be alienated. . . . Now if rights are founded in the nature of our moral being, then the *mere circumstance* of sex does not give to man the higher rights and responsibilities, than to woman.
ANGELINA GRIMKÉ TO CATHARINE BEECHER, 1836·

And what's her history?
A blank, my lord.
SHAKESPEARE, *Twelfth Night*

The Myth of "Republican Motherhood"

LIBERALISM, FAR BETTER THAN REPUBLICANISM OR Marxism, helps us to understand what Americans have done for themselves as individuals and as groups. One vast group, indeed a veritable majority, is women. In the academic world, the rise of women's history took place when the school of liberal consensus was being assaulted—thus that history has often been told in ways that obscure how liberalism might have set women free if it had been practiced as the universal principle that it was meant to be. For the history of women is inseparable from the Lockean liberalism through which it was to fulfill itself, no matter how its historians chose to express themselves. Black history, too, may be reinterpreted within the matrix of the same Lockean liberalism. The institution of slavery violated liberalism by depriving

African Americans of the right to free labor and property, thereby denying the natural law that all people ought to possess the means of their own self-preservation. And it was that same liberalism that provided the critique of plantation aristocracy as well as filial patriarchy.

When it comes to women's history, feminist scholars are determined to demonstrate that women in the past were by no means passive in, or absent from, the making of history, and that whatever the event in American history, women surely had a "role" in it.[1] No one today would write of women in American history the way Harvard president Charles Eliot described them a century ago. Of the majority of colonial women, he wrote:

> Generations of them cooked, carried water, washed and made clothes, bore children in lonely peril, and tried to bring them up safely through all sorts of physical exposure without medical or surgical help, lived themselves in terror of savages, in terror of the wilderness, and under the burden of a sad and cruel creed, and sank at last into nameless graves, without any vision of the grateful days when millions of their descendents should rise up and call them blessed.[2]

Such a bleak picture is a long way from the present portrait of women in American history. The new women's history rescues sisters of the past from their "nameless graves" and endows them with a sense of agency and identity. That women scholars would like to see things in ways that relate the past to the present is understandable. The demands of representation require establishing a presence for those who have been missing from the story. But no matter how much women of the past are now included in the present study of history, the real question is why they were excluded to begin with and why they accepted what was expected of them.

Were women better off after the American Revolution than before? Some historians argue that women enjoyed a high position in the eighteenth century, when the economy centered on the household and females took part in productive labor. Others argue that progress for women began only when they were free of ever-demanding household chores and had access to the public sphere. And for women scholars the public is always the political and rarely the economic—one possible reason why women made few advances until recent times, when they finally demanded entry into the world of business, law, medicine, and other professions. For historically the kind of "role" they were ready to accept in politics still required subservience. If women historians are right, women in the past desired to be virtuous republicans when they should have been, if I am right, assertive Lockeans.

For the past two decades the most discussed and debated idea in women's scholarship on the American Revolution is "Republican Motherhood" and its variations as "Liberty's Daughters" or "Republican Wife."[3] According to this body of scholarship, colonial women had high expectations that the Revolution not only would change the country's relationship with England but also would possibly give women a voice in public affairs. Whether or not the household became more egalitarian and the husband less domineering as a result of the Revolution remains unclear. It is acknowledged that divorce, property inheritance, and coverture (the laws governing the disposal of women's assets by her husband) changed little. Nevertheless, historians are happy to report that women found a new and improved position in taking on the task of teaching the youth of America, specifically "the role of guarantor of civic virtue."[4]

Women were assigned the task of upholding precisely what America had been abandoning, what could not be guaranteed, the idea of virtue that had failed to survive the Revolution itself and had been dismissed in the *Federalist* as an ancient and obsolete idea that "betrayed an ignorance of the true springs by which human conduct is actuated."[5] Even if the idea of civic virtue had survived, it is difficult to see how women would have benefited from it. If women had taken seriously the dictates of republicanism, they would have had to renounce their aspirations to equality, accept duty to the public as the highest priority, give up all notions of natural rights, and raise their sons to be warriors ready to die for their country. Ancient republics confined women to the *oikos*, the household, and that sphere went unchallenged in the history of republicanism. The most important thing you can do, Pericles said to the women of Athens, is as little as possible and thus not get yourselves talked about, "bruited on the lips of men." Republicanism in scholarship seems to have snookered women historians.[6]

The flowering of women's history has opened up new subjects seldom studied before: the culture of patriarchy, property law, child rearing, the domestic division of work, birth control, codes of courtship and bonds of love, impossible husbands and irresistible lovers (or vice versa), the story of single women, same-sex relationships, prostitution, free love, "the beauty myth" and the "new woman as androgyne," care work, philanthropy, factory inspection and protective labor legislation, social welfare, consciousness of self-perception, and so on. The reigning imperative is to show women in the past as active rather than passive, relatively independent if not completely free, involved, participating, and influencing, even if in the nineteenth century women were confined to separate "spheres," "roles," and "networks." With so much going on in women's lives, why did power elude them?

Could it be that women allowed themselves to be seduced by the politics of virtue and strove to be dutiful republicans when they might have considered trying to be defiant Lockeans? Reviewing the life of the reformer Dorothy Dix, the historian David J. Rothman writes that women were valued for being altruistic rather than assertive. "A woman would be accepted in the legislature's halls if she advocated the well-being of others and had no personal ambitions."[7] A contemporary of Dix, Sarah Josepha Hale, saw this situation as entirely normal. "Our men are sufficiently money-making," she wrote in a review of *The Frugal Housewife,* by the reformer and abolitionist Lydia Maria Child; "let us keep our women and children from the contagion as long as possible." "Hale's priorities are clear," wrote the literary historian Ann Douglas. "Male dollars must be ignored by female decorum; women should forget or at least appear to forget the sordid laws of acquisition and accumulation."[8]

Such attitudes persisted in American history, leaving many women with the conviction that their function in life is not to enjoy it but to change it. As dedicated reformers, women "had to fight for the right of fighting wrongs," observed the journalist Ida Tarbell.[9] In the nineteenth century a woman's choice of vocation involved moral duty rather than material ambition. Some of our contemporary historians have also sought to keep women in the past from the "sordid" contagion of money by focusing on politics at the expense of economics, only to wonder why politics fails to lead to power. Years later, the same historians often acknowledge that self-interest does so. Consider the odyssey of Ellen DuBois.

The Women's Movement and Feminism

In her pathbreaking study *Feminism and Suffrage,* DuBois, a professor of history at UCLA, comes close to staring political truth in the face but not close enough to perceive that women's beliefs blinded them to the realities of power. DuBois observes that women drew upon the Declaration of Independence and invoked the doctrine of natural rights as the basis of claiming political representation. DuBois also notes that the exclusion of women from public life rested on the assumption, prevalent in early American political culture, that wives and daughters lacked the independence necessary to vote their own will and judgment. Gordon Wood made winning freedom from dependency relations the essence of the American Revolution's "radicalism." But the legacy of '76 left women with neither freedom nor power, and the need to change their condition required them to become dependent not only upon one another but also on other political movements—abolitionism, temperance, the National Labor organization after the Civil War, and, with the feminists of the Greenwich Village era of 1912–18, the causes of socialism, anarchism, and pacifism. In all of these collective efforts women failed to win their own goals while vigorously supporting those of others. Earlier, with the passage of the Civil Rights Amendments, women had found themselves abjectly disfranchised; granting the vote to black men only made more emphatic their own exclusion from the Constitution. Why did power escape them?

DuBois offers two answers, both indicative of the difficulty of facing up to the limitations of democracy. First, DuBois tells us that the waning of the suffragist movement, and the divisions that fragmented the Equal Rights Amendment organizations, must be seen as "an aspect of the defeat of Reconstruction radicalism in general"—a curious explanation because radical Reconstruction, whether defeated or successful, had specified no place for women and their demand for rights and representation. Even more revealing is the historian's claim that the suffrage movement succeeded in teaching women some lessons about politics. "Activity in the women's suffrage movement itself did precisely what [Elizabeth] Stanton and others expected possession of the franchise to do as it demonstrated that self-government and democratic participation in the life of the society was the key to women's emancipation. Therein lie its feminist power and its historical significance."[10]

So presented, we are reassured that the "key" to power lies within the ideals and institutions of democracy itself. Actually democracy and power are mutually exclusive concepts; one waits on public opinion, the other moves independently of it. If we were to look at what was happening in the Fourteenth and Fifteenth Amendments to the Constitution, we might better appreciate why women, blacks—and, in many later instances, workers, dissidents, gays, abortion-rights advocates and other minorities having their own identities and interests— would have to circumvent democracy to realize some measure of power. Granting black Americans the rights and liberties guaranteed under due process was the first step (albeit, long deferred) in assuring that hitherto politically excluded Americans would have their freedoms protected by federal judiciary agencies, by courts rather than by Congress, by legal authority and not popular democracy. Yet many American historians naively continue to believe, like Bancroftians of the nineteenth century, that democracy is radically liberating and that if we are patient we will feel the progressive embodiment of reason working itself out through the will of the governed that radiates it.

Professor DuBois, however, has come a long way, all the way from republican idealism to liberal realism. In her recent essay "Making Women's History," written two decades after *Feminism and Suffrage,* DuBois distinguishes the older women's movement from modern feminism and, at last, she has found the true "key" to power:

> Whereas the women's movement stood for selflessness in the service of the cause, feminism stood for self-development as the route to women's emancipation. Whereas the women's movement rested on the principle of social purity, feminism went in search of female sexuality. Whereas the movement looked to the elevation of women collectively, feminism aspired to the liberation of individual women from social constraints, including those imposed by other women.[11]

It took women considerable time to become aware of value of Lockean liberalism, which makes self-development synonymous with conventional interest politics and puts women squarely in the consensus they had presumed to be battling with from the moment they entered the academic world. But has Professor Du Bois's important distinction between the women's movement and feminism any place in the writing of history standards for America's young students?

Women's History in the *National History Standards*

Many people have been left out of American history because of their non-western ancestry. Yet women have been left out of that same history despite having been born into a western culture that valued literacy, political rights, and the work ethic. The challenge of articulating women's history has stumped the best of minds. In *The Second Sex,* Simone de Beauvoir wrote seven hundred pages of excellent analysis, only to conclude that women had neither an event-making history nor a sense of sisterhood that transcended class and nation. But years earlier, in *Women as Force in History,* Mary R. Beard had insisted that the story of women could be found if students turned to hitherto unexplored sources. Beard also perceived that the fate of women depended upon the western idea of equality, and although she did discuss John Locke, she seemed unaware of Locke's role as the first philosopher to challenge the idea of patriarchy. But even with the legacy of Locke, which made women the rightful heirs to political rights, historiography written by men relegated the other sex to oblivion. Why this systematic exclusion of our mothers, sisters, wives, and daughters?

The obvious answer is that traditional history focused on politics, statecraft, wars and revolutions, the rise and fall of empires, the formation of government—in short, the spectacle of forces struggling for dominance and those leaders capable of transforming such events into history. Such is not the stuff of social history: even Catherine the Great, a woman leader, becomes troublesome because "greatness" itself has become suspect. In explaining how women have had no significant place in the "master narratives" of history, the new social historians seldom address the question of power but instead turn to rhetoric and its representations.

The current explanation of the absence of women in history blames the very function of re-presenting: using poststructuralist theory, historians insist that past linguistic representations rendered women out of sight and hence out of mind. Mistaking the effect for the cause, these scholars conclude that the absence of women was a matter of rhetorical strategies rather than power realities, and that the notion of gender is a construction waiting to be deconstructed. It is curious that American women have seized upon the writings of the French deconstructionists and have turned to masculine constructions to find out about female constraints. "The woman who is known only through a man is known wrong," warned the historian Henry Adams, the hero of Mary Beard's book. The lost status of women perplexed Adams, who once authored the little-known address "Primitive Rights of Women." Adams questioned the commonly held view that marriage originated in purchase or capture and the cult of patriarchy that subordinated women throughout history. His belief in sexual equality could hardly be based upon his skepticism of democracy; instead he sought to redefine feminine dignity in nature itself. "The idea that she was weak revolted all of history," he observed of the opposite sex; "it was a paleontological falsehood that even a Euocene female monkey would have laughed at." Yet history complicated matters. "Women had been supreme," he wrote in the *Education*: "in France she still seemed potent, not merely as a sentiment but as a force; why was she unknown in America?" At a dinner one evening Adams turned to the person next to him and asked whether there is a possible explanation as to why "the American woman was a failure." Without a moment's hesitation, she shot back: "Because the American man is a failure."[12]

Adams knew that history is the study of power and the play of forces that seek to possess it. Such an approach to history is by no means a masculine monopoly, as indicated in the writings of Antonia Fraser, Jeane Kirkpatrick, and Selya Benhahib. But the field of women's studies and the new social history that have shaped the *National History Standards* pay attention only to the distaff side of Adams's family.

Did the American Revolution affect the status of women? The standards ask students to "draw upon diaries, letters, and historical stories to construct a narrative concerning the daily lives of men, women, and children affected by such wartime developments as the participation of men and women in the front lines; [and] the need for women and children to assume men's roles in managing farms and urban business." They are also asked to "analyze how women's quest for new roles and rights for their gender" can be seen in Abigail Adams's well-known letter of 1776 to John Adams:

> Remember the Ladies, and be more generous and favourable to them than your ancestors. Do not put such unlimited power into the hand of husbands. Remember all Men would be tyrannts if they could. If particular care and attention is not paid to the ladies we are determined to foment a Rebellion, and will not hold ourselves bound by any laws in which we have no voice, or representation.[13]

But can one present this single letter as emblematic of "women's quest for new roles and rights"? According to Edith B. Gelles's biography, *Portia,* there is no evidence that the would-be First Lady had such intentions. "Abigail," writes Gelles, "disapproved of women who breached the prevailing code of female behavior."[14] If Abigail was not advocating new roles and equal rights, and hence was no precursor of modern feminism in questioning motherhood and wifehood, what was poor John to remember when he was asked to remember the ladies?

When female scholars remember women, they do so primarily through social history, a genre in ascendancy in the 1970s, when most of today's academic women entered graduate school. To concentrate heavily on the social is to privilege the ordinary over the exceptional, and hence women's historiography looks to "group consciousness," "separate spheres," "public space," "engendered selves," "social networks," and "discourse analysis" to demonstrate that women had a role in history—in areas such as the household in the colonial era and, with the beginnings of the industrial revolution, in textile factories and other workshops. The challenge, it seems, is to show above all that women were active rather than passive, intensely involved in this task and that duty. Women's unwaged domestic labor and remunerative work outside the household contributed to America's historical development, and thus mundane chores were no less important than masculine actions in the making of history. Such an emphasis also has political implications. Note this question from the *National History Standards:*

Construct a historical narrative using selections from a variety of primary
and secondary sources to analyze reasons for the strikes at Lowell in 1834
and 1836. *How did women use community bonds to mobilize protests in times
of crisis? Did the Lowell example influence others?*[15]

To teach young students that women in the past were able to be
effective through collective organization and action is certainly legitimate. But one of the aims of the *National History Standards* is
to address "historical-issue-analysis and decision-making" as people
confront specific problems involving "choices," "consequences," and
"core values." Unless the historian can show that options other than
collective action were available to young Lowell women, it is difficult to
see how the responsibilities of citizenship can be taught by studying
those who may have had almost no opportunity to express their own
preferred values and identities. In environments where the experience
of choice cannot be said to have existed and considerations of value
could hardly have been an option, "community bonds" may have been
formed out of necessity. Unless one is a Hegelian, necessity is scarcely
the best basis from which to teach the nature of freedom, which takes
on meaning and value only when it is chosen.

Given the utter neglect of women's history in the past, the amount
of attention devoted to it today is understandable. But sometimes the
overcompensation is a little silly. In the recently published *Companion
to American Thought,* George Kennan is given one brief paragraph
while Florence Kelley, a nineteenth-century reformer, is given three
full pages. Ultimately, however, it is not the allocation of space in print
that is the problem with women writing about women. The problem
lies in their theoretical floundering in radical categories of thought
that possibly preclude women from naming the problem that has no
name—the problem of freedom and its inextricable relation to power.

Throughout the *National History Standards,* students are continually asked to examine the "role" that women played in a given episode
in the past. This emphasis on role acting helps us understand that we
are creatures of society's expectations. In feminist theory the idea of
becoming aware that the self is socially constituted is liberating in that
gender can now be seen as something constructed rather than as an
essential aspect of nature. Since women as a social creation are "constituted discursively," the task of the historian, advises Joan Scott, is

"to interrogate the processes of their creation."[16] One would think, then, that women would partake of an Emersonian view of the self as "aboriginal," with the potential to be self-reliant and as autonomous as possible. But the idea of a self-made woman capable of resisting determination from without is anathema to feminist history.

Thus, whether it is because feminists see the individualistic self as "bourgeois" and too close to capitalism, or whether they prefer to see women in the past acting through groups as a source of strength, in the standards action is always presented in a given social framework, and women appear to be compelled to engage in life collectively. Such an approach to history, wherein human acts take on meaning only by externally referring them to society, may be incompatible with the *National History Standards'* goals of teaching "political intelligence" and the values of freedom. As François Furet has emphasized, "political history is primarily a narrative of human freedom" involving "the thought, choice, and actions of men—primarily great men. Politics is the quintessential realm of chance, and so of freedom." Social history, in contrast, deals with patterned structures and roles, often so determining that "society speaks and acts autonomously. According to this view, social agents simply enact their society's rules of operation and reproduction without knowing that they do so, and enjoy no other freedom than the possibility of entertaining the illusion of freedom."[17] Or, as Denise Riley put it in *"Am I That Name?": Feminism and the Category of "Women" in History,* to treat women as a social phenomenon carries many of the same deterministic implications as treating gender as an aspect of nature. In the past not only biology but society, too, Riley notes, "horribly circumscribed" women as a fixed category.[18] In *Three Guineas,* Virginia Woolf describes society as a "conspiracy": "You shall not learn; you shall not earn; you shall not own."[19] Does such a female mind need to be told that she has been "constituted discursively"? Must women be reduced to a role?

It seems that the role-stuck role that women are to play in the history standards deals more with the older women's movement than with modern feminism, more with social duty than individual opportunity. There seems to be a contradiction not only between what students are to value and what they are to learn, but also between past knowledge and present needs. Because youths going to school today do so to become educated, presumably for some vocation other than manual labor, one can only wonder why the new social history concentrates on factory work and the habitual routines of daily life. When one considers that most advances by women in American history have been made by virtue of institutions, especially the Constitution and its equal protection of the laws and civil rights mandated by the courts, one would think that women historians would emphasize political institutions as much as social relations. Moreover, with little attention to events, social history seems indifferent to change, progress, and some kind of achievement that can distinguish the dominant from the dominated. Reigning unquestioned, social history could quell a young woman's imagination.

Women's history only betrays its servitude to men's history by continuing a common disdain against all that is exceptional and outstanding. Consider what students could learn if the new social history allowed intellectual history to have a voice of its own, if it gave women a place in the American mind, particularly women who could do as they chose and were "great" precisely because they dared to be different.

It was a woman who first discerned the logical contradictions of Calvinism (Anne Hutchinson); who first portrayed the American Revolution in verse and drama (Mercy Otis Warren); who first brought Goethe to America (Margaret Fuller); who first assaulted plantation slavery by allegorizing it (Harriet Beecher Stowe); who first saw the implications of evolutionary biology for the female sex (Charlotte Perkins Gilman); who first wrote a Flaubertian novel on the silk cage of domesticity (Kate Chopin); who first earned a living as an author (Hannah Adams) and a million dollars as an entertainer (Lotta Crabtree); who first poeticized the "soft eclipse" of women by the requirements of wifehood (Emily Dickinson); who first made us aware of the environment's ecological fragility (Rachel Carson); who first appreciated modern art (Gertrude Stein), supported it (Peggy Guggenheim), and turned it into landscape realism (Georgia O'Keeffe); who first turned to music to make Parisian society swing (Josephine Baker), bring tears from the soul (Bessie Smith), and make an aria vibrate with the beauty of black spirituality (Leontyne Price); who first went back beyond modern America to understand human relations (Margaret Mead); and, most relevant to our subject, who first showed us that the American

Revolution succeeded because it had no need to address the "social question" of human misery and class oppression (Hannah Arendt).

The Idea of "The Public Sphere"

Perhaps as part of their effort to revere the ordinary woman of the past and to center her history in the social realm, much of the recent social history turns away not only from Lincoln but also from Margaret Fuller, assigning priority to women's role in politics and the mystique of republicanism and civic activity. Lincoln believed that America's formative political culture freed up the possibility of life beyond politics— a life of economic enterprise and individual pursuits—whereas Fuller saw herself as an intellectual with a mind devoted to minds, and she favored a life of revolutionary heroics to the routine procedures of democratic politics. Both Lincoln and Fuller esteemed the Declaration of Independence, and each felt disappointed in an America that failed to uphold its ideals. But what are those ideals? What followed from the American Revolution was not the imperative of "participatory democracy," to use the language of the New Left, but the impulse to ambition, opportunity, and industry. Lincoln grasped the uniqueness of America, its exceptionalism in breaking away from the Old World's commitment to dynastic succession, ethnic affinity, and religious community. When he invoked "liberty to all," he meant not only political rights but specifically *"enterprise,* and *industry* to all."[20]

Many women scholars are reluctant to listen to Lincoln's advice. No doubt women were excluded from enterprise and industry in American history as a matter of course, but they were also excluded from politics and government. Yet why the turn to one institution and not the other? The answer is that the 1960s generation galvanized around politics as a daily passion, and when that New Left generation became the Academic Left, it continued to regard politics—particularly democratic politics as opposed to economic liberalism—as radically emancipatory and resistant to capitalist individualism because it involves the civic and the public.

Historically women did participate in America's economic development not only by running farms and taking care of household chores but as entrepreneurs, managers, and salespersons, even when they suffered from a shortage of capital and no access to credit and loans. Women frequently operated boardinghouses, taverns, and inns, organized theater groups, and started publishing ventures, particularly women's magazines like the influential *Woman Banker*. Black women sold hair care products on commission, and Jewish immigrant women ran corner groceries or sewed dresses. Closer to our time, educated, professional women have successfully entered the corporate world, although frustrations at not having reached top executive positions may be due to the "glass ceiling" or the "mommy track," skeptical attitudes about women's abilities, doubts about their ultimate commitment, or perhaps simply male jealousy. The world of enterprise, innovation, risk, and profit is far from alien to American women.[21] Yet academic feminists regard business as a private affair and far removed from the redeeming public sphere and "civic space."

The notion that democracy springs to life in the civic space came to America by way of Germany, a fitting locale for the Bancroftian tradition, which also drew its romantic interpretation of history from German philosophy. The theory of the "public sphere" was first formulated by Jürgen Habermas, the neo-pragmatist political philosopher who believed that democracy requires certain social conditions—such as public conversation that takes place openly, freely, and without coercion—to fulfill its supposedly normative ideals. Yet as a pragmatist, Habermas, like John Dewey earlier, has no patience with the republican dialectic of "interest" and "virtue," or the idea of *auctoritas*, or any classical idea that aimed to discipline desires instead of realizing them. To the pragmatists the world becomes known to us only through our needs and interests, which makes pragmatism a logical extension of Lockeanism rather than republicanism, in which private interests are to be subordinated to the general good, or Marxism, where the "Furies of interests" represent the irrational state of "prehistory" that is to be overcome. Yet women would never deign to see themselves as Lockeans for fear of being identified with the liberal consensus that they think they are overthrowing.

Thus the idea of the "public" resonates to the feminist scholar, who remembers only too well that the historical status of women had been confined to the private domestic sphere. But how do women act when they enter the public sphere? Do they not, in fact, reveal themselves

to be Lockeans? The notion of participation rights is as much republican as liberal, but republicanism, in contrast to liberalism, calls upon
citizens to rise to virtue and civic duty by subordinating their interests
to the *res publica*, "the affairs of men." How do women historians
handle this classical demand, which even the founders had thought
preposterous?

In her essay "Gender and Public Access: Women and Politics in
Nineteenth-Century America," Mary Ryan, professor of history at the
University of California, Berkeley, reminds us that Habermas's theory
of democracy had no place for women historically until women had
pushed themselves into the forefront of American politics. But note
the reluctance with which she "shies away from" (the phrase Sean
Wilentz used when he, too, dealt with what he wanted to deny) endorsing Lockean self-interests, even though women in the past had to
privilege the reality of their own well-being in order not to be taken in
by the language of masculine politics:

> The history of women in and on the way to the public sphere suggests
> that the notion of interests and identity need not be antithetical to the
> public good. From the vantage point of women's history, the identifica-
> tion of a political interest of one's own was not a fall from virtue but a step
> toward empowerment. Because the second sex, like many marginalized
> populations, was socially dependent on their politically dominant supe-
> riors, their empowerment necessitated the construction of a separate
> identity and the assertion of self-interest in practice, inclusive representa-
> tion, open confrontation, and full articulation of social and historical
> differences are as essential to the public as is a standard of rational and
> disinterested discourse.[22]

Where the *Federalist* authors had wisely concluded that no faction
would be able to stand above its own interest to consider the public
good, Ryan invokes the idea of "differences" in order to endow women
with such attributes so that we are assured that seeking power and
interest by no means represents a "fall from virtue." Why do women
allow themselves to be taken in by language that historically has en-
trapped them? Nietzsche warned that those who see themselves as acting virtuously become a victim of their own pretensions. Hence "one
is best punished for one's virtues." The woman's mistake, George
Bernard Shaw wrote, "is doing things for reasons instead of finding
reasons for what she wants to do."[23] What, then, did she want to do?

Historically women have been asked to serve society's needs, and elite women's colleges like Smith and Wellesley were established in the late nineteenth century to prepare young girls for adult vocations. Rarely were such vocations in business or politics. Instead female doctors went into public health, lawyers into social work, liberal arts graduates into librarianship or teaching, and social scientists into factory inspection and urban reform. Perhaps such low-status occupations were fulfilling to some women, but they were far from empowering. The older feminists rejected considerations of power and professional ambition because they saw themselves as accountable to society. The new feminist scholars seek to see women in the past as they see themselves. Is this possible? "One of the new feminism's weaknesses," writes Melissa Benn, "is that it tends to subscribe to a trickle-down theory of political life, a belief that the forward march of some women is good for all women."[24] In the public sphere, the historian Ryan would have us believe that virtue cohabits with power and that interest politics need not be regarded as "antithetical to the public good." Looking into the mirror of politics, liberalism refuses to see its own face.

A Marxism for Mothers

Some women historians cannot resist the temptation to make a virtue out of a necessity. Consider the Yale historian Nancy Cott and her book *The Bonds of Womanhood*, which played an important part in pioneering feminist scholarship. Cott reports that the nineteenth-century notion of "separate spheres" relegated acquisitive self-interest to men out in the world and dutiful self-denial to women inside the home. She even quotes from Marx's essay on "Alienation" to reinforce the point that the household provided a refuge from the world of estrangement and reification that afflicted male workers. "The worker," Marx wrote in 1840, "feels at ease only outside work, and during work he is outside himself. He is at home when he is not working and when he is working he is not at home." Cott acknowledges that the cult of domesticity fell short of directly challenging capitalism and its discontents. Nevertheless, in her view, "the values of domesticity undercut opposition to exploitative pecuniary standards in the work world," instilling a different morality of "self-control" and responsibility in which the home served as the "haven in a heartless world." This *"cri de coeur* against modern work relations" led the wise and wry law professor Joan C. Williams to call women's sphere "a Marxism you can take home to mother."[25]

Presumably, then, work in the kitchen and the nursery was fulfilling rather than alienating. But why should women's work in the house be regarded as more wholesome than men's work in the factory and the field or, more recently, in the office? Is washing diapers more satisfying than brokering dividends? Simone de Beauvoir was fond of saying that women are not born but become such as society and custom shape their image. In recent historiography, women scholars have allowed republicanism to shape a role for sisterhood and Marxism to provide its identity—both of which are defined inside the house, even if it be *A Doll's House.*

What values do women, and others at the margins of power, insist on that supposedly make their politics so different from liberalism? Poststructuralist feminists such as Joan Scott have emphasized gender differences and the politics of identity as though such "conflicts" actually threaten "consensus" history:

> RADICAL HISTORY REVIEW: Let's go back to women's history and gender. What has been its impact on history?
>
> JOAN SCOTT: That's a large question. I think it has several answers. Women's history has clearly had an impact; it's raised many questions about the adequacy of historical narrative, standard courses in the university curriculum. Like African-American history, gay history, labor history, various ethnic histories, women's history points up the need for new ways of thinking about how historical knowledge is produced. All these "other" histories create a crisis for liberal pluralism.[26]

Women's history does indeed compel us to ask how historical knowledge in the past was produced in ways that neglected so many subjects. But Scott shares a widespread impression that the advent of women's history and all the "other" histories pose a threat to liberal pluralism. How can that be? Are not the advocates of such subjects merely repeating the pattern of liberal pluralism, continuing what was once called, in the Progressive era, "pressure group interest politics"? Those who write for such journals as *Radical History Review* may continue to delude themselves by claiming that their academic programs are revolutionary. The truth is that activists of the 1960s, frustrated about their inability to overthrow the "system," were content to infiltrate it and enjoy its benefits. Higher education has become a series of fragmented fiefdoms in which each department or program does its own thing. And new departments and programs are established for the same reason that Willie Sutton robbed banks: that's where the money is.

Joan Scott is the most philosophically daring of women social historians. Yet her theoretical positions of deconstruction announce a brave new methodology only to have it self-deconstruct. Scott goes so far as to advocate poststructuralism as a methodological means to reach democracy as a political end, without sensing the tension between the two ways of thinking about politics. How can one think as a poststructuralist and see only domination and at the same time promise that democracy, the American political paradigm for over two hundred years, shall deliver us from this domination? Meanwhile, Professor Ryan believes that the entry of women into the public sphere was in keeping with democracy and its alleged egalitarian ethos. Why? Because "demands for public access by once marginalized groups, or insurgent social movements, serve over time to accumulate and expand the rights of all citizens."[27]

After discovering how the abolitionists and labor movements kept women's demands at bay, one is perplexed to hear that the politics of the once-outsiders opens itself up to those further outside the sphere of power and influence. What women's history represents, when shed of its feminist hesitations about giving up "virtue," is the individualist demand for equal rights and access to power positions—a demand that continues the liberal tradition as an unending pursuit to expand, appropriate, and subjugate whatever stands in its way. Like men on the outside, women too had to say "me" oftener and louder than the majority.[28]

Yet some women historians regard individualism as the political disease that afflicts men only. Linda Kerber, a former president of the Organization of American Historians, declares that "the classic statements of American individualism are best understood as guides to masculine conduct."[29] This point may be true historically, but such an assertion repeats a fallacy that seems to be everywhere in scholarship: that egoism expresses itself only through the actions of individuals looking out for themselves, while the ego disappears when groups march together making collective demands. The desires of the "I" are elevated to the wants of the "We." Carol Gilligan's thesis that women have a different moral sensibility than men in their capacity for more connected relationships may or may not be entirely valid. But women cannot at the same time choose to become mired in a politics of difference and complain that history has left them behind. The moral sensibility that Gilligan describes has gone unrewarded in America's culture. It is only when women begin to move ahead politically, and especially economically, only when they take individualism seriously, that gender distinctions start to disappear.

Women's feminist history differs little from men's labor history in that both needed more than democracy to realize their respective ends. "Like aggressive men alive to their own interests," wrote Herbert Croly, "the laborer soon decided that what he really needed was not equal rights, but special opportunities." In order to contend with the power of big business, labor had to go around democracy and seek the authority of the state. "The labor unions, like the corporations, need legal recognition; and this legal recognition means, in their case, also, discrimination by the state in their favor."[30] Croly wrote these words in 1909. Today preferential treatment from the state is the mother's milk of identity politics. What older liberal consensus historians saw as a "democracy of cupidity" has become a democracy of hypocrisy to the extent that it does not recognize itself for what it is—a politics of disparate demands on the part of various groups who claim victimization in order to be entitled to some advantage over others. Once we disabuse ourselves of the rhetoric of "radical" republicanism and democracy, we can see why the egotism of liberal interest politics simply puts on a collective face and proceeds to request that the legal system mandate retributive justice on the basis of gender, class, or race. Such a strategy is the culmination of the older cupidity by newer means.

Today affirmative action programs have been criticized as a violation of the country's historical principles of democracy and equality.

Yet as Croly's observations make clear, and as Nietzsche and Weber anticipated, democracy itself, to the extent that people participate in its processes, results in escalating demands on the part of groups seeking benefits by whatever claims prove effective. The irony is that this new form of "clientelism" returns America to the very system of patronage that the Revolution was supposed to have extirpated.

CHAPTER 10

Black America and the Liberal Tradition

"Doomed to Subjection"

IF SUCCESSFUL AMERICAN FEMINISTS TURNED OUT TO be Lockeans who valued interest, power, self-development, and professional opportunity as much as parenting and domestic responsibility, one wonders if ambitious, achieving African Americans might also reveal a Lockean sensibility. Do black Americans constitute a separate culture or are they too part of the liberal consensus?

In the pre–Civil War era many suffragists likened their position to that of freed blacks who also were denied citizenship and the vote; occasionally they even identified with slaves themselves. The abolitionist and suffragist movements had much in common. Both blacks and women resented their subordinate status and saw themselves as enslaved and "degraded" by the deprivations surrounding their lives. Elizabeth Cady Stanton believed that both freed blacks and white women suffered from the same experience of humiliation to the extent that they could be well-off and cultivated and still feel the sting of "invidious distinctions." She singled out Robert Purvis, a Philadelphia black who, despite his wealth and learning, experienced "the humiliation of color" that brought on "ever-recurring indignities in daily life."[1] It may have been this common experience that led Frederick Douglass to regard his identification with the suffrage movement as an act of pure idealism. "When I ran away from slavery," he wrote, "it was for myself; when I advocated emancipation it was for my people;

but when I stood up for the rights of women self was out of the question, and I found a little nobility in the act."[2]

Certainly white women had no experience of the intimidation, fear, and sufferings endured by slaves. Yet many women could feel with the black race the dread of dependency and the desire for autonomy. They could also resent being told that their condition in the scheme of things was unalterable. Attitudes in the press indicated that some American opinion makers knew nothing of Locke's refutation of Filmer and thus continued to regard patriarchy and white supremacy as natural. "How did women first become subject to man as she now is all over the world?" asked the *New York Herald* in 1852. "By her nature, her sex, just as the Negro is and always will be, to the end of time, inferior to the white race, and, therefore, doomed to subjection."[3]

Angelina Grimké, writing to Catharine Beecher in 1836, understood well the actual liberal concept that rights belong to human beings as part of their species as moral creatures. "The investigation of the rights of the slave has led me to a better understanding of my own," she instructed.

> I have found the Anti-Slavery cause to be the high school of morals in our land—the school in which *human rights* are more fully investigated and better understood and taught, than in any other. Here a great fundamental principle is uplifted and illuminated, and from this central light, rays innumerable stream all around. Human beings have *rights*, because they are *moral* beings: the rights of all men grow out of their moral nature; and as men have the same moral nature, they have essentially the same rights. These rights may be wrested from the slave, but they cannot be alienated; his title to himself is as perfect now, as is that of Lyman Beecher; it is stamped on his moral being, and is, like it, imperishable. Now if rights are founded in the nature of our moral being, then the *mere circumstance* of sex does not give to man the higher rights and responsibilities, than to woman. To suppose that it does, would be to deny the self-evident truth, that the "physical constitution is the mere instrument of moral nature." To suppose that it does, would be to break up utterly the relations of the two natures, and to reverse their functions, exalting the animal nature into a monarch, and humbling the moral into a slave; making the former a proprietor, and the latter its property. When human beings are regarded as moral beings, *sex*, instead of being enthroned upon the Summit, administering upon rights and responsibilities, sinks into insignificance and nothingness.[4]

Grimké's letter is replete with rights axioms. Even though she may not have read Locke (her Christian-Calvinist sensibility was close to the philosopher's and may otherwise account for their likemindedness), she possessed a Lockean grasp of the idea that rights are inalienable. Rights may be "wrested" from slaves and women, but neither would voluntarily surrender the most basic right, the right to life and self-preservation. All people have an essential nature, she wrote in another letter; race, like sex, is only an "incident," not an essence, and hence all people enjoy the right to have rights.[5]

Such sentiment flowered shortly after the American Revolution, particularly in the North. With the natural-rights philosophy of the Declaration in mind, reformers began to demand that state laws protecting slavery as property be repealed. Between 1780 and 1804, legislation providing gradual emancipation passed in New York, Connecticut, and Pennsylvania. But the impetus to free the slaves died out, and with the Haitian uprising of 1800, many in the North as well as the South chose to look the other way whenever the subject of slavery came up. Even former president John Quincy Adams, who fought the fugitive slave law, had to be talked into defending the survivors of the *Amistad* uprising, in which Africans seized their slave ship and murdered its officers before being captured by the American navy and returned to New England for trial. After many legal battles, the Supreme Court ruled that the *Amistad* uprising did not constitute mutiny because the ship had originally been sailing illegally to a Spanish port in America in violation of the ban on international slave trade. The Africans were declared free and they sailed back to their homeland.

Slavery: "Our Republican Robe Is Soiled"

In recent years the subject of slavery has become one of historiography's most discussed and analyzed subjects. It was not always that way. In the early nineteenth century only abolitionists, particularly those who felt the fire of religious conscience, dared to bring up the subject publicly. Politicians, especially Democrats, suppressed the subject in Congress, and even many white intellectuals spent more time poeticizing about the beauties of nature than pondering humanity's inhumanity to its own species. But the subject anguished Abraham Lincoln. "Our Republican robe is soiled," declared Lincoln in reference to the existence of slavery. He reminded Americans that their ancestors were so ashamed of the institution that they had ignored it in their founding document. "Thus, the thing is hid away in the constitution," he observed, "just as an inflicted man hides away a wen or a cancer, which he dares not cut out at once, lest he bleed to death; with the promise, nevertheless, that the cutting may begin at the end of a given time."[6]

America almost bled to death in cutting out the cancer of slavery. The Civil War cost some 620,000 lives, and the Emancipation Proclamation of 1863, coming in the midst of the war, came as a surprise that left the status of black-white relations more complex than ever and racism more rampant. Many historians of the late nineteenth century chose to suppress both the subject of slavery and discussion of the plight of free blacks in the aftermath of the war, a war that itself came to be regarded as a mistake brought on by a "blundering generation" of politicians. When the Civil War reemerged in recent scholarship, the subject of slavery, not only in America but throughout the world, seemed not contingent and incidental but fundamental to the tragic story of humankind.

An early study that has been rediscovered and raised to the status of a seminal thesis is Eric Williams's *Capitalism and Slavery.* Williams's book appeared in 1944, the same year that Friedrich von Hayek's *The Road to Serfdom* was published. Von Hayek sought to demonstrate that adhering to free-market economics assured a nation that it would remain free; Williams strove to demonstrate that the market itself made slavery possible by using earned profits to finance the industrial revolution, after which the market had no use for a slave system that hindered British manufacturing and exports. The idea that slavery had its origins in economics and that the suppression of the slave trade itself also occurred for economic reasons has been questioned by historians, who have demonstrated that in the Caribbean and elsewhere slavery remained profitable. The price of slaves either continued to rise in all of the Americas or remained at a steady level in Africa at the same time that abolitionists were agitating to outlaw the system. The U.S. Constitution prohibited the slave trade after 1808, and England abolished slavery in its West Indian colonies in 1833, though the institution continued elsewhere in the Americas. Whatever the origins of slavery, its demise had more to do with conscience than with commerce.

But the question of origins continues to trouble scholars. While the distinguished black historian Williams (who once served as prime minister of Trinidad) argued that slavery was an economic system and not necessarily a racist attitude, a matter more of profit than of prejudice, the work of William D. Jordan and others has uncovered evidence of how blacks were seen as distinctly different from whites: they were regarded as "inferior" and associated with the "savagery" of African tribal life and its "heathen" cultures.[7] The question whether such prejudices allowed whites to rationalize trading in slaves, or whether the embarrassing presence of slavery itself gave rise to racist attitudes—whether, in short, racism was the effect of slavery or its cause—may seem irrelevant when one considers that the early colonists turned to African Americans only after they had failed to force others to work. Proud native Indians had refused to be coerced into laboring with their hands, and the system of white indentured servitude could barely meet the rising demand for field laborers. It has been estimated that one-third of the male population of colonial society arrived from Europe as indentured servants, having sold their muscle and skills in exchange for passage to the New World.[8]

To study anything historically requires the intellectual activity of attention; what goes unattended is ignored and possibly forgotten. Recently America has undergone a change of mind about Africa and African Americans that is nothing less than astounding. In the early nineteenth century, the era of the abolitionists, much of America harbored racist sentiments and remained inattentive to slavery as an institution. Today, on the contrary, to the extent that racism has been progressively reduced in many parts of the country and in government policies, the American people are made to feel all the more responsible for slavery. Six generations after the "peculiar institution" ceased to exist, Americans are still told that they must become attentive in order to bear the sins of the past. White Americans are to feel guilty about slavery while many black Africans feel neither regret nor remorse. Conor Cruise O'Brien, who taught in Ghana for several years and adopted two African children, has made an illuminating observation in an essay with the revealing title, "African Self-Righteousness Is as Tiresome as European":

> The notion of one continent "raping" another is a hollow trope. The reality was one of exploitation of weak people by strong people. The strong included many Africans, as well as Europeans. The Europeans, it is true, got most of the loot. Why not? They were the strongest of the strong. Liverpool did better out of the slave trade than Kumasi. But Kumasi, too, did pretty well. And I have never met an Ashanti who was anything but proud of the Ashanti Empire, or who was in the least ashamed of the part played by the slave trade in the growth of that powerful and predatory polity. The Fanti, who did even better out of the slave trade, are not exactly wracked by guilt either. Nor . . . do I know many Arabs, or members of the African peoples associated with the Arab slave-trade, who worry about that long chapter in the history of slavery.[9]

That the "predatory polity" of slavery existed centuries ago in Africa should suggest that race and racism may have had little to do with its origin and continuation. In early African history, where the possibility of converting crop surpluses into wealth was limited, acquiring people as servants and slaves remained a tempting option.[10] When the Portuguese arrived in Africa in the early fifteenth century, the captains of Prince Henry the Navigator had been sent to circle the globe in the hope of finding a route to India and the "spice islands." Landing on African shores, the captains set out to look for gold but ended up purchasing slaves, an act that marked the beginning of slavery's being associated with blacks (before the era of exploration it had referred to Slavs, the source of the word). Eventually the Portuguese transported more than 4.5 million slaves from their homelands.

By the time the Atlantic slave trade had developed in the seventeenth century, Arabs as well as Portuguese were involved, and both were soon joined by Europeans and New England sea captains. In Islamic west Africa, Muslim merchants dominated the slave trade. In the eighteenth century 60,000 people a year, mostly men and boys, were taken from their homes. In all, between the mid-fifteenth and late nineteenth centuries, roughly 13 million blacks left Africa, with 10 to 20 percent of them dying in the brutal Middle Passage before arriving in the Americas. It has been estimated that an even higher number of African slaves were sent to the Islamic nations of the Middle East and north Africa.

In ancient history slavery knew no color boundaries, but many classical authors had no quandaries about defending slavery by arguing that certain people are "by nature" incapable of leading independent lives (Aristotle) or that manual labor was incompatible with the life of the mind (Seneca). Although some scholars insist that Christianity put an end to slavery by pronouncing all men equal before the eyes of god, Saint Augustine proclaimed that slavery, while wrong in principle, was God's punishment for humankind's original sin, and Saint Paul reminded readers of scripture that religion required absolute obedience to authority.[11] Abraham Lincoln went against both an older classicism and Christianity when he endowed labor with dignity and valued freedom over submission.

Slavery was not always associated with black people, and it involved various religions. In the Middle Ages new slaves had often been white captives in holy wars, and some of them were shipped to Sicily and the Atlantic islands to work on sugar plantations. In Africa, the Muslim religion was instrumental in expanding the slave trade, though the religion forbade Muslims from enslaving one another. The Islamic countries of Africa and the Middle East put up the most resistance to ending the slave trade and slavery itself. The Jews in the Mediterranean were heavily involved in trade and commerce, but they remained relatively apart from the slave trade. They were restrained by the strictures of Hebrew law against treatment of slaves, including their possible sexual exploitation by masters, and were reluctant to see Muslims and Christians Judaized by means of slavery.[12]

With the discovery of Brazil in 1500, slavery entered the New World. There and in Spanish colonies a pattern started that would repeat itself in North America. At first Europeans tried to coerce indigenous Indians into working, but native people proved resistant to subordination—so white growers turned to black slaves as an answer to the labor problem. In the United States cotton became the single most important agricultural product of the South, all of it sown and picked by slaves. Today historians debate whether slavery was profitable or not and in what respect it led to the Civil War. Historians also debate whether slaves survived plantation life with a confident identity as they successfully resisted its oppressions, or whether the experience of chattel slavery did irreparable damage to slaves' culture and community, depriving them of pride and self-reliance.[13]

The ending of slavery has been as controversial for historians as its beginnings. A good deal of the writing on this subject has been undertaken by economic historians, with conservatives tending to follow Adam Smith and emphasizing such stages as the hunter, the shepherd, agriculture, and ultimately commerce and the market (which they argue helped end slavery); and radicals following Karl Marx and emphasizing such successive modes of production as Asian, slave, feudal, capitalist, and ultimately, in the future, socialist. Ironically, both the capitalist and the communist look to the stages and modes of economic development as liberating. Both believe that the stagnation of slavery stood in the way of releasing society's productive forces, and neither places much emphasis on intellectual history and the role of ideas. But when the focus is shifted to intellectual history, as it has been by several recent scholars, a telling question arises. If slavery was a violation of America's founding ideas, was anti-slavery a reaffirmation of them?

The Yale historian David Brion Davis created a controversy when he argued, in *The Problem of Slavery in the Age of Revolution, 1770–1820*, that the cause of anti-slavery "reflected the ideological needs of various groups and classes" and hence that it was in the interest of abolitionists to oppose slavery in order to sustain their status and power in an emergent capitalist economy. Even the gentle Quakers, Davis writes, were "selective" in their condemnation of forced labor: they protested the enslavement of blacks in the South but remained silent about wage laborers in the North. David depicts Quaker leaders as worried about the rise of an "undisciplined" labor force and as urging the abolition of slavery so that all workers, white as well as black, would regard themselves as free, responsible agents. Thus humanitarianism becomes a form of "social control" in which a "highly ethical purpose could disguise the effects of power." Quakers may have been unaware of the fruits of their thoughts and actions, but the historian cannot help but report them. "Although eighteenth-century Quakers were not responsible for the consequences of a nineteenth-century labor market . . . they unwittingly drew distinctions and boundaries which opened the way, under a guise of moral rectitude, for unprecedented forms of oppression."

The historian Thomas Haskell challenged Davis and other scholars who insisted that the rise of capitalism had much to do with the fall of slavery and that self-interest played a role in both phenomena, however much the abolitionist may have hidden from himself his own selfish motives. Drawing on Max Weber and other social theorists, Haskell argued that the ascendancy of capitalism "could have expanded the conventional boundaries of moral responsibility" to the extent that the "autonomous power of the market" influenced character and taught people to keep their promises and calculate the consequences of their actions. Capitalists were men of integrity and probity, Haskell urges, and "the defining characteristic of the 'man of principle,' the moral paragon of a promise-keeping, market-centered form of life, was his willingness to act on principle no matter how inconvenient it might be."[14]

Between Davis's contention that abolitionists were men of interest and Haskell's conviction that they were men of principle lies the heart of the liberal consensus and its dilemmas. When Weber discussed early capitalism, he had the conscience-struck Calvinist in mind, and by the time he moved on to Ben Franklin, he saw the "spirit" of capitalism sublimated into practical, mundane activities. Henceforth, from Ben Franklin to John Dewey, there would be no distinction between interests and principle. To Franklin all that is valuable can be reduced to the useful, and to Dewey the self cannot be separated from its actions or interests. Why, asked Dewey, is it right to do what is in the interest of others and wrong to do what is in the interest of ourselves?[15] When Lincoln replied to a similar sentiment uttered by defenders of slavery, he demonstrated, it may be recalled, that if it is in your interest to enslave others, it is also in the interest of others to enslave you. But Lincoln scarcely looked to the market as the agency that would enable people to keep their promises; instead, he looked to the Declaration.

Lincoln's contemporaries, the New England Transcendentalists, would have been amused to hear that capitalism gives people a "willingness to act on principle no matter how inconvenient it might be." Convenient, expedient behavior was all the Transcendentalists saw, prompting Thoreau to write his lament, "Life without Principle." Tocqueville would also have been perplexed to be told that market capitalism creates "the moral paragon of promise keeping." Tocqueville did see how voluntary associations that offered a measure of mutuality could assure local freedoms. But what troubled Tocqueville about America was precisely the *individualisme* released in a society of "equality of conditions" where people compete with one another and remain proudly independent. "As social conditions become more equal, the number of persons increases who . . . owe nothing to any man, [and] expect nothing from any man; they acquire the habit of always considering themselves as standing alone, and they are apt to imagine that their whole destiny is in their own hands."[16] When Tocqueville observed that classical virtue and a devotion to the public good had no existence in America, he also hastened to add that enlightened interest or self-interest rightly understood (*l'intérêt bien entendu*) could possibly make it "in the interest of every man to be virtuous." But Tocqueville never went as far as Montesquieu in defining virtue as requiring the "relinquishing" of one's interest for the good of society.

From a Tocquevillian perspective, it may have been in the interest of Quakers to champion the abolition of slavery. Lincoln, too, was not above using this line of reasoning when he warned northern workers that opening up the territories to slavery would jeopardize their ability to command wages. But Lincoln also called upon Americans to "sacrifice" upon the altars of the Declaration as rational, self-responsible subjects. Americans, in Lincoln's view, could scarcely find their identity and moral guidance from the fluctuations of the market or the vicissitudes of society and public opinion. The Declaration, in his view, is the source that obligates us to take into account the misery and happiness of others in weighing our motives for action. To leave the slavery question up to banks and polls is like leaving it up to popular sovereignty, "a most arrant Quixotism."[17] Lincoln believed that American democracy rested not upon popular will but upon fixed principles, on the "definitions and axioms of a free society."[18]

Slavery may have ended up in the western world, but it neither originated nor flourished solely there. To the contrary, opposition to slavery emerged primarily in the West as a violation of the Enlightenment's value of equality and humanity. Along the African coast, slaves were stockpiled in forts built by Europeans at the request of tribal leaders, who enjoyed the huge profits made by selling their own people. The movement to abolish slavery began mainly in in England and America. In *The Wealth of Nations*, Adam Smith condemned slavery as a hindrance to progress and a destroyer of human motivation, much as Lincoln would a century later. In the nineteenth century some African chiefs opposed the ending of the slave trade, while today, at the beginning of the twenty-first century, slave labor continues in the Sudan and in Mauritania, an Islamic regime on the coast of west Africa.

It seems clear that slavery derived from sinful humanity's temptation to exploit its own species for reasons of greed, power, or status. Today in the academic world bookstores are running over with titles on "postcolonial" and "subaltern" studies, which tell us that we whites in the West collapse into anxiety when we think about the "other" and come to understand our sins of oppression and exploitation.[19] But as the philosopher William James remarked, "the trail of the serpent is everywhere." The West, along with Africa and the Middle East, has been imperialistic, exploitative, and racist. Yet only in the West has imperialism been historically opposed, exploitation institutionally controlled, and racism legally prohibited.

Reconstruction

Yet we should not allow recent accomplishments in the area of human rights to cover up the enormity of the past violations of liberalism. It requires utmost integrity for liberalism to remain true to its own standards of fairness and justice, and the historian is obligated to remind us when a political philosophy failed to advance humankind.

If during the first half of the nineteenth century U.S. citizens ignored Lockean liberalism as it applied to black Americans, during the second half they betrayed it entirely. During the era of Reconstruction freed blacks were denied the land promised to them during the Civil War. They would also be denied the political freedoms promised in the Fourteenth Amendment, which made African Americans citizens and thereby entitled to all the rights, privileges, and immunities thereof; and in the Fifteenth Amendment, which prohibited the abridgment of the right to vote "by the United States or by any state on account of race, color, or previous condition of servitude." The eventual return of the white Democratic Party in the South, the collapse of southern Reconstruction, and the rise of the Ku Klux Klan all worked to intimidate blacks from voting. Such denials of freedom and equal protection of the law meant that the nearly 4 million slaves emancipated in 1863 lacked any civil status.

It was the ghost of Jefferson that won out, the philosopher who distrusted central government and the rule of the few and looked to the majority will to sustain popular democracy in diversified local communities. That will expressed itself not only in the South but throughout the nation as it denied blacks the rights that the Constitution had supposedly guaranteed. But in the South in particular blacks, who had no desire to return to the plantation, were forced to sign labor contracts that gave them bare subsistence wages. Thus whether slaves or freed persons, African Americans were excluded from the Lockean consensus because they were denied both the right to property and wealth as the fruits of one's labor and the right to self-government as a means of protecting oneself from interference by others. It should be recalled that Lockean liberalism was meant to reflect the will and interest of democratic majorities. Where, then, does liberalism leave numerical minorities?

In the post–Civil War era at least two policies were put forth as a response to the question, and both reflected the sustaining reality of liberalism as well as its limits.

The Civil Rights Act of 1875, which guarantees equal access to public facilities, was based on the laissez-faire assumption that once artificial barriers of racial discrimination have been eliminated, the field of opportunity is leveled and open to all. One black congressman declared: "Place all citizens upon the one broad platform; and if the Negro is not qualified to hoe his row in the contest of life, then let him go down."[20] In some respects the policy that looked to the rational efficacy of the free market contained the Lockean sentiment that freedom derives from productive and profitable work and that removing impediments to the capitalist economy would remove barriers to racial opportunity.

If the laissez-faire policy was implicitly Lockean, the land-labor policy was explicitly so, to such a degree that the second policy toward racial relations in post–Civil War America may be called "black Lockeanism." Freed African Americans expressed their deep desire to own the forty-acre plots that they had worked on as slaves. When they heard that the government intended to return land to the former plantation owners, the freed blacks petitioned both President Andrew Johnson and General O. O. Howard, head of the Freedman's Bureau. "General we want Homesteads; we were promised Homesteads by the government." They argued that the restoration of all land to white society left them "at the mercy of those who are combined to prevent us from getting land enough to lay our fathers bones upon." Freed blacks regarded themselves as entitled to some of the land of former plantation owners, on the grounds that they had been exploited and deprived of the fruits of their labor even though they had occupied the land and brought agricultural improvement to it:

> We have a right to the land where we are located. For why? I tell you. Our wives, our children, our husbands, have been sold over and over again to purchase the lands we now located upon; for that reason we have a divine right to the land. . . . And then didn't we clear the land, and raise crops of corn, of cotton, of tobacco, of rice, or sugar, of everything. And then didn't those large cities in the North grow up on the cotton and sugar and the rice that we made? . . . I say they have grown rich, while my people are poor.[21]

One can scarcely ask for a better version of Lockean liberalism. The statement virtually echoes one made two decades earlier in the anti-rent movement in New York's Hudson Valley. Protesting the manorial rule of landlords and their seigneurial prerogatives, poor white tenants held that it was they who "had spent the best years of their lives rendering the land valuable."[22] Similarly, the ex-slave realized that he and his people had created property and wealth by clearing the land and raising crops on it. The principle that people have property in themselves, that they own their own bodies, is also implied. In addition, they have a "divine right" to land as retribution for what Lincoln once termed the "sin of slavery" and for the Christian principle that all God's creatures have access to nature.

Where did black people, who had lived under conditions of slavery for more than two centuries, obtain their ideas of freedom, especially ideas that linked freedom to property and self-ownership and that, at least, glimpsed the possibility that land and liberty might result from individual effort?

Black Lockeans

In the past several years writers on African-American history have returned to slavery to recover the unsavory aspects of the system. But many more years ago three perspectives converged to paint a strangely pretty picture of slavery as an institution.

In the nineteenth century, Southerners, responding to abolitionist arguments before the Civil War and to the Reconstruction policy afterward, portrayed slaves as intelligent workers content with being part of the plantation family. In the 1930s, during the Depression, the federal government assigned the Works Project Administration to collect an oral history of aging former slaves, but the result was another benign view because those interviewed avoided bringing up painful memories of life under slavery and the interviewers themselves avoided raising such questions. Then in the 1960s and 1970s, historians began writing about slavery as a "culture" and "community" in which black people had proven to be resilient, with functioning families, healthy social relations, and firm identities based on a strong sense of place and belonging. Under slavery, we were told, blacks enjoyed a protective and caring paternalism far removed from the exploitative and alienating capitalism that presumably afflicted white wage earners in the North. Blacks survived the ravages of slavery, these historians argued, so the problems they are encountering today in contemporary society, particularly in the inner cities, must be due to white racism.

Without necessarily denying the extent of racism, a reaction to this "romantic" view of slave life on the plantation began to emerge in the 1990s. Recent research has revealed such previously glossed-over subjects as rape and other acts of violence, cruelty, and amputation as punishment for attempted escape. The idea that slavery could have nurtured the black family and community now seems unpersuasive if not preposterous. "Look," exclaimed the black Harvard sociologist Orlando Patterson, "how can you have 270 years of history in which the family was not recognized, women could be raped, beaten, stripped naked in the fields before their so-called husbands; where men were emasculated deliberately in the sense of having no authority, no say over their children, even though they are encouraged to reproduce; how can you have 270 years of that and claim that people came out with intact families with two parents? It's just absurd in the face of it." Patterson summed up the whole experience of slavery in two words: "social death."[23]

How then, out of undeniable social death, did there emerge an undying will to life and to labor? As an institution slavery deprived blacks of all of their political rights and privileges but not necessarily all of their economic freedoms and opportunities. Within the plantation's vast economy existed small informal or internal economies worked by slaves themselves. Often these were garden plots where vegetables could be grown to consume, exchange, or sell. This backyard sowing and tilling was especially prevalent in the Low Country of Georgia and South Carolina, where slaves owned land, cows, corn, and wagons and often traded and sold such items among themselves and occasionally with and to white people. Bartering and negotiating became part of the exchange mentality of some slaves. Commercial activity never freed the blacks from the state of dependency imposed by plantation owners. But the budding entrepreneurial itch among some slaves indicated how far the third and fourth generations of African Americans had been separated from their older roots in Africa's communal culture, where private property had been an alien notion and shared values a sacred sentiment.[24]

Before the Civil War northern abolitionists had assumed, as did Lincoln himself, that slavery denied blacks the fruits of their labor. Thus considerable surprise arose when the Southern Claims Commission, created by Congress in 1871, became aware that former slaves had lost their crops and surplus to a foraging Union army that had seized them during the war. When testimony was heard about garden plots and other possessions, it was revealed that northern officials, who had been convinced that only free people could own things, also had assumed, as the historian Dylan Penningroth put it, "that property could not own property." Federal agents of the commission set out to find traditional evidence of ownership—receipts, deeds, titles, bills of sale. But the former slaves proved their case less through paperwork than through oral testimony. The commission heard stories of how slaves had worked harder in order to have free time to work their own plots; how skills had become a portable form of property; how the giving of property had served in marriage ceremonies to affirm bonds between newlyweds; how hogs, cows, and chickens had come to be inherited among family members; and how slaves had established claims to their property by showing them off at public occasions. Thus claims to property rarely became part of the private sphere, for without written evidence of ownership, and with property passing through so many hands (and with each parcel possibly embodying the interests of several people, including the old master), resolutions about ownership became, in Penningroth's words, a public "interchange of display and acknowledgment."[25]

That disputes over property became a public affair may be no more significant than in today's society, where such disputes end up in civil court. But contemporary historians of American slave societies tend to look for every evidence of the public over the private and the communal over the competitive. A notable skeptic is Peter Kolchin, who has compared American slavery to Russian serfdom. Kolchin notes that slaves never achieved the isolated community of the *mir*, which was far removed from absentee owners and thus capable of fostering a collective sense of the peasants' common interests. But Kolchin also illuminates certain aspects of slave resistance that may bear on the hidden seeds of a potential liberalism within a presumptuous paternalism.

The rare slave uprisings over two centuries (Gabriel Prosser, Virginia, 1800; Denmark Vesey, South Carolina, 1822; Nat Turner, Virginia, 1831) may be seen as evidence that slaves hardly accepted their servile status. Yet all such collective efforts were suicidal in an environment without a jungle, forest, or hills to escape to and with well-armed resident masters and overseers. Slaves may have "resisted" their condition by moving sluggishly, feigning illness, breaking tools, and other acts that historians have termed "silent sabotage." But when efforts were made to escape, runaways had to head out on their own. "One of the most striking characteristics of that resistance—aside from its very existence—is that it was largely the work of individuals," writes

Kolchin. A collective confrontation with the ruling authorities would be sure to be suppressed, and a public protest would be regarded apprehensively. Slaves who ran away had to travel alone or in pairs in order to move through a white environment without attracting attention. Moreover, the decision to flee could scarcely be discussed with other slaves without risking an informer revealing the plot to the master. Frequently it was fear of punishment, a change of masters, or having been treated unjustly that prompted slaves to make their escape. But "a longing desire to be free," as one former slave put it, had to be acted upon in solitude and perhaps irrevocably, because running away meant leaving behind family and friends.[26]

In at least one important respect this resistance to slavery exemplifies the Lockean principle that humankind emerges from the state of nature and that natural rights are a possession of the individual. Had the right to property been the province of society as a whole, the individual would risk starvation waiting for others to act. The natural right to self-preservation belonged to the individual and not to the collective, for survival depends upon personal initiative and not necessarily community involvement. Whether or not plantation slavery sowed the seeds of a latent black individualism, those former slaves who testified before the Southern Claims Commission came close to echoing Locke's *Second Treatise on Government*. Locke defined property as that "whereof we may not be deprived without our consent."

"Driven with Peculiar Force into Economic Activity"

In *The Protestant Ethic and the Spirit of Capitalism*, Max Weber starts out by raising a riddle. Why in Catholic Germany are almost all modern enterprises "overwhelmingly Protestant"? The situation puzzled Weber, who saw capitalism as emanating not from established elites but from classes and religious groups that had experienced oppression and persecution. National and religious minorities in positions of subordination, excluded from positions of influence, are most likely "to be drawn with peculiar force into economic activity." This drive was true of Poles in Russia, non-conformists and Quakers in England, Puritans who came to America, and Jews worldwide for two thousand years. The "ablest members" of the minorities "seek to satisfy the desire for recognition of their abilities in their field, since there is no opportunity in the service of the state."

Weber taught scholars that they must study the values of human actors, for values not only motivate action but also illuminate the meaning of such actions. In his study of early America, Weber became convinced, after tracing a mentality of anxiety and ambition from the Puritans to Ben Franklin, that "the spirit of capitalism was present before the capitalist order." Capitalism was not simply the squalid scramble for profits but the deeper desire to prove one's self and succeed, and Weber believed that persecuted minorities' drive for recognition would express itself in the economic sphere of life.

The sociologist John Sibley Butler, in his study *Entrepreneurship and Self-Help among Black Americans,* drew upon the idea of "middle-man minorities" to suggest that among those discriminated-against are groups that have established a position within the structure of capitalism. Workers in these groups often serve as labor contractors, money lenders, storekeepers, and in other positions of liaison, negotiating the different demands of producer and consumer, owner and tenant, employer and worker. Butler also updated Gunnar Myrdal's classic, *An American Dilemma: The Negro Problem in Modern Democracy* (1944). Myrdal held that the Negro wage earner, while excluded from much of skilled work, had some possibility of entering such jobs, whereas the black professional worker in the middle or upper classes experienced a "much more complete and settled" exclusion due to social considerations of status as much as economics. All of this has changed, Butler notes, writing a half-century later. The post–World War II civil rights movement created a solid black middle class that, having benefited from a college education, entered the professions and in some instances even attained executive positions.[27]

But the burden of Butler's scholarship and that of others is to demonstrate that black enterprise existed long before the civil rights movement. The vast literature on this subject has been neglected. One of the seminal works is Abraham L. Harris's *The Negro as Capitalist,* a text that came out in 1936, at the heyday of American radicalism. Harris himself had been influenced by Marxism, but he had also delved into the work of Max Weber and Thorstein Veblen; hence his sociological sense of economics took on complexity and irony, with blacks driven by pride as much as profit. Although many blacks entrusted their savings to banks owned by whites, Harris discovered that in the period 1899–1934, no fewer than 134 banks had been founded and were managed by African Americans. After analyzing deposits, earnings, growth rates, assets, and loans, Harris concluded that the financial structure of the banks was confined almost completely to loans and discounts with little investment in stocks and bonds. Nevertheless, even though a segregated financial market precluded substantial investment, African-American banks went far beyond older primitive saving systems by offering rotating credit arrangements and other transactions that facilitated the circulation of money in black communities.[28]

A half-century before The Negro as Capitalist appeared, African Americans emerged from Reconstruction vying between themselves over two strategies of adapting to American society. One strategy, which accepted the realities of racism and its "Jim Crow" laws of segregation, concentrated on developing businesses within black neighborhoods. The other looked to joining the American workforce in the tradition of European immigrant groups. But in the trade unions most blacks faced exclusion or were allocated the most menial jobs, while in "homegrown" small enterprises involving banking, insurance, publishing, and store keeping, some blacks enjoyed a measure of economic success.

Savings Bank Salvation

The legacy of Reconstruction left African Americans with two very different possibilities: laissez-faire liberalism and Black Lockeanism. Laissez-faire liberalism stood opposed to government-sponsored land redistribution as departing from a universal standard of individual rights and opportunities, while Black Lockeanism held that such redistribution addressed the injuries to a race as a whole. I cannot address here whether land redistribution could have prevented southern blacks from falling into a subsistence economy, as some scholars suggest, or whether, as others insist, it could have been the beginning of the creation of black capital and economic independence. But the two policy positions developed in the Reconstruction era continue to characterize political discourse about race in America, particularly the question of civic inclusion.

One position, stretching from Frederick Douglass to Booker T. Washington to our contemporaries Shelby Steele and Thomas Sowell, emphasizes a liberal individualism based on initiative in the private sphere, self-development, work and thrift, the rationality of economic life, personal responsibility, and integration with the larger white society. The second position, which stretches from W. E. B. Du Bois to Martin Luther King Jr. to our contemporaries Henry Louis Gates and Cornel West, emphasizes a quite different point of view: race as a collective experience, power as residing in groups rather than individuals, the necessity of civil disobedience and non-violent coercion, a Christian understanding of the Fall and the limitations of reason, and a black aesthetic sensibility based on understanding language and rhetoric. In intellectual matters, these positions can easily overlap; hence Gates is close to Douglass in interpreting the taking up of writing by African Americans as a means of creating a self that slavery had denied it.[29]

A liberal consensus with foundations in American history can scarcely encompass the totality of black culture and politics. In the 1920s Marcus Garvey started the pan-African United Negro Improvement Association precisely to escape the dominant white culture. In our era the Los Angeles activist Ron Karenga advocates a separatist stance and the black Muslims see their future in Islamic religion, albeit with a strong emphasis on self-help and hard work.

For all of the contemporary clamor over multiculturalism and diversity, it is remarkable to find black intellectual history steeped in a liberalism that many of today's radicals scholars refuse to acknowledge. Booker T. Washington's support of vocational education for black youths, based on the premise that technical skills would make his students indispensable to the industrial economy, resonated in the thoughts of John Dewey and Thorstein Veblen, who also elevated the practical over the theoretical and hoped that America would value the useful rather than the wasteful. The status of work and its relationship to freedom and to wealth itself is also part of the legacy of black culture. "I found employment," Frederick Douglass remembered after arriving in New Bedford, "in stowing a sloop with a laid of oil. It was new, dirty, and hard work for me but I went at with a glad heart and a willing hand. I was now my own master."[30] The idea of "self-help" also characterized the thought of Martin Delany, Alexander Crummell, and other blacks. Their belief in the duty to work hard was close to, as Gayle McKeen has noted, the Lockean relationship of labor to "self-ownership" in that workers can rightly claim to own what they make.[31] James Weldon Johnson, the lawyer and literary intellectual who helped organize the National Association for the Advancement of Colored People, exclaimed "What an interesting and absorbing game is making money!" as he was about to take up real estate investment.[32] Amos Webber, the Philadelphia handyman and servant once active in the underground railroad, urged his people to become homeowners. A black New York newspaper editor, writing about a black woman who bought an apartment building with her earnings, exhorted that people of color "can profit by her example."[33] And in his address on the "Meaning of Business," Du Bois explained why entrepreneurial energy should be nurtured in his race and why the black bourgeoisie must learn to accumulate capital and put it to productive use. "The day the Negro race courts and marries the savings-bank will be the day of its salvation," he told an audience of businessmen. Thrift and wise investment, he stated in 1898, "would mean more to us today than the right of suffrage."[34]

Du Bois, as we saw in the introduction, appreciated Abraham Lincoln as a statesman who was desperately trying to both free the slaves and preserve the Union. Even more sympathetic to Lincoln's situation was Frederick Douglass, the former slave who called upon Lincoln several times at his summer cottage. Douglass also visited the White House at least three times. On the last occasion, a policeman, thinking Douglass could not have been invited because he was black, grabbed him and forced him out the door. But Lincoln saw what was happening and intervened. "Here comes my friend Douglass," he exclaimed as he left his company, took Douglass by the hand, and started chatting with him. Douglass would later write: "In all my interviews with Mr. Lincoln, I was impressed with his entire freedom from popular prejudice against the colored race. He was the first great man I talked with in the United States freely, who in no single instance reminded me of the difference between himself and myself, of the difference of color, and I thought that all the more remarkable because he came from a state where there were black laws."[35]

Today the mystique of "difference" is everywhere, as though the demand to be recognized requires a declaration of group uniqueness. Those who deny the thesis of "American exceptionalism" often regard themselves as exceptional—and thus uniquely qualified for some sort of benefit—because of their race, ethnicity, gender, or sexual preference. Yet the whole idea of natural rights presupposes that people are essentially the same and thereby entitled to similar opportunities and equal protection under the law. At a time when many Americans are told that their identity lies in being recognized as some kind of ethnic subspecies, it may be helpful to remember that Lincoln and Douglass could share a national identity and a common historical foundation in American liberalism.

Conclusion:
The "New Self" and the
"Tragic Ambiguity"

"The Pathology of American Democracy"

MUCH OF THE LIBERAL CONSENSUS THAT PERVADED
the American past has been lost to present historiography, and with it
the loss of any sense of the importance of property and wealth, the
value of the work ethic in a society that had to overcome slavery and
deal with leisure-class pretensions, and an economic way of life that
offered the possibility of equality of opportunity and the forging of
self-made identities. Instead of recovering the meaning of such a legacy as a live possibility, some scholars continue to write about dead
ends.

The young black historian Robin D. G. Kelley, for example, wants
his students not only to appreciate the story of "communism" but also
to approach history as a "hidden manuscript" in which may be found
evidence of black people's "resistance" to capitalism and other "oppositional practices" aiming at subverting mainstream politics and
culture.[1] If history were a laughing matter, the evidence would be
worthy of a good chuckle.[2] The result of retelling the American story
in this way, however, is quite serious. Can such an approach to the past
do anything other than condemn black Americans to powerlessness
and poverty? While blacks have good reason to protest racial discrimination, one wonders why some scholars remain addicted to a politics
of failure.

Similar doubts arise when we are told, as we have been by Cornel

West, a distinguished black philosopher at Harvard University, that America can find its political redemption in "prophetic pragmatism," "radical democracy," "political engagement," "organic intellectuals," and "an Emersonian culture of creative democracy." Never mind that Emerson saw democratic politics as "cunning" rather than creative.[3] Professor West has convinced himself that "postmodernism" offers the solution to "the crisis of the Left," and that one can find the way out of that crisis simply by invoking every fad that has sprouted in the groves of academe: "operations of otherness and marginality," "temporality, difference, and heterogeneity," "the demystification of European cultural hegemony, the destruction of western metaphysical traditions, and the deconstruction of North Atlantic philosophical systems," and "Derrida's deconstructionist version of poststructuralism [that] accents the transgressive and disruptive."

West, the son of a Protestant minister, also instructs fellow academic intellectuals to draw upon the "Christian tradition," and he cites Reinhold Niebuhr as exemplary. The Calvinist, sin-struck Abraham Lincoln was Niebuhr's political hero, and the theologian had a bust of the president in his apartment study. Yet in his book *The American Evasion of Philosophy*, West mentions Lenin and "Leninist" more than a dozen times, Lincoln not once. Lincoln, it will be recalled, believed America was founded upon "a philosophical idea" and that the country must face the problem of slavery and social justice on "a philosophical basis." West bids good riddance to philosophy and its foundations as he proudly hails the arrival of friction, faction, and fission. "The academic inclusion on a grand scale of the students of color, working-class origin, and women produced ideologies of institutional pluralism to mediate between the clashing methods and perspectives in the structurally fragmented humanistic departments and programs. Dissensus reigned and reigns supreme."[4]

If there is one diehard conviction held by our ismites in the academy, it is that dissensus goes hand in hand with democracy and that democracy itself is radical. The conviction has little basis in history. When has democracy ever been radical?

In the pre–Civil War era it was the Calvinist, conscience-struck Whigs who championed the abolition of slavery and granting equal suffrage to free blacks. The Democrats, the party of the democratic masses and the virtuous "common man," succeeded in the complete disenfranchisement of free blacks in the state of New York and elsewhere, thereby denying them the voting rights that they had once possessed and exercised. Eliminating property qualifications for whites while reimposing them on blacks was too much for Chancellor James Kent, the conservative legal jurist who responded to the democratic charge that the black man was "a degraded member of society and would, therefore, be always willing to sell his vote." "How came they so?" asked Kent. "Was it not by our fault and the fault of our fathers. . . . However we may scorn and insult, and trample upon this unfortunate race now, the day was fast approaching when we must lie down with them in that narrow bed appointed for all the living. . . . God has created us all equal; and why should we establish distinctions?"[5]

But white democratic society continued to make distinctions, and racial discrimination occurred precisely where the new social historians tell us to look to the site of action and contestation: history down below with democracy and the virtuous workers. Du Bois saw things differently. Even as a socialist, he grew so angry with the labor movement's hostility to blacks that he wrote in praise of business: "The white employers, North and South, literally gave the Negroes work when white men refused to work with him; when he 'scabbed' for bread and butter the employers defended him against mob violence of white laborers; they gave him educational institutions when white labor would have left him in ignorance."[6]

In 1928, Harry F. Davis, the leading black Republican in Ohio, observed that a "colored worker who is denied the protection and the benefits of organized labor because they will not take him in, has only one place of redress in case his right of employment is assailed, and that is in our courts." Speaking on the floor of Congress, Representative Davis explained why freedom of contract logically followed from the enumerated rights of property and liberty. "The groups I represent have not got very much physical or tangible property and their biggest asset is their right to a job, recognized as a contract, but an intangible right, and I maintain that if this bill [an injunction outlawing employer-employee contracts in which job applicants must agree not to join a labor union] becomes a law it would affect very materially their right to the biggest thing which they have, the right to earn a living."[7]

Older black leaders like Davis recognized the limits of democracy and regarded rights not as entitlements to benefits based on victimization but as immunities that are there to protect people from the actions of others. Newer scholars, in contrast, wax emphatic about democracy and regard the people they champion as deserving of entitlements as a consequence of their excluded and oppressed prior status. There may be good historical reasons for women to see themselves as having suffered from the same history as blacks, the same denial of political rights and exclusion from the labor market. But how are freedom, justice, and racial and gender equality to be derived from democracy?

To read the scholarship of black academic intellectuals today is to miss what earlier leaders like Du Bois and Davis were advocating. It is widely accepted in contemporary scholarship that black people desiring to get ahead in American life have only two options, one closed, the other open. Cut off from a local government controlled by white party bosses, feeling the effects of racism everywhere in American society, black intellectuals chose "culture" rather than "politics" for their means of self-expression. Blacks had "no choice," we are told, but to "bet on the only horse willing to run under their colors. The most pressing reason for the New Negro's decision to work through culture, not politics," writes Harold Cruise, "was that this was the closest Harlem could come to so-called real politics."[8]

Rarely do black academic intellectuals regard economics as a path to mobility and racial progress. Excluded from politics and access to government, blacks take to music and poetry. Why not the life of business? The world of athletics, where blacks have excelled in ferocious competition, and jazz and dance, where they have performed with the beauty of dissonance and the demands of discipline, are not too far removed from the world of business, which involves risks, innovation, entrepreneurship, profit, and success. Yet that domain of life remains closed to teachers of African-American history. The title of Manny Marable's book, *How Capitalism Underdeveloped Black America,* explains it all.[9] Ironically, authors of such books have no trouble asking capitalism to finance their own programs in the academic world. On the one hand, capitalism supposedly lives off the profits of exploited black labor; on the other hand, that same economic system must support an African-American Studies program whose future depends, it would seem, on the continuation of the allegedly unearned dividends of Wall Street. To use the terms of Thorstein Veblen, in the black academic world the captains of enterprise and the captains of erudition meet in a marriage of mendacity.

Like some recent black scholars, women historians tend to credit democracy for doing the work that should be credited to bureaucracy. Higher education itself, the very "system" that the New Left had set out to transform, has become more bureaucratized and administered by professional title-holders and paper-pushers than ever before in American history. Yet those who enjoy the benefits of bureaucracy see themselves as expanding the ideals of democracy. Seldom do they acknowledge that they and their sisters in the past had to, in Ralph Ellison's words, "go on struggling against the built-in conditions which comprise the pathology of American democracy."[10]

The Futility of Deconstruction

Curing that pathology may well require a well-placed push. Women's forced entry into the public sphere constituted one act of empowerment. But it remains questionable whether women's entry into history opened up access to other groups that had been excluded. Between 1920, when women won the vote, and 1960, when the Left had its rebirth, no national feminist organization supported the cause of black women or women working in factories and fields. Championing their own cause in close sisterly solidarity, feminists had to come to terms with power—and power leaves democracy behind; otherwise it dissipates to the extent that it expands its scope to encompass more and more people of differing views. Some feminist historians argue that power is not a problem because women possess what men lack: a basic sympathy and generosity enabling them to want for others what they desire for themselves. One would like to think that private egotism vanishes once people enter the public sphere and take part in civic affairs. But does it?

On the question of how we actually treat others in this situation, perhaps we should first look at what the radical historians have been reading. According to Professor Joan Scott, an eminent fellow at Princeton's prestigious Institute for Advanced Study, historians must take up poststructuralism and deconstruction to appreciate how language and other forms of representation have served to marginalize women and various minorities. Poststructuralism denies truth as a direct encounter with reality and holds that history can be nothing more than interpretations based on shifting perspectives, often those expedient to the historian's political purposes. What the public sphere and poststructuralism appear to offer is a new approach to history that emphasizes differences, diversity, and, above all, recognition of the "other." This notion of *altarity*, of becoming aware of our practices of exclusion in order to take responsibility for "otherness," has been elevated to an ethic in poststructuralist thought.[11] And deconstruction comes to the fore as a method that promises to uncover modes of representation that have in the past incorporated differences and silenced their meanings in order to create the appearance of consensus.

So much for theory. But the irony of ironies, today feminist scholars themselves seek to forge their own consensus through the apparatus of government commissions and bureaucratic monitoring. The formerly excluded have taken control of the mechanisms of exclusion at the expense of others holding differing views. Describing women's "unreflective complicity with modern forms of power," the philosopher Marion Tappen writes of the changes taking place in the academy: a "bureaucratization which operates with definite techniques of surveillance and normalization," with feminists "coopting these procedures" so that "course content must be relevant to women, teaching materials must not be sexist, students' essays must not include sexist language, all committees must include one woman."[12]

The proposal that historians take up French poststructuralist theory has generated controversy among scholars.[13] The more telling issue is not whether the proposal is controversial but whether it is feasible. Advocating poststructuralism as a methodology with which to gain a multiculturalist appreciation of the diversity of other cultures scarcely makes sense. Does not poststructuralism in fact make it more difficult to understand diversity? How can we start with the basic premise of poststructuralism—which holds that all knowledge is historical and so shaped by the conventions of language that no accurate representation of an object is possible—and arrive at a precise comprehension of cultures different from our own? Without access to the real, how do we study it without appropriating it for our own purposes, particularly when we are told that the only reality is the recognition that our minds have invented it?

Poststructuralists tell us that all we know is from reading a text and that there is nothing beyond the text. And because knowledge claims have no foundations but only contingent linguistic constructions, they remain to be deconstructed. Feminist scholars in particular may see the interrogation of truth as radical and liberating, but in the nineteenth century such a position was taken up by reactionaries and racists. It was John C. Calhoun, the apologist for slavery, who mocked the "self-evident" truths in the Declaration of Independence, which he claimed was a document that textualized with the materials of rhetoric premises that only seemed to refer to reality. In his debates with Abraham Lincoln, Stephen Douglas became the poststructuralist and his opponent the absolutist. While Lincoln looked to the Declaration and the Bible as providing the foundational truths of the Republic, Douglas claimed that there are no such truths other than what people believe, and because beliefs vary in different parts of the country, people in the territories have a sovereign right to vote for or against slavery. Feminists would like to insist that men do not have a right to be sexist, but since poststructuralism informs us that everything is a matter of interpretation and perspective, and that there is no truth but only varying beliefs and practices, does not the sexist have a right to be different and, moreover, exempt from universal standards of right and wrong?

Although the historian Scott takes her intellectual direction from the French poststructuralists Jacques Derrida and Michel Foucault, the dilemma she and other feminists face was actually presaged by another French thinker, Alexis de Tocqueville. Scott has come to recognize what Tocqueville had warned a century and a half ago. While equality abolishes differences, individuals may still experience more subordination than freedom, and while male privileges may be assaulted and the barriers to women's opportunity torn down, competitive life continues hierarchies and systems of domination that are driven by human pride and envy. Now that women have entered into the men's world, they confront Tocqueville's dilemma of humankind demanding to be both treated as equal and recognized as different.

Those who view history using poststructuralism believe that it enhances an appreciation of democracy as the means through which freedom can be realized. Arguing against Gertrude Himmelfarb's insistence that cultures require unifying historical narratives, Scott dismisses such advice as "a repudiation of the possibility of contest and conflicting interpretation, a refusal of change, and a rejection of the possibility of what I would call democratic history."[14] Once again the feminist embraces democracy and "democratic history" more as a mantra than as a methodology. When did people who had been precluded from participating in power benefit from the presence of democracy? Rather than democracy leading to power on the part of those struggling to overcome their subordinate status, democracy and power move in opposite directions. Democracy aims to expand, encompass, absorb, and, above all, include; power seeks to restrict, confine, limit, and, above all, exclude.

The idea that power itself can be democratized so as to lead to more inclusive representation may be wishful thinking. Democracy itself remains almost inert against what Weber called "the law of small numbers," the ability of concentrated minorities to locate themselves in strategic positions in order to impose their will and produce desired effects.[15] Democracy as representation and participation may promote rights, and it remains the best means of allowing more and more people to share the civic space of society. But poststructuralism, which enables us to transform linguistically what we cannot change politically, serves only to create illusions instead of exposing them, particularly illusions about republicanism and democracy as agencies of radical transformation. We can no longer delude ourselves into thinking that the rhetoric of democracy, however "radical" it seems when workers are said to chant its slogans, tells us anything about the truths that reside in power itself.

And such truths are elusive. "What is the force that moves nations?" asked Tolstoy as he proceeded to demonstrate that the answers given by historians are little more than tautologies:

> What is the cause of historical events? Power. What is power? Power is the combined will of the masses vested in one person. On what conditions are the wills of the masses vested in one person? On the condition of that person's expressing the will of all men. That is, power is power. That is, power is a word the meaning of which is beyond our comprehension.[16]

Does power contradict democracy, or does it move through it like a fish in water? Consider how power actually works within the institutions of democracy. The Equal Employment Opportunity Commission, established to reinforce Title VII of the Civil Rights Act of 1964, laid the basis for affirmative action by prohibiting discrimination in hiring practices. Later the Richard Nixon administration conducted the first compliance review of hiring policies toward women by institutions of higher education receiving federal grants, and the president issued an executive order adding sex to other categories of discrimination that were prohibited. Soon a plethora of committees and commissions were established to address the issue of gender as well as race. As Sara Evans put it: "Such commissions constituted a tacit admission that there was indeed a 'problem' regarding women's position in American society, that the democratic vision of equal opportunity had somehow left them out."[17]

In demanding to be allowed in, and in turning to the resources of government, women, like blacks and other once excluded groups, were in fact working against the theoretical presuppositions of the new social history. Instead of history arising democratically from the bottom up, it moved from the top down and the inside out as activists gained control of the offices of power, authority, and decision-making. Activists succeeded only when they posited themselves and engaged in government, and when they went after power they became part of the liberal consensus, however much they saw themselves in conflict with it. Acting for themselves for the first time in history, women finally accepted the legitimacy of interest politics and discarded older causes such as socialism and pacifism. By doing so, they showed their understanding that power resides in institutions and that politics is an exercise in force.

Lincoln's Heirs

For some feminists such a recognition became as much a burden as a blessing. In *Women, Money, and Power*, Phyllis Chesler faced directly "the basic dilemma" of "how women can gain enough money to literally change the world without being corrupted, co-opted, and incorporated on the way by the many value systems we must change."[18] According to Cynthia Fuchs Epstein, author of *Women in Law,* females who went into the legal profession gained confidence not by changing the world but by adapting to it; to the extent their abilities were recognized, their salaries increased, and their positions promoted, professional women achieved a "new self" in a male world.[19] In her essay "When Feminism Failed," Mary Anne Dolan, speaking of fellow workers at the *Los Angeles Herald,* wrote: "If we were passing on to our children merely the values of power, money, and status, it was because those were what we were clinging to. What was missing in the 'new' women I saw at the *Herald* was the joyful 'I am.' What remained was the fearful 'I want.' "[20]

The "fearful 'I want' " is the Lockean woman anxiously asserting what the seventeenth-century philosopher declared to be the attributes and rights of the human species: access to property and opportunity, the values of individualism and autonomy, and an egalitarian stance against hierarchy and patriarchy. Only by operating inside the dimensions of American history can the feminist succeed in her ambitions. If she moves from a sense of victimhood to a high plane of achievement, she will suddenly share in the broader story of American history. The colonists, after all, saw themselves as victimized by British colonial policies, and included a list of whining grievances in the Declaration. But the Declaration leads with a statement of noble human rights that eclipses in scope and grace these petty complaints. The colonists used Locke to overthrow monarchy. Today's feminists can act from within a similar liberal tradition in challenging patriarchy.

The plight of modern women is not too unlike the plight of the early Puritans, who also feared that with success comes compromise and self-recrimination; hence the jeremiad lamenting the failure to live up to earlier ideals. It is the fate of pathbreakers never to be conciliated, and one admires seeing in feminists what Santayana appreciated in the old Puritans: "an agonized conscience" on the part of those who experience "the joys of an unhappiness that confesses itself."[21] The feminist dilemma is as old as philosophy itself. Women once assumed that their access to the world of power would allow their unique capacity for nurturing and moral sentiment to help improve the world. But the desire to obtain something *by* one's efforts and the desire to be something *in* one's efforts are two different things. The race after power, money, and status is bound to be frustrating for, as Simone Weil reminds us, in an open, competitive society power is as unstable as it is contestable and, once obtained, one must use it or lose it.[22] In Henry Adams's novel *Democracy*, the heroine is attracted to Washington, D.C., because she wants to be close to the political workings of "POWER!" Once there, however, she is repelled by the discovery that with power comes corruption and flees the capitol.

The breakthrough of a "new self" in history has always been met with a tragic ambiguity," to use Kenneth Burke's apt phrase, and this applies to men as well as women. Historically ambition, the drive to rise and succeed, has been the seed of an emergent capitalist culture. But ambition and virtue have been uncomfortable bedfellows. In colonial America, political and religious authorities denounced selfishness as sin, as though the Calvinists could not be industrious while practicing self-denial. Goethe, Burke pointed out, both welcomed and feared his Faust, as did Shakespeare his Macbeth; each character gave expression to rising new economic and cultural trends that upset conventional moral standards. Margaret Fuller knew the feeling of a "vaulting ambition, which o'erleaps itself," and she continued to leap. The philosopher William James, in the late nineteenth century, called the cult of success a "bitch goddess." And today aspiring women and ethnic minorities run up against a similar "tragic ambiguity" because ambition still has both favorable and unfavorable connotations. In the eighteenth century Ben Franklin felt the ambiguous emotions about ambition and achievement to be at the heart of the liberal consensus. It still is.[23]

Perhaps those who openly fear the corruptions of power need not flee the centers of power, and those who sense they have been co-opted are expressing their ties with American history itself, which began in hopeful wonder and proceeded toward practical adjustment and pragmatic compromise. Indeed, however "radical" some contemporary historians would like their version of history to be, material reality is the "magnetic North Pole" on the compass of American history. "Power is what they want, not candy," Emerson wrote approvingly of the hustling entrepreneurs of the Jacksonian era. The poet-philosopher also noted that "politics is the activity of the soul illustrated in power," thereby making us aware that in American history freedom, rather than vying with domination, requires the strategic application of force for its realization.

One could well compare Emerson's essay "Self-Reliance" to Betty Friedan's *The Feminine Mystique*. Both sermons preach a consciously chosen autonomy in the face of social pressures to conform to conventional roles, and if Emerson showed men how to overcome fear, Friedan showed women how to overcome guilt. It is both an exasperation and an ecstasy to try to engage in what philosophers call "autodicy," the self's justification to itself. Even Lincoln anguished over his crucial decisions between freedom and order. His own ambitions also faced a "tragic ambiguity" as he tried to pursue the conflicting political values of liberty and democracy, the self-determination of the individual, and the social determinants of society.

The counter-narrative to the story told in these pages would emphasize community, an expression that conveys the more positive feelings of fraternity and solidarity. Historically a community of mutuality and common purpose moves all together or it moves not at all, and often communities resisted change rather than forging it. But the idea of community had a powerful appeal to the generation that witnessed the horrors of the Vietnam War: it blamed America's involvement on a culture of individualism and competitive capitalism that allegedly sought to dominate the world market. And here we confront an awkward irony.

While younger radical scholars accused older liberal historians of being responsible for war, poverty, and racism by either neglecting such topics or treating them nationalistically, and while the younger set called for turning away from a consensus outlook to a conflict-oriented interpretation of the American past, the subsequent fixation on community brought the American mind back to where it started. Various studies emphasizing community sought to show us that workers, women, blacks, and other ethnic and minority groups lived among themselves with no great conflicts as they enjoyed ideas and principles that were common and widely shared. So deep was the need to believe in community that historians who set out to find evidence of conflict may have had a deeper hunger for consensus wherever it could be found—among older Indian tribes, women's networks, and workers' moral economy, or the new cultural identities, generational loyalties, and hands-on Woodstock nations. One need only compare the *Federalist* of the 1780s to the *Port Huron Statement* of the 1960s. At Port Huron, Michigan, in 1962, the radical Students for a Democratic Society (SDS) met to discuss how best to reconceive America and organize its humanistic transformation. From the meeting came a moving manifesto written by Tom Hayden.

The two documents offer a telling juxtaposition. The *Federalist* grappled with conflict and the *Port Huron Statement* invoked consensus; one saw the inexorability of cursed old world factional rivalry, and the other hoped for the possibility of a brave new world of "fraternity," "honesty," "vision," and "love."[24]

It may be helpful to remember that what the 1960s activists once called for, as the early New Left, and what they ended up advocating, as the Academic Left, offer entirely different outlooks regarding America and its ideals. The turning away from America and the embrace of the non-western world and multiculturalism came two decades after the student rebellion of the 1960s. What is amazing about the earlier *Port Huron Statement* is how pro-American was its faith in the possibility for the country's self-regeneration. It may be a stretch to compare the *Port Huron Statement* and the Gettysburg Address, although the repeated references to "alienation" and "anxiety" in the 1960s text would have been understood by a president who had had his own bouts with melancholy and depression.

But what would Lincoln have said had he read that "work should involve incentives worthier than money or survival," and that students "would replace power rooted in possessiveness, privilege, or circumstance by power and uniqueness rooted in love, reflectiveness, and creativity"? Lincoln could well have cited his Lyceum Address to remind the New Left that power requires more than lofty sentiments for its control and that work driven by material reward and the elevation of mind has a worthiness all its own. But Lincoln would have been impressed by the New Left's efforts to awaken America to racial discrimination and poverty, and he would perhaps have been delighted to hear his own words in the text: "government of, by, and for the people." Above all, what the two documents have in common is that both, born of the agony of war, called upon Americans to rededicate their country by returning to earlier principles that had been violated. In ways that neither Lincoln nor the Left clearly understood, the egalitarian ideals of the Declaration would come to be realized in the legal protections of the Constitution: the "apple of gold" came to fruition in the "picture of silver."

Those with the will to work and the ambition to prosper have always made up the liberal consensus—a consensus that includes women, laborers, blacks and other ethnic minorities, all those who believe in the gospel of work and try to live for conviction as well as comfort. Call them Lincoln's heirs. His dreams of possibility symbolize both the foundations and the aspirations of American history, and his speeches on responsibility and moral obligation, and particularly the applause that often greeted such exhortations, continue to provide us with a conscience capable of feeling sin and guilt. Our anxieties today about power and success are part of this legacy of angst, a legacy that actually began the moment the Puritans landed on the shores of New England. From that time forward, the challenge of testing the possibilities of freedom, even against various dogmas of determinism, and even when success brought remorse instead of joy, has run like an unbroken thread throughout American history, a country that has always nurtured, as F. Scott Fitzgerald put it in the final passage from *The Great Gatsby*, our "capacity for wonder," our need to imagine beyond the horizon and to work to get there.[25] The thread still resides within our common history, and Lincoln's vision of our foundations offers the consensus with which we can retrace it.

Notes

Preface

1. J. G. A. Pocock, "Between Gog and Magog: The Republican Thesis and *Ideologia*," *Journal of the History of Ideas* 48 (1987): 325–46.
2. W. H. Auden, "Friday's Child," in *W. H. Auden: Collective Poems*, ed. Edward Mendelson (New York: Vintage, 1991): 675–76.
3. John Dewey, "Time and Individuality," in *John Dewey: The Essential Writings* (New York: Harper Torchbooks, 1999), 145–46.
4. Henry Adams, *The Education of Henry Adams* (1907; New York: Modern Library, 1931), 294.
5. Karl Marx, *Capital: A Critical Analysis of Capitalist Production* (1867; Moscow: Progress Publishers, n.d.), 1:21.
6. Max Weber, *The Protestant Ethic and the Spirit of Capitalism,* trans. Talcott Parsons (1930; New York: Routledge, 1992), 181–82. For further reflections by Weber on America, see John Patrick Diggins, *Max Weber: Politics and the Spirit of Tragedy* (New York: Basic, 1996).
7. *Federalist,* nos. 10 and 47.
8. Alan Bloom, *The Closing of the American Mind* (New York: Simon and Schuster, 1987), 136–56. While I am not entirely in agreement with Bloom's thesis that modern European thought has damaged the American mind, I admire his book for its bouncy brilliance and for its acknowledgment of Lockeanism at the foundation of America: "Americans are Lockeans: recognizing that work is necessary . . . and will produce well-being; following their natural inclinations moderately, not because they possess the virtue of moderation but because their passions are balanced and they recognize the reasonableness of that; respecting the rights of others so that theirs will be respected; obeying the law because they made it in their own interest. From the point of view of God or heroes, all this is not very inspiring. But for the poor, the weak, the oppressed—the overwhelming majority of mankind—it is the promise of salvation. As Leo Strauss put it, moderns 'built on low but solid ground' " (p. 167).

9. Gordon S. Wood, *The Radicalism of the American Revolution* (New York: Knopf, 1992); chapter 2 deals with Wood's widely influential book.

10. Edmund Burke, *Reflections on the Revolution in France,* ed. Conor Cruise O'Brien (1790; London: Penguin, 1983), 304.

11. Christopher Lasch, *The Culture of Narcissism* (New York: Norton, 1978); John Locke, *Second Treatise of Government,* ed. C. B. Macpherson (Indianapolis: Hackett, 1980), 27.

12. Joseph Brodsky, *On Grief and Reason* (New York: Farrar Straus, 1995), 137.

Introduction

1. *Federalist,* no. 1.

2. Abraham Lincoln, "Special Message to Congress, 1861," in *Abraham Lincoln: Speeches and Writings, 1859–1865,* ed. Donald Fehrenbacher (New York: Library of America, 1989; hereafter *S&W*), 2:250; *Notes on the Debates of the Federal Convention of 1787 Reported by James Madison,* introduction by Adrienne Koch (New York: Norton, 1966), 89.

3. Ralph Waldo Emerson, *Representative Men* (New York: Hurst, n.d.), 8–27. On this subject I am indebted to Perry Miller's "Emersonian Genius and American Democracy," in *Nature's Nation* (Cambridge: Harvard Univ. Press, 1967), 163–74.

4. *Lincoln in Martí: A Cuban View of Abraham Lincoln,* ed. Emeterio S. Santovenia, trans. Donald F. Fogelquist (Chapel Hill: Univ. of North Carolina Press, 1953), 66.

5. Walt Whitman, *Leaves of Grass* (Garden City, N.Y.: Doubleday, 1926), 125.

6. *Lincoln in Martí,* 66.

7. *Du Bois: Writings,* ed. Nathan Huggins (New York: Library of America, 1986), 1196–99.

8. Lincoln, *S&W,* 1:456.

9. John Locke, *The Second Treatise of Government,* ed. Thomas P. Peardon (New York: Liberal Arts Press, 1952), 120.

10. Quoted in William A. Henry III, "Beyond the Melting Pot," *Time,* Apr. 9, 1990, p. 31.

11. Thomas Wentworth Higginson, *Army Life in a Black Regiment* (New York: Norton, 1984), 60.

12. Margaret Fuller, "American Literature," in *Margaret Fuller: American Romantic,* ed. Perry Miller (Garden City, N.Y.; Anchor, 1963), 231.

13. Garry Wills, *Lincoln at Gettysburg: The Words That Remade America* (New York: Simon and Schuster, 1992), 38.

14. John C. Calhoun, "Speech on the General State of the Union" (1850), in *Union and Liberty: The Political Philosophy of John C. Calhoun,* ed. Ross M. Lence (Indianapolis: Liberty Fund, 1992), 573–601.

15. *The Collected Works of Abraham Lincoln,* ed. Roy P. Basler, 9 vols. (New Brunswick, N.J.: Rutgers Univ. Press, 1953), 4:128–29.

16. This is not to say that Lincoln was absolutely certain that the Revolution was about the principles enunciated in the Declaration. As will be indicated, Lincoln avoided the question of the causes of the Revolution and even suggested that the motive of the revolutionaries may have been as much hatred of the enemy as love for liberty. But Lincoln had a better grasp than Jefferson of the Lockean meaning of equality

even though there is no evidence that he had read Locke. Jefferson did read Locke, only to misunderstand him when it came to the natural equality of the human species. Without having read him, Lincoln intuited the Lockean meaning of equality in regard to the rights of labor.

17. Lincoln, S&W, 1:28–36.

18. Jefferson was perfectly aware of the Lockean meaning of property and labor as rights grounded in the laws of nature; he refers to it in, among other places, his 1801 inaugural address. Years earlier, warning Madison about the danger of the maldistribution of wealth, Jefferson wrote: "Whenever there is in any country, uncultivated lands and unemployed poor, it is clear that the laws of property have been so far extended as to violate natural right. The earth is given as a common stock for man to labour and live on. If, for the encouragement of industry, we allow it to be appropriated, we must take care that other employment be furnished to those excluded from the appropriation. If we do not the fundamental right to labour the earth returns to the unemployed." Thomas Jefferson to James Madison, Oct. 28, 1785, in The Portable Jefferson, ed. Merril D. Peterson (New York: Viking, 1975), 396–97.

19. On this point I am much indebted to the thoughtful essay of John H. Schaar, "And the Pursuit of Happiness," in Legitimacy in the Modern State (New Brunswick, N.J.: Transaction, 1981), 231–49. See also Howard Mumford Jones, The Pursuit of Happiness (1953; Ithaca, N.Y.: Cornell Univ. Press, 1966. Jefferson dismissed Ben Franklin's position, insisting that "those who mistake happiness for the mere absence of pain" are engaging in "a miserable arithmetic." Jefferson to Maria Cosway, Oct. 12, 1786, in The Life and Selected Writings of Thomas Jefferson, ed. Adrienne Koch and William Peden (New York: Modern Library, 1944), 403. Jefferson called himself an Epicurean, and his notions of happiness had a touch of the hedonic. Jefferson starts America out in pursuit of a goal that many Enlightenment philosophers thought could scarcely be reached because it could hardly be grasped. Jean-Jacques Rousseau thought that "to seek happiness without knowing where it is" could lead one to remain inactive for fear of going astray, whereas by not even thinking about it "I followed the road to happiness." Separated from will and intelligence, the idea of happiness seems to defy reason itself. See Rousseau, Emile; or On Education, trans. Allan Bloom (1762; New York: Basic, 1979), 442–43.

20. Whether it is defined as the gratification of desires or the pursuit of pleasures, happiness for Jefferson is unambiguously positive. He once defined happiness as "to be not pained in body, nor troubled in mind" (Schaar, "And the Pursuit of Happiness," 241). Lincoln was too troubled a thinker not be troubled about slavery.

21. Friedrich Nietzsche, Genealogy of Morals and Ecce Homo, ed. and trans. Walter Kaufman (New York: Vintage, 1989), 38.

22. The idea of happiness may be as politically mischievous as it is philosophically misleading. Reinhold Niebuhr's observations on Jefferson's formulation suggested how it easily led to the sin of pride as America equated prosperity with virtue and assumed its superiority to the rest of the world. What Niebuhr wrote in 1952, when the Korean War had turned into a tragic stalemate, could have been said with equal force a decade later during the Vietnam War: "There are many young men in Korea today who have been promised the 'pursuit of

happiness' as an inalienable right. But the possession of the right brings them no simple happiness. Such happiness as they may achieve is curiously mixed with pain, anxiety and sorrow. It is in fact not happiness at all. If it is anything, it may be what Lincoln called 'the solemn joy that must be yours to have laid so costly a sacrifice upon the altar of freedom.'" Reinhold Niebuhr, *The Irony of American History* (New York: Scribner's, 1952), 61; Jones, *Pursuit of Happiness,* 16.

23. William James, *A Pluralistic Universe,* cited in *The Writings of William James,* ed. John J. McDermott (New York: Modern Library, 1968), viii.

Chapter 1: Abraham Lincoln

1. On Marxism's departure from classical thought, see Hannah Arendt, *The Human Condition* (Chicago: Univ. of Chicago Press, 1958); Andrzej Walicki, *Marxism and the Leap to the Kingdom of Freedom* (Stanford, Calif.: Stanford Univ. Press, 1955); and George E. McCarthy, *Marx and the Ancients: Classical Ethics, Social Justice, and Nineteenth-Century Political Economy* (Savage, Md.: Rowland and Littlefield, 1990). The prevailing view is that the doctrine of natural rights begins with Hobbes and specifically with Locke, and that the idea of a state of nature presupposes that the individual exists prior to civil society, and rights are advanced against the state. A certain view of rights can be found in Aristotle's conviction that justice is a communal virtue and that all citizens are entitled to share in the good life. See the valuable work by Fred D. Miller Jr., *Nature, Justice, and Rights in Aristotle's Politics* (New York: Oxford Univ. Press, 1995).

2. William Appleman Williams, *The Contours of American History* (Chicago: Quadrangle, 1966), 285.

3. David Donald, *Lincoln* (New York: Simon and Schuster, 1995), 14.

4. Abraham Lincoln to Albert G. Hodges, Apr. 4, 1864, Lincoln, *S&W,* 2:585–86.

5. See Nicola Chiaromonte, *The Paradox of History* (Philadelphia: Univ. of Pennsylvania Press, 1970).

6. Pieter Geyl, *Debates with Historians* (New York: Meridian, 1958), 259.

7. Stendahl, *The Charterhouse of Parma,* trans. Margaret R. B. Shaw (New York: Penguin, 1958), 47, 59; see also Isaiah Berlin, *The Hedgehog and the Fox* (New York: Simon and Schuster, 1966).

8. Garry Wills, *Lincoln at Gettysburg: Words That Made American History* (New York: Doubleday, 1992), 32–40.

9. John C. Calhoun, "Speech on Union," in *Union and Liberty: The Political Philosophy of John C. Calhoun,* ed. Ross M. Lence (Indianapolis; Liberty Fund, 1992), 582.

10. Richard Hofstadter, *The American Political Tradition and the Men Who Made It* (New York: Knopf, 1948), i–ii.

11. Ibid., 93–136.

12. Ibid., 137–63.

13. Daniel J. Boorstin, *America and the Image of Europe: Reflections on American Thought* (Cleveland: Meridian, 1960), 99.

14. Ibid., 43–61.

15. Daniel J. Boorstin, *The Genius of American Politics* (Chicago: Univ. of Chicago Press, 1953), 1–35, 100–116; see also John P. Diggins, "Consciousness and Ideol-

ogy in American History: The Burden of Daniel J. Boorstin," *American Historical Review* 76 (1971): 99–117; John P. Diggins, "The Perils of Naturalism: Some Reflections on Daniel J. Boorstin's Approach to American History," *American Quarterly* 28 (1971): 153–80.

16. John C. Calhoun, "Speech on the Oregon Bill," in *Union and Liberty*, 564.
17. John C. Calhoun, "A Disquisition on Government," in *Union and Liberty*, 5–78.
18. *The Lincoln-Douglas Debates*, ed. Robert W. Johannsen (New York: Oxford Univ. Press, 1965), 37–48, 73, 130.
19. Ibid., 219–37.
20. Lincoln, *S&W*, 4:301–2.
21. John Locke, *The Second Treatise of Government*, ed. Thomas P. Peardon (1660? Indianapolis: Bobbs-Merrill, 1952), 6.
22. Pauline Maier, *American Scripture: Making the Declaration of Independence* (New York: Knopf, 1997), xix–xx; Wills, *Lincoln at Gettysburg*, 38.
23. Lincoln, *S&W*, 2:405, 520.
24. Ibid., 4:24–25.
25. Eric Foner, *Free Soil, Free Labor, Free Men* (New York: Oxford Univ. Press, 1970), 38.
26. Thorstein Veblen, *The Higher Learning in America: A Memorandum on the Conduct of Universities by Business Men* (1918; New York: Hill and Wang, 1957).
27. Gabor S. Boritt, *Lincoln and the Economics of the American Dream* (Urbana: Univ. of Illinois Press, 1994), vi; *The Historian's Lincoln: Pseudohistory, Psychohistory, and History*, ed. Gabor S. Boritt (Urbana: Univ. of Illinois Press, 1988).
28. Quoted in Boritt, *Lincoln*, xxiv.
29. Lincoln, *S&W*, 1:303.
30. Ibid., 1:307–48.
31. Ibid., 1:456.
32. At the heart of Lincoln's dilemmas was the tension between liberalism and conservatism that characterizes the Declaration and the Constitution: the Declaration gives the people the right to revolt in order to free themselves, whereas the Constitution instructs them of the need to establish institutions in order to preserve themselves. Two insightful analyses of Lincoln's dilemmas are Richard Weaver, *The Ethics of Rhetoric* (Chicago: Gateway, 1953), 85–114; and Kenneth M. Stampp, "The United States and National Self-Determination," in *Lincoln: The War President*, ed. Gabor S. Boritt (New York: Oxford Univ. Press, 1992), 123–44. The classic, pioneering work on Lincoln's political thought is Harry V. Jaffa, *Crisis of the House Divided: An Interpretation of the Lincoln-Douglas Debates* (Seattle: Univ. of Washington Press, 1959).
33. Ralph Waldo Emerson, "Lincoln," in *Selected Writings of Ralph Waldo Emerson*, ed. Brooks Atkinson (New York: Modern Library, 1992), 831.
34. See, for example, David Donald, "Abraham Lincoln and the American Pragmatic Tradition," in *Lincoln Reconsidered: Essays on the Civil War Era* (New York: Vintage, 1961), 128–43.
35. Lincoln, *S&W*, 1:28–36.
36. Reinhold Niebuhr, "Theology and Political Thought in the Western World," in *Faith and Politics*, ed. Robert Stone (New York: Braziller, 1968), 55.
37. Lincoln, *S&W*, 1:333.
38. Ibid., 1:484.
39. Emerson, "Lincoln," 829–36.

40. Ralph Waldo Emerson, "Greatness," in *Letters and Social Aims* (Boston: Houghton Mifflin, 1904), 318–19.

Chapter 2: America's Lockean Moment

1. Lincoln, *S&W*, 1:36.
2. Ibid.
3. Ibid., 1:35.
4. Ibid., 2:686.
5. Thomas Jefferson to Samuel Kercheval, July 12, 1816, in *The Life and Selected Writings of Thomas Jefferson*, ed. Adrienne Koch and William Peden (New York: Modern Library, 1944), 673–76; see also Daniel J. Boorstin, *The Lost World of Thomas Jefferson* (1948; Boston: Beacon, 1960), 194–213.
6. Allen C. Guelzo, *Abraham Lincoln: Redeemer President* (Grand Rapids, Mich.: Eerdmans, 1999).
7. The philosopher Santayana has Socrates articulating what could well be Lincoln's position and "The Stranger" that of Jefferson:

> SOCRATES: For who can have a greater stake in a country than its founders, whose whole soul and single hope was devoted to establishing it, that it might last and be true to their thought forever; or than the soldiers who in many wars have successively given lives to preserve it? Surely at every meeting of your assembly their votes are counted first, which they once cast so solemnly and sincerely, and at so great a sacrifice to themselves for your sake; and their veto is interposed beforehand against any rash measure that might undo their labours, stultify their hopes, and banish their spirit from the house which they built and loved.
>
> THE STRANGER: No; the dead have no vote among us. On the contrary, we think they have too much influence as it is without voting, because they have bequeathed institutions to us which encumber our playground and are not to our liking; and the inertia which these institutions oppose to our fresh desires seems to us a hateful force, which we call the dead hand.

George Santayana, *Dialogues in Limbo* (Ann Arbor: Univ. of Michigan Press, 1957), 115–16.
8. Speech at Lewistown, Illinois, Aug. 17, 1858, in *The Collected Works of Abraham Lincoln*, ed. Roy P. Basler, 9 vols. (New Brunswick, N.J.: Rutgers Univ. Press, 1953), 2:547.
9. Alexis de Tocqueville, *Democracy in America*, ed. J. P. Mayer, trans. George Lawrence (1835–40; New York: Harper, 1969), 2:331, 484; Lincoln, "Second Inaugural," "Gettysburg Address," in *The Portable Lincoln*, ed. Andrew Delbanco (New York: Viking, 1992), 269, 295.
10. C. B. Macpherson, *The Theory of Possessive Individualism* (Oxford: Oxford Univ. Press, 1962).
11. Quoted in Howard Mumford Jones, *The Pursuit of Happiness* (1953; Ithaca, N.Y.: Cornell Univ. Press, 1966), 21.
12. When a few years ago I submitted to the *American Historical Review* a paper making this argument, it was roundly rejected by anonymous readers, all of

whom upheld the school of classical republicanism. Yet more recently in the field of political science Lockeanism is enjoying a revival. See Joshua Foa Dienstag, "Saving God and Mammon: The Lockean Sympathy in Early American Political Thought," *American Political Science Review* 90 (1996): 497–511; Michael Zuckert, *Natural Rights and the New Republicanism* (Princeton, N.J.: Princeton Univ. Press, 1994); A. John Simmons, *The Lockean Theory of Rights* (Princeton, N.J.: Princeton Univ. Press, 1992); and James Tully, *An Approach to Political Philosophy: Locke in Context* (New York: Cambridge Univ. Press, 1993).

13. Chris Nyland, "Locke and the Social Position of Women," *History of Political Economy* 25 (1993): 39–63.

14. John Locke, *The Second Treatise of Government*, ed. Thomas P. Peardon (1660?; Indianapolis: Bobbs-Merrill, 1952), 29.

15. Gordon S. Wood, *The Radicalism of the American Revolution* (New York: Knopf, 1991), 95–212.

16. Kenneth Burke, *Attitudes toward History* (1937; Boston: Beacon, 1961), 229–30.

17. Newt Gingrich, *To Renew America* (New York: Harper, 1995), 32.

18. Ibid., 33.

19. Wood, *Radicalism,* 96.

20. See. J. G. A. Pocock, *The Machiavellian Moment: Florentine Political Thought and the Atlantic Republican Tradition* (Princeton, N.J.: Princeton Univ. Press, 1975).

21. *Federalist,* nos. 9, 14, 18.

22. Boorstin, *Lost World of Jefferson,* 204–12.

23. Karl Marx, "The Eighteenth Brumaire of Louis Bonaparte," in *The Marx-Engels Reader,* ed. Robert C. Tucker (New York: Norton, 1978), 596.

24. "Their task cannot be," Gordon Wood has said of fellow scholars, " 'to unravel the truth of the situation as distinct from the myth that is current about it.' Ideas do not mask reality; they define and create it." Wood, "Intellectual History and the Social Sciences," in *New Directions in American Intellectual History,* ed. John Higham and Paul K. Conkin (Baltimore: Johns Hopkins Univ. Press, 1979), 33. Whether or not political language represents or creates reality, the historian has an obligation to study how language is used and possibly abused. Consider the following passage from Wood's book: "The Revolution brought to the surface the republican tendencies of American life. The 'Suddenness' of the change from monarchy to republicanism was 'astonishing.' 'Idolatry to Monarchs, and servility to Aristocratical Pride,' said John Adams in the summer of 1776, 'was never so totally eradicated from so many Minds in so short of time.' Probably Adams should not have been astonished, for the truncated nature of American society with its high proportion of freeholders seemed naturally made for republicanism. Yet adopting republicanism was not simply a matter of bringing American culture more in line with the society. It meant as well an opportunity to abolish what remained of monarchy and to create once and for all new, enlightened republican relationships among people" (Wood, *Radicalism,* 169). Contrary to Wood's contention, Adams had every right to be "astonished" at the "suddenness" with which a republican sentiment broke out. For Adams understood that the colonists, instead of having been long-abiding republicans, as Wood holds, remained sympathetic to monarchism until 1775, when they heard that George III had denounced them as "rebels," whereupon they felt betrayed and abandoned; and many continued to harbor monarchist sympathies until the Declaration of Inde-

pendence. Yet historians feel the need to reiterate the expression "republic" and "republicanism" here and elsewhere in contemporary scholarship without situating the expression within a quotation so that we can be assured that eighteenth-century Americans actually used the terms.

25. Thomas Paine, "The Rights of Man," in *Thomas Paine: Representative Selections,* ed. Harry Hayden Clark (New York: Hill and Wang, 1961), 210.

26. Wood, *Radicalism,* 3–8, 96, 229–32.

27. When Daniel Bell wrote *The End of Ideology* (New York: Free Press, 1960), he had in mind Marxism as an extension of the Enlightenment's dream that history is moving rationally, both by its own inexorability and by human agency, to the point where it becomes conscious of controlling the forces of history and hence crosses over from necessity to freedom. In his seminal work *The Ideological Origins of the American Revolution* (Cambridge: Harvard Univ. Press, 1965), Bernard Bailyn's notion of ideology derived more from Clifford Geertz and the idea that belief systems are constructed out of symbols that mediate meanings and guide political conduct. This mid-twentieth-century notion of cultural symbols is a long way from DeStrutt de Tracy's *Elements d'idéologie,* which offered a "science of ideas" and held out such utopian hopes that Napoleon was to dismiss its followers, *idéologues,* as visionaries and John Adams was to ridicule the term itself as "idiocy." See George Lichtheim, *The Concept of Ideology and Other Essays* (New York: Vintage, 1967), 3–47.

28. Bernard Bailyn would probably reject the description "paranoid," but in his *Ideological Origins of the American Revolution* the colonists are accurately described as suspicious and in the grip of anxiety about power, convinced that its very presence is a threat to liberty. In the *Federalist,* Hamilton had to deal with this fear of power as he tried to remind his country that power can enable as well as oppress.

29. Consumption for the sake of social prestige, rather than "loosening the bonds of society," reinforces them, as was pointed out by Adam Smith in *A Theory of Moral Sentiments* (1725), John Adams in *Discourses in Davilia* (1796), and Charlotte Perkins Gilman in *Women and Economics* (1898). Instead of engendering a capacity for independence, "emulation" leaves the cultural hegemony of the upper classes unchallenged. "How much more worthwhile was such emulative consumption in America, where distinctions of rank were more blurred," writes Wood in making a comparison to England (*Radicalism,* 135). More worthwhile indeed, but the blurring of class distinctions makes consumption not only a ritual but also a race in which citizens struggle to stay ahead in social strata that are shifting and being re-formed. Consumerism may indicate that the social order is opening up, but to ape the gentry class by buying commodities for the sake of their display value is hardly a declaration of independence from social dependency. Thinkers from Adams to Tocqueville, from Thorstein Veblen to Georg Simmel, saw such a race as expressing the human need for approbation and the "passion for distinction," and feminists would come to see that consumption relegated the wife to a buyer of the ornamental and wasteful as a validation of the husband's leisure-class status, while at the same time reinforcing the categories of "economic man" and "domestic woman." The coming of consumer culture could be considered as much inhibiting as liberating in regard to two categories that have no significant place in republicanism: women and workers, both of

whom were made to feel the status of leisure and the stigma of labor. Moreover, all of this drive for recognition through consumption says something about human ambition on the part of people unsure of themselves, an uncertainty at the very heart of liberal individualism. See *Gender and Stratification,* ed. Rosemary Crampton and Michael Mann (London: Polity, 1986); John P. Diggins, *The Bard of Savagery: Thorstein Veblen and Modern Social Theory* (New York: Seabury, 1978).

30. Wood, *Radicalism,* 78.
31. Ibid., 303–4.
32. "Public office in the olden time was looked upon as a free-hold designed by nature for the care of certain families. This idea came to America with the settlers and held firm place throughout the colonial era. The theory did not depart with the Loyalists. The radicals, who had had a slight chance of office, were glad to see the Tories go and helped them off. They seized their offices and adopted their ideas of office holding. After having once fed at the public crib, it seemed a perfectly natural thing to continue the feeding there." Edward Channing, *A History of the United States,* vol. 4: *Federalists and Republicans* (New York: Macmillan, 1917), 50–56; Henry Adams, "Civil Service Reform," in *The Great Secession Winter of 1860–61 and Other Essays,* ed. George E. Hochfield (New York: A. A. Barnes, 1958), 95–128; Max Weber, *Zur Politik im Weltkrief: Schriften and Reden, 1914– 1918,* ed. Wolfgang J. Mommsen (Tübingen: J. C. B. Mohr, 1988).
33. Hannah Arendt, *The Human Condition* (Chicago: Univ. of Chicago Press, 1958).
34. Burke quoted in Conor Cruise O'Brien, *The Suspecting Glance* (London: Faber, 1972), 39–49.
35. A. J. Ayer, *Thomas Paine* (New York: Atheneum, 1988), 79.
36. The poem and Trumbell are quoted in Kenneth Silverman, *A Cultural History of the American Revolution* (New York: Columbia Univ. Press, 1987), 505.
37. Ibid., 506.
38. "A new generation of democratic Americans," Wood wrote of the Jacksonian era, "was no longer interested in the revolutionaries' dream of building a classical republic of elitist virtue out of the inherited material of the Old World" (Wood, *Radicalism,* 369).
39. *Federalist,* no. 9; Michael Lienesch, "Interpreting Experience: History, Philosophy, and Science in the Constitutional Debates," *American Politics Quarterly* 11 (1983): 379–401; John P. Diggins, *The Lost Soul of American Politics: Virtue, Self-Interest, and the Foundations of Liberalism* (New York: Basic, 1984).
40. *Federalist,* no. 10.
41. See Yehoshua Arieli, *Individualism and Nationalism in American Ideology* (Baltimore: Penguin, 1966), 180.
42. Quoted ibid., 247.
43. Hector St. John Crèvecoeur, *Letters from an American Farmer* (1782; Garden City, N.Y.: Dolphin, n.d.), 50; Pauline Maier, *American Scripture: Making the Declaration of Independence* (New York: Knopf, 1997).
44. Wood, *Radicalism,* 369.
45. François Furet, *The Passing of an Illusion: The Idea of Communism in the Twentieth Century* (Chicago: Univ. of Chicago Press, 1999), 9.
46. See Aron's valuable essay "The Myth of Revolution," in his *The Opium of the Intellectuals,* trans. Terence Kilmartin (New York: Norton, 1962), 33–65.

47. U.S. Senate, "The Nature of Revolution," *Hearings: Committee on Foreign Relations,* 19th Congress, 2d sess., Feb. 19, Feb. 21, Feb. 26, Mar. 7, 1968 (Washington: Government Printing Office, 1968), 140–41.

48. Horace Bushnell, "Barbarism, the First Danger" (1842), in *On Intellectuals,* ed. Philip Rieff (Garden City, N.Y.: Anchor, 1970), 183–202.

Chapter 3: American Identity in an Age of Political Correctness

1. Ho Chi Minh is quoted in Susan Dunn, "Enlightenment Legacies," *Partisan Review* 66 (1999): 532–54; on the controversy, see Michael Lind, *Vietnam, the Necessary War: A Reinterpretation of America's Most Disastrous Military Conflict* (New York: Free Press, 1999).

2. Quoted in Susan Mueller, "An Instant That Lingers" *Media Studies Journal* 12 (Fall 1998): 8.

3. The *National History Standards* are actually titled *National Standards for United States History* (Los Angeles: National Center for for History in the Schools, n.d.), 3. (Hereafter *NHS.*)

4. *NHS,* 75.

5. Franco Venturi, *The End of the Old World Regimes in Europe,* trans. R. Burr Litchfield (Princeton, N.J.: Princeton Univ. Press, 1991), 2 vols.

6. Marx is quoted in Edmund Wilson, *To the Finland Station: A Study in the Writing and Acting of History* (1941; New York: Farrar Straus Giroux, 1971), 377; Engels in Lewis S. Feuer, *Marx and the Intellectuals: A Set of Post-Ideological Essays* (Garden City, N.Y.: Anchor, 1969), 214.

7. Hannah Arendt, *On Revolution* (New York: Viking, 1963), 49.

8. Max Eastman, "The Wisdom of Lenin," *Liberator* 7 (1924): 24.

9. Max Eastman, "The Religion of Patriotism," *Masses* (July 1917): 8–12; Randolph Bourne, "The State," in *War and the Intellectuals: Collected Essays,* ed. Carl Resek (New York: Harper, 1964), 65–104.

10. Margaret Fuller, "Fourth of July, 1845," in *Margaret Fuller: American Romantic,* ed. Perry Miller (Garden City, N.Y.: Anchor, 1963), 210–13.

11. Ernest Hemingway, *A Farewell to Arms* (1929; New York: Scribner's, 1957), 184–85.

12. Richard Rorty,"The Unpatriotic Academy," *New York Times,* Feb. 13, 1994; Nussbaum's essay is in *For the Love of Country: Debating the Limits of Patriotism,* ed. Joshua Cohen (Boston: Beacon, 1996).

13. G. K. Chesterton, "Paying for Patriotism" in, *The Common Man* (New York: Sheed and Ward, 1933), 50–52.

14. John H. Schaar, "The Case for Patriotism," in *Legitimacy in the Modern State* (New Brunswick, N.J.: Transaction, 1989), 285–311.

15. Maurizo Viroli, *For Love of Country: An Essay on Patriotism and Nationalism* (New York: Oxford Univ. Press, 1995).

16. Benedetto Croce, "Patriotism: A Disused Word," in *My Philosophy: Essays on the Moral and Political Problems of Our Time* (New York: Collier, 1962), 132–33.

17. *Bonds of Affection: Americans Define Their Patriotism,* ed. John Bodner (Princeton, N.J.: Princeton Univ. Press, 1996).

18. John Dewey, "Education as Politics," in *Character and Events,* ed. Joseph Ratner, 2 vols. (New York: Henry Holt, 1929), 2:776–781.

19. Arthur M. Schlesinger, "Historical News," *American Historical Review* 46 (July 1941): 1003–4.

20. R. G. Collingwood, *Essays on the Philosophy of History,* ed. William Debbins (New York: McGraw-Hill, 1965), 77–78.

21. Nathaniel Hawthorne, *French and Italian Notebooks* (Cambridge, Mass.: Houghton Mifflin, 1871), 456–57.

22. Quoted in Edmund S. Morgan, *The Genius of George Washington* (New York: Norton, 1980), 51.

23. *Federalist,* no. 1.

24. See Blandine Kriegel, *The Rule of Law: A Case for the State* (Princeton, N.J.: Princeton Univ. Press, 1995), 93–96.

25. Conor Cruise O'Brien, *The Long Affair: Thomas Jefferson and the French Revolution, 1785–1800* (Chicago: Univ. of Chicago Press, 1996).

26. Tocqueville, *Democracy,* 367.

27. Quoted in John Keane, *Tom Paine: A Political Life* (Boston: Little, Brown, 1995), xiii, 231.

28. There are, of course, many Enlightenments. German philosophers like J. G. Herder did emphasize differences and cultural relativism or pluralism. Much of the American political founding had its intellectual origins not in the French but in a Scottish Enlightenment that was distrustful of reason. Alexander Hamilton was steeped in David Hume, as was John Adams in Adam Smith. Even the European Enlightenment was open to non-western cultures, as indicated in Montesquieu's *The Persian Letters.* Those contemporary scholars who continue the critique of the Enlightenment first articulated by German émigré scholars, the program of "Critical Theory" associated with the Frankfurt school, scarcely take into account this influence of Calvinism and Scottish skepticism on the American Enlightenment.

29. Nell Irvin Painter, "Bias and Synthesis," *Journal of American History* 74 (1987): 109–12.

30. Thomas Bender, "Wholes and Parts: The Need for Synthesis in American History," *Journal of American History* 73 (1986): 120–36; Eric. H. Monkkonen, "The Dangers of Synthesis," *American Historical Review* 91 (1986): 1146–57.

31. John Fonte, "We the Peoples: Multicultural Agendas," *National Review* 48 (Mar. 24, 1996): 47–49.

32. Lincoln, speech in Chicago, July 10, 1858, *S&W,* 1:58.

33. Friedrich Nietzsche, *On the Use and Disadvantage of History for Life,* trans. Peter Preuss (1873; Indianapolis: Hackett, 1980), 7–35.

34. Ralph Waldo Emerson, "Memory," *The Portable Emerson,* ed. Mark Van Doren (New York: Viking, 1946), 284.

35. This position is held more by the philosophical conservative than the free-market libertarian. "Conservatism assumes the existence of an objective moral order based upon ontological foundations," wrote Frank Meyer when an older conservatism was at its intellectual height in America. See Frank S. Meyer, "The Recrudescent American Conservatism," in *American Conservative Thought in the Twentieth Century,* ed. William F. Buckley Jr. (Indianapolis: Bobbs-Merrill, 1970), 80. Lockean liberalism promises that modern life can get along without ontological foundations as the mind turns toward the practical tasks at hand. Reason, Locke wrote, cannot get to the bottom of things, for knowledge enters the mind through impressions, notions, habits, and other external stimuli that leave their

inscriptions. "Reason does not lay down a foundation, even though oftentimes it erects a superb structure, and raises as far as heaven the summits of the sciences." John Locke, *Questions Concerning the Law of Nature,* ed. Robert Horwitz, Jenny Strauss Clay, and Diskin Clay (Ithaca, N.Y.: Cornell Univ. Press, 1990), 121.

36. Charles Kelser, "The Founding of American Unity," and Harvey Mansfield, "The Twofold Meaning of 'Unum,' " in *Reinventing the American People: Unity and Diversity Today,* ed. Robert Royal (Grand Rapids, Mich.: Eerdmans, 1955), 93–114.

37. *Federalist,* no. 2.

38. Randolph Bourne, "Trans-National America," in *The Radical Will: Randolph Bourne; Selected Writings, 1911–1918,* ed. Olaf Hansen (New York: Urizen, 1977), 248–64.

39. Iris Marion Young, *Justice and the Politics of Difference* (Princeton, N.J.: Princeton Univ. Press, 1990), 98–99.

40. *Federalist,* no. 10.

41. Arthur O. Lovejoy, *The Great Chain of Being: A Study in the History of an Idea* (New York: Harper, 1960), 6, 208–25.

42. *Federalist,* nos. 6, 10, 24, 51.

43. *Federalist,* nos. 28, 51, 56, 60.

44. *Federalist,* nos. 10, 51, 85. In the last of the papers, Hamilton quotes David Hume and esteems his "judicial reflections."

45. John Adams, *A Defense of the Constitutions of the Government of the United States of America,* 3 vols. (1787–88; New York: Da Capo, 1971), 3:488–89.

46. *Federalist,* nos. 1, 2, 6, 51; Adams, "Preface" to *Defense,* in *The Political Writings of John Adams,* ed. George Peek (Indianapolis: Bobbs-Merrill, 1954), 115; Adams to Jefferson, Oct. 9, 1787, in *The Adams-Jefferson Letters,* ed. Lester J. Cappon (New York: Simon and Schuster, 1971), 202–3; Thomas Jefferson, *Notes on the State of Virginia,* ed. Thomas Abernathy (New York: Harper, 1964), 156.

47. An excellent analysis of Jefferson's thoughts on human variety is Daniel J. Boorstin, *The Lost World of Thomas Jefferson* (1948; Boston: Beacon, 1960).

48. Adams is quoted in Adrienne Koch, *Power, Morals, and the Founding Fathers* (Ithaca, N.Y.: Cornell Univ. Press, 1961), 82.

49. Alexander Hamilton, "Report on Manufacturers," *The Papers of Alexander Hamilton,* ed. Harold C. Syrett and Jacob E. Cooke, 26 vols. (New York: Columbia Univ. Press, 1966), 10:83, 293–94.

50. Quoted in George Wilson Pierson, *Tocqueville in America* (1938; Baltimore: Johns Hopkins Univ. Press, 1996), 129.

51. On Marx's critique of capitalism, see Chapter 8; on Hamilton's view of a money economy, see Forest McDonald, *Alexander Hamilton: A Biography* (New York: Norton, 1982).

52. Henry Adams, *The History of the United States of America During the Administrations of Thomas Jefferson and James Madison,* 2 vols. (New York: Library of America, 1986), 2:1331.

Chapter 4: American Exceptionalism

1. Reagan's inaugural address, reprinted in the *New York Times,* Jan. 21, 1981.

2. Henry Adams, *Democracy: An American Novel* (1880; New York; Airmont, 1968), 44.

3. See John Patrick Diggins, "The National History Standards," *American Scholar* 65 (1996): 495–522; the convergence thesis was first formulated in Gary B. Nash's *Red, White, and Black: The Peoples of Early America* (Englewood Cliffs, N.J.; Prentice Hall, 1974); it was then uncritically incorporated into the *National History Standards*.

4. Perry Miller, *The New England Mind: From Colony to Province* (Cambridge: Harvard Univ. Press, 1953), 3–26.

5. Daniel J. Boorstin, *The Lost World of Thomas Jefferson* (1948; Boston: Beacon, 1960), 29–80.

6. Alexis de Tocqueville, *Democracy in America*, ed. J. P. Mayer, trans. George Lawrence (1835–40; New York: Harper, 1969), 525–30.

7. See John P. Diggins, *Up from Communism: Conservative Odysseys in American Intellectual History* (New York: Harper, 1975), 142–43.

8. Quoted in Seymour Martin Lipset, *American Exceptionalism: A Double-Edged Sword* (New York: Norton, 1996), 79.

9. Thomas Paine, *Common Sense*, ed. Isaac Kramnick (New York: Penguin, 1982), 63.

10. Boorstin, *Lost World of Jefferson*, 228.

11. Quoted in Joyce Appleby, "Recovering America's Historical Diversity: Beyond Exceptionalism," *Journal of American History* 79 (1992): 419–31.

12. Quoted in Susan Dunn, "Conflict or Consensus? Lessons from the Sister Revolutions," *Partisan Review* 65 (1998): 195–213.

13. Louis Hartz, *The Liberal Tradition in America* (New York: Harcourt, 1955), 85–86.

14. Gurowski and Belloc are quoted in C. Vann Woodward, *The Old World's New World* (New York: Oxford Univ. Press, 1991), 72.

15. Tocqueville, *Democracy*, 251, 634–45.

16. Ibid., 31–49, 290–301.

17. Max Weber, "Capitalism in Rural Society in Germany," *From Max Weber: Essays in Sociology*, ed. H. H. Gerth and C. Wright Mills (New York: Oxford Univ. Press, 1946), 363–85.

18. Abraham Lincoln, "Fragment on the Constitution and Union," in *The Collected Works of Abraham Lincoln*, ed. Roy P. Basler, 9 vols. (New Brunswick, N.J.: Rutgers Univ. Press, 1953), 4:168–69.

19. Karl Marx, "The Eighteenth Brumaire of Louis Napoleon," in *The Marx-Engels Reader*, ed. Robert Tucker (New York: Norton, 1978), 602; Karl Marx, *Capital: A Critical Analysis of Capitalist Production* (1867; Moscow: Progress Pub., n.d), 1:21.

20. Hartz, *Liberal Tradition*, 134.

21. The consensus outlook on American society was seen as troublesome by the New England Transcendentalists, whose doctrine of "self-reliance" attempted to inculcate the virtues of solitude and steer the democratic citizen away from what Tocqueville called the "tyranny of public opinion."

22. On the Academic Left, see John Patrick Diggins, *The Rise and Fall of the American Left* (New York: Norton, 1992).

23. Herbert Butterfield, *The Whig Interpretation of History* (1931; New York: Norton, 1965).

24. Charles Sellers, *The Market Revolution: Jacksonian America, 1815–1846* (New York: Oxford Univ. Press, 1991), 3–69, 268, 340–41; Sean Wilentz, *Chants Democratic: New York City and the Rise of the American Working Class, 1788–1850* (New York: Oxford Univ. Press, 1985), 61–103.

25. Simon Middleton, "Rights, Privileges, and the Place of the Artisan in Colonial New York," Ph.D. thesis, City University of New York, 1998.

26. George Santayana, "Emerson the Poet," in *Santayana on America*, ed. Richard Colton Lyon (New York: Harcourt, 1968), 268–83.

27. Tocqueville, *Democracy*, 506–13.

28. Lincoln, *S&W*, 2:415.

29. The philosopher Richard Rorty hungers for a politics of solidarity and exhorts the Left to cease its bickering and factionalism. Yet his historical advice is problematic. He urges the academic intellectual to return for guidance to the 1930s, the most divisive and sectarian decade in modern American history. See Rorty, *Achieving Our Country* (Cambridge: Harvard Univ. Press, 1998).

30. William James, "What Pragmatism Means," in *The Writings of William James*, ed. John J. McDermott (New York: Modern Lib., 1968), 384.

31. Barry Alan Shain, *The Myth of American Individualism: The Protestant Origins of American Political Thought* (Princeton, N.J.: Princeton Univ. Press, 1994).

32. Quoted in Raymond Aron, *Main Currents in Sociological Thought*, trans. Richard Howard and Helen Weaver (Garden City, N.Y.: Anchor, 1968), 1:265. See also Hartz, *Liberal Tradition*.

33. Quoted in George Wilson Pierson, *Tocqueville in America* (1938; Baltimore: Johns Hopkins Univ. Press, 1996), 129.

34. Reinhold Niebuhr, *Moral Man in Immoral Society* (1932; New York: Scribner's, 1960), xi–xii.

35. Hartz, *Liberal Tradition*, 283.

36. William James, "Pragmatism's Conception of Truth," in McDermott, *Writings of William James*, 429–43.

37. Mary Nolan, "Review Essays: American Exceptionalism," *American Historical Review* 102 (1997): 748–74.

38. John Adams, from his "Defense of the Constitution," in *The Works of John Adams*, 10 vols., ed. J. F. Adams (Boston: Little, Brown, 1850–56), 4:290–98.

39. *Federalist*, nos. 10 and 51.

40. John Adams to Benjamin Rush, Feb. 2, 1807, in *The Spur of Fame: Dialogues of John Adams and Benjamin Rush*, ed. John A. Shutz and Douglass Adair (San Marino, Calif.: Huntington Library, 1966), 75–77; Tocqueville is quoted in Aron, *Main Currents* 1:258.

41. On Tocqueville and Weber on America, see John Patrick Diggins, *Max Weber: Politics and the Spirit of Tragedy* (New York: Basic, 1995).

42. Richard Rodriquez, "The Birth Pangs of a New L.A." *Harper's* (July 1993): 20.

Chapter 5: The Pride and the Pain

1. Ralph Waldo Emerson, "The American Scholar," in *The Portable Emerson*, ed. Mark Van Doren (New York: Viking, 1946), 23–48.

2. Emerson, "History" and "American Scholar," in *Portable Emerson*, 139–64, 31.

3. Abraham Lincoln to David Hunter, Dec. 31, 1861, in Lincoln, *S&W*, 2:298–99; M. Houser, *Lincoln's Education and Other Essays* (New York: Bookman, 1957), 45; see also Douglas L. Wilson, "What Jefferson and Lincoln Read," *Atlantic Monthly* 267 (Jan. 1991): 51–62.

4. Quoted in David Herbert Donald, *Lincoln* (New York: Simon and Schuster, 1995), 53.

5. Emerson, "Politics" and "Wealth," in *Portable Emerson*, 188–204, 431–43.

6. Quoted in Judith N. Shklar, *American Citizenship: The Quest for Inclusion* (Cambridge: Harvard Univ. Press, 1991), 83.

7. *Federalist*, no. 10.

8. Thomas Jefferson to the Chiefs of the Cherokee Nation, Jan. 10, 1806, in *The Life and Selected Writings of Thomas Jefferson*, ed. Adrienne Koch and William Puden (New York: Modern Library, 1946), 578–80.

9. A vast literature exists on the debate over America's early political culture. A valuable introduction to the subject is Joyce Appleby, *Liberalism and Republicanism in American Historiography* (Cambridge: Harvard Univ. Press, 1992); see also Daniel T. Rogers, "Republicanism: The Career of a Concept," *Journal of American History* 79 (1992): 11–38.

10. Alexis de Tocqueville, *Democracy in America*, ed. J. P. Mayer, trans. George Lawrence (1835–40; New York: Harper, 1969), 386.

11. Henry Adams, *The History of the United States of America during the Administrations of Jefferson and Madison*, 2 vols. (1889–91; New York: Library of America, 1986), 1:440.

12. *Judgment at the Smithsonian*, ed. Philip Nobile (New York: Marlowe, 1995); *History Wars: The "Enola Gay" and Other Battles for the American Past*, ed. Edward T. Linethal and Tom Engelhardt (New York: Henry Holt, 1996); "History and the Public: What Can We Handle? A Roundtable about History after the *Enola Gay*," *Journal of American History* 82 (1995): 1029–1135.

13. Thucydides, *The Peloponnesian War*, trans. Rex Warner (New York: Penguin, 1972), 46–49.

14. Linethal and Engelhardt, *History Wars*, 2.

15. Paul Goldberger, "Historical Shows on Trial: Who Judges?" *New York Times* (Feb. 11, 1996).

16. Todd Gitlin, "The Big House: The Library of Congress's Cowardice," *New Republic* (Jan. 22, 1996): 12–14.

17. Robert W. Snyder, "The Wild Harp of Erin," *Culturefront* 4 (Fall 1996): 53–55, 86.

18. Michael J. Ybarra, "Limitations of Statues in Light of Today," *New York Times* (June 9, 1996); "A Monument Caught in the Middle," *New York Times* (May 6, 1996).

19. All quotes are from Marie Collins Swabey, *The Judgment of History* (New York: Philosophical Library, 1954), v, 38–39.

20. Quoted in "Nations and Their Past: The Uses and Abuses of History," *Economist* (Dec. 21, 1996): 70–74.

21. Aristotle, *The Politics*, trans. Carnes Lord (Chicago: Univ. of Chicago Press, 1984), 35; A. D. Momigliano, *Studies in Historiography* (London: Weidenfeld and Nicolson, 1966); Benjamin I. Schwartz, *The World of Thought in Ancient China* (Cambridge: Harvard Univ. Press, 1985).

22. *The Varieties of History: From Voltaire to the Present*, ed. Fritz Stern (London: Meridian, 1957).

23. Harvey Gross, *The Contrived Corridor: History and Fatality in Modern Literature* (Ann Arbor: Univ. of Michigan Press, 1971); Nicola Chiaromonte, *The Paradox of History* (Philadelphia: Univ. of Pennsylvania Press, 1985).

24. Lord Acton, *Lectures in Modern History* (New York: Meridian, 1961) 41.

25. Friedrich Nietzsche, *Beyond Good and Evil* (Chicago: Gateway, 1955), 219–39; Paul Valéry, *The Outlook for Intelligence,* trans. Denise Folliot and Jackson Mathews (Princeton, N.J.: Princeton Univ. Press, 1962), 114.

26. Robert D. Kaplan, "Fort Leavenworth and the Eclipse of Nationhood," *Atlantic Monthy* 278 (Sept. 1996): 75–90.

27. John Dos Passos, *The Ground We Stand On* (London: Routledge, 1942), 3; Edmund Burke, *Reflections on the French Revolution* (New York: Penguin, 1982); José Ortega y Gasset, *Concord and Liberty* (New York: Norton, 1946), 92.

28. Henry Adams, *The Education of Henry Adams* (1907; New York: Modern Lib., 1931), 300–301.

29. Emerson, "History," in *Portable Emerson,* 139–63; Emerson quoted in Frank Kermode, "Whose History Is Bunk?" *New York Times Book Review* (Feb. 23, 1992), 33.

30. Tocqueville, *Democracy,* 50–57, 551–54, 508, 584–89.

31. Friedrich Nietzsche, "Thus Spoke Zarathrustra," in *The Portable Nietzsche,* ed. Walter Kaufman (New York: Penguin, 1968), 251.

32. John Patrick Diggins, *The Promise of Pragmatism: Modernism and the Crisis of Knowledge and Authority* (Chicago: Univ. of Chicago Press, 1995).

33. Diane Ravitch, "Decline and Fall of Teaching History," *New York Times Magazine* (Nov. 17, 1985), 50–54.

34. Ibid., 55.

35. Ken Burns, "Thoughts on Telling History," *American History Illustrated* 26 (Mar.–Apr. 1997): 27; George Orwell, "Such, Such Were the Joys," in *The Orwell Reader* (New York: Harcourt, 1956), 426.

36. Paul Gagnon, "Why Study History?" *Atlantic Monthly* 262 (Nov. 1988): 43–66.

37. Tocqueville, *Democracy,* 30.

38. Ibid., 538.

39. Ibid., 705.

40. Quoted in Jean-Claude Lamberti, *Tocqueville and the Two Democracies* (Cambridge: Harvard Univ. Press, 1989), 103.

41. Quoted in George Wilson Pierson, *Tocqueville in America* (Baltimore: Johns Hopkins Univ. Press, 1996), 117–18.

Chapter 6: 'The 'Last Best Hope" or the "Suicide of the West"?

1. Lincoln, *S&W,* 1:4.

2. The Harvard political theorist Seyla Benhabib does not necessarily associate herself with such positions; rather she discusses them with astute reservations in her book *Situating the Self: Gender, Community, and Postmodernism in Contemporary Ethics* (New York; Routledge, 1992), and in *Democracy and Difference: Contesting the Boundaries of the Political,* ed. Seyla Benhabib (Princeton, N.J.: Princeton Univ. Press, 1996).

3. Gary B. Nash, *Red, White, and Black: The Peoples of Early America* (Englewood Cliffs, N.J.: Prentice Hall, 1974).

4. Lincoln, *S&W,* 2:213.

5. Lincoln, *S&W,* 1:3–11.

6. The impression of America as degenerate and decadent begins in the eighteenth century and reaches a crescendo in the writings of many modern European intellectuals influential in America. See the recent book by James Ceasar, *Reconstructing America: The Symbol of America in Modern Thought* (New Haven: Yale Univ. Press, 1997).

7. Theodor W. Adorno, "Scientific Experiences of a European Scholar in America," in *Perspectives in American History*, vol. 2: *The Intellectual Migration: Europe and America, 1930–1960* (Cambridge: Charles Warren Center for American Studies, Harvard Univ., 1968), 338–70.

8. Max Weber, "Capitalism and Rural Society in Germany," in *From Max Weber: Essays in Sociology*, ed. H. H. Gerth and C. Wright Mills (New York: Oxford Univ. Press, 1946), 369.

9. Anatole Broyard, *When Kafka Was the Rage* (1993; New York: Vintage, 1997), 15.

10. Max Horkheimer, "The End of Reason," in *The Essential Frankfurt School Reader*, ed. Andrew Arato and Eike Gebhart (New York: Continuum, 1993), 26–48.

11. Iris Marion Young, *Justice and the Politics of Differences* (Princeton, N.J.: Princeton Univ. Press, 1990).

12. *Essential Frankfurt School Reader*, 118–37.

13. Charles A. Beard, *The American Spirit: A Study of the Idea of Civilization in the United States* (New York: Macmillan, 1942); Carl Becker, "What Is Still Living in the Philosophy of Thomas Jefferson?" *Proceedings of the American Philosophical Society* 87 (1943): 201–10.

14. Reinhold Niebuhr, *The Children of Light and the Children of Darkness* (New York: Scribner's, 1944).

15. James Burnham, *Suicide of the West* (New York: John Day, 1965), 15.

16. David Gress, *From Plato to NATO: The Idea of the West and Its Opponents* (New York: Free Press, 1998).

17. George Santayana, *Egotism in German Philosophy* (New York: Scribner's, 1915).

18. *NHS*, 14.

19. Adams and Voltaire are quoted in Daniel J. Boorstin, *The Lost World of Thomas Jefferson* (Boston: Beacon, 1960), 74–75.

20. Theodore Zeldin, *The Intimate History of Humanity* (New York: Harper, 1995), 50–51.

21. Roy F. Baumeister, "Should Schools Try to Boost Self-Esteem?" *American Educator* 20 (Summer 1996): 14–19, 43.

22. David S. Landes, *The Wealth and Poverty of Nations: Why Some Are So Rich and Some So Poor* (New York: Norton, 1998), 513.

23. Gary Nash, "Multiculturalism and History: Historical Perspectives and Present Prospects," in *Public Education in a Multicultural Society: Policy, Theory, Critique*, ed. Robert E. Fullinwider (New York: Cambridge Univ. Press, 1996), 102.

24. Friedrich Engels and Karl Marx, *The German Ideology* (London: Lawrence and Wishart, 1970), 59–60.

25. Jane S. Jacqueete, "Women in Power: From Tokenism to Critical Mass," and Mayra Buvinic, "Women in Poverty: A New Global Underclass," both in *Foreign Policy* 108 (Fall 1997): 23–53; "Is Multiculturalism Bad for Women?" *Boston Review* 22 (Oct.–Nov. 1997): 2–40.

26. Iris Marion Young, *Justice and the Politics of Difference* (Princeton, N.J.: Princeton Univ. Press, 1990), 4–11.

27. Charles Taylor, "The Politics of Recognition," in *Multiculturalism and "The Politics of Recognition,"* ed. Amy Gutman (Princeton, N.J.: Princeton Univ. Press, 1992), 37–43.

28. Joseph Chan, "A Confucian Perspective of Human Rights," paper presented at the conference on "The Growth of East Asia and Its Impact on Human Rights," Carnegie Council on Ethics and International Affairs, Bangkok, 1996; see also *Confucianism and Human Rights,* ed. William Theodore De Bary and Tu Weiming (New York: Columbia Univ. Press, 1998).

29. Nathan Glazer, *We Are All Multiculturalists Now* (Cambridge: Harvard Univ. Press, 1998).

30. David Lowenthal, *Possessed by the Past* (New York: Free Press, 1997).

31. *NHS,* 1.

32. Ibid., 2.

33. Ernest Gellner, *Conditions of Liberty: Civil Society and Its Rights* (New York: Penguin, 1994), 185; José Ortega y Gasset, *History as a System and Other Essays toward a Philosophy of History* (1941; New York: Norton, 1962), 203.

34. *NHS,* 1.

35. Paz was referring to pre-Columbian Aztec and Inca cultures; see Octavio Paz, *Claude Lévi-Strauss: An Introduction,* trans. J. S. Bernstein and Maxine Bernstein (New York: Delta, 1967), 90.

36. Lincoln, *S&W,* 1:271.

37. Abraham Lincoln, "Your Race Are Suffering," in *Lincoln on Democracy,* ed. Mario M. Cuomo and Harold Holzer (New York: Harper, 1990), 251–52.

38. Thomas Hobbes, *The Leviathan,* ed. C. B. Macpherson (1651; London: Penguin, 1981), 186.

39. John Locke, *The Second Treatise of Government,* ed. Thomas P. Peardon (1660; Indianapolis: Bobbs-Merrill, 1952); for an excellent discussion of Hobbes and Locke, see Pierre Mament, *An Intellectual History of Liberalism,* trans. Rebecca Balinski (Princeton, N.J.: Princeton Univ. Press, 1994).

40. James Tully, *An Approach to Political Philosophy: Locke in Context* (New York: Cambridge Univ. Press, 1993).

41. Landes, *Wealth and Poverty of Nations.*

42. John Patrick Diggins, *Max Weber: Politics and the Spirit of Tragedy* (New York; Basic, 1996).

43. Amartya Sen, "Human Rights and Asian Values," *New Republic* 217 (July 14–21, 1997): 33–40.

44. Fareed Zakaria, "The Rise of Illiberal Democracy," *Foreign Affairs* 76 (Nov.–Dec. 1997): 22–43.

45. Lincoln, *S&W,* 1:399–400.

Chapter 7: Politics at the Center, Professors at the Peripheries

1. Gary Nash, *The Urban Crucible: Social Change, Political Consciousness, and the Origins of the American Revolution* (Cambridge: Harvard Univ. Press, 1979), vii–xv, 258–70; for a learned corrective to the "history from below" school, see Martin J. Burke, *The Conundrum of Class: Public Discourse on the Social Order in America* (Chicago: Univ. of Chicago Press, 1995).

2. Louis Hartz, *Economic Policy and Democratic Thought: Pennsylvania, 1776–1860* (Chicago: Quadrangle, 1968), 80, 118–48.

3. Louis Hartz, *The Necessity of Choice: Nineteenth-Century Political Thought*, ed. Paul Roazen (New Brunswick, N.J.: Transaction, 1990), 203.

4. The political theorist Karen Orren has challenged Hartz's thesis regarding the absence of feudalism. She argues that in nineteenth-century labor relations the courts drew on ancient common law regarding servants and masters to uphold the subordination of workers to employees. When strikes broke out, Orren writes, the state intervened to force workers to return to their jobs, thereby precluding their having a viable role in democratic politics. See Karen Orren, *Belated Feudalism: Labor, the Law, and Liberal Development in the United States* (New York: Cambridge Univ. Press, 1991). The collusion of corporate industry with the state and the judiciary, it seems to me, may be no more evidence of the presence of feudalism than was the later collusion of labor unions and government bureaucracy. If feudalism persists in contemporary society it may be seen on the American campus, where teaching assistants do all the work and professors enjoy all the pay and privileges.

5. Louis Hartz, *The Liberal Tradition in America* (New York: Harcourt, 1955), 145–200.

6. Quoted in Gabor S. Boritt, *Lincoln and the Economics of the American Dream* (Urbana: Univ. of Illinois Press, 1994), 90.

7. Louis Hartz, *A Synthesis of World History* (Zurich: Humanity, 1984), 91; see also Patrick Riley, "Louis Hartz: The Final Years, The Unknown Work," *Political Theory* 16 (1988): 377–99.

8. Michel de Certeau, *The Mystic Fable*, trans. Michael B. Smith (Chicago: Univ. of Chicago Press, 1992), 10–11.

9. *Report of the Committee of the Senate upon the Relations Between Labor and Capital* (Washington: Government Printing Office, 1885), 1:456–57.

10. Van Wyck Brooks, *America's Coming-of-Age* (1915; Garden City, N.Y.: Anchor, 1958).

11. Ezra Pound, *Hugh Selwyn Mauberley* (1920), in *Diptych: Rome-London* (New York: New Directions, 1994), 37–42.

12. George Santayana, "The Genteel Tradition in American Philosophy," in *Santayana on America*, ed. Richard Colton Lyon (New York: Harbinger, 1968), 36–56.

13. John Adams, *The Works of John Adams*, ed. Charles Francis Adams, 10 vols. (1850–56; Boston: AMS, 1971), 6:216; Alexander Hamilton, *Federalist*, no. 9.

14. Leon Fink, *In Search of the Working Class: Essays in American Labor History and Political Culture* (Urbana: Univ. of Illinois Press, 1994); for an earlier critique of labor historians who as academic intellectuals never seem to grasp what workers really aspire to, see Aileen S. Kraditor, *The Radical Persuasion: Aspects of the Intellectual History and Historiography of Three American Radical Organizations* (Baton Rouge: Louisiana State Univ. Press, 1981).

15. Harry Levin, *The Power of Blackness: Hawthorne, Poe, Melville* (New York: Vintage, 1960), 5.

16. "This revised narrative of political change in America begins boldly, with the bearers of a transformative idea, but concludes all-the-more paradoxically with adaptations that strengthen established governing arrangements. We have in this way sharpened our appreciation of the New Deal's original radicalism, and how it was tamed (Brinkley); of Progressivism's bright 'promise,' and how it was 'lost'

(Eisenach); of the Populist's stirring 'moment,' and how it was coopted (Goodwin), of labor's own 'vision,' and how it was constricted (Hattam); of the zealous Reconstruction, and how it was eviscerated (Foner); of the pre-Revolution republicanism, and how it was transmuted (Wood). There can be no denying the gap between the end results of American politics and their full-blown and authentic opposition. But that is the point. Proceeding from 'vision,' from 'alternative Americans,' whatever changes ensue become interesting namely for the shortfall. The 'real' changes, the 'meaningful,' the 'fundamental' changes will be the ones that don't happen, and our incremental adaptations will remain pretty much as Hartz described them." Karen Orren and Stephen Skowronek, "In Search of Political Development," paper delivered to the American Political Science Association, San Francisco, Aug. 28–Sept. 1, 1996.

17. Ralph Waldo Emerson, "Experience," in *Essays by Ralph Waldo Emerson* (Boston: Houghton Mifflin, 1865), 71.

18. Leon Fink, "The New Labor History and the Powers of Historical Pessimism: Consensus, Hegemony, and the Case of the Knights of Labor," in Fink, *In Search of the Working Class*, 89–111; Mark Twain, *Collected Tales, Sketches, Speeches, and Essays* (New York: Library of America, 1992), 945.

19. James Joyce, *Ulysses* (New York: Vintage, 1986), 21, 28, 175.

20. George Santayana, "Lovers of Illusion," in *Dialogues in Limbo* (1948; Ann Arbor: Univ. of Michigan Press, 1957), 80.

21. Hamilton, *Federalist*, nos. 1, 6, 9, 15.

22. The subject of "Republican Motherhood" and other matters in women's history are dealt with in Chapter 9; on working-class culture as supposedly "counterhegemonic," see Fink, *In Search of the Working Class*, 69–115, 175–200, esp. 105.

23. In the twentieth century three American Lefts came and went, each lasting less than a decade; but it seems that a fourth, today's Academic Left, will always be with us. See John Patrick Diggins, *The Rise and Fall of the American Left* (New York: Norton, 1992).

24. This is the apt title of the chapter on Calhoun in Richard Hofstadter's still splendid *The American Political Tradition and the Men Who Made It* (New York: Knopf, 1948).

25. George Fitzhugh, "Sociology for the South," in *Antebellum*, ed. Harvey Wish (New York: Capricorn, 1960), 57.

26. Richard Hofstadter, *The Progressive Historians: Turner, Parrington, Beard* (New York: Knopf, 1968); John P. Diggins, "Consciousness and Ideology in American History: The Burden of Daniel J. Boorstin," *American Historical Review* 76 (Feb. 1971): 99–118.

27. Godfrey Hodgson, *American in Our Time* (New York: Vintage, 1978), 67–98; Ann Douglas, "The Failure of the New York Intellectuals," *Raritan* 17 (1998): 1–23.

28. The first statement articulating a consensus interpretation was Richard Hofstadter's *The American Political Tradition and the Men Who Made It*, published in 1948. Hofstadter had been working on the book toward the end of World War II, a time when U.S.-Soviet relations remained friendly and few foresaw the coming rivalry between the superpowers.

29. Hofstadter offered this note in his introduction to the Israeli edition of *The American Political Tradition*, later published in the United States with a preface by Christopher Lasch (New York: Vintage, 1973).

30. Lewis Corey, *The Crisis of the Middle Class* (1935; New York: Columbia Univ Press, 1992), 365.

31. Quoted in Raymond Aron, *The Opium of the Intellectuals,* trans. Terence Kilmartin (New York: Norton, 1962), 69.

32. Sean Wilentz, "Against Exceptionalism: Class Consciousness and the American Labor Movement, 1790–1920," *International Review of Labor and Working Class History* 26 (1984): 1–24.

33. Karl Marx, "The Eighteenth Brumaire of Louis Bonaparte," in *The Marx-Engels Reader,* ed. Robert C. Tucker (New York: Norton, 1978), 595.

34. Rogers M. Smith, "Beyond Tocqueville, Myrdal, and Hartz: The Multiple Traditions in America," *American Political Science Review* 87 (1993): 549–66; see also Smith's comprehensive study of American political culture, *Civic Ideals: Conflicting Visions of Citizenship in U.S. History* (New Haven: Yale Univ. Press, 1997).

35. Tom Callender, Esq., *Letters to Alexander Hamilton: King of the Feds* (New York: Reynolds, 1802).

36. *Federalist,* nos. 6, 9, 14, 38, 63.

37. Charles Sellers, *The Market Revolution: Jacksonian America, 1815–1846* (New York: Oxford Univ. Press, 1991).

38. Michael Kazin, *The Populist Persuasion: An American History* (New York: Basic, 1995), 38–39.

39. Randolph Bourne, "A Mirror of the Middle West," in *The Radical Will: Randolph Bourne, Selected Writings,* ed. Olaf Hansen (New York: Urizen, 1977), 271–74; Thorstein Veblen, "The Country Town," in *The Portable Veblen,* ed. Max Lerner (New York: Viking, 1948).

Chapter 8: What Do Workers Want?

1. Adams quoted in Daniel M. Friedenberg, *Life, Liberty, and the Pursuit of Property* (Buffalo: Prometheus, 1992), 328.

2. Alexis de Tocqueville, *Democracy in America,* ed. J. P. Mayer, trans. George Lawrence (1835–40; New York: Harper, 1969), 621.

3. *Ralph Waldo Emerson: Selected Prose and Poetry,* ed. Reginald L. Cook (New York; Holt, Rinehart, 1950), 480; "Wealth," in *The Complete Works of Ralph Waldo Emerson,* 12 vols., centenary ed., (New York: AMS, 1979), 11:86–127.

4. Gordon Wood, "The Would-Be Gentleman," *New York Review of Books* (Aug. 8, 1996), 36–39; see also Wood's excellent article "Inventing American Capitalism," *New York Review of Books* (June 9, 1995), 44–49.

5. See the forum "How Revolutionary Was the Revolution? A Discussion of Gordon S. Wood's *The Radicalism of the American Revolution,*" in the *William and Mary Quarterly* 51 (1994): 677–715.

6. Virginia Woolf, *A Room of One's Own* (1929; New York: Harcourt, 1957), 3–37.

7. W. E. B. Du Bois, *The Soul of Black Folk* (1903; New York: Dover, 1994), 48–49.

8. E. P. Thompson, *The Making of the English Working Class* (New York: Vintage, 1963), 12.

9. Edmund Burke, "Speech on Conciliation with the Colonies," in *Selected Writings of Edmund Burke,* ed. Walter J. Bate (New York: Modern Library, 1960), 130.

10. George Rawick, "I Dissent," in *History and the New Left: Madison, Wisconsin, 1950–1970*, ed. Paul Buhle (Philadelphia: Temple Univ. Press), 57.

11. "Preface," *Making Histories: Studies in History Writing and Politics*, ed. Richard Johnson, Gregor McLennan, Bill Schwarz, and David Sutton (Minneapolis: Univ. of Minnesota Press, 1982), 8–12.

12. Karl Marx, "Economic and Philosophical Manuscripts" (1844), in *Writings of the Young Marx on Philosophy and Society*, ed. Loyd D. Easton and Kurt H. Guddat (Garden City, N.Y.: Anchor, 1967), 306.

13. Karl Marx, "Alienation and Social Classes," in *The Marx-Engels Reader*, ed. Robert C. Tucker (New York: Norton, 1978), 133–35.

14. Karl Marx, "Economic and Philosophic Manuscripts of 1844," in *The Marx-Engels Reader*, 103–4.

15. Georg Simmel, *The Philosophy of Money* (London: Routledge, 1978), 89.

16. Marx, "Economic and Philosophic Manuscripts," 104.

17. Robert E. Weir, *Beyond Labor's Veil: The Culture of the Knights of Labor* (University Park: Pennsylvania State Univ. Press, 1996).

18. Charles Sellers, *The Market Revolution: Jacksonian America, 1815–1846* (New York: Oxford Univ. Press, 1991), 157; Weir, *Beyond Labor's Veil*, 317; Leon Fink, *In Search of the Working Class: Essays in American Labor History and Political Culture* (Urbana: Univ. of Illinois Press, 1994), 190.

19. Lincoln, *S&W*, 2:90–111, 296–97.

20. Richard Hofstadter, *The American Political Tradition and the Men Who Made It* (1948; New York: Vintage, 1957), viii.

21. Quoted in Richard J. Ellis, *The Dark Side of the Left: Illiberal Egalitarianism in America* (Lawrence: Univ. of Kansas Press, 1998), 147–74.

22. J. G. A. Pocock, *The Machiavellian Moment: Florentine Political Thought and the Atlantic Republican Tradition* (Princeton, N.J.: Princeton Univ. Press, 1975). I undertook an opposing interpretation in *The Lost Soul of American Politics: Virtue, Self-Interest, and the Foundations of Liberalism* (Chicago: Univ. of Chicago Press, 1987); see also Joyce Appleby, *Liberalism and Republicanism in American Historiography* (Cambridge: Harvard Univ. Press, 1992), and Daniel T. Rogers, "Republicanism: The Career of a Concept," *Journal of American History* 79 (1992): 11–38.

23. The distinction made by social-labor historians—that in pre-industrial times a "moral economy" of mutuality, community, and solidarity prevailed and gave way to an environment of competitive materialism only when a market economy arrived—is, at least in early American history based more on faith than fact. In seventeenth-century colonial America, bakers, carters, and other workers were forever taking each other to court in disputes over contracts and overdue payments. More competitive strife existed within a class than between classes. See Simon Middleton, "Rights, Privileges, and the Place of the Artisan in Colonial America," Ph.D. thesis, City University of New York, 1997.

24. Sean Wilentz, *Chants Democratic: New York City and the Rise of the American Working Class, 1788–1850* (New York: Oxford Univ. Press, 1984), 61–103, 153–55. Wilentz seems unaware that republicanism, unlike liberalism, has no place for the right of workers as such and no labor theory of value. Never have historians of Wilentz's generation been more taken in by one ism in the hope of exchanging it for another. The story that Wilentz tells is, among other things, the struggle on the part of an embryonic labor movement to secure control of the workplace in

opposition to modernization and the coming of capitalism. From the Jacksonian era to that of the Populists and beyond, the struggle between the producers and the profiteers appear to dramatize conflict—which would be true if the producers were as dedicated only to making goods as the profiteers are only to making money. As Hofstadter would remind us, the world of production and the world of profit are simply two expressions of different forms of property.

25. Thomas Paine, "The Rights of Man," in *Reflections on the Revolution in France and the Rights of Man* (Garden City, N.Y.: Dolphin Books, 1961), 279.

26. Sellers, *Market Revolution*, 32, 268.

27. Eric McKitrick, "The Great White Hope," *New York Review of Books* 39 (June 11, 1992), 33–37.

28. Sellers, *Market Revolution*, 340–41, 363.

29. Parker quoted in Vernon L. Parrington, *Main Currents in American Thought*, vol. 2: *The Romantic Revolution in America* (New York: Harcourt, 1954), 415.

30. Michael Kazin, "The Historian as Populist," *New York Review of Books* (May 12, 1988), 48–50; see also the intelligently critical reappraisal by Nick Salvatore, "Herbert Gutman's Narrative of the American Working Class: A Reevaluation," *International Journal of Politics, Culture, and Society* 12 (1998): 43–79.

31. Friedrich Nietzsche, *The Will to Power*, trans. Walter Kaufman and R. J. Hollingdale (New York: Vintage, 1967), 274.

32. Quoted in Bernard Mandel, *Samuel Gompers: A Biography* (Yellow Springs, Ohio: Antioch, 1963), 64.

33. Wilentz, *Chants Democratic*, 92.

34. Emerson, "Journals," in *Ralph Waldo Emerson: Selected Prose and Poetry*, ed. Reginald L. Cook (New York: Rinehart, 1950), 481.

35. Quoted in Wood, *Radicalism*, 246.

36. This is the argument that James Henretta once held in his provocative "Families and Farms: *Mentalité* in Pre-Industrial America," *William and Mary Quarterly* 35 (1978): 3–52, and reconsidered in his *The Origins of American Capitalism: Selected Essays* (Boston: Northeastern Univ. Press, 1994).

37. Jerry Z. Muller, *Adam Smith in His Time and Ours: Designing the Decent Society* (New York: Free Press, 1993); Istvan Hunt and Michael Ignatiev, "Needs and Justice in the *Wealth of Nations*," in *Wealth and Virtue: The Shaping of Political Economy in the Scottish Enlightenment*, ed. Istvan Hunt and Michael Ignatiev (New York: Cambridge Univ. Press, 1983), 1–44.

38. Herbert Hill, "The ILGWU Today: The Decay of a Labor Union," *New Politics* 1 (1962): 6–17; on the teamsters and longshoremen's unions, see Daniel Bell, *The End of Ideology: On the Exhaustion of Political Ideas in the Fifties* (New York: Basic, 1960), 175–209.

39. Maurice Isserman, review of John Patrick Diggins, *The Rise and Fall of the American Left*, in the *New York Times Book Review* 97 (Mar. 8, 1992): 9.

40. Herbert Hill, "Myth-Making as Labor History: Herbert Gutman and the United Mine Workers of America," *International Journal of Politics, Culture, and Society* 2 (1988): 132–200.

41. Stanford M. Lyman, *Chinese Americans* (New York: Random House, 1974); "The Race Question and Liberalism: Casuistries in American Constitutional Law," *International Journal of Politics, Culture, and Society* 5 (1993): 183–247; David R. Roediger, *The Wages of Whiteness: Race and the Making of the American Working*

Class (London: Verso, 1991); Alexander Saxton, *The Rise and Fall of the White Republic: Class Politics and Mass Culture in Nineteenth-Century America* (1990; London: Verso, 1996).

42. David R. Roediger, *Towards the Abolition of Whiteness* (London: Verso, 1994), 12.

43. Lyman, "The Race Question and Liberalism," 183–247; on the I.W.W. I have drawn upon the paper by Phillip J. Mellinger, "The IWW's 1917 Return to Arizona: The 'Old' and 'New' Western Labor History."

44. Noel Ignatiev, *How the Irish Became White* (New York: Routledge, 1995); Iver Bernstein, *The New York City Draft Riots: Their Significance for American Social and Political History in the Age of the Civil War* (New York: Oxford, 1990); Michael Patrick MacDonald, *All Souls: A Family Story from Southie* (Boston: Beacon, 1999).

45. Hayden White, "Getting Out of History," *Diacritics* (1982): 2–13.

46. Saxton, *Rise and Fall of the White Republic*, 205–25.

47. For Lincoln on labor, see the valuable work of Gabor S. Boritt, *Lincoln and the Economics of the American Dream* (1978; Urbana: Univ. of Illinois Press, 1994), 13–24.

48. Lincoln, *S&W*, 1:28–36.

Chapter 9: Outside Demanding In

1. A major inspiration is Mary Beard's *Women as Force in History: A Study in Traditions and Realities* (1946; New York: Persea, 1983). Significantly, Beard avoided using the term "role" and instead preferred "force," a word she had adopted from the historian Henry Adams. Adams did believe that at certain times in history women as leaders presided forcefully and often charismatically; he mentioned such figures as the Virgin Mary of the Middle Ages, legendary Polynesian princesses, or figures from the works of Homer and other classical authors. But so far as I am aware, he did not claim to see such a feminine force in American history.

2. Quoted in Arthur Schlesinger, *New Viewpoints in American History* (New York: Macmillan, 1925), 127.

3. Linda K. Kerber, *Women and the Republic: Intellect and Ideology in Revolutionary America* (Chapel Hill: Univ. of North Carolina Press, 1980); Mary Beth Norton, *Liberty's Daughters: The Revolutionary Experience of American Women, 1750–1800* (Boston: Little, Brown, 1980); Jan Lewis, "The Republican Wife: Seduction in the Early Republic," *William and Mary Quarterly* 44 (1987): 689–721; see also the Forum "Beyond Roles, Beyond Spheres: Thinking about Gender in the Early Republic," *William and Mary Quarterly* 46 (1989): 565–85.

4. Kerber, *Women and the Republic*, 200.

5. *Federalist*, no. 15.

6. Pericles quoted in Thucydides, *The History of the Peloponessian Wars*, ed. Sir Richard Livingstone (New York: Oxford Univ. Press, 1960), 117.

7. David J. Rothman, "The Politics of Virtue," *New York Times Book Review* (Aug. 6, 1995).

8. Ann Douglas, *The Feminization of American Culture* (New York: Knopf, 1977), 57.

9. Quoted in Schlesinger, *New Viewpoints*, 136.

10. Ellen DuBois, *Feminism and Suffrage: The Emergence of an Indispensable Women's*

Movement in America, 1848–1869 (Ithaca, N.Y.: Cornell Univ. Press, 1978), 201–2.

11. Ellen DuBois, "Making Women's History: Activist Historians of Women's Rights, 1880–1940," in *Intellectuals and Public Life: Between Radicalism and Reform,* ed. Leon Fink, Stephen T. Leonard, and Donald M. Reid (Ithaca, N.Y.: Cornell Univ. Press, 1996), 214–35.

12. Henry Adams, *The Education of Henry Adams* (1907; New York: Modern Library, 1931), 383–85, 442–43; "Primitive Rights of Women," in *The Great Secession Winter of 1860–61 and Other Essays,* ed. George E. Hochfield (New York: Barnes, 1958), 333–60.

13. *NHS,* 81.

14. Edith Gelles, *Portia: The World of Abigail Adams* (Bloomington: Indiana Univ. Press, 1992), 1–36.

15. *NHS,* 103.

16. Joan Wallach Scott, *Gender and the Politics of History* (New York: Columbia Univ. Press, 1988), 1–163; see also Scott's argument for the primacy of language in "The Evidence of Experience," *Critical Inquiry* 17 (1991): 773–97.

17. François Furet, *In the Workshop of History,* trans. Jonathan Mandelbaum (Chicago: Univ. of Chicago Press, 1984), 20.

18. Denise Reily, *"Am I That Name?": Feminism and the Category of "Women" in History* (Minneapolis: Univ. of Minnesota Press, 1988), 66.

19. Virginia Woolf, *Three Guineas* (New York: Harcourt, 1938), 105.

20. *The Collected Works of Abraham Lincoln,* ed. Roy P. Basler, 9 vols. (New Brunswick, N.J.: Rutgers Univ. Press, 1953), 4:128–29.

21. Angel Kwolek-Folland, *Incorporating Women: A History of Women and Business in the United States* (New York: Twayne, 1998).

22. Mary P. Ryan, "Gender and Public Access: Women's Politics in Nineteenth-Century America," in *Habermas and the Public Sphere,* ed. Craig Calhoun (Cambridge: MIT Press, 1992), 258–88.

23. Friedrich Nietzsche, *Beyond Good and Evil,* trans. Marianne Cowan (Chicago: Regnery, 1955), 83; George B. Shaw, *The Quintessence of Ibsenism* (New York: Dover, 1994), 6.

24. Melissa Benn, "Making It," *London Review of Books* (Feb. 5, 1998), 20–23.

25. Nancy Cott, *The Bonds of Womanhood: Women's Sphere in New England, 1780–1835* (New Haven: Yale Univ. Press, 1977), 67–69; Joan C. Williams, "Virtue and Oppression," in *Virtue,* ed. John C. Chapman and William A. Galston (New York: New York Univ. Press, 1992), 309–37.

26. "Interview with Joan Scott," *Radical History Review* 45 (1989): 41–59.

27. Ryan, "Gender and Public Access," 285.

28. *The Philosophy of Nietzsche,* ed. Geoffrey Clive, trans. Ocscar Levy (New York: New American Library, 1965), pp. 365–497.

29. Linda K. Kerber, "Can a Woman Be an Individual? The Discourse of Self-Reliance," in *American Chameleon: Individualism in a Trans-National Context,* ed. Richard O. Curry and Lawrence B. Goodheart (Kent, Ohio: Kent State Univ. Press, 1991), 151–66. For a learned discussion of this issue, see Wilfred M. McClay, *The Masterless: Self and Society in Modern America* (Chapel Hill: Univ. of North Carolina Press, 1994).

30. Herbert Croly, *The Promise of American Life* (1914; Boston: Northeastern Univ. Press, 1989), 386–90.

Chapter 10: Black America and the Liberal Tradition

1. Stanton is quoted in Jean V. Matthews, "Race, Sex, and the Dimensions of Liberty in Antebellum America," in *The Liberal Persuasion: Arthur Schlesinger Jr. and the Challenge of the American Past,* ed. John Patrick Diggins (Princeton, N.J.: Princeton Univ. Press, 1977), 109–10.

2. *The Life and Writings of Frederick Douglass: Reconstruction and After,* ed. Philip Foner, 5 vols. (New York: International, 1955), 4:452.

3. Quoted in Matthews, "Race," 108.

4. Grimké's letter is in *The Feminist Papers: From Adams to de Beauvoir,* ed. Alice S. Rossi (New York: Bantam, 1973), 320–21.

5. Quoted in *The Public Years of Sarah and Angelina Grimké: Selected Writings, 1835–1839,* ed. Larry Ceplair (New York: Columbia Univ. Press, 1989), 265.

6. *Collected Works of Abraham Lincoln,* 2:276; 4:22.

7. Winthrop D. Jordan, *White over Black: American Attitudes toward the Negro, 1550–1812* (Baltimore: Penguin, 1969).

8. Edmund S. Morgan, *American Slavery, American Freedom: The Ordeal of Colonial Virginia* (New York: Norton, 1975).

9. *Conor Cruise O'Brien: An Anthology,* ed. Donald Harmon Akenson (Ithaca, N.Y.: Cornell Univ. Press, 1994), 241.

10. John Reader, *Africa: A Biography of the Continent* (New York: Knopf, 1998); on the slave trade, see Philip D. Curtain, *The African Slave Trade: A Census* (Madison: Univ. of Wisconsin Press, 1969); David Eltis, *Economic Growth and the Ending of the Transatlantic Slave Trade* (New York: Oxford Univ. Press, 1987); Hugh Thomas, *The Slave Trade* (New York: Simon and Schuster, 1997).

11. Zvi Yavetz, *Slaves and Slavery in Ancient Rome* (New Brunswick, N.J.: Transaction, 1988).

12. David Brion Davis, *Slavery and Human Progress* (New York, Oxford Univ. Press, 1984).

13. The classic older study on the "damage" thesis is Stanley Elkins, *Slavery: A Problem in American Institutional and Intellectual Life* (Chicago: Univ. of Chicago Press, 1958); the most notable challenge to that thesis is Eugene D. Genovese, *Roll Jordan Roll: The World the Slaves Made* (New York: Pantheon, 1974); for a valuable survey, see Peter Kolchin, *American Slavery, 1619–1877* (New York: Hill and Wang, 1993).

14. The debate between Davis and Haskell, which first appeared in the *American Historical Review,* has been compiled in the anthology, *The Antislavery Debate: Capitalism and Abolitionism as a Problem in Historical Interpretation,* ed. Thomas Bender (Berkeley: Univ. of California Press, 1992).

15. John Dewey, "Egoism versus Altruism," in *Lectures on Psychological and Political Ethics* (1898; New York: Macmillan, 1976), ch. 6.

16. Alexis de Tocqueville, *Democracy in America,* ed. J. P. Mayer, trans. George Lawrence (1835–40; New York: Harper, 1969), 104–6.

17. Lincoln, *S&W,* 1:463.

18. Ibid., 2:19.

19. See *Colonial Discourse and Post-Colonial Theory: A Reader,* ed. Laura Chisman and Patrick Williams (New York: Columbia Univ. Press, 1994).

20. Representative Richard H. Cain of South Carolina, 1875, quoted on p. 11 of Carol Horton, "Liberty and Equality and the Civic Subject: Identity and Citizenship in

Reconstruction," paper delivered at the University of Chicago in 1996 at a conference in honor of the late David J. Greenstone.

21. Quoted ibid., 12–14.

22. Quoted in Martin Bruegel, "Unrest: Manorial Society and the Market in the Hudson Valley," *Journal of American History* 82 (1996): 1393–1424.

23. Quoted in an interview in the *New York Times*, May 1, 1999; see also Orlando Patterson, *Slavery and Social Death: A Comparative Study* (Cambridge: Harvard Univ. Press, 1982).

24. Ira Berlin, *Free at Last: A Documentary History of Slavery, Freedom, and the Civil War* (New York: New Press, 1992).

25. Dylan Penningroth, "Slavery, Freedom, and Property Among African Americans," *Journal of American History* (Sept. 1997): 405–30.

26. Peter Kolchin, *American Slavery, 1619–1877* (New York: Hill and Wang, 1993), 133–68.

27. John Sibley Butler, *Entrepreneurship and Self-Help among Black Americans: A Reconsideration of Race and Economics* (Albany: SUNY Press, 1991); Butler, "Myrdal Revisited: The Negro in Business," *Daedalus* 124 (Winter 1995): 199–221.

28. Abraham L. Harris, *The Negro as Capitalist* (College Park, Md.: McGrath, 1936).

29. Henry Louis Gates, "Frederick Douglass and the Language of Self," in *Figures in Black: Words, Signs, and the "Racial" Self* (New York: Oxford U.P., 1987), 106–10.

30. Frederick Douglass, *The Life and Times of Frederick Douglass* (1892; New York: Macmillan, 1962), 209–12.

31. Gayle McKeen, "Self-Help in African-American Political Thought," paper delivered at the University of Chicago in 1996 at a conference in honor of the late David J. Greenstone. McKeen notes that Douglass deeply valued wealth derived from honest work as a means of cultivating the mind and affording the leisure to contribute to civic responsibility. "Work," she explains, "could stand as a single word summary of the theme of the 'Self Made Men,' in which Douglass praises work, labour, effort, industry, exertion, fortitude, and perseverance" (p. 11).

32. James Weldon Johnson, *Autobiography of an Ex-Colored Man* (1912; New York: Dover, 1995), 92.

33. Quoted in Nick Salvatore, *We All Got History: The Memory Book of Amos Webber* (New York: Times Books, 1996), 271–72.

34. Francis L. Broderick, *W. E. B. Du Bois: Negro Leadership in a Time of Crisis* (Stanford, Calif.: Stanford Univ. Press, 1959), 66; David Levering Lewis, *W. E. B. Du Bois: Biography of a Race, 1868–1919* (New York: Holt, 1993), 179–237.

35. Quoted in Richard Nelson Current, *Speaking of Abraham Lincoln: The Man and His Meaning for Our Times* (Urbana: Univ. of Illinois Press, 1983), 36.

Conclusion

1. Robin D. G. Kelley, "The Black Poor and the Politics of Opposition in a New South City, 1929–1970," in *The "Underclass" Debate*, ed. Michael Katz (Princeton, N.J.: Princeton Univ. Press, 1993), 293–333.

2. Since at least the nineteenth century, it has been a challenge to historians to try to interpret what people in the past were doing and why when they had no opportunity to write down their thoughts. Max Weber, for example, made meaning

(*Sinn*) a basic component of human action and asked us to try to understand what sense it made to a person or group of person to be engaged in a line of action. The task is to get at interpretive subjective understanding, the meaning that the subjects attach to their actions. Professor Kelley has no trouble with this intellectual quandary. As evidence that poor people are capable of "self-activity" and that black youths especially are capable of "the politics of opposition," Kelley offers the following in regard to riding city buses in Birmingham in the 1930s: "African American passengers adopted a score of other oppositional practices. The most common forms include hiding or moving color dividers, insisting on paying only part of the fare, holding the center door open while dozens of unpaid passengers forced their way onto the bus, and vandalism. Perhaps the most fascinating and often overlooked form of resistance was the use of sound to invade space designated for whites. Black passengers were rejected frequently for making too much noise" (p. 307). Such a description reads like the juvenile antics of almost any American generation of any race. The impassioned aim of younger scholars is to look to social history for evidence of "opposition," "resistance," "transgressivity," and whatever purportedly symbolizes some kind of blow against capitalism and the establishment. I am a little puzzled to think that that my generation of the 1950s carried out "oppositional practices" on the streets of San Francisco when, just horsing around, we did pretty much the same things as did the youths in Birmingham. (Only we didn't just sneak onto the bus; we stole it!)

3. Ralph Waldo Emerson, "Politics," in *The Portable Emerson*, ed. Mark Van Doren (New York: Viking, 1946), 189–204.

4. Cornel West, *The American Evasion of Philosophy: A Genealogy of Pragmatism* (Madison: Univ. of Wisconsin Press, 1989), 235–39.

5. *Reports of the Proceedings and Debates of the Convention of 1821* (1859; New York: DeCapo, 1970), 304, 364–65.

6. W. E. B. Du Bois, "The Denial of Economic Justice to Negroes," *New Leader* (Feb. 9, 1929), 43–46.

7. Davis's statement from the congressional hearing is in an article to which I am indebted. See David E. Bernstein, "Roots of the 'Underclass': The Decline of Laissez-Faire Jurisprudence and the Rise of Racist Labor Legislation," *American University Law Review* 43 (1993): 85–138, quotation on 105.

8. Cruise's seminal *The Crisis of the Negro Intellectual* is quoted in Ann Douglas, *Terrible Honesty: Mongrel Manhattan in the 1920s* (New York: Farrar Straus, 1995), 323.

9. Manny Marable, *How Capitalism Underdeveloped Black America: Problems in Race, Political Economy and Society* (Boston: South End, 1985).

10. Ralph Ellison, "Going to the Territory," in *The Collected Essays of Ralph Ellison*, ed. John F. Callahan (New York: Modern Library, 1995), 594.

11. Mark C. Taylor, *Altarity* (Chicago: Univ. of Chicago Press, 1987).

12. Marion Tappen, "Ressentiement and Power," in *Nietzsche, Feminism, and Political Theory*, ed. Paul Parton (New York: Routledge, 1993), 131–43.

13. See the symposium "On Language, Gender, and Working-Class History," *International Labor and Working-Class History* 32 (Spring 1987); and Scott's reply in *International Labor and Working-Class History* 32 (Fall 1987): 39–45.

14. Joan Scott, "History in Crisis," *American Historical Review* 74 (1989): 691.

15. On Weber's theory of "small numbers," see Richard Pipes, "Max Weber and Russia," *World Politics* 7 (1955): 371–401.

16. Quoted in Nicola Chriamonte, *The Paradox of History* (Philadelphia: Univ. of Pennsylvania Press, 1970), 26.

17. Sara Evans, *Personal Politics: The Roots of Women's Liberation in the Civil Rights Movement* (New York: Knopf, 1979), 16–17. On civil rights legislation pertaining to women, see Joan Hoff Wilson, *Law, Gender, Injustice: A Legal History of U.S. Women* (New York: New York Univ. Press, 1991).

18. Phyllis Chesler, *Women, Money, and Power* (New York: Morrow, 1976).

19. Cynthia Fuchs Epstein, *Women in Law* (New York: Basic, 1981).

20. Mary Anne Dolan, "When Feminism Failed," *New York Times Magazine* (June 26, 1988), 20–23, 66.

21. George Santayana, "The Genteel Tradition in American Philosophy," in *The Winds of Doctrine and Platoism and the Spiritual Life* (New York: Harper, 1957), 165–99.

22. Simone Weil, *Oppression and Liberty* (Amherst: Univ. of Massachusetts Press, 1973), 66–69.

23. Kenneth Burke, *Attitudes toward History* (1937; Boston: Beacon, 1959), 29.

24. The full text of the *The Port Huron Statement* is reprinted as an appendix in James Miller, *Democracy Is in the Streets: From Port Huron to the Siege of Chicago* (New York: Simon and Schuster, 1987), 329–74.

25. More than any other American novel, *The Great Gatsby*'s tragic end confirms what earlier moralists worried about when fearing that capitalism would result in a culture that celebrated wealth without work. How Mr. Gatz came to possess his fortune remains veiled in the novel, with a hint that it had something to do with racketeering. But we learn at the end of the story that young Gatz had kept a notebook with Franklin's aphorisms about serious study and hard work—the advice of Abraham Lincoln. Fitzgerald's own life charted the same decline from youthful ideals to adult indulgence, from, to use the eulogy of his friend John Dos Passos, "the conscientious worker" to "the moneyed celebrity." John Dos Passos, "A Note on Fitzgerald," in *The Crack-Up*, ed. Edmund Wilson (New York: New Directions, 1945), 238–43.

Index

abolitionism, 8, 25, 38, 39, 203, 232, 235, 240, 253, 256–58, 263–66, 269, 270, 279

Academic Left, 112, 248, 290, 312n23

Acton, Lord, 142

Adams, Abigail, 244

Adams, Hannah, 247

Adams, Henry, 22, 60, 99, 130, 135, 143–44, 159, 243, 316n1; *Democracy*, 102, 288; *The Education of Henry Adams*, 144, 243

Adams, John, 53, 64, 92, 95–97, 108, 110, 121–23, 166, 174, 196, 211, 214, 215, 244, 299n24, 300n29, 303n28

Adams, John Quincy, 258

Adorno, T. W., 159–61; *The Authoritarian Personality*, 159–60; *Dialectic of Enlightenment*, 160–61

advertising, 18, 50

affirmative action, 119, 120, 171, 254, 286

Africa, 165, 170, 175, 180, 231; deportation to, 175–76; history, 175–77, 260; slave trade, 258–66

African Americans, 3–5, 7, 13, 28, 48, 70, 133, 178, 196, 199, 230, 241, 249, 278, 286, 289, 320n2; black Lockeanism, 268–74; citizenship, 133–34, 256, 266; colonization, 175–76; *Dred Scott* decision, 36, 133; enterprise, 272–76, 281–82; free, 133–34, 176, 256, 258, 259, 266–69, 279–80; history, 19–28, 236–37, 256–77; and liberal tradition, 256–77; mob violence against, 38, 235; property disputes, 20–24, 39, 267–75, 280; and racism in labor, 230–35, 256–72, 280–82; Reconstruction, 266–69, 274; slave trade, 258–66; vote, 256, 267, 279–80; and

wealth, 211–14, 259–66, 272–76. *See also* civil rights; slavery

agriculture, 31–32, 47, 97, 203, 229; black, 262–63, 268–71

Alger, Horatio, 188

American Historical Association, 80–81, 146

American Revolution, 4, 10–12, 38, 41–70, 71–74, 82–83, 90, 106, 110, 181, 183, 195, 211, 229, 238, 240, 258, 294n16; causes and consequences, 41–70; consumerism and patronage, 58–61; and Lockeanism, 48–70; national history standards, 71–74; and patriotism, 82–87; and radicalism, 53–55, 58–61, 63–66; and women, 240–48

Amistad uprising, 258

ancestry, 6, 53, 87, 165–69

Anderson, Marian, 7

anti-communism, 200–203

anti-Federalists, 93

anti-foundationalism, 18, 27–28

antiquity, 53, 54, 64, 84, 87, 95, 98, 107, 130–35, 140, 142, 146, 147, 172, 196–97, 205, 238, 262

Arendt, Hannah, 61, 74, 248

Aristotle, 53, 93, 140, 215, 262, 296n1

Aron, Raymond, 67

Articles of Confederation, 95

atomic bomb, 78

Augustine, Saint, 262

authority, 1, 6, 24, 44, 87–92, 96, 112, 132, 143, 163, 165, 177, 187, 192, 204, 231, 235, 286; and American identity, 87–92; Lockeanism vs., 48–49; patriarchal, 53, 113, 179; and revolution, 56–58; Roman, 53, 54